reel
spirituality

Engaging Culture

WILLIAM A. DYRNESS
AND ROBERT K. JOHNSTON,
SERIES EDITORS

The Engaging Culture series is designed to help Christians respond with theological discernment to our contemporary culture. Each volume explores particular cultural expressions, seeking to discover God's presence in the world and to involve readers in sympathetic dialogue and active discipleship. These books encourage neither an uninformed rejection nor an uncritical embrace of culture, but active engagement informed by theological reflection.

reel
spirituality

theology and film in dialogue

second edition

robert k. johnston

Baker Academic
Grand Rapids, Michigan

© 2000, 2006 by Robert K. Johnston

Published by Baker Academic
a division of Baker Publishing Group
P.O. Box 6287, Grand Rapids, MI 49516-6287
www.bakeracademic.com

Printed in the United States of America

Library of Congress Cataloging-in-Publication Data
Johnston, Robert K., 1945–
    Reel spirituality : theology and film in dialogue / Robert K. Johnston.—2nd ed.
        p.   cm.
    Includes bibliographical references (p.   ) and index.
    ISBN 10: 0-8010-3187-7 (pbk.)
    ISBN 978-0-8010-3187-8 (pbk.)
    1. Motion pictures—Religious aspects. I. Title.
PN1995.5.J59 2006
261.5'7—dc22   2006023923

For Cathy

my companion in

faith, film, and life

Everything you need to know about life is in the movies.

Travis, *Grand Canyon*

I didn't want you to enjoy the film. I wanted you to look very closely at your own soul.

Sam Peckinpah, director

contents

illustrations

Photos

Figures

d. = director, directed by.

preface to the
second edition

Sister Rose Pacatte, a film educator and reviewer for the *St. Anthony Messenger*, tells of going to the cineplex. Dressed in street clothes, she had come to see *The Missing* (2003). Sitting next to her was a young professional woman with whom she struck up a conversation. Sister Rose asked, "Why did you come to the movies today?" To which the woman replied, "This is the third movie I've seen today. I think my boyfriend is going to propose to me today, and I'm not sure I am ready. I always come to the movies when I have to figure out my life." "So you needed a retreat or spiritual direction," Sister Rose commented, "but you came to the movies." "That's what I and my friends always do," was the reply. "We can always find solutions in the movies."[1] Sister Rose told this story at a consultation on theology and film where filmmakers, church leaders, and academics were all present. In the discussion that followed, a filmmaker responded, "That's rather worrying!" But Sister Rose countered, "If you don't find meaning in church, you go and search it out elsewhere."[2]

It is a fact. Movies function as a primary source of power and meaning for people throughout the world. Along with the church, the synagogue, the mosque, and the temple, they often provide people stories through which they can understand their lives. Sister Rose no doubt spoke to us in hyperbole when criticizing the church for its irrelevance. There are, of course, places of worship that are vibrant and meaningful. But people both within the church and outside it recognize that movies are also providing primary stories around which we shape our lives. Movies block out the distractions around us and encourage an attentiveness toward life. Presenting to viewers aspects of their daily lives, both intimate and profound, movies exercise our moral and religious imagination. They allow us to try things on. From the stories we see on the screen (or in our living rooms), our spirits quicken. Or so I argued in the first edition of *Reel Spirituality* and will again suggest in the pages that follow.

Although the overall continuity between editions of this book will thus be apparent to anyone who reads both, there are also important changes in both the book's tone and its content. First, while the power of movies both for good and for ill has long been recognized (Sister Rose's experience, for example, finds its on-screen equivalent in Woody Allen's 1985 movie, *The Purple Rose of Cairo*), the non-liturgical branches of Protestant churches have been slower to accept, let alone embrace, this truth. Moreover, churches and synagogues, whether conservative or liberal, have until recently failed to act on this reality—to realize the importance of engaging spiritually with movies as part of their congregational activity. Thus, the first edition of this book attempted an apologia; it mounted an argument in favor of movie watching by Christians. Not everyone thought this necessary, however. Some reviewers, particularly from more mainline Protestant and Catholic traditions, criticized the book for being too defensive—for even bothering to justify the church's engagement with film. Jim Friedrich, for example, wrote in his review of this book in *Episcopal Life*, "His evangelical background compels him to make arguments in favor of movie-going that Anglicans take for granted."[3] Friedrich is no doubt right. The question today for most Christians is not *whether* the church should engage Hollywood, but *how* that engagement should best be done—*how*, that is, Christians might best relate their practice of faith to their moviegoing. Thus, readers of this second edition will find the dialogue between theology and film more assumed than argued, even as we seek to better understand its artistic power and theological possibilities.

A second criticism of *Reel Spirituality*'s first edition centered on my perceived overdependence on a literary model of filmic interpretation.[4] For some, their critique includes with it the more radical rejection of story as central to a film's power and meaning. I disagree with any attempt to jettison story, as chapter 6 argues. If anything, the role of narrative in film is more recognized today than when the first edition was written. It is the use of narrative technique within documentaries, for example, that is partly responsible for the increased popularity of these movies today. But the more general critique of this book's first edition still has force. It is simply true that movies "tell" their stories in a different way than novels. Unlike literature, movies make use of a threefold narrative technique—telling their stories through script, music, and image. The first edition of this book, while noting this fact, failed (as do most studies in theology and film) to give adequate treatment to music and to image, centering more on text alone. The criticism of reviewers was thus justified. Readers of this volume will therefore note that a whole chapter has been added discussing the importance of music and image for understanding a film's power and meaning.

Students who have used *Reel Spirituality* in my classes have often voiced a third concern, one this edition also addresses. They have frequently expressed a desire for a more explicit treatment of ethical issues that arise out of people's experience with film. Viewers not only experience movies; they also reflect on those experiences regarding their adequacy for life. Because I wanted to locate the primary source of the power and meaning of a movie in viewers' experience of it and also wanted to avoid the typical "judgmental" tone of an earlier generation of theological reflection on film, I did not adequately address the secondary ethical reflection that arises naturally in the dialogue following people's encounter with a movie's story. To remedy this omission, this second edition includes a new chapter that moves the discussion of theological ethics beyond the church's fixation with the rating system.

In addition to these three "internal" course corrections, readers will also note changes in the new edition based on "external" factors. The most obvious outside factor is the gap of six years since the first edition was published. These years have brought with them a whole spate of superb movies, many inviting our best theological reflection. Thus, the second edition examines many more recent movies. (I have also attempted to add breadth to the volume with additional references to certain film classics.) Second, since the initial publication of *Reel Spirituality*, there has been an explosion of interest in the study of theology and film both in the church and in the academy. David Ford's third edition of *The Modern Theologians* (2005), for example, has a chapter devoted to this emerging field, written by Jolyon Mitchell.[5] The number of books and monographs on this topic have soared over the last five years. Thus my chapter "Theological Approaches to Film Criticism" has been reworked to take into account new and important insights that colleagues are offering.

However, for all the changes, what remains central to my argument is the importance of film for people of faith. There is also the concomitant recognition that the spiritual and the religious can be important to Hollywood. Not just *The Chronicles of Narnia: The Lion, the Witch and the Wardrobe* (2005) or *The Passion of the Christ* (2004)—both obvious choices—have triggered phone calls to my office by members of the press seeking theological reflection, but also *Brokeback Mountain* (2005) and *Spider-Man 2* (2004) as well. There is a growing realization that movie stories offer diverse perspectives on life that, along with other types of reflection, invite religious dialogue. *Reel Spirituality* is meant to facilitate such engagement—in the church, in Hollywood, and in the larger society.

Pasadena, California
June 2006

acknowledgments

For Second Edition

This second edition of *Reel Spirituality* has again benefited from the insight of my students and colleagues. I wish to thank in particular students at Fuller Theological Seminary who were in my 2005 theology and film class. They read a draft of the manuscript and offered their perceptive comments on it. Especially helpful were the insights of Zachery Holt, Doug Zukunft, and Jessica Raymond, as well as the ongoing dialogue I had with my student assistant for the class, Matt Webb. I wish also to thank three of my doctoral students—Tony Mills, Nelleke Bosshardt, and Brian Pounds—for helping me with research and editing.

I am grateful as well for the insightful critique of the first edition offered by Ken Myers, whose audio journal, *Mars Hill Audio*, continues to inform Christians on a broad range of issues relating to theology and culture. I have also benefited from numerous book reviews and from colleagues in the field who have entered into conversation with the book through their writings. Of particular help were the comments of Terry Lindvall, Steve Nolan, Clive Marsh, Jolyon Mitchell, John Lyden, and Gordon Lynch (see the bibliography for relevant citations). My students (and colleagues) Barry Taylor and Craig Detweiler, both with extensive experience in the film industry as well as in university teaching, continue to be mentors, helping me shed my overdependence on literary models of filmic interpretation. So too do filmmakers Ralph Winter, Norman Stone, and Scott Derrickson, as well as the filmmakers and film educators who serve with me on planning committees for both the City of Angels Film Festival and the Reel Spirituality Institute, which is part of the Brehm Center for Theology, Worship and the Arts at Fuller Theological Seminary. My wife, Catherine Barsotti, is my movie-viewing partner. Her insights are everywhere present throughout these pages.

It is to the Henry Luce Foundation, however, and its president, Michael Gilligan, that I am particularly indebted. Their generous support allowed me to take leave in the spring and summer of 2005 from my work at Fuller Theological Seminary to write much of this second edition. Their support also allowed me to gather in Pasadena, California, a group of filmmakers, scholars, and church consultants for four days of conversation over two years for the purpose of brainstorming how the discipline of theology and film might best move forward. These colleagues critiqued the first edition of *Reel Spirituality*, and they provided fresh insights regarding the change and development required to move the discipline to its next level of maturity. I am indebted to each of them.

The following colleagues were part of the Luce Consultations in 2004 and 2005:

Mitch Avila (philosopher and author/teacher in theology/philosophy and film)

Catherine Barsotti (theology and film educator, reviewer, and author)

Jonathan Bock (screenwriter and president of a film marketing company)

Craig Detweiler (screenwriter, author, and chairperson of a university film department)

John Drane (professor of practical theology)

Brad King (filmmaker/producer)

Terry Lindvall (historian of religion in film and former chair of a university film department)

Gerard Loughlin (theologian and author in theology and film)

Clive Marsh (church administrator and professor/author in theology and film)

Sally Morgenthaler (church consultant in worship)

Barbara Nicolosi (screenwriter, consultant, and film educator)

Gaye Williams Ortiz (communications professor and author in theology and film)

Rose Pacatte, FSP (theology and film educator, reviewer, and author)

Norman Stone (award-winning filmmaker/writer and director)

Barry Taylor (film composer and music director, pastor, and educator/author in theology and popular culture)

Rebecca Ver Straten-McSparran (director of a film program for university students)

The goodwill and keen insight of these interdisciplinary colleagues have contributed greatly to the pages that follow, and I am grateful to them.

For First Edition

Reel Spirituality has been shaped and formed by the five classes in theology and film that I have taught at Fuller Theological Seminary. The first three of these were co-taught with Robert Banks. Much of what is written on these pages developed in dialogue with Rob and our students. It is impossible to credit (or even know) all that were originally Rob's ideas. Suffice it to say, I am deeply in debt to my former colleague for his creativity, his stimulation, and his encouragement.

Many of the film descriptions in this book first appeared as reviews in the pages of *The Covenant Companion*, a monthly publication of the Evangelical Covenant Church. I am thankful to Jane Swanson-Nystrom, managing editor of the *Companion*, for asking my wife and me to be regular contributors to that magazine. The reviews were co-written with my wife, Catherine Barsotti. It is with Cathy that I have seen most of the movies described in this book, and it is with her that I have had my fullest discussions about them. Her insights have consistently stretched my thinking and broadened my experience. It is to her that I dedicate this book.

In one of the film columns that we co-wrote, we asked readers to suggest titles for this book. Among the suggestions we received were

Rumors of Glory
God in Hollywood: Resident Alien?
Action! Hearing God's Voice in the Midst of the Movies
Why I Am Not Afraid to Share My Popcorn with Jesus
Jesus the Film Critic
Movies That Changed My Life

However, the title I chose, *Reel Spirituality*, comes from another source. It is borrowed from a conference I co-chaired in 1998 with Hollywood producer Ralph Winter (*Star Trek IV* and *VI*; *Mighty Joe Young*; *X-Men*). We brought fifty pastors and church leaders together with fifty Hollywood writers and directors to discuss "Storytelling as Common Ground." I am indebted to Ralph and to those on the planning committee for teaching me much about storytelling in the movies.

I am also indebted to a number of individuals who read a draft of this book and offered helpful suggestions as to how I might improve it: Ken Gire, who has written widely on the spirituality of everyday life; screenwriter Craig Detweiler; Fuller Theological Seminary colleagues Rob Banks and Bill Dyrness; and students Ginger Arnold, Chad Pecknold, and Neal Johnson. I am thankful as well to students in my class on Theology and Film, which I taught in the fall of 1999. All forty students were given a copy of the manuscript and asked to write a response to it. Their criticisms and encouragements have helped shape this book as well.

introduction

The task I'm trying to achieve is above all to make you see.

D. W. Griffith

Barry Taylor, a musician who has pastored a church for those in the Hollywood entertainment industry, was asked by a producer friend to go to the Warner Sound Studios for a test screening of a new movie. It was a rough cut, that is, one with temporary music, unedited sound, and some special effects missing. Over one hundred people were invited that evening in order to provide the producers and directors feedback about the film, which has since been released with the title *The Third Miracle* (1999). Barry provided music for the movie.

The movie's story is about Frank Shore, a Catholic priest who has lost his faith and is living a dissolute life. The lapsed priest has a gift no one else has, however—one that is needed by the church. He can expose fraudulent miracles. As the story unfolds, the diocese calls on Shore to help with an investigation of a series of apparent miracles. The source of the unexplainable phenomena seems to be a mysterious woman, now deceased, whom some people consider a saint. When Shore meets the woman's daughter, there begins for him a journey toward the recovery of faith and hope.

After the screening, the producers tried to elicit from the audience their opinion about technical aspects of the film. Specifically, they wanted to know whether or not the story held up, the characters were compelling, the scenes made sense, and so on. But, recounted Taylor, "They didn't get the information they were looking for. Instead they got an hour-long discussion that they had to forcibly stop about God, faith, and miracles. And apart from my friend, I was the only person in the room who had set foot in the church in the last five years." Barry said he sat in a theater that night and heard people arguing about the nature of faith, and whether miracles could happen. They were asking, What makes a saint? Who is part of the church? And who are we as human beings? The conversation simply erupted, and it was theological to the core. Taylor concluded his remarks to a group of faculty and fellow-students at Fuller Theological Seminary by saying that "there is a very, very serious conversation going on in our culture, in Western culture at the end of the twentieth century, about God. And the church is not a part of it. We're not invited to the conversation most of the time . . . and we are not aware."[1]

Conversation about God—what we have traditionally called theology—is increasingly found outside the church as well as within it. One of the chief venues for such conversation is the movie theater with its adjacent cafés. With attendance at church stagnating and with movie viewing at theaters and through video stores at an all-time high, Christians find themselves wanting to get back into the conversation but often are not able to do so effectively.

This book is intended to help Christian moviegoers enter into theological conversation with film. As image, film assumes an artist and a viewer. As story, film assumes a speaker and a hearer. That is, although we might be watching a movie while sitting silently in a theater, we are still part of a dialogue. For movies seek to engage us, their viewers, as whole human beings. They invite—we might almost say, demand—our response. And it is easily given. After seeing a film, we go with friends to Starbucks or a restaurant to have a cup of coffee and to talk about whether we liked the film or not. We want to share our reactions and responses.

For many Christians, however, this conversation with film remains partial, both naive in its judgments and disconnected from our faith and beliefs. How can we enter into the conversation with Hollywood in a way that goes beyond bumper stickers and sloganeering? How can we engage this alternate form of storytelling, both emotionally and intellectually?

Too few of us have developed the skills of movie watching, let alone of film criticism, so as to make authentic dialogue from a Christian perspective possible. Even fewer have reflected theologically on how God might be using film to reveal something of the divine to us. Many Christians assume that movies are neither the context for theological discussion nor the occasion for revelatory event. When they go into a theater, they do not expect to see anything but celluloid and therefore are not disappointed! But they are impoverished. Moreover, they are increasingly out of step with those outside the church who resonate strongly with Hollywood's spiritual fare.

Many people in our society are seeking spirituality, even if they have little interest in organized religion. The situation is not entirely new, but it is surely more pronounced of late. In an introduction to his classic book, *Basic Christianity* (1971), John R. W. Stott states that "large numbers of people, especially young people" are "hostile to the church, [but] friendly to Jesus Christ."[2] They believe what Annie Savoy did in the movie *Bull Durham* (1988), that the church produces too much guilt and is boring, and thus they reject it. But many today, particularly young adults, are willing to examine their spirituality and the spirituality of others. They even "believe" in Jesus. If religious ideas or experience can be put into an irreverent or interesting package, so much the better. Here is the appeal of Kevin Smith's edgy but God-affirming movie *Dogma* (1999) and Ron Howard's *The Da Vinci Code* (2006).

Wanting to help Christians better connect with Hollywood—wanting, that is, to help Christians get back into the conversation on that which concerns us most—this book risks being one-sided. If film is a powerful tool for engaging its viewers spiritually, surely it can be used for bad as well as good. If it can be the occasion for divine encounter, can it not also undercut and destroy belief? Must not Christians be selective in what they see? The answer is, "Of course." The violence that was integral to *Saving Private Ryan* (1998) and *Schindler's List* (1993) helped viewers discover the horror of war and the Holocaust. It is easily distinguished from *Saw II* (2005). But what of *Pulp Fiction* (1994) or *Unforgiven* (1992)? The sexuality of *The Thomas Crown Affair* (1999) can be distinguished from *Caged Heat* (1974) or *Frankenhooker* (1990). But do viewers understand the larger intention of these movies, or are they all just occasions for many in the audience to engage in murder and sex from the safety of their seats? From the typical applause at showings of these movies, it is safe to say that most of the irony and subtlety of these films is lost on the average viewer. Christian discrimination is called for, but in two senses of that word. Not only should Christian moviegoers be at times selective, but they must also become knowledgeable film viewers as well.

Though discrimination is called for, something that will vary depending on an individual's personal and spiritual maturity, the church has swung the pendulum so far in that direction for so long that another danger seems the bigger problem today. Currently, the church risks irrelevancy without its walls and complacency within. We have boxed in God and the results are proving disastrous. New eyes are called for as we attempt to see God anew.

Henry David Thoreau wrote in his journal, "The question is not what you look at, but what you see."[3] *Reel Spirituality* is a book about "seeing." And "responding." Again I take my cue from another of our great nineteenth-century humanists, John Ruskin: "The greatest thing a human soul ever does in this world is to see something, and tell what it saw in a plain way."[4]

The focus of *Reel Spirituality* is on *film* and *theology*, two words that demand clarification from the outset. Movies were invented just over one hundred years ago. Yet they are one of our most popular art forms. For this reason, perhaps, movies have not been taken seriously either by art critics or by theologians. In an attempt to help legitimate their discipline, film critics in the fifties and sixties turned from Hollywood "movies" to European "films" in order to concentrate on the more serious fare of directors like Fellini and Bergman. As a result, the early seventies evidenced a spate of books on the theological significance of serious and noncommercial European films. While American movies were thought to put entertainment first and soul-searching second, if at all, foreign films were considered to be just the opposite. Now, almost fifty years later, such distinctions seem artificial, though they are occasionally still voiced.[5] By *film* I mean *movies*, whether seen in theaters, on video, or on TV; whether produced in Hollywood or Europe, by a major studio or the independents.[6]

While writing the first edition of this book, I was on sabbatical living near Malaga, Spain. When it was time for the Oscars, I was amazed. Hollywood's premier event was now a world event. For two days, the Spanish news, both on television and in the papers, was filled with Oscar discussion. It is estimated that in 1999, over one billion viewers in 117 nations watched the awards ceremony live, many getting up in the middle of the night to do so. In 1999, the Best Picture Award was given to the English movie *Shakespeare in Love* (1998); Best Actor went to the Italian Roberto Benigni for *Life Is Beautiful* (1998), a film he also wrote and directed; and the American Steven Spielberg won Best Director for his movie *Saving Private Ryan* (1998). European "films" are Hollywood "movies," and Hollywood movies are film. This book is about Hollywood and its worldwide industry. It is, after all, the movie that became the twentieth century's major form of storytelling, and nothing yet, not even video games or the Web, seems ready to supplant it.

The word *theology* is at least as ambiguous as *film*. For some, it means an academic, and perhaps arcane, discipline that systematically discusses the doctrines of Christianity. It is the equivalent of academic discussions of European "art house" films in the sixties—something best left to the critics. But what has become a technical subdiscipline in the study of Christianity, abstract and for many lifeless, has a much broader history. In the early centuries of the church, theology meant simply the study *of* God. It was first-order reflection, much closer to what a word like *spirituality* might mean today. Edward Farley notes that in the early centuries after Christ's birth, theology meant a habit of the human soul, a way of knowing God and what God reveals. Theology had to do with "a personal knowledge of God and the things of God in the context of salvation. Hence, the study of divinity (theology) was an exercise of piety, a dimension of the life of faith." To be interested in theology was to be interested in knowing God directly.[7]

With the rise of the universities, theology came chiefly to mean study *about* God. Theology was now understood as second-order reflection, though it was still viewed comprehensively and holistically. In the words of Farley, *theology* in this second sense "refers to a cognitive enterprise using appropriate methods and issuing in a body of teaching."[8] Theology, that is, was to be seen not first of all as an experiential enterprise but as a critical task—a discipline whose end was an integrated knowledge about God.

It is in both of these two original senses of the term that I will use the word *theology* in this book. For movies, like other art forms, help us not only to know about God, but to actually experience God as well. And they do so with an artistic power unique to their medium.

the power of film

[Movie characters'] ideals become our ideals. Their thoughts become standards of our thinking and language. Their style of dress and movement are seen on the streets of our nation. And their moments of triumph and defeat become our successes and our failures.

Jodie Foster, as quoted in *Movie Nights*

Seen any good movies lately? The question is a common one. In our contemporary world, watching movies has become as normal an activity as eating, sleeping, or using the computer. According to one pollster, viewers in the United States watched on average thirty-eight movies in 2003 (57 percent of all Americans watched *Finding Nemo*; 45 percent saw *Pirates of the Caribbean: The Curse of the Black Pearl*; and 42 percent saw *Bruce Almighty*!). Among adults 95 percent saw at least one movie that same year while only 47 percent read one book the previous year.[1] Movies are huge business, with $9.3 billion spent in the United States in 2003 in box-office sales, $23.8 billion on the exponentially growing sales and rentals of DVD and video, and $12.6 billion more being expended on cable, satellite, and pay-per-view television (much of which is film based).[2] In Spain, as in most of Europe, movies (and music) are the entertainment of choice.[3] And, in India, sales of movie tickets outpace those in America by over two to one.[4] Movies are truly a worldwide phenomenon.

Besides advances in DVD and satellite technologies, other transformations in the delivery of movies are taking place. Netflix and Blockbuster Online are making available the pleasures of hard-to-locate movies from around the world, as well as providing viewers a constantly renewable source of DVDs without even the need to put down the remote control and go to the local video store! The production of commentary and special features on DVD supplements has become a specialty in its own right, giving viewers a master class in directing, lighting, editing, music, and camera placement for the price of the movie. Personal DVD libraries are increasingly common and will continue to become more so.

The influence of movies in our society can be noted in other ways as well. In 2005, White House policymakers were reported to be lobbying major studios, writers, and directors to add anti-drug messages within their films. When Revlon, BMW, Chanel, and Amazon.com sought to increase sales in 2004, they created short "movies" starring Halle Barry, Nicole Kidman, Clive Owen, and Minnie Driver.[5] Such examples are easily multiplied. When the planes crashed into the towers on 9/11, people said it looked like a scene from a disaster movie. Reality seemed, on that day, less real than the reels at the cineplex. Our only frame of reference for this kind of terrorism was what we had already witnessed in movies like *Independence Day* (1996) and *Air Force One* (1997).

Movies, however, are more than profits and box office, Netflix and DVD supplements, advertising and messages. They remain in the twenty-first century our primary storytelling medium, interpreting reality for us and acting as a type of cultural glue. Given its importance as a means of cultural communication, the cinema has become a significant contemporary language in need of understanding and explication. Thus, the University of Southern California is now requiring all its undergraduates to take at least one cinema/television course in order to learn how to "read and write" with media; other colleges are sure to follow suit. Moreover, movies are commonly used as part of the core curriculum in such disparate fields as philosophy, sociology, English, religion, and psychology. And some even believe that cinema studies is positioned to become the new MBA, a means of general preparation for careers in fields as diverse as law and the military.[6]

"Seeing" Life

The importance of film for both our world economy and our culture is obvious, but it is important not to forget that the power of a movie lies first of all in what transpires within the individual viewer as she or he gazes at the screen. In the movie *Smoke* (1995), Paul Benjamin stops in one evening at the tobacco shop of Auggie Wren, located on a street corner in Brooklyn.[7] Paul is a writer, but his pen has been silenced by the senseless death of his pregnant wife from random gunfire. Whiling away the time, Paul notices Auggie's camera sitting there. Auggie explains that he uses it every day and invites Paul to look through his photo album. What Paul discovers seems odd to him—picture after picture of the same scene; people passing by Auggie's corner store. The photographs were all taken from the same spot, at the same time—8 a.m., one each morning—and there are several thousand. As Auggie explains, "It's my corner. Just a small part of the world, but things happen here, too." Paul, however, sees nothing except the same picture!

As Paul leafs through the pages, Auggie says to him, "Slow down. You'll never get it if you don't slow down, my friend." And as Paul does, he begins to see small differences in each of the photos. The light changes; the seasons pass. There are bright mornings and dark mornings, summer light and autumn light. There are weekdays and weekends. Different people pass through the photographs, some repeatedly. In several pictures, Paul even discovers his wife walking to work. The pictures bring tears to his eyes as he begins to see life afresh. He discovers the variety and vitality of life once again, this time through a small slice of Brooklyn captured on film.

This scene from *Smoke* is both a metaphor for what can happen when we watch a movie and a movie clip capable of evoking from those in its audience what it itself portrays. For movies help us to "see." They focus life for the viewer, giving us a richer variety of experience than would otherwise be possible. Carl Sandburg, the poet laureate, once commented,

> I meet people occasionally who think motion pictures, the product Hollywood makes, is merely entertainment, has nothing to do with education. That's one of the darndest fool fallacies that is current. . . . Anything that brings you to tears by way of drama does something to the deepest roots of our personality. All movies, good or bad, are educational and Hollywood is the foremost educational institution on earth. What, Hollywood more important than Harvard? The answer is not as clean as Harvard, but nevertheless farther reaching.[8]

For some, going to the movies is still a last resort for what to do on a free evening. And a video is what we rent for our children when we are going out for some more important "cultural" event. But for an increasing number of people, watching a movie is simply part of our normal routine. Movie stories, including some that "make us cry," have become a regular part of our informal education. When I ask my students how many movies they have seen in the theater or on DVD in the last month, the typical response is eight or nine (an identical number to what polls suggest for adults in Spain). When I ask them to share with a classmate the last movie that brought them to tears, they easily recount the experience.

Yet, though most of us watch movies and are affected by them, we seldom try to understand what we have seen, let alone relate it to our wider religious beliefs and practices. After all, film is one thing, and our religious faith is quite another. Such a disconnect is understandable, at least on the surface. Movies are, on one level, mere entertainment—escapism. Our spiritual faith, on the other hand, concerns our vocation and destiny; it is foundational. But such easy dichotomies crumble under closer scrutiny. Worship services also entertain (consider the pageantry and music), while movies sometimes engage us at the core of our being.

Reflecting on his experience of the movie theater as a young boy, Martin Scorsese remembers how he was taken there by his family:

> The first sensation was that of entering a magical world—the soft carpet, the smell of fresh popcorn, the darkness, the sense of safety, and, above all, sanctuary—much the same in my mind as entering a church. A place of dreams. A place that excited and stretched my imagination.[9]

As the French filmmaker Eric Rohmer recognized earlier, the cinema was for Scorsese "the cathedral of the twentieth century."[10]

It is easy to become cute when making comparisons between screen and sanctuary: popcorn and Coke in place of the bread and wine; ticket price for tithe; high ceilings to suggest transcendence; attendees speaking in hushed tones while they expectantly await the start; a certain ritual involved with where we sit and how often we go; a sense of disappointment—even betrayal—if the film/religious service falls short of expectations. But behind all such forced analogies is the primary fact that both cinema and church provide "life-orienting images."[11] As Read Mercer Schuchardt suggests in one of his online *Metaphilm* commentaries, "Like religion, a good movie really does answer the only three questions worth asking in life: who you are, where you come from, and what you should do."[12]

Or listen to George Miller, the producer of *Babe* (1995) and *The Witches of Eastwick* (1987),

> I believe cinema is now the most powerful secular religion and people gather in cinemas to experience things collectively the way they once did in church. The cinema storytellers have become the new priests. They're doing a lot of the work of our religious institutions, which have so concretized the metaphors in their stories, taken so much of the poetry, mystery and mysticism out of religious belief, that people look for other places to question their spirituality.[13]

In the pages that follow, we will need to consider whether Christian theology, as Miller suggests, has become overly rationalized to the detriment of the life-transforming power of its original story. Perhaps it is enough, by way of introduction, to recognize subtly that movies provide for many alternate forms of transcendence. They provide a *reel spirituality*.

Reel Spirituality is one of a growing number of books attempting to bridge the chasm that exists for many between movie viewing and faith. The rift is deep and historic, even if it is now increasingly out of vogue. For while early motion pictures showed the passion play of Oberammergau (1898)[14] and the temptation of St. Anthony (1898),[15] the growth of the film industry was so dramatic that the church and Hollywood soon came into conflict. Between 1913 and 1916, twenty-one thousand theaters opened in the United States. One of the most engaging portrayals of this early confrontation is John Updike's *In the Beauty of the Lilies*,[16] a novel about America in the twentieth century, hence the title's allusion to the "Battle Hymn of the Republic."

As the story opens, we find ourselves in Patterson, New Jersey. It is the spring of 1910. D. W. Griffith is filming *The Call to Arms* with Mary Pickford, his teenage star. As the actress faints in the heat, across town the Reverend Clarence Wilmot stands in the pulpit of Fourth Presbyterian Church, feeling "the last particle of faith leave him." Both Hollywood and the church are struggling, but the novel's trajectory is clear from the outset: as the church grows old and loses its faith amid the onslaught of culture, film is destined to grow. After all, Mary Pickford is only seventeen. Clarence eventually must resign and is reduced to selling encyclopedias. His son, Teddy, stops going to church. Later, when he is an adult, Teddy finds his daughter Essie, even as a little girl, wanting most to go to the theater, where she is enraptured by the images on the screen.

As the novel proceeds through four generations of the Wilmots, Essie becomes the Hollywood star Alma DeMott. Life is not easy for her, however. Hollywood is a wilderness that invites moral compromise. Her son, Clark, thus pays the price for her profligacy. Clark ends up in a cult similar to the Branch Davidians. He is not so much a believer as someone searching for life's meaning. With a plot that spans most of the twentieth century, John Updike has chronicled modern American life in terms of the conflict between the church and Hollywood, the sanctuary and the movie theater. Neither side really "wins" the war, but the secularization of society is clearly evident.

In Updike's fictional world, we used to have giants of the faith. Now we are left merely with struggling artists. In an earlier novel, *The Centaur*, Updike recounts the conversation of the narrator, Peter, with his mistress, as he lies with her in his painter's loft in Greenwich Village. He is trying to tell her how life was good in his childhood, despite the fact that his grandfather had lost his faith as a Lutheran minister, and his father had struggled with self-doubt about the meaningfulness of his vocation as a high school teacher. Nevertheless, Peter had felt a sense of place. Now, as a poor artist, he confesses his rootlessness—his lack of a firm foundation on which to stand—and comments, "Priest, teacher, artist: the classic degeneration."[17] Again Updike confronts us with the question, is the movie theater simply a poor substitute for the church? He leaves the answer ambiguous, but the gap between art and faith remains wide.

The Power of Film

As with the characters in Updike's novels, the theater and the church have sometimes seemed to be in competition with each other. My friend Paul Woolf, a screenwriter and *maggid* (ordained Jewish storyteller who teaches people about God), tells of growing up Jewish in Brooklyn. He had a strong feeling about Judaism even as a young boy, but the rabbis did not connect with him. The spiritual experiences that he had were more often the result of simple things. He remembers walking down the street when he was four, holding his mother's hand and realizing that he was in the presence of God. His consciousness seemed enlarged to the point that he could hear every bird singing and every leaf rustling. A similar experience happened when he was ten, as he stayed out playing with fireflies late into the summer evening. He says, "Here were these creatures twinkling their lights, and the summer had breath. I could hear everything. The faraway tinkling bells of an ice-cream truck, dogs barking, my friends laughing. Again, it was a shift of awareness, away from the self to a wider awareness."[18]

The next time this happened, Woolf was fourteen. It was the days of movie road shows, and he got dressed up to go into Manhattan to see *Spartacus* (1960). Woolf sat transfixed as he watched Kirk Douglas, the gladiator Spartacus, say to his wife, played by Jean Simmons, "Anyone can kill, can be taught to fight; I'm not interested in that. I want to know where the wind comes from . . . why we are here." Woolf describes that all of a sudden there was this "incredible flight of questioning about life. In a film, no less."[19] As the movie ended the audience just sat there, stunned. Woolf concludes: "On the train ride back to Brooklyn, I kept thinking, how can this be? Why had I never experienced this in a house of worship? That's when I made my decision. I said to myself, I'm going to Hollywood to make movies."[20]

Woolf's story is told repeatedly. Perhaps the best known example is from a movie—*Cinema Paradiso* (1988; English version, 1989). It is a small film, recounting the story of a young, fatherless boy, Salvatore (Toto), who loves the movies and eventually becomes a famous producer. In the story, which is set in Sicily, Salvatore returns home for the funeral of his friend Alfredo, reminiscing about his childhood and his friendship with this man who was the projectionist at The Paradiso. Although Toto would fall asleep in church, movies captivated him; Alfredo became his mentor. The story's most memorable metaphor involves motion picture kisses. We see the young, wide-eyed Toto peek into the theater as the local priest, watching the coming attractions in solitude, censors out all the scenes of kissing (even while enjoying them!) by ringing his altar bell to cue the projectionist that he must cut this from the film if it is to play that night to a packed house. As the story comes to an end, Salvatore receives, as a bequest from his friend, a montage of all the movie kisses that the church had forced him to excise. As Salvatore watches these wonder-filled moments, we too experience his rich sadness and joy.

Or again, the well-known Methodist pastor William Willimon tells of growing up in Greenville, South Carolina. One Sunday evening in 1963, in defiance of the state's blue laws, the Fox Theater opened its doors. Willimon, together with six of his buddies, entered the front door of their church as if to go to the

Methodist Youth Fellowship, but then slipped out the back to join John Wayne at the Fox. He says that evening was "a watershed in the history of Christendom, South Carolina style":

> Greenville, South Carolina—the last pocket of resistance to secularity in the Western world—served notice that it would no longer be a prop for the church. There would be no more free passes for the church, no more free rides. The Fox Theater went head to head with the church over who would provide the worldview for the young. That night in 1963, the Fox Theater won the opening skirmish.[21]

The power of film extends far beyond any such youthful skirmishes with the church, however. In his introduction to *Screening the Sacred,* Joel Martin tells of a friend who, after watching Sylvester Stallone in *Rocky* (1976), was inspired to begin seriously working out. For a significant period of time, Martin recounts how he had "no less than a conversion experience."[22] The actress Rosalind Chao tells of growing up in Orange County, California, as the only Asian (actually the only minority) in her school. Her entire world was white, creating a number of insecurities in her. Her favorite movie moment came while watching her first movie, *My Fair Lady* (1964), at the Egyptian Theater in Hollywood. As Audrey Hepburn stood at the top of the stairway ready to go to the ball, she had been transformed from a lowly street urchin into a sophisticated young lady. Rex Harrison sees her, dressed in a breathtaking gown, for the magnificent woman she is. As she walks down the stairs, the song "I Could Have Danced All Night" swells around her. Chao relates how the movie became "a near obsession with [her]. I kept going back to see it."[23]

Movies can also have a significant social impact. When a cartoonist named Walt Disney created the character Bambi, deer hunting nose-dived in one year from a $5.7 million business to $1 million.[24] In 1934, after the opening of the movie *It Happened One Night*, sales of men's undershirts dropped dramatically. The movie's star, Clark Gable, was dressed sans undershirt in order better to display his "manliness." As a result, it was not until World War II, when men were retrained to wear undershirts by the military, that high sales levels were reestablished. On a more trivial note, sales of Reese's Pieces shot up 65 percent after their use in *E.T.—The Extraterrestrial* (1982), while Tom Cruise helped boost sales of two brands of sunglasses, first Ray Ban, which he wore in *Risky Business* (1983) and then Oakley, whose sales increased 39 percent after the company paid to have Cruise use its glasses to receive instructions in *Mission: Impossible 2* (2000). More recently, sales of pinot noir increased 44 percent in one year and became the wine of choice after being featured in *Sideways* (2004). The movie also spawned a tour of the Santa Barbara County wineries used as locations in the movie, just as Omaha has had a tour of sites used in other Alexander Payne movies—*Citizen Ruth* (1996), *Election* (1999), and *About Schmidt* (2002). *Amelie* (2001) has sparked similar tours of Paris, rejuvenating the corner of Montmartre where she "lived," and New Zealand tourism is up significantly as a result of both *The Lord of the Rings* (2001, 2002, 2003) and *The Chronicles of Narnia: The Lion, the Witch and the Wardrobe* (2005).

In 1984, Jessica Lange, Sissy Spacek, and Sally Field were all incongruously invited to testify before congressional subcommittees on agricultural matters because of their supposed expertise stemming from the roles they played that year in *Country, The River,* and *Places in the Heart*, respectively![25] Actresses Tilda Swinton and Rebecca Romijn-Stamos were similarly asked to help interpret fashion at the 2003 showings in Paris, while the opposite happened in 2004 to well-rounded diva Deborah Voigt, who was dropped from the Royal Opera's production of Strauss's *Ariadne auf Naxos* at Covent Garden in London because she was too large to play the role *convincingly*. The influence of movies in dictating image would seem now to include even "the mythic opera star" known for her ample proportions!

In a different arena, observers have noted that increasingly the public learns history from film. *Good Night, and Good Luck* (2005) helps us recapture the McCarthy era. It is *The Deer Hunter* (1978) and *Platoon* (1986) that give us our understanding of Vietnam; *Mississippi Burning* (1988) that shows us the civil rights struggle; and *Dances with Wolves* (1990) that teaches us about Native Americans. Some have even argued that a film such as *M*A*S*H* (1970), though ostensibly about the Korean War, was meant to teach its contemporary viewers about the irrationality and inhumanity of the Vietnam War, which was then being waged. And through its humor, it did a good job. But if such an interpretation is open to differing opinions, no one harbors any illusion about Steven Spielberg's intention in his film *Saving Private Ryan* (1998). As he hoped, it has become a primary shaper of opinion concerning World War II. Tom Hanks, the lead actor, has taken up the cause of veterans as a result of his experience. For some whose fathers and mothers fought in these wars but came home silent about the horrors they experienced, the film has brought new dialogue and healing. Several weeks after the film came out, the *Los Angeles Times* ran an article describing how some younger people were saying that they understood for the first time something of the sacrifices that were made. After seeing the film, some twenty-year-olds were even going up to people in their seventies and thanking them for what they had done.[26]

Culturally, the power of film is not limited to congressional hearings, merchandising, or history lessons. In his provocative book *Life the Movie* (1998), Neal Gabler goes so far as to view American culture itself as taking on the characteristics of a movie. Life in the West has become show business for many, where we each play a role and long for our moment of celebrity. Gabler argues that it is not politics or economics but entertainment "that is arguably the most pervasive, powerful, and ineluctable force of our time—a force so overwhelming that it has finally metastasized into life."[27] Fun, accessible to everyone, sensuous, and providing a release from order and authority, motion picture entertainment has captured the American spirit.

The conversion of life into an entertainment medium is pervasive. Gabler observes that in the late nineties, we were coached in our roles by Martha Stewart, and our costume designer was Ralph Lauren. For many, this still holds true. Our makeup artists are plastic surgeons. In the words of Andre Agassi in a commercial for Canon cameras, "Image is everything." Theme restaurants sell atmosphere more than food. Stores like Niketown have become entertainment centers. Ideas have become sound bites. Politicians appear on Jay Leno and David Letterman. Athletic events are often subordinated to the athlete's story. Books need promotional tours if they are to sell. News programming is for our enjoyment; it is prime-time fare. Hard news is increasingly written using the techniques of fiction, so that it can be read at Starbucks.

Today everyone seems to own a camera—on a cell phone or a camcorder, with an iPod, or attached to the computer. Our concern to capture it all on "film" causes many people to experience life primarily through the lens of the camera. Brides and grooms, for example, video their weddings so that they can replay the event at their wedding receptions (as if the real event is the showing, and the ceremony the taping). Images of John F. Kennedy Jr. and Princess Diana have allowed these individuals to become not only icons but personal friends to be mourned. Twenty-four-hour videocams in dorm rooms and apartments allow viewers on the Internet to see the "lifies" that others are playing, as do the reality shows of the Osbournes, Anna Nicole Smith, and *Amish in the City*. With these phenomena beginning just months after the release of the movies *The Truman Show* (1998) and *Edtv* (1999), we would seem to have a classic example of life imitating art. If life is not a cabaret, it is at least a movie!

Even if Gabler overstates his case, the fact that movies play an increasingly significant role in defining both ourselves and our society seems beyond dispute. As Elia Kazan, the controversial filmmaker of the fifties, sixties, and seventies (*On the Waterfront* [1954], *A Streetcar Named Desire* [1951], *The Last Tycoon* [1976]) said, film is now "the language of [hu]mankind."[28] Movies broaden our exposure to life and provide alternate interpretations of life's meaning and significance. Values and images are formed in response to life's experiences, with movies providing the data of countless new stories. In fact, as society's major means of telling its stories, movies have become a type of lingua franca. Who doesn't know the story of *Titanic* (1997)? Think of the millions of children who have seen *Finding Nemo* (2003) or *The Incredibles* (2004). When we go to a party and must make conversation with new people, is it not a recent movie that provides the smile of recognition and the conversation starter? Even in the church or the synagogue, theological discussion is often more likely to happen following a movie than a sermon.[29] Movies cannot be dismissed as simply entertainment and diversion, though they are also that. Rather, movies are life stories that both interpret us and are being interpreted by us.

The power of film can change lives and communicate truth; it can reveal and redeem. Consider the following examples.

Schindler's List (1993)

Schindler's List tells the story of a group of Jews condemned to the Krakow ghetto by the Nazis during World War II. Threatened with annihilation, they are saved by a German businessman and munitions manufacturer named Oskar Schindler. Initially more interested in obtaining cheap labor, Schindler comes to care about his Jewish coworkers. They become his family, and he goes to extraordinary lengths to rescue them. As the war winds down, Schindler must flee, for he is a war criminal. In a moving sequence, we see his Jewish workers gather around him as he is about to drive off from the factory. They hand him a signed letter telling of all he has done for them, hoping that the Allies will read it if Schindler is picked up. They also give him a gold ring made from the fillings of their teeth on which is engraved in Hebrew a Talmudic saying, "Whoever saves one life, saves the world in time." Schindler is overcome with emotion as he reflects on how his gold lapel pin might have been bartered for a Jewish life and his car for ten or more people. "I could have got more," he cries.

Oskar Schindler (Liam Neeson) welcomes workers to his factory. *Schindler's List* (d. Spielberg, 1993). Photo by David James. © 1993 Universal City Studios Inc. and Amblin Entertainment, Inc. All rights reserved.

Toward the end of the movie, we are fast-forwarded to the present. We see some of the actual survivors from Schindler's factory, along with the actors who played their parts in the movie, gathering almost fifty years later in Jerusalem at Schindler's grave to pay homage to him. While the survivors move past his gravestone, two sentences are superimposed on the screen: "There are fewer than four thousand Jews left alive in Poland today." "There are more than six thousand descendants of the Schindler Jews." Just as his Jewish foreman said, there are generations alive because of what Oskar Schindler did.

Though the movie ends this way, it is not the end of the story. The scene now shifts to Switzerland, October 1996, and Christoph Meili has just seen *Schindler's List* at a local theater. He realizes that he does not know a single Jew personally. After all, there are very few Jews living in Switzerland today. Three months pass, and Meili is making his routine rounds as a young security guard at the bank in Zurich where he is employed. Passing by the room where the paper shredders are located, he sees two large containers filled with old books. He has never seen anything like this before. Looking more closely, he discovers that the books contain records dating to World War II. Meili stuffs one book under his clothing and then completes his rounds. After he takes the book home, he finds that it is a ledger documenting Jewish-owned property that had been confiscated in Berlin and turned over to the Nazis.

What should Meili do? He remembered scenes in *Schindler's List* of Nazis stealing valuables from Jews, and he remembered that Schindler did something. In a later newspaper account, Meili said, "I have the feeling I also have to do something." And do something he did. The next day he found two more over-sized ledgers in the garbage that had been too big to fit through the shredder. He then tried to contact a Zurich newspaper but was put off. When he spoke to a Jewish cultural organization in town, they told him that they would not do anything. As they put it, "This is dynamite, too hot to handle." Finally, Meili contacted a small Jewish newspaper, and at a press conference the next day, the story exploded around the world.

Meili was soon accused by his fellow Swiss citizens of being an Israeli spy. Others threatened his life. After all, Swiss banks are a national institution and considered sacrosanct. A police investigation was instigated because it was said that he "stole" bank secrets. Even his father asked him, "Are you crazy? Why are you helping the Jews?" Ironically, Meili was forced to become the first Swiss in history to ask for and receive political asylum in the United States. As a result of his action, however, the Swiss banks were forced to reach a settlement with Holocaust survivors, their families, and Jewish groups. The amount was one and a quarter billion dollars! Could the Jewish director Steven Spielberg, who had owned the rights to the movie for ten years before making it, have dreamed of a better response to his film story? Here is the power of film.[30]

Beauty and the Beast (1991)

Disney's animated fable *Beauty and the Beast* tells the story of Belle, a teenager living in an eighteenth-century French village. Belle loves books and is not interested in the romantic advances of the muscular Gaston. As the opening sequence of the movie reveals, Belle is compassionate, intelligent, and liberated. She is not one to be easily outsmarted, having a clear mind of her own. After her father is imprisoned in the forest castle of a ferocious beast, Belle sets off to rescue him. She too becomes a prisoner of the beast in his crumbling but formidable castle. We know from an earlier sequence that the beast is actually a young, handsome prince who has been cursed because he was unkind. Unless someone loves him, he will be a beast forever. As you can guess, after great adventures, the two young people eventually fall in love, and the results are magical.

Belle, a beautiful and independent teenager, sings of her desire to lead a full life. *Beauty and the Beast* (d. Trousdale and Wise, 1991). © The Walt Disney Company. All rights reserved.

The film is one of Disney's best animated features. Roger Ebert, writing in the *Chicago Sun-Times* (22 November 1991), says, "Watching the movie, I found myself caught up in a direct and joyous way. I wasn't reviewing an 'animated film.' I was being told a story, I was hearing terrific music, and I was having fun." Here is a film to take you back to your childhood. But that is not why I describe the film. I tell the story because of a book by Gerry Sittser titled *A Grace Disguised*. Gerry is a religion professor at Whitworth College in Spokane, Washington. The book relates his response to the catastrophic loss of his wife, his mother, and one of his daughters in a car crash in 1991. The van he was driving was hit by a drunk driver, and only Gerry and three of his other young children survived. Five years later, he wrote his book, reflecting on how a person might grow through loss.

Sittser shares that among the things that helped him and his children to cope were the stories of countless others—whether friends, strangers who wrote to him, or even those they read about or saw on the screen. After commenting on those stories that had helped him personally, Sittser turns to reflect on the stories that were meaningful to his children, Catherine (eight years old at the time), David (seven), and John (only two). Quoting Sittser:

> The children read books and watched movies that somehow touched on the theme of loss. John asked me to read *Bambi* dozens of times after the accident. He made me pause every time we came to the section that told the story of the death of Bambi's mother. Sometimes he said nothing, and the two of us sat in a sad silence. Sometimes he cried. He talked about the similarity between Bambi's story and his own. "Bambi lost his mommy too," he said on several occasions. Then he added, "And Bambi became the Prince of the Forest." . . . Catherine found comfort in Disney's movie version of *Beauty and the Beast* because the main character, Belle, grew up without a mother and, as Catherine has observed, became an independent, intelligent, beautiful person.[31]

If the compelling power of *Schindler's List* was in the scope of its revelation concerning the value of all persons, and particularly the Jews, here a movie story spoke on a more personal level, helping to redeem the life of one small girl. And who could ask for more?[32]

Becket (1964)

Nominated for twelve Academy Awards and starring Richard Burton and Peter O'Toole, the film *Becket* tells the story of Henry II, the Norman king of England, and his drinking buddy, Thomas à Becket. King Henry wanted free rein to live and act as he chose, to whore and wage war and tax the citizenry as he saw fit. His one obstacle to complete license was the archbishop of Canterbury, who had his own independent authority as leader of the Church of England. The archbishop often frustrated Henry's designs. In order to solve his problem, King Henry ingeniously decided to appoint his companion in "wine, women, and song," Thomas, as the next archbishop. Brilliant, except for one problem: Thomas decided to take his new vocation—his calling to be God's servant—seriously and to serve God rather than the king. King Henry tried to persuade him to compromise and accommodate to his old friend's (and king's) wishes. But Thomas remained steadfast. As a result of his faithfulness, Thomas was martyred in Canterbury Cathedral on the altar steps.

King Henry II (Peter O'Toole) tries to persuade Becket (Richard Burton) to compromise his position as archbishop. *Becket* (d. Glenville, 1964). Courtesy of Photofest, New York, New York.

When I first saw this film as a freshman in college, I did not much identify with Thomas's martyrdom (or subsequent sainthood!). But I did hear God calling me to the Christian ministry. My struggle with accepting the call to become a minister was with my image of the pastor as needing *first* to be a holy person. My Young Life leader, who ministered to me during high school, was such a person, as was my church counselor. I knew I was no saint. In the film, however, I heard God saying to me through his Spirit, "You need not be holy. Thomas was not. You only have to be obedient to my call." And I responded like Thomas and said, "God, I will be loyal to you with all my being." Here again is the power of film. Not only can it reveal and redeem, but also it can be the occasion for God to speak to the viewer.

I told of my call into the ministry at the first conference titled "Reel Spirituality," which several of us organized in the fall of 1998 and from which the title of this book is taken. Fifty Hollywood screenwriters and directors and fifty leading pastors and church leaders had gathered to discuss "Storytelling as Common Ground: The Church and Hollywood." When I was finished, one of the other speakers, Father Gregory Elmer, a Benedictine monk, commented that he too had heard God speak to him, calling him into the monastic life, while watching the same movie! We could even identify the different scenes in the film where God had made himself known to us.

What is noteworthy in this "coincidence" is that the two of us saw the same movie, *Becket*, yet heard God's call in unique ways. For me, the issue was obedience to the call to active service in the world, and I became a Protestant minister who teaches theology and culture. For Father Elmer, the call was to purity of heart and single-minded devotion, and he became a Catholic mystic. In the chapters to come, we will consider the importance of the viewer in understanding what makes a film work. We will also consider film as the occasion not only to know about God but to know God. At this point it is enough to note again that a movie's story has the power to transform life.

a brief history
of the church
and hollywood

Critics debate about when the first movie was shown. Some claim its origin to be October 6, 1889, when Thomas Edison and his associate William Dickson, working with film from George Eastman, projected moving pictures across a screen. Edison later linked the images up to a phonograph. But Edison did not secure an international patent for his invention, a machine that by 1896 allowed a single viewer a "peep show" for thirty seconds. Soon there were a variety of rivals to Edison's Kinetograph camera and Kinetoscope machine, with such exotic names as Zoëtrope, Cinématographe, and Bioscope. All provided the lucky few with magical demonstrations of flickering pictures.

The more usual date for the beginning of the cinema, however, is December 28, 1895, when the first paid exhibition was put on by the Lumière brothers at the Grand Café in Paris. Earlier that year, Louis and Auguste had patented their projector, which used a strip of celluloid with perforations down the center. With it, they could easily transport their moving pictures. For a time, Lumière projections were offered in special showings for the rich, but very soon the cinema moved to the fairgrounds of Europe and the nickelodeons of America's cities.

Mutual Experimentation

Early movies showed a train arriving at a station, a man sneezing, a gardener being squirted with his own hose, or a staged fistfight. Some early patrons were so perplexed by these moving images that they ducked the ocean waves that crashed on the screen and jumped out of the way of the oncoming train. The novelty of seeing uninterpreted reality soon wore off, however, and filmmakers began to record theatrical plays and to develop their own tableaus. But even this cinema tended "to show or display, to be looked at rather than looked through."[1] It was more exhibition than compelling story, something Andre Gaudreault and Tom Gunning have called a "cinema of attractions."[2] Many of these early "movies" had religious themes.[3] *The Horitz Passion Play* was shot in 1897 on a vacant lot in Paris; the more popular *Passion Play of Oberammergau*, a nineteen-minute movie filmed in the snow in New York City (!), but claiming to be an authentic version of the German passion play, premiered in 1898.

Some of these early religious movies were even made by evangelists. Just after the turn of the century, Herbert Booth, son of Salvation Army founders William and Catherine Booth, was appointed Commandant for Australia. In order to interest people in coming to the Sunday night lectures and prayer meetings, he experimented with the use of slides and film.[4] Booth, with the help of Joseph Perry, produced a multimedia show titled *Soldiers of the Cross* (1900), which combined short films with slides, hymns, sermons, and prayers. The production used a Lumière machine to show film sequences performed by nonprofessional actors chosen from Salvation Army personnel. The shorts depicted Stephen being stoned to death, Christ in agony on the cross, martyrs burning at the stake, animal maulings in the Coliseum, human torches in the gardens of Nero, and Christian women jumping into vats of lime rather than forsaking their Lord. Both the secular and the religious press gave the performances high praise.

Not all movies were religious in theme, however, and not all the religious films were reverent. *The Great Train Robbery* (1903) was an instant success, partly due to the shock of seeing a man in a cowboy hat pull out his gun and fire straight into the camera. Some one-reel short subjects poked fun at clerics, showing them drinking and being involved with women. But many movies continued to portray religious life with reverence, and churches were often used as movie theaters. At least seventy movies based on biblical themes were shot prior to the First World War. Reverent and straightforward, these movies were embraced by churches for they proved effective competition against other forms of amusements, drawing crowds, particularly on Sunday evenings when blue laws closed most other venues. Soon the adaptation of Lew Wallace's novel *Ben Hur* (1907), the Jesus story *From the Manger to the Cross* (1912), and the Italian religious epic *Quo Vadis* (1912) all made it to the big screen and were widely successful as feature films. *Quo Vadis* even opened on Broadway and went head-to-head with the traditional stage.

Almost from the start, motion pictures were spectacularly successful with the public. In 1902, Thomas Tally opened the Electric Theater in Los Angeles, the first theater in the United States devoted exclusively to showing motion pictures. By 1907, the American market for movies had grown so large that the gross income of the movie industry was larger than the combined receipts of vaudeville and traditional theater. *Harper's Weekly* labeled it "nickel delirium."[5] One contemporary estimate suggests that by 1911, there were ten thousand theaters in the United States showing movies to a daily audience of over four million persons.[6] Ronald Holloway calls these early years of the twentieth century "the inventive age of cinema."[7] Developing techniques as they went, many of these first-generation moviemakers also had a deep mystical sense. As the poet Vachel Lindsay wrote in 1915 concerning the new cinema: "The real death in the photoplay is the ritualistic death, the real birth is the ritualistic birth, and the cathedral mood of the motion picture which goes with these and is close to these in many of its phases, is an inexhaustible resource."[8]

In these early years, the church and Hollywood seemed to be mutually reinforcing each other's needs and values. The Congregational minister Herbert Jump perhaps best expressed the church's optimism. In his pamphlet "The Religious Possibilities of the Motion Picture" (1911), Jump compared the religious possibilities of the movie to Jesus' use of parables, particularly the dramatic story of the Good Samaritan in Luke 10:30–37:

> And now we come to the point: the objections which you and others thus make against the religious use of motion pictures can all of them be urged with equal force against the use of the most convincing parable which the Christ ever uttered. The films that have value for religious education today are those which portray truth as the Good Samaritan portrays it—in a dramatic story, of contemporary experience, exciting in character and thus interesting even to the morally sluggish, picturing negative elements such as crime, accident, ignorance, sin, and thus commending itself as true to life, but in the end showing the defeat and expulsion of these negative elements by positive qualities, virtuous souls, God-like traits.[9]

Jump encouraged his fellow clergy to use movies in their Sunday Schools, evangelistic outreach, social ministry to the needy, and sermons, as well as in providing entertainment for their parishioners.

Growing Criticism

After the First World War, however, things began to change. Although attendance continued to soar (from 4 million daily customers in 1911, to 8.5 million in 1916, to 12.5 million in 1920), commercialism and a reaction in the larger culture to nineteenth-century attitudes began to alter the motion picture landscape. The star system was born as Mary Pickford and Charlie Chaplin received salaries of over ten thousand dollars per week. One estimate suggests that during these years over 80 percent of the paying public went to a movie in order to see a particular star. Movie magazines were produced showcasing Rudolph Valentino and Greta Garbo.

Paralleling the growth of the star system was the evolution of the movie theater. Its architecture no longer resembled nineteenth-century neoclassical churches, but dream palaces, expressing the romantic and exotic. In Hollywood, two of these "theme" palaces, the Egyptian and the Chinese, attracted huge crowds, as did the Roxy in New York, with seating for six thousand in its "royal" hall.

Increasingly, movies became escapist fare. Gangsters and monsters, intrigue and romance filled the screen. But instead of risking a fresh, imaginative portrayal of life, whether through fantasy or realism, movies too often reverted to formulas. Although large studios and chains of theaters had created financial health for the industry, the artistic heart of the motion picture business was put in jeopardy, as was its cordial relationship with the church.

In 1919, as a tribute to his mother, D. W. Griffith volunteered to film the Centenary Celebration of the Methodist Episcopal Church where seventy-five thousand congregants would assemble. Key filmmakers were invited to address the throng, and a giant, eight-story screen allowed attendees to view film. Those in attendance were encouraged to use any means possible, including movies, to share the Christian gospel. But the key figure with regard to the church and Hollywood during the period between World War I and the Depression was not Griffith. It was Cecil B. DeMille, who recognized in the increasingly secular culture a growing market for the illicit. Religious himself, DeMille nevertheless understood the new morality of the flapper era and gave the public what they wanted—a religious gloss over salacious scenes. After viewing one of DeMille's movies, D. W. Griffith was reportedly so upset with DeMille's tactics that he said to his star Lillian Gish, "I'll never use the Bible as a chance to undress a woman!"[10] DeMille's "bathtub" and "bathrobe" epics all had a similar shape and feel to them. Based on the rationalization that indiscretion could be presented on the screen as long as the sin was eventually corrected, his spectacles were little more than glorified melodramas that included an effective combination of debauchery and piety. They were, however, hits with the public.

In *The Ten Commandments* (1923), which was produced for the then-astronomical figure of one-and-a-half million dollars, DeMille housed his portrayals of orgies within a larger moral framework of the giving of the Law. In his next film, on the life of Christ, DeMille realized that he was on even more sensitive ground, so he used Protestant, Catholic, and Jewish clergy as advisors (perhaps to co-opt the opposition!). He even had Mass celebrated on the set each morning. But DeMille also turned to the best-selling author Bruce Barton, who had written his life of Christ as if Jesus were a Madison Avenue executive. Again, the formula of biblical veneer (some of the heroic postures are held so long that they bring to mind a religious painting) and contemporary recasting is evident. *The King of Kings* (1927) opened with DeMille's usual formula of sex and piety, this time beginning with an apocryphal scene in Mary Magdalene's lavish pleasure palace, where she is expressing anger about the loss of her boyfriend, Judas, who has forsaken her to follow a preacher from Nazareth. Leaving her guests in the middle of the party, Mary rides off on her chariot to get Judas back and is converted upon meeting Jesus. And so the biblical story is not only retold but rewritten.

Confrontation

It was the continuing excesses of DeMille's orgies that finally ushered in a period of direct confrontation with churches. This was particularly true of the Roman Catholic Church, which realized the power of film to shape opinion. DeMille's *The Sign of the Cross* (1932) portrayed both pagans and Christians in Nero's Rome. Again, DeMille gave his viewers an "immoral morality play."[11] It is Nero's fiddle that sounds most loudly as the camera pauses voyeuristically to capture the pagan excesses. The movie's most famous scene shows the empress Poppea, played by Claudia Colbert, bathing in milk and saying to the Christian Dacia, "Take off your clothes, get in here, and tell me all about it." The camera shows Colbert's back and legs, while not quite exposing her breasts. But it was enough; the sensual effect accomplished its intention. So, too, did the scenes of torture and suffering. Many, in fact, when looking at the film today, think DeMille was almost obsessed by cruelty. There was in the film such a heavy dose of sex and sadism that a growing number of leaders, both in the Protestant and in the Catholic Church, found it offensive.

Public opposition to Hollywood had been growing since the early twenties. Coming hard on the back of the Chicago White Sox baseball scandal in 1919, when several of the sport's idols were accused of game-fixing, several high-profile scandals involving Hollywood people caused a popular backlash. Mary Pickford, "America's Sweetheart," proved to be not quite the innocent that she portrayed on the screen as she divorced her husband to marry her lover, Douglas Fairbanks. Then, in 1922, "Fatty" Arbuckle was accused of rape and contributing to the death of an actress. Though he was never convicted, the lurid stories in the press ruined his successful career. Just as the baseball establishment had looked for a "czar" to bring back into the game a perception of morality, so the movie industry moved quickly to appoint a head of their association whose character was beyond reproach.

(The industry already had a loosely rendered list of thirteen prohibitions that included proscriptions of such subjects as drunkenness, nudity, crime, gambling, and illicit love. But the vague and omnibus quality of these standards, plus the lack of any enforcement tool, made them ineffective.) Faced with the growing threat of government censorship, the industry organized itself as the Motion Picture Producers and Distributors of America (MPPDA) and appointed Will Hays to develop and supervise a self-censorship program. An elder in the

Presbyterian Church, Postmaster General of the United States, and chairman of the Republican Party, Hays brought prestige to the office. His new production guidelines were approved in 1927. Similar to the earlier attempt, they included a ban on swearing, any suggestive nudity, ridicule of the clergy, anti-patriotism, and so on. But Hays made the standards more effective than the previous effort. Through his office, over one hundred scripts were rejected between 1924 and 1930. Self-control seemed to be working.

With the rise in production costs and the loss of editing flexibility given the advent of sound in movies, a greater codification of the rules seemed necessary, however. Studios were unwilling to modify their product once it was largely finished. Martin Quigley, a Catholic film journal publisher, and Daniel Lord, a Jesuit priest who had consulted with DeMille on *The King of Kings*, were brought in. After a series of meetings with Hays and with representatives of the studios, a new Production Code was adopted in 1930.

But the start of the Depression quickly changed matters with regard to Hollywood's willingness to live by the Code. Faced with growing red ink, the studios turned to sensationalism—to sex and violence—to lure back the public. As James Skinner opines, "Nothing succeeds like excess."[12] Gangster films such as *Little Caesar* (1930), starring Edward G. Robinson and Douglas Fairbanks Jr., and *Public Enemy* (1931), with James Cagney, were thought by many to glorify crime. *Blonde Venus* (1932), starring Marlene Dietrich, took prostitution as a theme, even if the star became a hooker for the sake of her child. Neither the Hays Office nor its Production Code Administration, which was created to grant a seal of approval, could stem the tide of the sensational and seductive. It was perhaps the production of *The Sign of the Cross* (1932) that best symbolized that a voluntary system of restraint would no longer work. When Will Hays asked Cecil B. DeMille what he was going to do about a provocative dance scene in the movie, DeMille replied, "Not a damned thing." And the scene was left in the final cut. But if Hollywood would not do something itself, then the church felt it had to step into the void.

The response of the Catholic Church was the creation of the Legion of Decency. In 1933, the Vatican's Apostolic Delegate in the United States announced that "Catholics are called by God, the Pope, the bishops and the priests to a united and vigorous campaign for the purification of the cinema, which has become a deadly menace to morals."[13] This was followed later in the year by the appointment of an Episcopal Committee on Motion Pictures, which was charged with coming up with a plan to stem the tide of Hollywood excess. Bishops around the country were also beginning to act unilaterally. In 1934 Cardinal Dougherty of Philadelphia instructed his faithful with regard to movies to "stay away from all of them. . . . [T]his is not merely a counsel but a positive command, binding all in conscience under pain of sin."[14] As a result, attendance in Philadelphia theaters quickly fell by 40 percent. Flush with a new sense of power, the Episcopal Committee came up with the idea of a pledge of decency that it would ask Catholics to abide by.

The Legion of Decency asked its members to "remain away from all motion pictures except those which do not offend decency and Christian morality."[15] Within a few months, seven to nine million Catholics had taken the pledge. With the Legion of Decency providing the strong arm, the Production Code got a new lease on life. Joseph Breen was appointed to administer the Code, and he began working with both producers and the Legion to ensure that acceptable movies were screened. The Code's "first principle" set the tone for its twelve(!) commandments: "No picture shall be produced which will lower the moral standards of those who see it. Hence the sympathy of the audience shall never be thrown to the side of wrong-doing, evil or sin." Its eighth restriction stated, "No film or episode may throw ridicule on any religious faith."[16]

Though the Code was only advisory, the Legion gave it teeth through its threat of boycott. But, to be effective, the Legion needed a standardized system for rating what was unacceptable for viewing by members in the church. Thus, the bishops turned to the International Federation of Catholic Alumnae, a film-reviewing group of the Catholic Church that dated back to 1924 and was located in New York City, away from the pressure of Hollywood. While this group of educated women had heretofore only rated acceptable movies by placing them in two categories—suitable for church halls and suitable for mature audiences but not for church and school settings—they now were asked to rate unsuitable movies as well. And their power in influencing the Code for well over two decades is legend.

The initial results of the Hays Office, working in conjunction with the Legion, were impressive. By 1936, 91 percent of the movies that the Legion reviewed were given an "A" (approved) rating, and only 13 out of 1,271 movies were labeled "C" (condemned). The stories of how various film projects were altered to avoid the wrath of the censors make interesting, if dated, reading. If producers accepted the advice of Joseph Breen in the Hays Office, then the Legion usually followed with the granting of acceptable ratings.

Again, however, larger pressures from society intervened. With the advent of World War II, two-piece swimsuits were justified on the patriotic grounds of saving fabric! Women became common in the workplace, and pinup calendars were everywhere. Standards with regard to sexuality in the movies seemed hopelessly dated. The Hays Office responded by subtly easing its Code, but the Legion of Decency remained adamant that morality would be preserved. Howard Hughes's movie *The Outlaw* (1943), publicized with pictures of Jane Russell wearing a cantilevered bra that enabled her breasts to be maximized regardless of her posture, became a focal point. When in 1940 the Production Code Office warned Hughes that Rio (Jane Russell) was not to be leaning over in her peasant blouse in front of the screen, Hughes ignored the warning. Approval was therefore denied pending thirty-seven cuts. Hughes was not through, however, and he went to the Appeals Board. The result was a capitulation by the Production Code Office and the ordering of cuts of only one minute. Breen had lost most of the battle. Though the wrangling over this film would last for six more years before *The Outlaw* went to national release, and though the Legion's own censors were eventually able to extract another twenty minutes of cuts, the tide was turning.[17]

By the fifties, the system of censorship was clearly failing. Society's standards had changed concerning what was deemed acceptable. In 1956, the Code was revised, but to no avail. The Catholic Church, on the other hand, tried to stand firm. For example, when the Broadway play *The Moon Is Blue* was adapted for the screen by Otto Preminger in 1953, the Legion opposed its use of the words *pregnant* and *virgin* (words not then heard in American movies) as well as its easy posture toward girls being seduced, even though the heroine herself remained a virgin. Although the Legion condemned the movie with a "C" rating and Cardinal Spellman warned Catholics against attendance, *Life*, *Variety*, and *Newsweek* all gave the movie strong reviews, and the courts ensured that theaters could not ban films from being shown without better reason. Over ten thousand theaters screened the movie, and it proved a box-office success, with Catholics attending in the same proportion as the general population.

To make matters worse, the Catholic rating systems worldwide were proving to be inconsistent. For example, the International Catholic Film Office awarded Fellini's *La Strada* (1954) a major prize, only for the Legion to rate it unacceptable for the general public. On the other hand, when Fellini's *La Dolce Vita* came out in 1960, there was a papal condemnation of the film, but this was not enough to keep the Legion from dividing into two camps with regard to the acceptability of the movie. The opening scene has a large granite statue of Christ being carried over the people by helicopter for installation at St. Peter's Square. In this way, Christ is symbolized as out of touch with the people. Moreover, hedonism and immorality among the rich make up the bulk of the story. Nevertheless, the artistic strength of the movie caused the Legion ultimately to deem it acceptable for mature audiences. The era of the Code and the Legion was over.

A New Rating System

In the sixties, society's standards and Hollywood's tastes changed even more quickly. *The Pawnbroker* (1965), *Who's Afraid of Virginia Woolf?* (1966), and *Alfie* (1966) appeared and—with their flashbacks of concentration camp memories, vitriolic domestic argument, and immoral and abusive seduction—set new standards of openness in Hollywood. The Production Code was now largely ineffective, and the Legion was increasingly ignored. In one year, the Legion's listing of objectionable movies rose from 15 to 24 percent. A means of providing more nuanced ratings was clearly necessary.

The growing popularity of international films was as important to the changing context as was the Code's demise. Students were flocking to cinemas to see the "artistic" films of European and Asian directors. How could the Legion give their highest rating to *Godzilla versus Mothra* (1964) and condemn Antonioni's *Blowup* (1966)? The wide popularity of serious, subtitled films in the late fifties and early sixties—movies by Kurosawa, Bergman, Buñuel, and Fellini—together with the ineffectiveness of the Production Code caused Hollywood to scrap the old system of self-regulation.

In its place, there was adopted in 1966 a variant of the current ratings system, one self-administered by the major studios without church intervention. The code was developed under the direction of Jack Valenti and the Motion Picture Association of America, beginning just prior to the release of *The Graduate* (1967) and *Bonnie and Clyde* (1967). Things had changed forever in Hollywood. Sympathy could now be thrown to the side of wrongdoing and sin. Movie critic Pauline Kael noted that by the end of the seventies, the "old mock innocence" had too often been replaced by "the sentimentalization of defeat" and a movie culture that seemed to "thrive on moral chaos."[18] It is understandable, as well, that in some movies a backlash against the church and its clerics was portrayed. After all, Hollywood had not been able to present anything but pietistic glosses on Christianity for most of its existence. Michael Medved is no doubt right that some in Hollywood swung the pendulum too far.[19] But there was surely that within clergy and church practices also deserving of criticism.

If theologians and church-related film critics were to have any voice at all in this new situation, they would need a broader and more informed approach to a Christian understanding and interpretation of film than the traditional rhetoric of caution or even abstinence. Dialogue, not censorship, was being called for. It was in this changing context that the church began to interact theologically in a new way with Hollywood.

1979 to the Present

Other forces were also acting on the church's relationship with Hollywood. With the advent of television after World War II, movies became a staple of most people's diet, as ubiquitous as the living room in their homes. In the process, church censorship was made next to impossible, even for the faithful. In 1979, however, George Atkinson helped popularize home viewing of Hollywood films in a more far-reaching way. That year he opened the first video rental store, making viewing-on-demand a possibility. For the first time, the viewer controlled the market. By the 1970s, Hollywood executives had begun making feature-length movies available on videocassette, charging fifty dollars each. There were few takers. But Atkinson saw an opportunity and with fifty movies that he purchased—including *The French Connection* (1971), *The Sound of Music* (1965), and *Butch Cassidy and the Sundance Kid* (1969)—he offered customers rentals for ten dollars. People came in droves. Other innovations have followed, the DVD being the most significant to date. In 1999, the packaging of DVDs with extra features began in earnest with Larry and Andy Wachowski adding two documentaries to their DVD version of *The Matrix* (1999). By 2005, there were more than 24,000 video stores in the United States, according to the Video Software Dealers Association. Customers rented 2.6 billion DVDs and VHS cassettes in 2004, generating more than $8 billion in revenue. We had become a movie culture.

What about the church during this same period? Though statistics vary, it is clear that, since 1979, church attendance has fallen in the United States, and commitment to the institutional church has slackened. Increasingly, churches are losing people "to the weekend," as one pastor observed. Arts festivals, beaches, bookstores, bicycles, Starbucks—people are using Sundays for leisure activities and turning to more individual expressions of faith for their spirituality—Internet prayer sites, movies, reading. A Gallup Poll in 2004 found that about 31 percent of Americans say they attend worship services once a week.[20] Yet actual attendance would seem to be far less. According to actual attendance counts in 2003, adults who went to church in a given week—rather than those who said they did—numbered barely over 18 percent of the national population, and the figure is declining.[21]

The church's response to these new realities has varied, as we will document in chapter 3. A few continue to resist (and often get media attention), believing that greater purity and a reassertion of doctrinal priorities is the best "defense" against such growing secularism. But a larger and increasing number of Christians have recognized that since the church's message is a story, and since movies are our culture's primary storytelling medium, dialogue and interaction are called for. As Rodney Clapp observes, "In our very busy, overly hectic lives and society, people don't pause for any kind of contemplation or second thoughts about what's the meaning of life except in places like movie theaters. At my church, we have people who see films together and then talk about it."[22]

Churches are also doing more than just talking. According to one research group, in 2004, 29 percent of all U.S. churches used video clips at least once a month, up from just 4 percent in 1999. In another survey, the Calvin Institute found that in 2003, 21 percent of all churches were using film clips each week.[23] If the church is to have any influence in society, if it hopes to continue to relate even to its own members (particularly its youth), let alone communicate its story effectively to those outside its doors, the church must use film creatively in its various ministries. However, Sally Morgenthaler, a consultant to the Emerging Church movement, complains that, at present, worship pragmatism is too often undermining the quality of the worship service in churches. That is, although movies are increasingly being used, they are being used poorly.[24] Congregants are seeking the Light but are instead being treated to worship lite. There is no doubt that the quality of dialogue and usage needs to improve (and no doubt will) in the years ahead. But there is also this new reality: the astounding proliferation of film usage by churches as they enter the twenty-first century.

Support for the use of media and the arts is coming from multiple quarters. Pope John Paul II, for example, in his *Address to the Festival for the Third Millennium*, December 1999, asserted:

> People created in the image and likeness of God are naturally called to peace and harmony with God, with others, with ourselves, and with all creation. The cinema can become an interpreter of this natural propensity and strive to be a place of reflection, a call to values, an invitation to dialogue and communion. . . .
>
> The cinema enjoys a wealth of languages, a multiplicity of styles, and a truly great variety of narrative forms. . . . It can contribute to bringing people closer, to reconciling enemies, to favoring art and ever more respectful dialogue between diverse cultures.[25]

This pope, himself a poet and playwright who saw several of his plays turned into movies, also affirmed in an address to participants of the Pontifical Academies in 2004 "the *via pulchritudinis* [the 'path of beauty'] as the best way for the Christian faith and the culture of our time to meet, besides being a valuable instrument for the formation of the young generations."[26]

Bishop T. D. Jakes, who appeared on the cover of *Time* in 2001 as America's best preacher and had his movie *Woman, Thou Art Loosed* (2004) reviewed favorably by the *New York Times*, was asked by *Time* magazine if cinema is the next frontier of evangelism. He responded, "It can be. The gospel is not about standing and saying 'Come to me.' It's about going where they are, and the world is at the theater."[27] As the church enters the twenty-first century, it is indeed trying to "go where they are." Richard Corliss, *Time* magazine's film critic, observed in an article discussing the church's use of film in its ministries:

> For decades America has embraced a baffling contradiction. The majority of its people are churchgoing Christians, many of them evangelical. Yet, its mainstream pop culture, especially film, is secular at best, often raw and irreligious. It's hard to see these two vibrant strains of society ever coexisting, learning from each other. Yet, the two are not only meeting, they're also sitting down and breaking bread together.[28]

The church is now recognizing that theology is often being done outside its doors. Thus, a spate of books on film have appeared since 1990 whose primary intention is to bring movies into the church's life and witness. Terry Lindvall's bibliography of religion and film (2004, 2005) stretches to almost eighty pages![29] Some of these books have a more catechetical function, using movies to interpret the Apostles' Creed, for example.[30] Other books use movies to illumine biblical texts.[31] Still others provide pastors help with their preaching.[32] Some of the most popular books encouraging film's use in the church (though they are often quite superficial) are those intended to suggest appropriate clips that youth leaders might utilize.[33] There is also a growing number of books and Internet resources meant to facilitate group discussion with adults and teens,[34] as well as some seeking to be an aid to spiritual growth.[35]

Supporting and encouraging the church's rapid adoption of film as a resource for its life and witness is the escalating number of Christian websites that review movies and/or provide resources on movies for Christian study and reflection. Gordon Matties, a professor of biblical studies and theology at Canadian Mennonite University, has created a website titled "Movie Theology: Movie Reviews and Resources," which provides users a link to multiple websites offering movie reviews from a Christian perspective.[36] As of June 2006, Matties listed forty-eight such websites, six blogs, two film discussion groups, and five review sites geared to parents wondering about a film's use of sex, vulgar language, and violence. The granddaddy of these sites is HollywoodJesus.com, where webmaster David Bruce has attracted 700 million hits since its inception in 1997. He provides multiple reviews, visuals, links to the movie's websites, a reader's forum, and much more. Another excellent site is *Christianity Today*'s Film Forum,[37] a weekly digest by Jeffrey Overstreet of comments by both Christian and mainstream newspaper critics, together with his own helpful perspectives.

The church and Hollywood are in dialogue in other ways too. Many seminaries and Christian colleges are moving quickly to add theology (or religion) and film classes to their curriculum, while others have instituted film discussion nights on their campuses. The City of Angels Film Festival (CAFF), a retrospective festival held at the Directors Guild of America Theaters in Hollywood is in its twelfth year as it seeks to foster discussion about film from a spiritual perspective to assist the renewal of the city. Other cities have followed suit. The Damah Film Festival, for example, which was located in Seattle for its first three years and is currently in Los Angeles, has spotlighted new movies that feature spiritually meaningful images on film. Reel Spirituality has held a yearly conference in conjunction with CAFF that has brought church leaders and film professionals together to discuss storytelling as common ground. Similar conferences, both in Great Britain and the United States, are becoming regular fixtures of the church's life. At the congregational level, churches are regularly offering cinema cafés or similar venues where films are shown, food is provided, and discussion is facilitated.

Common to many of these ventures is the belief that movies provide a helpful occasion for spiritual dialogue and insight. One of my students recently narrated his experience in leading a film discussion with a small group in his church, of which he had been a member for some time. The group had reached a plateau relationally despite their attempts to create a more genuine Christian community. They decided to watch *Italian for Beginners* (2002), a film that portrays a group of characters dealing with self-doubt, loss, and the need for acceptance and love. The student related:

As we began to discuss the movie, it became apparent that it served the group in a role none of us had consistently found the courage to take on, by initiating and modeling a level of vulnerability and disclosure that gave the group permission to respond in kind. As a likeable, funny, but unflinchingly honest and deeply reflective participant in our conversation, the movie was the catalyst for a "healthier small-group dynamic," allowing us to share from our truer selves.[38]

A movie provided this group the occasion to reflect on their individual and collective faith, to receive one another as partners in the story's shared joys, uncertainties, failures, and undeserved gifts of life, and to receive moments of grace within these intimate realities.

As the church moves more fully into the twenty-first century, the old hostilities are still present in some quarters. And given the sensationalism and commercialism of some Hollywood movies, a prophetic voice is still appropriate, as we will discuss in a later chapter. But movies are also increasingly recognized as serving the church and the synagogue, the mosque and the temple. They are providing a resource in our personal and societal search for meaning and transcendence; they are helping those in the church develop a clearer understanding of how religion is both perceived and expressed today; and they have become the occasion for relating missionally with those outside the church and for theological reflection for those within it.

theological approaches to film criticism

Since the invention of motion pictures a century ago, we can observe a variety of theological responses that the church has made to film as it has learned from and has sought to influence Hollywood. These responses fall into one of five types: avoidance, caution, dialogue, appropriation, and divine encounter.[1] They can be depicted graphically on a linear timeline:

Figure 3.1 The Theologian/Critic's Posture

Although these approaches developed more or less chronologically over the last eighty-five years (1920–2005), we can still find good contemporary representatives of all five of these types of theologian/critic. Moreover, as each approach is more a "type" than a firm category, some theologians have adopted, over time, multiple perspectives, while others have proven somewhat eclectic in their approach. Despite this fluidity, these options are nonetheless identifiable.

These same five theological approaches to Hollywood can also be graphed using a matrix to show (1) whether a given theologian/critic begins his or her reflection with the movie itself or with a theological position, and (2) whether a given response centers on the movie more ethically or aesthetically:

55

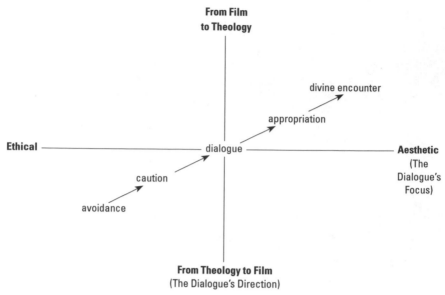

Figure 3.2 The Theologian/Critic's Approach

Theologians who articulate an avoidance strategy do so from an ethical posture (often their books even have words like "morality" and "values" in their titles) and always move from their given theological perspective to the film under consideration, never vice versa. On the other hand, those interested in exploring a divine encounter through film begin with the film and only in light of the film itself attempt to make theological judgments. When they do, moreover, the criticism tends first of all to be aesthetic, not ethical, in nature.

Spread out along the diagonal that we can draw between these contrasting approaches are the three other positions. Those expressing caution take the film itself more seriously but still focus their responses on the film's ethical stance, beginning their deliberations from a given biblical/theological posture. Those wishing for theological dialogue want theology to inform their film viewing and film viewing to inform their theology in a lively two-way conversation that is both ethical and aesthetic in nature. Those desiring to appropriate the movie's meaning begin their deliberations with the movie itself but bring their own theological perspectives more strongly into the conversation than those who would explore divine encounters.

Both Jewish and Christian theologians/critics have often proven more eclectic in their approach than the graph might suggest. They have in practice made use of more than one of these approaches, depending on the films being considered and the audience intended. (That not all persons fit neatly into a given category is typical of any typology, for these are simply artificial constructs to help organize data.) But many have tended in their theological criticism to use a dominant perspective toward the movies.

Avoidance

The stance of some Christians has been to continue the boycott mentality that characterized conservative Protestantism and Roman Catholicism of an earlier era. Writing in the forties in an introduction to Herbert Miles's *Movies and Morals*, Hyman Appelman labeled movies to be "next to liquor, the outstanding menace to America and to the world."[2] Miles, if anything, was even stronger in his condemnation: "They [movies] are the organ of the devil, the idol of sinners, the sink of infamy, the stumbling block to human progress, the moral cancer of civilization, the Number One Enemy of Jesus Christ."[3] The best that Miles could say about Hollywood was, "There are some good teachings in the movies. Yes. And there is some good paper in the waste basket, but it is only to be used when it is impossible to secure paper from any other source."[4]

Such rhetoric seems to come from a bygone day, certainly one before the advent of television. But Carl McClain, writing for a Nazarene publishing house in 1970, expressed a similar sentiment: "I submit that a frequenter of the theatre or movie house cannot at the same time be a spiritual force for good, a vital Christian leader or Sunday school teacher."[5] Bryan Stone, author of the book *Faith and Film: Theological Themes at the Cinema* (2000), begins his case for the importance of cinema becoming a dialogue partner for Christians by recalling: "I grew up in a conservative Christian denomination that taught that it was wrong to go to the movies. The cinema was spelled *s-i-n-ema*, and Hollywood, we were taught, was an industry that was as opposed to Christian values as anything could be."[6]

More typical today than such blanket condemnation, however, is the argument for a selective boycott of films judged to be morally objectionable. It is, after all, difficult to condemn *The Sound of Music* (1965) or *The Straight Story* (1999). For example, writing to the organizers of the City of Angels Film Festival, Dr. Ted Baehr, chairman of the Christian Film and Television Commission, complained that the Festival had chosen to show Peter Weir's *The Year of Living Dangerously* (1982) and Martin Scorsese's *Taxi Driver* (1976). He attached to his memorandum several pages from the *Communist Manifesto* and complained that Weir's film "takes the side of the Communists in the Indonesian struggle for freedom from Communism. I was there at the time," he writes, "and can tell you firsthand that the communists were killing thousands of people, particularly Christians, and were not the good guys as portrayed in the film." He continues, "My question for *Taxi Driver* would be: What was it about the movie that influenced John Hinkley to shoot President Reagan? When you start to answer that question you will start to understand the spiritual significance of the movie, as you well know."[7] For Baehr, there is a great divide between much of Hollywood and the church. "By supporting the good and rejecting the bad, Christians can make a difference."[8] The religion portrayed in the majority of movies is not Christianity but "materialism, consumerism, eroticism, hedonism, . . . humanism, . . . the cult of violence."[9] Many films should just not be shown, thinks Baehr. Or if they are, Christians should protest by not going to movie theaters and instead relying on DVDs and videotapes, which they can selectively view.

Similarly, Larry Poland has written of his leadership in boycotting *The Last Temptation of Christ* (1988). In his book *The Last Temptation of Hollywood*, which was rushed to press just months after the release of Martin Scorsese's film, Poland chronicles what he calls "this century's most passionate conflict between Christians and Hollywood."[10] What he calls "the hideous distortions of the person and work of Jesus," both in the novel by Nikos Kazantzakis[11] and in the screenplay by Paul Schrader, caused Poland and a small group of other concerned Christians eventually to organize a boycott that was partially effective.

There is no question that Universal Studios was duplicitous in trying to quiet those like Larry Poland whom they thought would criticize their interpretation of the Christ event. They lied, were purposely deceptive, and tried to use their power and influence to cover up their high-handedness. Their marketing attempts and damage-control plans lacked ethical conviction. Poland, for his part, tries to avoid the "C" word (censorship), which was exploited by the press to characterize his efforts. But the boycott that he organized with Bill Bright, James Dobson, Donald Wildmon, and other Christian leaders, together with their publicly announced attempt to buy all copies of the film from the studio in order to destroy them, had the same feel to much of the American public. For Poland, Hollywood, like other businesses, must be morally accountable for its actions or accept the consequences: "If there is no 'chilling effect' for film and TV producers from the deeply religious majority in America, we will be seeing child molesting, cannibalism, sado-masochism, bestiality, and even 'snuff' films soon accepted as 'art' on the major movie screens of America."[12]

Although many remain unconvinced by Poland's logic, some churches continue to use boycott as a primary strategy for dealing with Hollywood. The Catholic League for Religious and Civil Rights, for example, mounted a vigorous boycott campaign in 2002 against distribution in the United States of the Mexican film, *El Crimen del Padre Amaro*. The movie was one of four films released that year that were critical of the Catholic Church: the French movie *Amen* highlighted the alleged silence of Pope Pius XII concerning the Holocaust; the Italian film *The Bankers of God* focused on recent Vatican bank scandals; the English movie *The Magdalene Sisters* told the story of young women who, when judged promiscuous by their families and priest, were "locked away" in laundries run by Irish nuns (this practice continued into the 1960s); and then this Mexican film, "The Crime of Father Amaro," which tells the story of Padre Amaro, played by Gael Garcia Bernal, who has an affair with a teenager. In the movie, the church is portrayed as morally passive, choosing neither to confront drug lords nor to connect with the people as this padre could. Cardinal Carrera of Mexico criticized the movie as "an atheistic smear on the church and its priests, designed to stir intolerance."[13] This judgment was seemingly shared by the Catholic League, which mounted a large letter-writing campaign. Yet Mexican viewers made the movie the biggest box-office hit in the country's history, with exit polls finding that 70 percent of audiences approved of the story. As is often the case, opposition helped draw a crowd. Despite (or perhaps because of) the official opposition of the Catholic Church, often in the news for its sexual abuse scandals, these movies found a wider and more receptive audience than might otherwise have been the case.

The Catholic League for Religious and Civil Rights is perhaps better known in the United States for its opposition to *Dogma*. When Kevin Smith's irreverent yet God-affirming movie opened at the New York Film Festival in October 1999, it did so over the objections of Cardinal John O'Connor and Mayor Rudolph Giuliani. That the movie exuberantly affirms the existence of God and tells the story of a woman's recovery of faith, or that Smith is a practicing Catholic, was thought irrelevant. It was simply enough that organized Christianity was mocked and theology questioned.

In *Dogma*, a thirteenth apostle (played by Chris Rock) claims to have been cut out of the Bible because he is black! There are pot-smoking prophets, the crucifix is replaced by the statue of a "Buddy Christ" winking and giving the thumbs-up, and scatological and sexual humor abounds. The plot revolves around two fallen angels, banished from heaven and now living in Wisconsin, who seek to reenter heaven against God's wishes through a loophole in church dogma. A plenary indulgence has been granted to any who pass through the arch of a particular Catholic church in New Jersey, allowing them to be read-mitted to heaven.[14] The story, like jokes in the movie, is irreverent, but it also affirms the importance of faith, the benevolence of God, and the divinity of Christ. Here is a movie that is not agnostic or un-Christian in viewpoint, even if it is sacrilegious and sexy in design. After all, as Smith commented, if he were to talk about God to his generation, he wouldn't make *The Song of Bernadette* (1943). Instead, Smith wanted "to do something full of faith that was entertaining enough to keep [viewers] in their seats."[15]

A spokesperson for the Catholic League for Religious and Civil Rights, how-ever, wrote that "the entire plot is one situation after another of making fun of the Catholic faith."[16] It mattered not that when the criticism of *Dogma* was made, no one had yet seen the movie. Reading an early version of the script with its assorted vulgarities and anti-religious jibes and noting that George Carlin was cast as the cardinal and Alanis Morissette as God was enough for the League to institute a letter-writing campaign and for the United States Catholic Conference to give the film its worst rating of "O" ("morally offensive"). Smith has said that the idea for the movie came as he sat in church and listened to homilies that condemned sinners rather than invigorated the faithful. As one of the characters in the movie says, "I have issues with anyone who treats God as a burden, not a blessing." Such theology was lost on many churchgoers but not on the wider public. As the headline in the *Los Angeles Times* announced following the movie's opening, "*Dogma* Opens in New York to Protesters' Jeers, Audience Cheers."[17]

Caution

> I vacillate between the peril of pleasure
> And the value of the experience.
>
> Augustine, *The Confessions*
> *of Saint Augustine*

A more common attitude among contemporary conservative Christians is that of caution. With the advent of television, few Christians continued to argue for abstinence as a viable strategy. But many remain worried over the entertainment industry's influence. Writing about the Academy Award nominations in 2005 for Best Picture, the Protestant Chuck Colson complained that "the films Hollywood chose to honor had little to do with quality and everything to do with philosophy and worldview." Quoting Barbara Nicolosi, a Catholic who is executive director of *Act One: Writing for Hollywood*, a screenwriting workshop for Christians held in several cities around the United States each year, he complained: "Hollywood's choices affirm, once again, 'just how very, very sick America's storytellers have become.'"[18] Nicolosi's comments were, in part, her reaction to the Academy's snub of Mel Gibson's *Passion of the Christ* (2004), a movie that affected her deeply. But her language is unguarded. She suggested in the article Colson quotes that it might even be a sin against the Holy Spirit for the industry to be "throwing accolades at films that are essentially depraved in their themes." Why, she asks, "would the Academy want to give awards to mediocre films?"[19]

From firsthand experience, I know that both Colson and Nicolosi are committed to a vibrant engagement with popular culture. For both, however, that engagement is seen as a "culture war." Thus Nicolosi, the screenwriter, states in an interview with ZENIT, the Catholic news agency: "The best way to change Hollywood is to get more of *our people* in this town" (italics added).[20] And Colson, the culture critic, advises readers both in his *Breakpoint Commentary* and in his devotional book, *How Now Shall We Live?* of their need to "demystify movie magic" by learning to unpack its techniques and by identifying the filmmaker's worldview.[21] Both critics are quick to add that Hollywood can sometimes get it right, but they also bemoan the fact that the percentages are so low. As Colson writes, "Yes, there are too many bad movies out there—films that celebrate depravity. But there are good ones too. Films we can use to teach our kids and our neighbors good lessons."[22]

The title of Lloyd Billingsley's book *The Seductive Image* suggests its content and approach. He writes that since his "expectations of film are low," he is rarely disappointed: "My basic posture toward film as a medium is increasingly skeptical, and any list of all-time favorites I could put together would be rather short. That said, I stress the medium's power, and add that to ignore it would be folly."[23] John Butler is similarly cynical and introduces his discussion of movies by saying that "the second part [of the book] goes to the movies with a look at some of the moral issues served up in between the popcorn and candy bars. Tips on choosing a movie and possibly saving up to five dollars by skipping that new movie, depending on where you live, are examined in chapter ten."[24]

In their arguments, Billingsley and Butler stay tightly within the Christian sphere, but their skeptical rhetoric is self-defeating with regard to influencing any serious moviegoer. I say this despite the obvious strength of their position in arguing for a necessary moral discrimination when it comes to critiquing a movie. Their books remind me of the pastor who wrote a letter to the editor about an article I wrote putting the movie *The Shawshank Redemption* (1994) into conversation with the Old Testament book of Ecclesiastes. On the strength of my recommendation, he said he had taken his preteen daughters to see the movie and was horrified by the prison rape scenes and the disgusting language. Only at the end of the letter did he admit that he hadn't really taken his daughters, but he might have (and how could a Christian recommend an R-rated movie?). My answer is twofold. First, most adults will find the portrayal of hope, friendship, and justice in *The Shawshank Redemption* moral to the core, despite its realistic prison setting. And second, what is suitable for a twenty-eight-year-old viewer is not necessarily appropriate for an eight-year-old. Just as with the other arts, cultural exposure must always be correlated with personal and spiritual maturity.

Viewer discrimination is obviously necessary for Christians of all ages. One of my single students in her mid-thirties explained to me that although she understood why I had assigned the classic baseball movie *Bull Durham* (1988) for those in the class, its glorification of casual sex was so well done that it was a temptation to her as she struggled to live a Christian life. She said she would not ordinarily go to such a movie. She did not need it. I said I agreed. Not everyone should see all movies. Discrimination is called for, but so too is sensitivity and maturity in film viewing.

Michael Medved serves as a good example of a cautious but thoughtful critic of Hollywood's values. Although a faithful Jew, Medved does not assume a Jewish readership as he argues that by constantly pushing the ethical envelope, the entertainment world "encourages" (even if it does not cause) antisocial activity.[25] Though moviemaking might function within a contemporary cultural consensus of values, Hollywood also seeks to transform it. In chapter after chapter of his book *Hollywood vs. America* (1992), Medved wages war with Hollywood because he sees that movies promote promiscuity, malign marriage, encourage illegitimacy, and belittle parents. Moreover, they are hostile to heroes, bash America, use foul language, often offend, and gravitate toward violence.

In his section titled "The Attack on Religion," Medved argues that there is today a one-sided vicious stereotyping of the church. In the thirties and forties we had handsome stars who were lovable priests (e.g., Spencer Tracy in *Boys Town* [1938] and Bing Crosby in *The Bells of St. Mary's* [1945]), and there was a feeling of religious uplift in many movies. In the 1980s, by contrast, it was more typical to see Christians portrayed as crazed killers and the clergy as vicious, morally corrupt, and bizarre looking. Hollywood seems intent on affronting the religious sensibilities of ordinary Americans. Medved asks rhetorically, If movie after movie shows this, will not viewers begin to believe it? Anti-religious movies typically lose money, Medved notes, but moviemakers do not seem to care. They have an axe to grind.

Perhaps Medved has overstated his case. Given that the Hollywood Production Code banned any unfavorable treatment of religion, that clergy and nuns were once portrayed more positively should not surprise anyone. Consider the analysis provided by Mark Hulsether, who notes a study done in 1996 that surveyed top grossing films between 1946 and 1990: "It reports that the portrayal of religious characters moved from being far more sympathetic than that of nonreligious characters to being comparable with nonreligious characters over the period studied." Hulsether asks rhetorically, "Should clergy be alarmed that after 1976 they were heroes only 50 percent of the time . . . about the same as other characters? Still, religious characters remained more likely to be good than the nonreligious (56 percent vs. 52 percent) and almost as likely (54 percent vs. 57 percent) to succeed."[26]

Les and Barbara Keyser question Medved's conclusions from another perspective. This is what they have to say concerning the Production Code's ban on portraying clergy in a bad light: "In practice, the sanction against evil or comic ministers became a benediction for virtuous and gleeful clerics. If one couldn't laugh at the religious, one could laugh with them. And if clergy couldn't be evil, they could be supernaturally innocent. The priest became a new unearthly creature, full of smiles and cheery lessons, singing songs of innocence to confound the world of experience; nuns worked their own magic by flying or, at the least, singing in perfect key."[27] Lacking any real spiritual dimension, priests could be interested only in saving their church's architecture.[28]

Just before the Oscars in 1999, Medved wrote an article for *USA Today* in which he refers to a study by Kagan Media Appraisals, a Hollywood consulting firm, which analyzed the return on investment of every nationally released film between 1988 and 1997: "The resulting study of 2,380 films revealed a consistent and unmistakable public preference for family fare. In fact, the average G-rated film generated eight times greater profit than the average R-rated film, though R-rated films remained 17 times more common than their G-rated counterparts." While PG-13 films drew a 35 percent better return on investment than R, G-rated films earned even more, a 78 percent better return on investment than R-rated movies. Why, then, would studios continue to produce adult-oriented movies? One answer, thinks Medved, is that Oscars typically go to such films. Films for adult audiences might not be as financially successful, but they "disproportionately draw industry acclaim and critical endorsement." Medved concludes:

> Contrary to the cliché, it's not pure greed that drives Hollywood's emphasis on gore, vulgarity and gratuitous sex. Statistics, new and old, show that the public welcomes less-disturbing (and sometimes less-challenging) alternatives. This means that petition campaigns and even boycotts will achieve very limited success, since the big studios already work against their own financial self-interest by defying heartland sensibilities with their emphasis on R-rated entertainment.[29]

It is not just those on the religious "right" who suggest caution, however. Those on the religious "left" are sometimes equally suspicious. Margaret Miles, the former dean of the Graduate Theological Union in Berkeley, seeks to identify and analyze the values imaged in films.[30] Hollywood, Miles recognizes, continues to shape our attitudes toward race, gender, class, and sexual orientation through its patterns, stereotypes, and symbolic markers. For example, it is often the male gaze that is captured by the camera's point of view. Even as a child, Miles understood from movie marquees that fat people were laughable, people of color were subservient, and beautiful, heterosexual people were the norm. The portrayal of a set of values in this way is not "accidental or incidental to religious perspectives," she argues, "but, as a concrete way religious perspectives are articulated, [is] central to religious values."[31] Miles also notes, with Medved, that in its direct portrayals of religion, Hollywood is typically hostile to Christianity. A student of iconic art, Miles chides the motion picture industry for its inability to inspire religious devotion through the images it projects. Often, it seems able only to caricature fundamentalism, as in *The Rapture* (1991) and *The Handmaid's Tale* (1990).

Miles, like Medved, approaches film from an ethically driven theological stance, but she also seeks to be a student of the films she considers. Few films escape her critical pen. She understands *Thelma & Louise* (1991) to be a cautionary tale about the consequences of women trying to escape a male-dominated world. She castigates two recent "Jesus" movies, *The Last Temptation of Christ* (1988) and *Jesus of Montreal* (1989), for not offering heroes to their audiences. And so on. Hers is a hermeneutic of suspicion. She views movies from her ethical/theological point of view and judges whether they fit. Though she seeks to be a student of film, she does not try to see a movie on its own terms. As John Lyden comments at the end of his discussion of Miles's book: "It is ironic that leftist critics of culture may find themselves in harmony with right-wing conservatives in their wholesale denunciation of popular culture."[32]

Miles and Medved, Colson and Nicolosi have a sense of style and discrimination with regard to their movie judgments, even if this reader finds them overly suspicious and does not always agree with their conclusions on particular movies. Butler and Billingsley, on the other hand, seem overly controlled by their dogma. All, however, come to film from a defined theological perspective and see a one-sided imbalance between Hollywood and the church, between movies and theology. For the most part, they see that movies are too often in the business of theological subversion. Thus, they advise caution for the religious viewer.

Dialogue

My comments about avoidance and caution should have been sufficient to signal the direction I believe Christian film criticism must go. Although theoretically the critical dialogue can begin anywhere along the continuum from avoidance to encounter, the danger of theological imperialism is high enough in practice that I would argue that Christian moviegoers should first view a movie on its own terms before entering into theological dialogue with it. The movie experience, like all play activities, functions best when it is a parenthesis within life's ongoingness. That is, when people enter the theater (or go to the opera or the ballpark, or play handball or dance), they must, when at play, set aside the issues of the larger world around them and be caught up in the movie experience itself. Whether listening to Mozart or looking at a Paul Thomas Anderson film, the audience must focus exclusively on the "present" of the experience, if it is to be authentic. In a sense, the real world must for a time "stand still." Moviegoers must give to the screen their "as-if" assent and enter wholeheartedly into the movie's imaginative world, or the experience risks being stillborn. With motion pictures, moreover, this happens naturally, as the darkness of the theater and the community of viewers, not to mention the surround sound and oversized screen, combine with the images and story to capture the audience's attention.

To give movie viewing this epistemological priority in the dialogue between film and theology—to judge it advisable to first look at a movie on its own terms and let the images themselves suggest meaning and direction—is not to make theology of secondary importance. Religious faith is primary. In fact, I argue that the nature of both moviegoing and religious faith demands that film viewing be completed from a theological perspective. But such theologizing should follow, not precede, the aesthetic experience.

I am reminded of the classic essays on reading literature by T. S. Eliot and R. W. B. Lewis. Writing in 1932, Eliot argued that "literary criticism [substitute "film criticism"] should be completed by criticism from a definite ethical and theological standpoint." But he also recognized that "whether it is literature or not can be determined only by literary standards."[33] In his 1959 essay, Lewis recalled "the remark made to Emerson by an old Boston lady who, talking about the extreme religious sensibility of an earlier generation, said about those pious folk that 'they had to hold on hard to the huckleberry bushes to hinder themselves from being translated.'" Lewis uses the story to illustrate his point that although people's religious beliefs are fundamental, they should not necessarily begin their criticism there. He writes that "absolutely speaking, as between religion and literature, religion no doubt comes first; but in the actual study of a particular literary text, it probably ought to follow, and follow naturally and organically and without strain—for the sake of the religion as well as the literature."[34] Although theology is the final authority for life, or should be, people are best served in the dialogue between theology and film if the movie's vision of life is first received with a maximum of openness before it is brought to the bar of judgment. J. C. Friedrich von Schiller's *On the Aesthetic Education of Man* is a helpful, even if extravagant, reading on the nature of the experience of play (and thus of moviegoing):

> In the midst of the awful realm of powers, and of the sacred realm of laws, the aesthetic creative impulse is building unawares a third joyous realm of play and of appearance, in which it releases mankind from all the shackles of circumstance and frees him from everything that may be called constraint whether physical or moral. . . . *To grant freedom by means of freedom* is the fundamental law of this kingdom.[35]

We thus turn from those approaches that begin theologically and judge movies from a predetermined norm to those critical perspectives that first view a movie on its own terms. The first of these options I have labeled "dialogue."

Even those who express caution with regard to film viewing recognize there are some movies that have identifiably religious themes or elements and thus invite/demand dialogue with them from a theological perspective. Like *The Passion of the Christ* (2004) or *Jesus of Montreal* (1989), they might be about Jesus, or like *Sister Act* (1992) or *Chocolat* (2000), might center their story on the nature of the church. They might portray a preacher's redemption, as in *The Apostle* (1997), or someone going insane out of jealousy at another's divine gifting, as with *Amadeus* (1984). Their posture can be either that of renunciation, as in *Hardcore's* (1979) or *Bull Durham's* (1988) portrayal of the church, or of affirmation, as in *Chariots of Fire* (1981) and *Keeping the Faith* (2000), both of which focus on Jewish and Christian vocation. They might even include both as does *The Mission* (1986). Theological critics are not imposing an outside perspective on these movies when they enter into conversation with such films. Rather, the movies themselves explicitly deal with religious matters and thus invite a theological response.

Some movies are simply inexplicable except from a theological perspective. In an analogous discussion of the relationship of theology and literature, Amos

Wilder discusses the works of Hawthorne, Emerson, Dickinson, Blake, Henry James, and Dostoyevsky and rightly concludes that "the time is past when literary appreciation (can) slight the theological aspects of the work of art, as though all such elements were external."[36] The same is true of film. For certain works of art, Christianity, or religion more broadly, has contributed specifically to their characterizations and symbols and must be taken into account if one's criticism is to be adequate, let alone total. To comment on film theologically in this sense is not to isolate one's theological observations from an artistic critique of the work as a whole. Nor is it to bring in an outside perspective as the lens through which the movie is seen. Rather, there can be real engagement and two-way dialogue between Christian theology and the movie, for the movie itself invites it.

A dialogically centered approach to theology and film is not limited to such obvious examples, however. Any good story invites such conversation. Beginning with Clive Marsh and Gaye Ortiz's edited volume, *Explorations in Theology and Film: Movies and Meaning* (1997), the last decade has produced a spate of dialogically directed books, mostly from a Protestant perspective. Although their individual perspectives are diverse, they share a commitment (belief/understanding/perspective) that film and theology invite a two-way conversation.

Roy Anker's *Catching Light: Looking for God in the Movies* (2004) uses the metaphor of light to suggest that film, using physical light to display its images, can be the vehicle for presenting divine Light itself.[37] Anker's thick readings of more than a dozen film classics set a critical benchmark for its close "textual readings," for its care in unpacking cinematic stories. However, the provocative descriptions invite further theological dialogue, as Anker consistently leaves the reader at the "conversational" door, rather than actually moving beyond the movie into theological dialogue with it. Peter Malone and Rose Pacatte, on the other hand, focus their movie-dialogue books on how film can actually be used by the viewer for spiritual growth, whether in individual reflection, homilies, or parish study. Their multivolume companion to the three-year cycle of the church lectionary, *Lights Camera . . . Faith!: A Movie Lover's Guide to Scripture* (2001, 2002, 2003), suggests an appropriate movie for conversation with each Sunday's readings throughout the church year.[38] Their goal is to help Christians relate the movies they view to their Christian convictions to provide a form of spiritual exercise.

Brian Godawa, a Christian screenwriter (*To End All Wars* [2001]), is more word-oriented and story-driven in his book, *Hollywood Worldviews: Watching Films with Wisdom and Discernment* (2002). Separating himself from both cultural "anorexics" and "gluttons," he helps viewers discern and then express "the worldviews and philosophies that are communicated through Hollywood movies."[39] Tim Cawkwell in his *Filmgoer's Guide to God* (2004) dialogues with three dozen religiously themed movies "which engage with the meaning and purpose of human existence as it might be found in faith in a Trinitarian, Christian God."[40] Cawkwell focuses particular attention on the directors of these films, on those masters of the use of religious stories: the Frenchman Robert Bresson, the Dane Carl Theodor Dreyer, the Italian Roberto Rossellini, and the Russian Andrey Tarkovsky.

While Anker primarily concentrates on the film "text," Malone and Pacatte turn to the film "viewer," Godawa to the film's "worldview," and Cawkwell to the film's "maker." Here is a range of dialogue across the artistic-critical circle (see chapter 7). Given their focus on the education of the viewer, the Malone and Pacatte books might also fit as easily in the next category ("appropriation"), while given his focus on "worldview," Godawa's "dialogue is lined with caution," to quote one of my students who read the book.[41] Yet all four are, first and foremost, calling for dialogue between film and faith.[42]

Over the last decade, several New Testament professors have also written books on Hollywood movies, again using approaches that are dialogical in nature. Bernard Brandon Scott's *Hollywood Dreams and Biblical Stories* (1994) seeks a critical correlation between themes that are embedded in movies and the Bible.[43] In *Saint Paul at the Movies* (1993) and *Saint Paul Returns to the Movies* (1999), Robert Jewett brings films and biblical texts into conversation by means of an interpretive arch rooted on one end in the ancient world of Paul and on the other in the contemporary situation reflected in a particular film. Jewett provocatively asks, "Could it be that certain movies afford deeper access to the hidden heart of Paul's theology than mainstream theologians like myself have been able to penetrate?"[44] Jewett calls his approach "dialogue in a prophetic mode"[45] and wants to be sure that the films he chooses for correlation with biblical texts "become a full partner in conversation with Paul the apostle."[46] Given his choice to start from the biblical text and his commitment (one I also share) to have Scripture function authoritatively—as first among equals—Jewett always risks imposing a theological perspective on the films he considers. For example, not everyone will agree with him that *Amadeus* (1984) is a movie about sin. At times, however, he is superb, as with his treatment of *Grand Canyon* (1991), both in his film analysis and in his theological dialogue.

My own recent work, *Useless Beauty: Ecclesiastes through the Lens of Contemporary Film* (2004), is another example of such intertextual hermeneutics, as is New Testament scholar Richard Burridge's *Faith Odyssey* (2003).[47] Burridge correlates fifty daily Bible readings with reflections on *2001: A Space Odyssey* (1968) and its sequels, two of the *Star Trek* movies (1982, 1984) and the five TV series, the *Star Wars* films (1999, 2002, 2005, 1977, 1980, 1983), *E.T.* (1982), the Harry Potter books and films (2001, 2002, 2004, 2005), *The Lord of the Rings* movies (2001, 2002, 2003), *The Matrix* (1999), and C. S. Lewis's science fiction trilogy and children's novels (*The Chronicles of Narnia: The Lion, the Witch and The Wardrobe* [2005] had not yet come out). In my book, a careful viewing of *American Beauty* (1999), *Magnolia* (1999), *Run Lola Run* (1998), *Monster's Ball* (2001), *Signs* (2002), and *About Schmidt* (2002) provides a parallel picture to what is described in Ecclesiastes, helping to bring to life this enigmatic yet fascinating portion of Scripture.

There are other interesting subgenres of dialogical criticism. Three recent books, for example, seek an intertextual dialogue between film and the Apostles' Creed (perhaps the most important early distillation of what early Christians believed). Bryan Stone, in his book *Faith and Film: Theological Themes at the Cinema* (2000), argues that "the relationship between film and theology cannot be solely a relationship in which theology merely uses film to illustrate or advance its own ideas. We must also become more responsible as Christians for engaging film theologically—for attending to its tacit faith claims and critiquing its implicit pretense of mirroring reality. The relationship between Christian theology and popular film is, in short, an interfaith dialogue."[48] Stone then enfleshes his premise by dividing the Apostles' Creed into fourteen sections and putting these affirmations into dialogue with fourteen companion movie texts. In *Nourishing Faith through Fiction* (2001), John May, the dean of Roman Catholic writers on theology and film, offers his reflections on his favorite books and films, again bringing these into dialogue with the Apostles' Creed. His stated goal is to present an understanding of "the meaning for our daily lives" of the articles of the Apostles' Creed.[49] Third, and perhaps most substantively, David S. Cunningham reads the Christian faith through both literature and film in a book titled *Reading Is Believing* (2002). Cunningham's goal, like May's, is not so much interreligious dialogue as it is making the creed a living statement. He believes that students of Christianity do not need more historical explanation, or even theology, but rather an engagement with other stories. Consequently, he turns to novels and film to help Christians "understand, embrace, cherish and practice their faith."[50]

Other writers have focused on movies about Jesus or which contain Christ figures. Peter Malone's *Movie Christs and Antichrists* (1990) and Lloyd Baugh's *Imaging the Divine: Jesus and Christ-Figures in Film* (1997) are two of the best. Some movies whose interpretive center focuses on Jesus Christ take a discursive approach in retelling the Jesus story. George Stevens's biblical spectacular *The Greatest Story Ever Told* (1965) and Pasolini's *The Gospel according to St. Matthew* (1964), as well as *Jesus Christ Superstar* (1973) and *The Last Temptation of Christ* (1988), are examples of this approach, as is the more recent *The Passion of the Christ* (2004).

James Wall proved prophetic in 1970 when he editorialized on the end of the traditional biblical saga following the disappointing reception for Stevens's movie.[51] Wall suggested that the basic mood of modern Westerners in the 1970s was secular, whether they were churchgoers or not. Without the basic religious presuppositions that operated prior to World War II, the pietistic Jesus epic lacked persuasive force. It had become little more than an audio-visual aid for the already informed. Thus, it is not surprising that attempts at portraying Jesus on screen in the seventies and eighties turned from the spectacular to the genre of musicals (e.g., *Jesus Christ Superstar* [1973]; *Cotton Patch Gospel* [1988]) or to reinterpreting Jesus in more human and, at times, even shocking terms (e.g., *Jesus of Montreal* [1989]; *The Last Temptation of Christ* [1988]), before falling silent in the nineties. But with Western society's recent turn to postmodernity, with its embrace of both story and spirituality, the Jesus story has resurfaced as a narrative that once again fascinates the moviegoer. *The Miracle Maker* (2000), an animated retelling of the story of Jesus from the perspective of the young daughter of Jairus who was healed by Jesus; *The Gospel of John* (2003), a surprisingly well-made adaptation of John's Gospel with the film narrative a word-for-word reading of that text; and Mel Gibson's dynamic icon, *The Passion of the Christ* (2004), are the best of a larger group.

An alternative to the explicit Jesus movie is the movie that makes metaphorical use of a Christ-figure in significant and substantive ways. There is a danger, as anyone teaching in the field of Christianity and the arts knows, in having overenthusiastic viewers find Christ figures in and behind every crossbar or mysterious origin. This is to trivialize both the Christ-figure and the work of art. But in certain films, the Christ-figure is a primary metaphor or the Christ-story functions significantly as a defining theme, giving shape to the narrative. When this is the case, any criticism of the movie that fails to notice this theme is incomplete criticism. *Shane* (1953), *Dead Man Walking* (1995), *Star Wars* (1977), *Cool Hand Luke* (1967), *Babette's Feast* (1987), *The Green Mile* (1999), *The Passion of Joan of Arc* (1928), and *One Flew over the Cuckoo's Nest* (1975) are all examples of such movies. We will discuss many of these films later in the book. Here it is important to note the dialogical posture of such theological criticism. Consider Baugh's analysis:

> The Christ-figure [in film] is a foil to Jesus Christ, and between the two figures there is a reciprocal relationship. On the one hand, the reference to Christ clarifies the situation of the Christ-figure and adds depth to the significance of his actions; on the other hand, the person and situation of the Christ-figure can provide new understanding of who and how Christ is: "Jesus himself is revealed anew in the Christ-figure."[52]

Dialogue between theology and movies can take many forms: It can note the explicit theological themes of given films or dialogue with the motifs embedded both in movies and the Bible. It can bring film and biblical (or theological) text into conversation, or it can compare and contrast the Christ of the Gospels with the metaphorical use of a Christ-figure to advance the meaning of a given movie. A few movies are even explicit depictions of the Jesus story, inviting correlation and critique. But whatever the shape, the common denominator in such approaches is the attempt to bring film and theology into two-way conversation, letting both sides be equal partners in the dialogue.

Appropriation

In his keynote address at the 2001 Conference on Religion and Cinema at Princeton University, the filmmaker Nathaniel Dorsky spoke of how he has attempted for almost forty years to create a "devotional cinema." A movie, Dorsky believes, has "the potential to be transformative, to be an evocation of spirit, and to become a form of devotion." His concern, both in his avant-garde films and when viewing other films, has been with those "moments of revelation or aliveness," when the film evokes "something meaningfully human." Here, the focus is not so much on encountering God as on finding ourselves, our spiritual center. According to Dorsky, something in the actual nature of film can "produce health or illness in an audience."[53] In the lecture, Dorsky then discussed how the elements of filmmaking and film viewing—the illuminated room, montage, the juxtaposing of absolute and relative time, the uncompromising and self-confirming "present" of a film, a movie's shots and cuts—all contribute to this alchemy. We will return to a discussion of how to unpack a film in a later chapter. For now, it is enough to note the suggestion that the postfilm experience can at times be transformative, as viewers realize that a movie has both mirrored and realigned their understanding of life itself.

The title of Neil Hurley's book *Theology through Film* (1970) offers an early example of a book written from the perspective of one seeking to appreciate such a possibility for film. Hurley seeks to appropriate the religious wisdom and insight that film can offer. Will movies simply confirm our prejudices, he asks, or will they "serve that reason which, after all, is the universal spark of the divine which the Stoic philosophers believed to bind all men together in some mysterious cosmic fraternity?"[54] It is telling that when the book was reissued in 1975, the title was changed to *Toward a New Humanism*.

Those, like Hurley and Dorsky, who see a material overlap between film and theology believe that film is capable of expanding the viewer's understanding. They see this happening particularly with regard to a religious humanism that is embedded within film itself. Movies can tease out for their viewers greater possibilities for being human and present alternative selves not otherwise available to the moviewatcher. Thus, it is not to theology that the critic must first turn, but to a film itself. And the goal in relating theology and film is not, first of all, to render moral judgments, as was the case with earlier options we considered, but to achieve greater personal insight.

In our introduction to the book *Finding God in the Movies* (2004), Catherine Barsotti and I give two examples of such an appropriation.[55] The one concerns the movie *Life as a House* (2001), which I assigned in one of my classes. The movie tells the story of Sam, an angry, isolated teenager and his father, George, who is dying of cancer and has been fired from his job with an architectural firm. Together (with some coercion on George's part), they rebuild a house on cliffs overlooking the ocean. The construction becomes a metaphor for the rebuilding of their lives, which happens concurrently. When students were asked to respond to the movie, one man in his late twenties volunteered that given his estranged relationship with his father, he "wept hard in the arms of [his] wife." A woman in her mid-thirties offered, "I've reached out to my dad." Later in the course, we had the opportunity to join others for a screening of *Field of Dreams* (1989) and an interview with Phil Alden Robinson, the film's writer and director. Robinson said he had no explicit theological intention for the movie but recognized it had spiritually affected scores of people in much the same way that *Life as a House* had affected some of my students. It had encouraged reconciliation. Respectful of the possibility that this film might have had a spiritual influence beyond his original intentions, Robinson spoke humbly and thanked those who had shared what the film had meant to them.

Gareth Higgins, in his *How Movies Helped Save My Soul: Finding Spiritual Fingerprints in Culturally Significant Films* (2003), offers a number of personal reflections on how moviegoing has affected him. He warns, "Film should be treated with the same respect as church or poison, for it can change your life."[56] For example, after recalling the "incredible scene" in *Fight Club* (1999) in which Tyler recounts how he is part of "the middle children of history. . . . We have no Great War, no Great Depression. Our Great War is a spiritual war. Our Great Depression is our lives," Higgins confesses, "When I watch it, I want to shout 'Amen!' That's us, people."[57] Responding similarly to *The Royal Tenenbaums* (2001), he writes, "This is a painful film to watch; because surely we must all be able to identify with some of it; it's such a knowing film. Aren't we all weird like this? I wouldn't know a 'normal family' if it ran up and bit me." "There is no other film like this—epic in scope, intimate in focus, magisterial in structure; it's the truth of all our families."[58]

To give a final example from Higgins, after giving his readers a primer in antiheroes (*Reservoir Dogs* [1992], *The Usual Suspects* [1995], *American Beauty* [1999], *The Apostle* [1997], *Once Upon a Time in the West* [1968], *The Wild Bunch* [1969], *Amadeus* [1984], *Quills* [2000], *The Field* [1990], *One Flew over the Cuckoo's Nest* [1975], *Network* [1976], *Nixon* [1995], *Cape Fear* [1991], *Fargo* [1996], *Taxi Driver* [1976], even *Lawrence of Arabia* [1962]), he asks what these antiheroes "do for us." He answers personally by noting their honesty in giving us the reflection of our darkest potential, of showing our need to integrate light and shadow, in declaring that we all are capable of both extraordinary good and extraordinary wickedness. Higgins writes, "As a member of the most psychologically disintegrated generation in history, I can't do anything but welcome this."[59]

Tony Campolo comments in his foreword to Higgins's book, "What Gareth offers us is not so much a series of interpretations as it is a methodology for engaging movies. He calls upon us to engage films with hungry eyes, and he echoes Jesus in saying that those with eyes to see will see truths in films that speak to the existential conditions of our times and to the spiritual conditions of our souls." Campolo compares Higgins's approach to movies to what the Danish philosopher Søren Kierkegaard calls "indirect" communication. Kierkegaard likens this form of communication to standing at a corner with a crowd of people waiting for the traffic to clear and overhearing two people who are unaware of your presence say revealing things about you. Campolo continues, "For Gareth Higgins, like Kierkegaard, church sermons are too direct, and therefore, those in the pews are able to prepare defenses against them, whereas in movies, those who make the movies do not even know who the viewer is, but indirectly communicate to him or her those messages that the viewer needs to hear."[60] Higgins himself begins his book by quoting Marcel Proust: "In reality, every reader is, while he is reading, the reader of his own self. . . . And the recognition by the reader in his own self of what the book says is proof of its veracity."[61]

While Higgins is highly personal and anecdotal in his book on cinematic appropriation, Clive Marsh's *Cinema & Sentiment: Film's Challenge to Theology* (2004) stands back from the process and assesses the theological relevance of cinema-going and film watching, something most studies in theology and film have largely ignored. Marsh recognizes a religion-like function in film watching. In their intensification of experience, movies have the ability to shape viewers' lives. "Something happens, or can happen, to people who watch films because of how films work, because of where they are watched, and who they are watched with."[62] Films provide narratives through which people find themselves and make choices about how to live. When people watch films such as *Schindler's List* (1993), *The Pianist* (2002), *Apocalypse Now* (1979), *Platoon* (1986), *Born on the Fourth of July* (1989), and *JFK* (1991), they do so for reasons that are "more than entertainment, and not just to get themselves educated." They do so, thinks Marsh, as "an exercise in spirituality":[63]

> As soon as film-watching is seen not merely as entertainment, but as a "life practice" around which so much else revolves, then its similarities to religious practice are clear. Seeing film-watching as a life practice, a discipline which one undertakes for many reasons and which has a broad impact on life, (raises) the question whether it helps shape a "spirituality." Perhaps it even *is* a spirituality for the most regular of cinema-goers.[64]

Cinema-going is a spiritual discipline for Marsh in that it shapes a pattern of living and serves as a channel through which thoughts, feelings, and aesthetic and moral sensibilities are developed. Film watching, however, is not a wholly adequate substitute for religion, despite how much it might function as such for many people in Western culture today. Instead, Marsh's contention is that film watching, like religion, "is a crucial element in contemporary life which opens up the emotional life for scrutiny. [He] contend[s] further that theology helps in the task of critical reflection upon the emotional life and is itself challenged as to its purpose in the process." Theology through film, that is, does not seek "to 'correct' films or their impact, or merely to impose a worldview upon a film or its watchers."[65] Rather, theology is in large part the cognitive structuring of the emotional life, provoked by the multidimensional experience of film watching.[66]

Joel Martin and Conrad Ostwalt Jr. provide a final example of those who seek dialogue. Influenced by the judicious perspective of Wesley Kort, they caution in their book *Screening the Sacred* (1995) against baptizing film as unconsciously Christian. It is enough to say that movies can and do perform religious functions in today's culture as they communicate a society's myths, rituals, and symbols and provide a web of fundamental beliefs. They agree with Thomas Martin when he writes that "no story can develop without some underlying construct. . . . [A]ll constructs, even in the most banal of stories, are seen as presenting one with a fundamental option about life. And, therefore, every story one encounters has some effect on or challenge to one's sense of reality."[67] Appropriation is inevitable. For people to appropriate insights from film, however, the beliefs and values embedded in a movie need not be called "Christian" or even "religious." Better to make the claim, like William Jones in his *Sunday Night at the Movies* (1967), that "Christians of our generation are becoming increasingly aware that the contemporary arts are pleading the same question the church is committed to holding before society: the question of the essential meaning of human experience."[68]

In his masterful study of the sacred in art, Gerardus van der Leeuw writes: "There is only a single art, and it is, first of all, art. There is only a single religion, and it is always and everywhere religion."[69] Though this is true, observes van der Leeuw, we also can discern again and again an essential unity between art and religion, for holiness and beauty appear in the same guise. "Climb up upon this height and you will see how the paths of beauty and holiness approach each other, growing distant, until finally, in the far distance, they can no longer be held apart. . . . We erect no ultimate truths, but remain modestly to one side. We believe that we have noticed something there, and so we point it out."[70] Noting similarities, yet choosing to remain simply descriptive, van der Leeuw speaks of a "mere analogy" between art and religion.[71] The one can be a schema of the other without their coinciding. Applying van der Leeuw's caution to the study of film, we can say that film portrays something about life that is religion-like, and thus dialogue and even appropriation is invited.

Having said this (and it is a significant caution), we realize that whether we call a film that causes viewers to celebrate humanity "religious," or "religion-like," or whether we speak of a film's axiological convictions or webs of significance, or of having an informing vision about life, the intention is largely the same. Those theologians who would seek to appropriate a movie's vision of life recognize that movies can offer insight to the viewer about the nature of the human. There is something new that a movie can provide a Christian. More than dialogue is called for. The theologian must be receptive to encountering spirit in a new guise and only then turn to respond from the viewer's own theological point of view.

Divine Encounter

John May has provided a helpful typology of the responses that theologians and Christian film critics have developed, starting from the 1960s. There are differences in his schematic structure from the one I have just presented, but the two overlap. May sketches out five distinct approaches to the religious interpretation of film, which he lists in their order of emergence, recognizing that all five theological approaches continue to be practiced. He labels these "religious discrimination," "religious visibility," "religious dialogue," "religious humanism," and "religious aesthetics."[72]

May sees that over the last forty years there has been a general shift in emphasis in theological discussion of film. From an earlier concern with (1) the morality of films and (2) the explicitly recognizable religious elements in a film, theological critics have turned to (3) a desire for theological conversation with film, and a more recent focusing on the (4) humanistic and (5) aesthetic sensibilities of movies. In particular, May believes that "religious aesthetics,"[73] what I have called "divine encounter," is the most fruitful arena for current inquiry. Movies have, at times, a sacramental capacity to provide the viewer an experience of transcendence. This was my experience with the movie *Becket*, and so too Father Gregory Elmer's.

This was also the experience of one of my former students, while watching the movie *Magnolia* (1999). The movie ends with Aimee Mann's song "Save Me" ("You look like the perfect fit / a girl in need of a tourniquet" / "Can you save me / come on and save me") as Jim goes to Claudia, the fragile young woman who has suffered sexual abuse at the hands of her father. While the song continues, "If you could save me / from the ranks of the freaks / who suspect they could never love anyone," we look over Jim's shoulder at Claudia. Over the song, we faintly hear Jim's voice saying, "You are a good and beautiful person." The camera remains focused on Claudia as she struggles to accept Jim's gift of love. Miraculously, she smiles briefly for the first time as the movie ends. The student commented that the final moment was a divine encounter for him. "It let me know there was still grace available because I had long given up hope that there was." In the margin of his paper on the movie, he wrote,

I see a lot of myself in Claudia's character and a lot of Jesus in Jim. The fact that Anderson kept Jim out of the frame for much of this scene while his voice bestowed grace from off camera was simply brilliant. This enabled the scene to transcend the film and become a conversation between me and Jesus. This film served as a catalyst for my return to faith after a decade of apostasy.[74]

May's emphasis on divine encounter is what you might expect from a leading Roman Catholic scholar in the field. For, as Andrew Greeley writes, "Catholicism has always believed in the sacramentality of creation," that it can be "a revelation of the presence of God."[75] The Catholic Church has held that God is known through the experiences, objects, and people we encounter in our lives. Catholic theologian Richard McBrien defines sacramentality as a way of seeing "God in all things (St. Ignatius of Loyola): other people, communities, movements, events, places, objects, the environment, the world at large, the whole cosmos. The visible, the tangible, the finite, the historical—all these are actual or potential carriers of the divine presence."[76] Or as Greeley would say, "grace is everywhere."[77]

Leaning heavily on the insight of Catholic theologian David Tracy in his book *Analogical Imagination*,[78] Greeley writes:

> Tracy noted that the classic works of Catholic theologians and artists tend to emphasize the presence of God in the world, while the classic works of Protestant theologians tend to emphasize the absence of God from the world. The Catholic writers stress the nearness of God to His creation, the Protestant writers the distance between God and His creation; the Protestants emphasize the risk of superstition and idolatry, the Catholics the dangers of a creation in which God is only marginally present. Or, to put the matter in different terms, Catholics tend to accentuate the immanence of God, Protestants the transcendence of God.[79]

Greeley, like Tracy, believes that Catholics tend to be more mystical, Protestants more prophetic. Catholics more likely emphasize manifestations of God's goodness; Protestants, the proclamation of God's judgment. Catholics will more often say, "God is like . . ."; Protestants, "God is not like . . ."[80] Or to use my framework, Catholic theology and film critics will cluster in the upper right quadrant of figure 3.2, while Protestant theology and film critics will cluster in the bottom left quadrant.

For Greeley, film is especially suited to the making of sacraments and the creating of epiphanies because of its "inherent power to affect the imagination." Moviemakers might not call their intention the celebration of grace, but that is what Christians recognize it to be. Greeley even goes so far as to posit that the filmmaker (as artist) can, at times, disclose God's presence "even more sharply and decisively" than God has chosen to do through creation itself. Be that as it may, "the pure, raw power of the film to capture the person who watches it, both by its vividness and by the tremendous power of the camera to concentrate and change perspectives, is a sacramental potential that is hard for other art forms to match."[81]

Writing in the preface to Greeley's *God in the Movies*, which he co-wrote with Albert Bergesen, Roger Ebert recalls a conversation with Paul Schrader, who was then working on *Touch* (1997), a story about a former Franciscan monk who had the stigmata (the wounds of Christ) on his hands, and who could help people by touching them. In the story, a woman offers to do the man's laundry but then pauses, wondering whether it is right to put stigmatic blood through the wash! Ebert then writes: "The films considered by Andrew Greeley and Albert Bergesen in this book all put the blood through the wash, in one way or another. They dare to consider the divine in the context of the carnal—not only in their stories, but in their very form, which is the Hollywood entertainment film."[82]

In more recent years, it is not just Catholics like Greeley and May who speak of the transcendent possibilities of movies. The Protestant David Dark, in his book *Everyday Apocalypse: The Sacred Revealed in Radiohead, The Simpsons and Other Pop Culture Icons* (2002), finds in *The Truman Show* (1998) and *The Matrix* (1999), as well as in the movies of the Coen brothers, apocalyptic visions that open unto epiphany.[83] Just as Nathan's story to David provided David a transcendent perspective, an apocalyptic moment, so movies can serve an identical function for us today. And the Presbyterian Edward McNulty, in his two volumes *Praying the Movies* (2001, 2003), says that in his film discussion, he is "seeking that elusive moment . . . an 'Aha!' moment, when the spirit awakens us to something special in the film. It may be an act of one of the characters, a word, a song, an image, or the way all the elements of a shot or scene come together in the perfect way, making us aware that we are on holy ground."[84]

Perhaps the most influential Protestant who has wrestled with the Transcendent in art has been screenwriter and director Paul Schrader. In his oft-quoted book, *Transcendental Style in Film* (1972), he argues that the revelatory kinship between theology and film is not accidental but rooted in "two universal contingencies: the desire to express the Transcendent in art and the nature of the film medium."[85] As with the other theologians/critics we have considered, Schrader has been influenced in his thinking by van der Leeuw's *Sacred and Profane Beauty: The Holy in Art*. He writes:

> "Art can be religious," the late Gerardus van der Leeuw wrote, "or can appear to be religious; but it can be neither Mohammedan nor Buddhist nor Christian. There is no Christian art, any more than there is a Christian science. There is only art which has stood before the Holy." The proper function of transcendental art is, therefore, to express the Holy itself (the Transcendent), and not to express or illustrate holy feelings.[86]

So far so good. But when Schrader turns to a discussion of how this is done, his Protestant stress on God's transcendence asserts itself.

Schrader believes the filmmaker must eschew such normal filmic conventions as character identification and special effects, which play on the viewers' emotions. According to Schrader, "with comparative ease he [the filmmaker] can make an ardent atheist sympathize with the trials and agonies of Christ. But he has not lifted up the viewer to Christ's level, he has brought Christ down to the viewers."[87] Such "abundant" means are tempting but ultimately do not bring people closer to the Holy who is other than us, thinks Schrader. Rather it is in the "sparse," abstract forms of three classic movie directors—Ozu, Bresson, and Dreyer—that Schrader believes he has uncovered a universal form of presentation. That is, in their ascetic aesthetic—their long takes and slow camera movement, their repeated use of silence, their restrained acting and editing—there is found a "common expression of the Transcendent in motion pictures."[88]

Not everyone agrees with Schrader's emphasis on stasis, on filmmakers denying the sensate and removing all vestiges of empathy and psychological realism from a film if they want to invite transcendence. Craig Detweiler, for example, believes such films demand too much of contemporary audiences. "They are rigorously, doggedly sparse art created in an era of abundance."[89] Schrader's own films, thinks Detweiler, which attempted to enflesh his theory, brought largely the same reaction as did the movies of Ozu, Bresson, and Dreyer, "critical kudos and audience indifference." Only when the screenwriter Schrader was able to link his scripts, which focused on protagonists racked with doubt and searching for a moment of light, with Martin Scorsese's abundant, visual Roman Catholic style, which reveled in the bloody, did Schrader find success. Writes Detweiler, "Enduring films such as *Taxi Driver, Raging Bull, The Last Temptation of Christ*, and *Bringing Out the Dead* resulted. Schrader's sparse means needed an abundant interpreter, a visual stylist *par excellence* to bring transcendence to the silver screen."[90]

As Detweiler argues in his book *A Matrix of Meanings* (2003, co-written with Barry Taylor), it is the new, ultra-abundant generation of filmmakers that holds the most promise of helping younger moviegoers progress from the profane to the sacred. Wes Anderson, Paul Thomas Anderson, Tom Tykwer, David Fincher—here are cinema's new high priests. "Loud, fast, and manipulative can also be profoundly, surprisingly spiritual." What needs to be recognized, Detweiler argues, is the growing generation gap. The younger generation has "evolved into a much more discerning, sophisticated, visual culture"[91] and thus need a more visual style of storytelling if it is to evoke wonder.[92]

Terry Lindvall, W. O. William, and Artie Terry make similar observations with respect to African American films and, by inference, their viewers. They question the disembodied spirituality of Schrader's Calvinistic residue, recognizing in the African American context a vibrant spirituality emphasizing animated singing, testimony, prayer, and call-and-response preaching. It is not the image of the monkish ascetic but the almost carnival joy of voices lifted up in spiritual song that provide the archetypal images of the African American religious experience. The way of affirmation, not the *via negativa,* has power. Referencing *The Color Purple* (1985), they write:

> The battle between flesh and spirit is not accompanied by a slow devolution into stasis, but a series of stuttering starts and stalls, characterized by sin and repentance,

seductions and sermons, fear and joy, tears and laughter, jazz and hymns, denial and desire, passion and prayer, fury, separation, and finally renewal and reunion, marked by the joy and gladness of community. The Transcendent is characterized by joy, forgiveness, reconciliation, and accessibility. Elijah's "still, small voice" is stylistically implicit, but the overwhelming image in relief is that of the Pentecost of God's charisma upon his needy children.[93]

A Theological Parallel

Those familiar with H. Richard Niebuhr's *Christ and Culture* will note the similarities between the models presented above and those of Niebuhr.[94] One might, in fact, see the preceding discussion as an application of Niebuhr's classic typology to the medium of film, film being one particular cultural expression. In his volume, Niebuhr presented five orientations that the church has taken as it has sought to understand the relationship between Christian theology (knowing "Christ") and the culture in which it is embedded. These are (along with their contemporary American equivalents): (1) "Christ against culture," the Anabaptist (and fundamentalist) option; (2) "Christ and culture in paradox," the Lutheran (and conservative evangelical) perspective; (3) "Christ the transformer of culture," an understanding of Reformed Christians (and mainstream Protestants and progressive evangelicals); (4) "Christ above culture," the Catholic (and more sacramental mainline and evangelical Protestant) option; and (5) "the Christ of culture," the liberal Protestant understanding.

In order to be more descriptive of the chronological development of theology and film criticism, and in order to represent on a continuum the options with regard to theology or film taking the lead in the conversation, I have labeled one of the poles in my typology "divine encounter," exchanging the positions of liberal Protestant and Roman Catholic thought in the process. But the similarities should be apparent nonetheless.

Critics of Niebuhr believe his understanding of culture to be too static and monolithic, his presentation biased in favor of the transformative option, and his historical examples to illustrate his typology unfair, particularly with regard to Anabaptists.[95] Are these criticisms also relevant with regard to my model? Perhaps we have not given equal weight to the avoidance option, but this is in part because so few currently embrace this position. Most of those who might previously have argued for abstinence, given their more conservative or even fundamentalist theologies, now argue for caution instead. Given the advent of the television age, abstinence is less and less a practical (or practiced) option.

More typically, those critical of Niebuhr reject his implicit theological position, finding in his presentation a bias in favor of the transformational paradigm. It should be clear that in my use of Niebuhr, I have not followed him in this regard and instead have chosen to reorder his typology to fit a more chronological pattern. Although some reviewers of the first edition of this book found me to be arguing for a dialogical paradigm (given the subtitle of the book), others rightly noted the importance this book places on appropriation and divine encounter (and perhaps on the inclusion of "spirituality" in the book's title). Though a Protestant, I have been deeply influenced by discussions of general revelation and common grace. Perhaps it would be fair to say I am a Protestant deeply influenced in my theology of culture by Catholic sacramentality.

It is also the case that as a Protestant, I continue to understand Scripture as normative. Thus, following Scripture itself, I see all five approaches as useful theologically, depending on the context and situation: 1 John might be judged as paradigmatic of avoidance; Paul's Epistle to the Romans, of caution; Paul's sermon on Mars Hill, which is recorded in the book of Acts, dialogue; the wisdom sayings in Proverbs, of appropriation; and the story in Genesis of the blessing of Abraham by Melchizedek, an example of divine encounter. An eclecticism in methodology is called for if we are to be faithful to the biblical account.

That I have wrongly pigeonholed critics by placing them in rigid categories while they actually are more fluid in their approach is also possible; but typologies are artificial constructs built to help sort out critical options. It is clearly the case that a given theologian/critic might adopt several different approaches to the conversation between movies and theology, depending on the film in view or the audience addressed. James Wall, for example, published in 1971 perhaps the classic expression of "theology and film in dialogue" in his *Church and Cinema: A Way of Viewing Film*. Just a year earlier, however, Wall's chapter for the edited volume *Celluloid and Symbols* ("Biblical Spectaculars and Secular Man") argued for theological appropriation and response. And his editorials from 1991 to 1997 in *The Christian Century* are published as *Hidden Treasures: Searching for God in Modern Culture* (1997). Here Wall argues for a sacramental view in which "God is active but often in disguise, and where signs of the spirit are waiting to erupt from novels, movie screens, and bully pulpits."[96] We can be eclectic about critical methodology and still find it useful to develop constructs for understanding how we proceed.

Two examples:

Saving Private Ryan (1998)

In assessing the adequacy of this chapter's typology from the side of movies themselves, it might be helpful to turn concretely to two particular films and consider how each form of criticism might work with reference to them. Steven Spielberg's *Saving Private Ryan* (1998) provides our first example. Some people might argue, for example, that the corpses and carnage are so graphic that this R-rated movie should be *avoided*. After all, the Christian is called to think on what is pure and commendable (Phil. 4:8). One of the older men in the church

I attend said he did not like the movie, not because of the violence, but because of the foul language. The vulgarities were superfluous and off-putting. Most soldiers would probably question whether the language was in fact superfluous, but that it was off-putting to this viewer is no doubt true. As a result, he thought such films should be *avoided*.

Captain John Miller (Tom Hanks, left) finally meets up with Private James Ryan (Matt Damon). *Saving Private Ryan* (d. Spielberg, 1998). Photo by David James. ©1998 DreamWorks LLC/Paramount Pictures/Amblin Entertainment. All rights reserved.

Others might recognize the validity of a realistic depiction of World War II but would express *caution* concerning the film, for its graphic twenty-five-minute opening sequence seems excessive. They might, however, as I once heard a pastor do, consider Captain Miller to be a Christ-figure. After all, he does arrive from the outside with a group of disciples on an errand of mercy and eventually lays down his own life so that another might live. In the process, they might begin to cautiously dialogue with the film, though the film often in such cases becomes little more than an illustration of a biblical text or theological topic.

Other Christians, however, might argue that the movie does not have a significant and substantial rooting in the Christ-story, but is rather an occasion for real *dialogue* about whether war, any war, is just and/or justified. World War II is thought by many to be the textbook case of a "just war." But can eight lives be risked in order to save one? And how are we to understand Captain Miller's comment, "Every man I kill, the further I feel away from home"?

The "mission" portrayed in the film is not, however, to win the war, but to save a man. It is the value of human life and of a family's continuity that Spielberg shows. Thus, others might use the gripping human portrayals within the inferno of war to appreciate anew the humanity of an older generation of soldiers who came back from World War II too horrified to speak of their experiences to their families. In the process of experiencing through Private Ryan their true humanity, the viewer might *appropriate* new insight into the nature of one's own humanity.

Finally, despite the saying "There are no atheists in a foxhole," this movie would seem to have little in its portrayal that is potentially sacramental in nature. It is literally mired in the mud. I doubt too many viewers had a sense of awe and wonder that seemed transcendent in nature, though perhaps the sacrifice of human life might have been the occasion for a *divine encounter*. If we were to consider other Spielberg movies, however—*Schindler's List*, *Amistad*, or even *E.T.*, they might better speak with reference to a potential transcendent dimension in the film.

Where is the heart of *Saving Private Ryan*? Some viewers might focus their attention on its portrayal of war and seek theological dialogue here. A theology of war can better be considered in the concrete, where the experience of actual soldiers can be reflected on. It is too easy to get lost in abstract political theory and ignore the praxeological dimension that any adequate theology must have. Here is a movie for a Christian ethics class to discuss.

Although all such criticism has its place, the theologian/critic is best served by letting the movie itself suggest the starting point for critical evaluation and dialogue. In the case of *Saving Private Ryan*, this would be its concern with the value of human life, with saving Private Ryan. The film's portrayal of humanity provides the interpretative center of this movie. I am reminded of the line by William Holden in *The Bridge on the River Kwai* (1957) where he observes that the point is not to die like a gentleman but to live like a human being. What is the nature of the human that so many would be sacrificed for the one? As the film ends, Private Ryan, now an old man, has returned with his family to the grave of the man who saved his life. His question as he begins to cry is whether he has lived a good enough life to justify this other man's death. Was saving his life worth the death of those who were sent to rescue him? The viewer is left to ponder.

Sideways (2004)

The movie *Sideways* (2004) was one of the most honored films of 2004, on almost every critic's list of best movies. The movie's screenplay by Alexander Payne and Jim Taylor received top honors, including Golden Globes, Oscars, and BAFTAs (the British Oscars). The movie was nominated for an Academy

Award for Best Picture, Best Director (Alexander Payne), Best Supporting Actor (Thomas Haden Church), and Best Supporting Actress (Virginia Madsen). The Screen Actors Guild awarded it Best Performance by an ensemble cast (Church, Madsen, Sandra Oh, and Paul Giamatti), its equivalent of best picture. The Golden Globes also awarded it Best Motion Picture—Musical or Comedy.

Stephanie (Sandra Oh), Jack (Thomas Haden Church), Maya (Virginia Madsen), and Miles (Paul Giamatti) enjoy the vineyards on California's central coast. *Sideways* (d. Payne, 2004). © Fox Searchlight Pictures.

Sideways is an odd-couple road movie that follows the (mis)adventures of two friends, Jack (Thomas Haden Church) and Miles (Paul Giamatti), both struggling with midlife crises as they look forward to Jack's upcoming wedding. In both its choice of genre and its general theme, *Sideways* thus mirrors the director's previous movie, *About Schmidt* (2002), another road movie dealing with human transitions, this time the crisis of retirement. Typical of the genre, it is not the straightforward action or plot that carries the story, but rather the "sideways" insights derived from the interaction between the two protagonists and the people they meet along the way. (The title also refers to the proper way to store a bottle of wine, for the qualities of wine are the primary metaphor within the movie.) Miles and Jack both sense that their lives are slipping away. As one of Miles's students recites in his English class, reading from John Knowles's novel *A Separate Peace*: "I could not escape a feeling that this was my own funeral, and you do not cry in that case." Instead, Miles uses wine while Jack uses women to escape loneliness and failed ambition.

As the movie opens, Miles is paralyzed by a two-year-old divorce. He is an oenophile (wine connoisseur) and frustrated novelist with a rejected manuscript ("The Day after Yesterday"), who finds little fulfillment as a middle-school English teacher. Jack is a bit actor, who does mostly voice-overs for commercials while seeking to seduce as many women as possible to reassure himself of his continued good looks (this despite his upcoming marriage). One of the duo is damaged and afraid; the other self-absorbed and sexually fixated. Though this odd couple would seem to have nothing in common, the two are buddies who still care for each other. Having been asked to be Jack's best man, Miles chooses, instead of a bachelor party, to give Jack a week-long trip to the vineyards of Santa Barbara in search of good food, good golf, and great wine. In particular, he desires to offer Jack a lesson in discerning the wonders of a bottle of pinot noir. Jack has other plans, however. As he tells Miles, his goal is for the two of them to "get laid." Here will be his gift to Miles, a way for him to move beyond his debilitating divorce. And so the story unfolds. The two meet Maya, a waitress at The Hitching Post restaurant whom Miles has known for some time but has been too shy and insecure to pursue. When they also meet Stephanie at one of the wineries they visit and she turns out to know Maya, a double date is arranged and the escapades are on. Miles tries to get Jack to appreciate the subtleties of the pinot grape, and Jack tries to get Miles to experience once again the risk of romance. The score at the end? One for two!

The movie is full of humor (there are stock pieces: Miles meeting Jack's fiancé, Jack and Miles on the golf course being harassed by the foursome behind them, Miles being chased out of the house by the stark naked, overweight husband of a waitress Jack has had a tryst with), lush photography (the breathtaking hills of Santa Barbara), and a wonderful retro-jazz score. The movie is, you could say, all about "wine, women, and song," but it is the screenplay, full of honesty and insight, that makes it. The scene at the end of the first double date when Miles and Maya retreat to the back porch captures the movie's essence in a nutshell. The two begin talking about what they most enjoy about wine. Miles says he prefers the pinot: "It's a hard grape to grow. As you know. It's thin skinned, temperamental, ripens early. It's not a survivor like the cabernet that can grow anywhere and thrive even when neglected. Pinot needs constant care and attention. . . . And only the most patient and nurturing growers can do it really, can tap into pinot's most fragile, delicate qualities." Maya responds that wine is "a living thing," "it's constantly evolving and gaining complexity. That is, until it peaks—like your '61—and begins its steady, inevitable decline." One needs to drink it when it is ready. And so, almost accidentally, we are given a lesson, not only about wine but about life, not only theirs but our own. These two wounded characters reveal their own vulnerability—their need for patience and constant care—as well as their need to "seize the day." The movie's tagline says it all: "In search of wine. In search of women. In search of themselves."

A simple road movie with heart, *Sideways* nonetheless earns its R rating with scenes of drunkenness, sexual encounters, foul language, and even violence. Given its focus on women and wine, on the one hand, and its existential search for meaning, on the other, the movie predictably elicited a wide range of responses from Christians, from objections to its glorification of drinking, to deep concern for its portrayal of sexual amorality, to deep appreciation for and identification with the characters' struggle to find meaning in life.

A few Christian critics did indeed dismiss the movie, though often because they missed its meaning. Andrew Coffin of *World Magazine* wrote, "*Sideways* is a well-observed, sometimes subtle comedy—unfortunately it's also a miserable story. Most critics would like you to believe that these scenes make worthwhile wallowing in the depravity of these sad, pathetic characters. But it's simply not true."[97] Charles Colson wrote in his *Breakpoint Commentary*: "There's the nasty little film called *Sideways*. This film suggests that it's fine—even funny—for a man to engage in an orgy of sex with strangers just before his wedding."[98] Another questioned the movie's preoccupation with Miles's drinking, referencing an article in the *New York Times* protesting the alcohol-fuel of this movie's road trip.[99] Though there might have been lyrical wine epiphanies, Miles also guzzled from the spit bucket at the winery, stumbled out of a bar, and chugged wine straight from the bottle. Here was someone with classic signs of alcohol abuse: not wanting to get up in the morning, drinking while driving, failed relationships, and money problems. The benign view of wine in the movie was judged to mask a serious issue within society.[100] Others found Jack, the Thomas Haden Church character, rude and offensive. All he wanted to do was bed any woman he could seduce, or so it seemed, and this on the eve of his own wedding! Despite the strong acting and interesting character development, some critics advised potential viewers to exercise caution before watching. Several websites commented that this R-rated movie, with its vulgar language, implied violence, sex, and alcohol abuse, should be viewed only by adults and then only by those with a tolerance for life's underbelly.

What surprised me as I surveyed over twenty Christian film Internet sites, however, was not the warnings, or even that a few reviewers missed the core of the movie. Rather, it was the overwhelming praise given the film by Christian critics, even by some of the most conservative. Here was a story that invited, even demanded, dialogue, perhaps even appropriation, from a Christian perspective. Reviewers found the conversations, especially between Miles and Maya, poignant and revealing. The screenplay was rightly praised as the strength of this movie. We were presented with four flawed yet authentic individuals, desperately trying to find meaning and relationship. We were shown that "the wages of sin" (Rom. 6:23) have a steep price tag. We were shown the truth that "two are better off than one, because together they can work more effectively. If one of them falls down, the other can help him up" (Eccles. 4:9–10 GNT). We might not be sure of the outcome as the movie ends, but there is hope.

Even more surprising was the fact that many of these reviewers did not remain at arm's length in their dialogue with the movie. Reviewer after reviewer found that, if they were honest, they discovered themselves in these four characters. They were deeply moved by the honesty of the portrayals and the desperate reach for love, in the absence of any guarantee of meaning. For them, the movie was a small epiphany. They found their spirits quickened.

We end this chapter with a sampling of their comments: "A bittersweet meditation on love, loneliness, fellowship and failed ambition."[101] "*Sideways*—like the typical bottle of wine, as explained in the film—is a reflection on real life: emotional, occasionally ugly, sometimes heartwarming, and often hilarious."[102] "[E]ven better are the moments of recognition, where we see ourselves in a particular character and then chuckle over our own foibles."[103] "It speaks to our need to enter into life and into relationships in such a way as to experience the fullness of our lives."[104] Craig Detweiler, writing in *Metaphilm*, concludes: "*Sideways* touched us all with its broken dreams and endless deceits. We've seen them. We've lived them."[105]

why look at film?
a theological
perspective

4

In the past, Christians raised the question, What has Athens to do with Jerusalem? That is, what value does pagan culture have for people of faith? Today, we might substitute Hollywood for Athens and ask a similar question: Why should Hollywood movies and Christian theology be brought together for dialogue and mutual understanding/insight? Isn't there a giant "disconnect"? The most common answer to such a question, first voiced in 1910 by the Reverend Herbert Jump, a Congregationalist minister, was that movies are modern-day parables. Jump believed that the parables of Jesus shared certain similarities with contemporary movies. These dramatic stories were rooted in everyday experience and proved effective means of communication with his audiences. The parable of the Good Samaritan, in particular, seemed paradigmatic: the story was taken from contemporary experience rather than from the Scripture of Jesus' day; its depiction of a violent robbery was exciting; and its realism allowed morally negative (the religious leaders are hypocritical) and ambiguous (the robbers leave victorious) features to remain. All that was lacking, thought Jump, was a better title, perhaps "The Adventure of the Jerusalem Merchant."[1]

Since Jump, the comparison of parable and movie has become almost ubiquitous, one used by both theological conservatives and liberals, by both Protestants and Catholics. In 1990, for example, Ed McNulty named his pioneering theology and film journal *Visual Parables*. David DiCerto, film reviewer for the U.S. Conference of Catholic Bishops' Office of Film and Broadcasting, states,

87

"Movies are modern parables. Christ used the mass medium of his time. I think storytelling has always been the most effective way of getting the message across."[2] Bob Smithouser of Focus on the Family echoes DiCerto in his book *Movie Nights*; so too do evangelical youth pastors Doug Fields and Eddie James in their *Videos That Teach*; and Peter Malone, president of the Organization Catholique Internationale du Cinéma, in his introduction to movies for the church, *On Screen*.[3] Even contemporary West African videos are labeled "moral parables" by their producers.[4]

Parables provide stories drawn from everyday life that capture the attention of their viewers/hearers by focusing on what is not usually seen, teasing their recipients into an active engagement with them through their open-endedness. In this way, Jesus' parables caused those present to see life in a new way.[5] So, too, do movies. In her perceptive article "Parable, Metaphor, and Theology" as well as in her book *Speaking in Parables*, Sally McFague argues that Jesus' parables should, in fact, be used as models for theological reflection today; for they unite language, belief, and life into a whole. "If theology becomes overly abstract, conceptual, and systematic, it separates thought and life, belief and practice, words and their embodiment." Our theological language must be "ordinary, contemporary, and imagistic (as it is in the parables)," she argues. "In the parabolic tradition people are not asked to be 'religious' nor are they taken out of the world; rather, the transcendent comes to ordinary reality and disrupts it."[6] McFague thinks that a theology that took its cues from Jesus' parables would surely find poetry, novels, and autobiographies to be prime resources. Written in 1974, McFague's article predates our video/DVD age. Today, she would no doubt add "movies" to her list.

Of course, not everyone has been persuaded by such "logic," particularly those committed to more propositional and less narrative forms of theology. Writing in 1995, evangelical scholars Mark Noll, Cornelius Plantinga Jr., and David Wells bemoan the fact that theology is largely ignored by the church today, even by evangelicals. Theology seems to possess little force or impact. Why is this so? Part of the explanation, they admit, is that there is too little good theology actually being written. Chief among the reasons, they think, is the church's aggressive embrace of certain forms of popular culture. Christians are contaminated by worldliness, by "Christian bodybuilding and beauty-queening." We are marginalized by an entertainment culture that glories in self-absorption. They answer that any new interest in theology by laypeople must "await success in getting people to read and think again, getting people to walk over to their TV set [and DVD player] and pull an enormous condom over it." Yet, they think getting people "to practice safe TV" (and perhaps movie abstinence?) will prove difficult.[7]

A Theology of Everyday Life

> Believing is not commanded by beliefs. Beliefs come from believing, and believing is generated in experience.
>
> Richard R. Niebuhr, *Experiential Religion*

If Christians are to live lives of modesty, reflection, and contentment, then why look at movies, many of which seem to encourage the antithesis? One answer is to say that at their best, movies, like parables, help viewers to see life more clearly. They "offer an existential challenge to 'all who have ears to hear (and eyes to see).'"[8] In an increasingly visual culture (something our above theologians bemoan, betraying perhaps their Calvinistic bias), film images have become an important source of knowledge. Movies provide viewers "imaginative possibility, without which we would be unable to try new models, new roles, new theories, new combinations of behavior."[9] Because the viewer cannot control the images, they catch us off guard and tell us things about others and ourselves. Viewed in this light, movies are part of the toolbox that most people use as they respond to and give shape to their lives. As such, they are a significant ingredient in a person's individual formation.

Others note that movies help us understand and critique our culture. It is from movies that we get our "collective" images of ourselves, our values, and our social world. Movies both identify our anxieties and reveal our society's values; they "tell" us something about the age in which we live. Like the canaries used to sniff out poisonous gas in the coal mines in nineteenth-century England, movies can smell the currents in our society, exploring dimensions of reality which we have not fully perceived. Of course, there is a range of values present, so movies often become the context for presenting these ambiguities and conflicts, and thus enabling dialogue. Margaret Miles summarizes film's cultural influence:

> In the decade 1983–93, issues related to race, age, ecology, family, education, addiction, abortion, violence, gender, class, United States foreign policy, fundamentalist Christianity, the New Right, "family values," reproductive technologies, AIDS—to name only a few—permeated popular films. In short, film supplies the historian of the present with an incomparable resource for describing and prescribing for the problems and struggles of the moment.[10]

While movies can provide their viewers both experiences of life and greater understanding of their culture, there is a third reason that Christians should engage film, one we might label "A Theology of Everyday Life." It was Michel de Certeau who first called attention to the importance of the practices of everyday life for understanding today's spiritual searching.[11] As we enter the twenty-first century, we are experiencing "the desecularization of the world" (or to put it positively, "its re-enchantment"), and this is happening outside our normal institutional channels.[12] For example, David Hay and Kate Hunt have discovered that while church attendance in England dropped more than 20 percent in 1987–2000, to something like 8 percent on any given Sunday, during the same period, those reporting having had a religious or spiritual experience grew almost 60 percent, from 48 percent to slightly more than 76 percent of the national sample.[13]

These researchers speculate that though the percentage increase is startling, perhaps the reality has not changed so drastically; in fact, they posit that spiritual awareness is a human universal. Maybe only people's sense of social permission to mention such an experience has changed. Nonetheless, this new sense of social permission is just the point. Our theological context is radically changing, or perhaps has already changed as we have moved into a postmodern world. The spiritual and the inexplicable are no longer taboo. John Drane notes,

> Because we no longer trust prescriptive ways of being, we find it difficult to trust religious institutions and the rationalized sacramentality which they offer. Alongside this is a profound questioning of the nature of truth as propositions, for that in itself can too easily become a fragmenting influence. "Faith" is more likely to be understood as a verb rather than a noun, and non-rational experiences (tactile, visual, emotional) are likely to be prioritised over the exclusively rational. There is a concern for relational wholeness, searching for personal healing and community in the midst of life's brokenness, but developing new forms of both rather than accepting what already exists, which tends to be seen as false and meaningless, and quite possibly controlling and exploitational.[14]

In such a situation, moviegoing and the subsequent conversation it engenders—one of our common practices of everyday life—has become an important alternate source for spiritual exploration. David Brown, for example, notes the number of directors who have turned to films involving sports, not to convey its rampant commercialism or adrenaline highs, but to provide viewers experiences of transcendence. He mentions Phil Alden Robinson's *Field of Dreams* (1989), Norman Jewison's *The Hurricane* (1999), and Robert Redford's *The Legend of Bagger Vance* (2000). Brown adds, "[B]y that [the experience of transcendence] I understand more than merely human transcendence. Religious language and imagery, dramatic scenery and strange coincidences and appearances are all invoked to create a sense of a larger mysterious presence." None of these movies approaches its theological explorations from the perspective of formal religious belief, certainly not from that of Christianity. Rather they seem to want "to highlight one way in which an apparently human pull beyond one's present capacities can be met with a transcendent experience of a quite different order."[15] Or, if sports movies are not your choice, then substitute the likes of *Magnolia* (1999), *American Beauty* (1999), *The Sixth Sense* (1999), *Garden State* (2004), or perhaps *The Color Purple* (1985).

Some theologians might belittle such expressions of spirituality, believing them to be a dumbing down of God, a desire to disregard fact and responsibility, a trivializing of the spiritual exercises that have characterized the great religious traditions of the world.[16] But though the experiences presented in these films might offer only a limited understanding of God, this need not negate its value. Partial does not necessarily equate with wrong, as Paul himself recognized in his dialogue with the Athenians. As recorded in the book of Acts (17:16–34), Paul addressed the curious at the Areopagus, praising them for being extremely religious and agreeing with their spiritual instinct in recognizing that they are inseparably related to the Creator (they were right in their worship of an "unknown god," v. 23). He even quoted with approval from their non-Christian poets: "For we too are his offspring" (Aratus of Soli) and "In him we live and move and have our being" (Epimenides), v. 28. What is surprising about Paul's use of these lines of poetry is the fact that these quotes are direct references to Zeus. Rather than criticizing such *half*-truths, Paul chooses to honor these half-*truths*. Such understandings of the Creator are commendable, he states, even as he moves to distance them from idolatrous images (v. 29) and to relate this general understanding of God to the special revelation of the risen Christ (v. 31). What is important is to recognize that the Athenians' limited knowledge is validated by Paul, even as he builds on it.

The poet-theologian Samuel Coleridge writes: "The almighty goodness does not dwell in generalities, nor abide in abstractions."[17] Rather, it is in the particular concrete experiences of life, including moviegoing, that a sense of the divine is being conveyed, experiences that, though partial, invite our theological reflection. Can or should the Christian community embrace such a theology from below? This is the crux of the issue for Christian believers. Let me suggest six theological reasons why Christians should enter wholeheartedly into dialogue with film: (1) God's grace is continually present throughout human culture; (2) theology should be concerned with the Spirit's presence and work in the world; (3) God speaks to us through all of life; (4) image as well as word can help us to encounter God; (5) theology's narrative shape makes it particularly open to interaction with other stories; and (6) the nature of constructive theology is a dialogue between God's story (as presented through the Bible, Christian tradition, and a particular worshiping community) and our stories (from the surrounding culture and our life experiences). If we hope to interest Christians in serious and ongoing dialogue, we need to explore these reasons in depth.

God's Grace and Human Culture

God has blessed all of creation, including human culture. This is clear from the opening chapters of Genesis, where the foundations of culture are sketched out for us. The fourth chapter describes the development of cities, agriculture, the arts, and technology (vv. 17–22). Although human invention can be used wrongly, as the subsequent story of the tower of Babel suggests, there is no negative judgment given against the beginnings of human civilization. Rather, culture is seen as part of life itself, part of life that God blessed by calling it "good" (Gen. 1:31).

This focus on the goodness of created life takes a secondary place in the biblical text as the narrative of God's mighty acts in history is told. Rainbow, Red Sea, Jericho, five smooth stones—these stories of God's involvement in his own people's lives retain their ability to convict and convince. The Bible tells the story of salvation history; yet Scripture's alternate, complementary theology, rooted in creation itself, is not totally absent. The goodness of life, all life, remains central to the Old Testament's wisdom literature—to Job, Proverbs, Ecclesiastes, Song of Songs, and selected Psalms. It was Walther Zimmerli who reminded modern scholarship that biblical wisdom thinks resolutely within the framework of creation theology.[18] In the last forty years, his thesis has become nearly axiomatic.

For example, the book of Proverbs does not ground its admonitions in the Law. Neither does it mention God's saving actions in the Exodus event. Rather, the authority and power of Proverbs is found in life itself.[19] Occasionally, the book of Proverbs even borrows its material from non-Israelite sources. There is in its pages an international outlook. The compiler of Proverbs makes use of the thirty sayings of the Egyptian *Instruction of Amenemope*, for example, as he proffers God's wisdom in 22:17–24:22. The sayings are freely adapted and put into the larger context of trust in Yahweh, but a reliance on pagan sources is evident. Alluding to *Amenemope*, the wisdom writer reflects:

> Have I not written for you thirty sayings
>   of admonition and knowledge,
> to show you what is right and true,
>   so that you may give a true answer to those who sent you?
>
> Proverbs 22:20–21

The sage did not himself organize his borrowed thoughts into thirty sayings, but he nevertheless is comfortable with finding in *Amenemope*'s thirty sayings God's wisdom. Proverbs' authoritative words can even come verbatim from those outside of Israel, as with the sayings of Agur, son of Jakeh (Prov. 30:1–2) and those from the mother of King Lemuel (Prov. 31:1–2).

That God would choose to speak his truth to Israel through nonbelievers should not surprise us. The prophets recount such scenarios. The book of Habakkuk records the argument between the prophet and his God when Habakkuk learns in a vision that God will use the Chaldeans as his instrument of justice against the wicked in Judah. How could Yahweh, who is good and just, use an evil nation to judge a "less evil" nation (Hab. 1:13)? Such an unholy alliance could not be, reasons Habakkuk. But he is wrong. God's mysterious ways can be mediated even through sinful, human agents (cf. King Neco of Egypt, who speaks God's word to King Josiah in 2 Chron. 35:20–24).

But lest we wrongly conclude that the non-Israelite cultural agents are always themselves evil, consider the biblical accounts of Melchizedek and Abimelech, Ruth and Cyrus. Or recall the book of Jonah. Here, it is the non-Israelite sailors who recognize God's possible involvement in their predicament long before Jonah. Only after the lot falls on Jonah and he is questioned by the sailors as to why he is being divinely punished does Jonah respond: "'I am a Hebrew,' he replied. 'I worship the LORD, the God of heaven, who made the sea and the dry land'" (Jon. 1:9). The emphasis, it should be noted, is on God as Creator and Sustainer. What follows next is full of irony. It is not the believer in Yahweh who acts in a godly way, but the pagan sailors: (1) they are the first to recognize that God is at work in the storm; (2) they consult with Jonah and one another as to the best course of action; (3) even when Jonah says, "Throw me overboard," they seek a more "ethical" solution; (4) they cry out to God for mercy for their contemplated action; and (5) after tossing Jonah overboard, they offer a sacrifice to Yahweh and make vows. We would hardly expect the actions of non-Israelite sailors to be wise and godly, but such is the case. Is there any doubt as to whom the writer intends for us to see as being models of true humanity? If so, we might note that later in the text it is the people of another non-Israelite culture, the Ninevites, who repent, while Jonah pouts. The irony is comical; the theology, crystal clear. God is involved with all of humankind and uses the wisdom and insight of nonbelievers to communicate his truth to those who believe.

I remember the personal impact of a scene in *One Flew over the Cuckoo's Nest* (1975). Inspired by McMurphy, Jack Nicholson's character, the patients want to see the World Series on television. Nurse Ratched, however, refuses to let them, fearing that a break in their routine will upset them. McMurphy is livid at such patronizing control. Fighting back, he begins to narrate an imaginative World Series game. When Sandy Koufax strikes out Mickey Mantle, there is pandemonium. The men on that mental ward feel a new sense of celebration and camaraderie. Simply by the power of his imagination, McMurphy has created a shared community, breaking the bonds of a society that would falsely restrict. As I watched, I too cheered, realizing as I did that I too have the potential to create that which could help others, if I would but seize the day.

As Christian theology has rightly concentrated its understanding of human-kind on our pervasive sin and consequent need of redemption, it has sometimes wrongly emptied human culture both of its actual achievement and of God's ongoing presence. Theology has too often failed to see that God is still at work throughout his creation. In doing so, we have lost the biblical balance, ignor-ing the prophet's creational counterpoints as well as wisdom's "kerygma" of life in all its fullness.[20] We have failed to recognize human culture's strength and possibilities. We have failed to see that God is in all of human culture, both in the way of life of a people and in the expression of that identity through human creativity.

Spirit and spirit

> God is interested in a lot of things besides religion. God is the Lord and Creator of all life, and there are manifestations of the holy in its celebration or in its repudiation—in every aspect of the common life.
>
> Joseph Sittler, *Gravity & Grace*

Christian theologians recognize the truth of Sittler's claim. Yet they have often had trouble expressing the nature of God's "presencing" through his Spirit in the lives of women and men. This is, in part, because no definition of the Spirit is given in Scripture; rather, the Spirit is "narrated as an event—as happening."[21] The Spirit becomes known as God reveals his personal presence in creation and re-creation, in animating and sustaining power and wisdom, and in inbreaking expectation.[22] It is the Spirit (*ruach* in Hebrew and *pneuma* in Greek) who gives life ("breath") to the body (Gen. 6:17) and makes humans understand (Job 32:8), who endows some with artistic excellence (Exod. 31:3–4) and others with a gifted mind (Gen. 41:38). It is the Spirit who empowers all of us to desire good and to act with integrity (Ps. 51:10–11). It is the Spirit who leads us into both freedom (2 Cor. 3:17) and truth (John 14:17).[23]

Understood as such, the Spirit is to be identified with the divine presence in all of life. "In him we live and move and have our being" (Acts 17:28). In the words of John Taylor, the Spirit is the "Go-Between God."[24] Over the centuries, theologians have tried to understand this presence theoretically, but these second-order descriptions unfortunately have a removed, sterile quality. The Spirit, after all, blows where it will. John Calvin writes that "it is the Spirit, who everywhere diffused, sustains all things, causes them to grow, and quickens them in heaven and in earth."[25] Martin Luther believed that godless persons can do good things "through the merit of the Holy Spirit"[26] and that "all the functions of the Christians, such as loving [one's spouse], procreating children, governing the family, honoring the parents, being obedient to the magistrate, etc., which in themselves are secular and of the flesh, are fruits of the Spirit."[27] John Wesley describes the "creative grace" of the Holy Spirit as the loving, sustaining, and convicting presence of God in all human beings.[28] Commenting on Paul's speech to the Athenians, for example, he notes: "We need not go far to seek or find [God's Spirit]. He is very near us; in us. It is only perverse reason which thinks [God's Spirit] is afar off."[29]

In the twentieth century, Karl Barth recognized that we encounter "parables of the kingdom," human expressions of God's grace, "not merely in the witness of the Bible and . . . the Christian Church, but also in the secular sphere."

This is the work of the triune God through the Spirit.[30] Paul Tillich recognized that the Divine Spirit is manifest in the human spirit, both in morality and culture.[31] While agreeing, Jürgen Moltmann extends the Spirit's role to nature as well—to all of life. He proposes that there is in life a paradoxical "immanent transcendence": "There are no words of God without human experiences of God's Spirit. So the words of proclamation spoken by the Bible and the church must also be related to the experiences of people today."[32]

Such statements are helpful for our understanding of the Spirit's role in our lives, but they all suffer from abstraction. They seem removed from the inspiring Spirit and certainly distant from our experience with movies. Though true, they remain inert. We may gain a better understanding of the Spirit, I believe, by listening to the countless witnesses to the happening of the Spirit in the spirits of humankind. For our purposes here, let me offer four examples, three from "real" life that are rooted in artistic experience and one from "reel" life.

In his autobiography, *Surprised by Joy*, C. S. Lewis describes several experiences of his youth in which he was pointed "to something other and outer." The first such experience occurred when he played with a toy garden his brother made for him in the lid of a biscuit tin. In the years that followed, similar experiences came as he smelled a flowering currant bush, as he discovered autumn in Beatrix Potter's *Squirrel Nutkin*, and when he listened to Wagner's romantic music. This "Joy," as Lewis came to call it, was known primarily as a longing until Lewis chanced to read George MacDonald's *Phantastes*. Lewis writes: "It was as though the voice which had called to me from the world's end were now speaking at my side. It was with me in the room, or in my body, or behind me. If it had once eluded me by its distance, it now eluded me by proximity—something too near to see, too plain to be understood, on this side of knowledge." Lewis goes on to relate: "That night my imagination was, in a certain sense, baptized."[33] Lewis had encountered the Spirit, the divine presence in all of life.

Paul Tillich's theology of correlation is based autobiographically in a similar "baptismal" experience.[34] Living amid the horror of war as an army chaplain during World War I, Tillich traveled to Berlin during his last furlough. There he saw a painting by Botticelli titled *Madonna and Child with Singing Angels*. The experience was transformative of his spirit (he calls it "almost a revelation"), opening him to an element of depth in human experience and providing him a "potent analogue" for talking about religious experience more generally. What happened to him was a "breakthrough."[35] In a lecture titled "Human Nature and Art" (1952), Tillich labels this early experience with Botticelli's painting "revelatory ecstasy." He says, "A level of reality opened to me which had been covered up to this moment, although I had some feeling before of its existence." Tillich had, he says, "an encounter with the power of being itself."[36] Here again is the presence of the Spirit in the human spirit, though Tillich uses other language in his description.

Peter Berger has called this same awareness *A Rumor of Angels*. Although some would trumpet the demise of the supernatural in our contemporary world, this need not be the case, Berger argues. (Berger was writing in the 1970s, before the current rebirth of interest in spirituality in American culture.) For "'in, with and under' the immense array of human projections, there are indicators of a reality that is truly 'other' and that the religious imagination . . . ultimately reflects." In short, Berger believes that there is possible an inductive approach to theology, one anchored in fundamental human experiences—in "prototypical human gestures." There are experiences of the human spirit that point beyond their own reality, that have an "immediacy to God." These include for Berger our propensities for order, play, hope, damnation (for example, of Eichmann, Hitler's henchman), and humor. He writes, "Both in practice and in theoretical thought, human life gains the greatest part of its richness from the capacity for ecstasy, by which I do not mean the alleged experiences of the mystic, but any experience of stepping outside the taken-for-granted reality of everyday life, any openness to the mystery that surrounds us on all sides."[37]

These testimonies of and reflection on experience, particularly the experience of art, offer us an important theological resource for understanding the Holy Spirit's presence within the human spirit through film. However, more needs to be said about this experience of "Joy," this witness to a "baptismal" presence, this "rumor" of the divine. If we are to be true to our own dialogical methodology, these human stories must be put into conversation with God's story—with Scripture. Can we take this witness back into the biblical text and find further insight concerning what is the persistent and cross-cultural testimony of people through the ages?

In his book *Saint Paul at the Movies*, New Testament scholar Robert Jewett does just that, finding in the "miracles" (the Joy, the baptismal presence, the rumors of angels) experienced in the daily life of characters portrayed in the movie *Grand Canyon* (1991) an expression of Paul's teaching in Romans 2. Jewett asks, What are we to make of Simon, the black tow-truck driver, who risks his life to rescue a white motorist, caught at night in an all-black section of the city? Or what of Claire, who finds an abandoned infant and convinces her husband they should adopt it? Are these righteous actions not also a work of the Spirit in the human spirit? Can we not see in these individuals an example of people who are "patiently doing good" (Rom. 2:7), who "do instinctively what the law requires" (Rom. 2:14)? Are these not persons "who live obediently in accordance with the revelation they have received"?[38]

And what of the Hollywood producer in *Grand Canyon* who is shot in a random act, only to have a "vision" while in the hospital, suggesting that he stop making films that glorify violence? Later, when the man is healed, he turns away from this "calling," again deciding to make violent movies. Is this not an example, thinks Jewett, of one who has "exchanged the glory of the immortal God" (Rom. 1:23) for (other) images? An example of those who "though they knew God, they did not honor him as God or give thanks to him, but they became futile in their thinking, and their senseless minds were darkened" (Rom. 1:21)?

According to Klyne Snodgrass, whom Jewett references, Paul is not speaking in Romans 1 and 2 of a "works righteousness" by which people make a claim upon God, but of a salvation and a damnation that "are a result of one's actions, taking into consideration the amount of revelation given."[39] Here, thinks Jewett, is a description of the characters in the film *Grand Canyon*. The "obedience" that is portrayed in the film and described in Romans 2:7, 14–15, and 29 is a direct result of God's activity. Romans 2 speaks of the law written on humankind's heart "to which their own conscience [their spirits] also bears witness" (v. 15) and of the circumcision of the heart (v. 29). Both are works of the Spirit. In this biblical passage, Paul seems to have in mind those righteous individuals who lived prior to the coming of Jesus. Their salvation is according to their response to the light they were given, the amount of revelation they received. But his argument would seem to apply equally to all who have experiences of God's Spirit, regardless of time or place, whether they prove salvific or not.

Here is an appeal to the work of the Spirit in our spirits at its most rudimentary, the reach of our spirits that is met by the Spirit, the inbreaking of the Spirit into our spirits.[40] Such is the possibility that books like *Phantastes*, paintings like *Madonna and Child with Singing Angels*, and movies such as *Grand Canyon* offer their readers and viewers. If the Spirit is active in and through the human spirit, then the potential for the sacred is present across our human endeavor. Yet Christian theology, though it might give lip service to the presence of the Spirit in all of life, continues largely to ignore such works of the Spirit in the mundane, the ordinary experiences of human life. This seems particularly the case among those who define the human in "spirit-ual" terms. In some circles, there has been an unfortunate narrowing of the Spirit's role to the Christian community and a limitation of the Spirit's relation with our spirit to the extraordinary. The result of this constriction of the Holy Spirit's role has been a denial of the human spirit.

Hearing God through Non-Christians

As a college freshman at Stanford, I heard Robert McAfee Brown ask those of us in his class, "How is it possible to see the hand of God in the work of non-Christian writers?"[41] Though Brown had in mind contemporary novelists and playwrights, his question is equally applicable to screenwriters and filmmakers. If God is the source of all wisdom and beauty, how is it that unbelievers can create wonderful things and speak wisely? Brown suggests that over the centuries theologians have given three different answers to this question.

The first response claims that non-Christian artists are the unconscious inheritors of the Christian tradition. To the degree that such artists portray truth, goodness, and/or beauty, it is because they have been nurtured in a cultural milieu formed by Christian convictions that they have unintentionally absorbed. Following this line of reasoning, we might conclude that when Peter Weir or Woody Allen, the Coen brothers or Alexander Payne regard humankind with reverence and portray our significance and worth, these filmmakers are covertly affirming a Christian perspective, even if outwardly they disavow that they are Christians. The difficulty with such an argument should be apparent. While Christianity has without doubt influenced world culture, it is disingenuous to say that filmmakers covertly affirm what they overtly deny. I remember a well-known scholar in the field of religion and literature, Nathan Scott Jr., once calling Ernest Hemingway a "Christian writer" because his portrayal of human sin was Christian in viewpoint. Surely that does not merit the descriptor "Christian" for Hemingway, nor would he have wanted it.

There are other problems with falsely "baptizing" filmic truth as well. Though Christians sometimes want to give the Christian faith credit for the good a filmmaker portrays, they rarely are willing to take responsibility for those images of life that don't ring true. As we know, however, Christians have been responsible through the centuries for much evil as well as much good. Moreover, it is evident that filmmakers who have grown up in non-Christian societies and who have not been nurtured by the Christian faith at all have still produced masterpieces of cinema. The films by the Japanese master Yasujiro Ozu, for example, who was influenced not by Christianity but by Zen (cf. *Tokyo Story* [1953]), come to mind. In an increasingly post-Christian and multicultural society, few theologians take such an imperialistic approach any longer. It simply seems dishonest to use whatever Christian "remainder" there is in society to whitewash the secular or other-religious as Christian. Any kind of direct Christian influence on film must remain occasional, the result of a particular Christian filmmaker.

A second theological approach that Brown describes is much more widely subscribed to by contemporary Christians. Recognizing that non-Christian culture has produced much of value, some say, "All truth is God's truth." This argument for the general availability of truth has its roots in Justin Martyr, who claimed, "Whatever has been well said anywhere or by anyone belongs to us Christians."[42] That is, since truth comes from God, truth is to be welcomed in whatever garb it appears. Augustine and perhaps John Calvin represent other examples of those who have given voice to this common Christian perspective toward the wider culture. Such a theological stance has much to commend for itself vis-à-vis contemporary film, not the least being the humility and openness that it evidences toward Hollywood. Christians have applauded such movies as *Chariots of Fire* (1981), *The Iron Giant* (1999), *Places in the Heart* (1984), *Shawshank Redemption* (1994), *Simon Birch* (1998), *The Rookie* (2002), *Antwone Fisher* (2002), and *Tender Mercies* (1983) for the theology they embody. We can learn from these stories more of the Story.

But there are limitations to this approach, which Brown recognizes. Rather than allowing film to expand our understanding of life, the critic comes to movies with the "truth" pretty well in hand. Christian affirmations of the truth contained in a movie, thus, will tend to be selective, a cut-and-paste affair. Since Christians, as they watch a film, already have the "truth," they will be tempted to concentrate only on those insights that illustrate their independently established viewpoints and to ignore the rest. The result is often a warping of a movie's larger vision or an ignoring of films that do not initially fit their theological grid. While Christians holding this perspective commend a movie like *Tender Mercies* (1983), they avoid other movies like *Mar Adentro* (*The Sea Inside* [2004]), *Million Dollar Baby* (2004), *American Beauty* (1999), or *Thelma & Louise* (1991). But if film is to work its full charm, if it is to enrich and enliven us, then we must approach it as viewers with openness and humility.

A contemporary example of this second theological option is provided by Os Guinness in his book *Dining with the Devil* (1993). He writes:

> We should therefore heed Origen's ancient principle: Christians are free to plunder the Egyptians, but forbidden to set up a golden calf. By all means plunder freely of the treasures of modernity, but in God's name make sure that what comes out of the fire, which will test our life's endeavors, is gold fit for the temple of God and not a late-twentieth century image of a golden calf.[43]

Guinness's suspicion of full involvement in the wider culture is evident. Moviegoers must remain leery of becoming "worldly." And his metaphor of "plundering" pagan culture is a particularly unfortunate one. His warning echoes the overinterpretation of Romans 12:2 by Eugene Peterson, in his best-selling paraphrase of the Bible, *The Message*: "Don't become so well-adjusted to your culture that you fit into it without even thinking. Instead, fix your attention on God. . . . *Unlike the culture around you, always dragging you down to its level of immaturity,* God brings the best out of you" (italics mine).[44] What is not considered in Peterson's interpretation (which adds the ideas to the actual biblical text) is the possibility that God might attempt to bring the best out of us through the work of our wider culture (including the film industry).

Rather than holding to either of the above approaches, Brown believes Christians must recognize that "God can use *all* things for the fulfillment of the divine purposes, including the *full* message of non-Christians rather than only selected congenial portions."[45] He reflects on the Christian's conviction that God is able to use all things for his purposes—truth and untruth. Brown turns by way of illustration to the tenth chapter of Isaiah. Just as Isaiah recognized in his day that God could speak a true word to his people, Israel, through the unbelieving, unethical Assyrians, so Christians should affirm today, argues Brown, that God in his freedom can speak not only through believers but through "Assyrians in modern dress."[46]

In the tenth chapter of Isaiah, we read that the Israelites (who believed they were "God's people") were being threatened by the Assyrians (who certainly were not "God's people"). Instead of Isaiah telling Israel that God was about to judge these pagans through his people of Israel in order that justice might reign, the scenario is reversed. It is the raping, pillaging Assyrians whom Isaiah claims will be God's spokesmen to make known God's way to Israel:

> Ah, Assyria, the rod of my anger—
>> the club in their hands is my fury!
> Against a godless nation I send him.
>
> Isaiah 10:5–6a

God's people (here called "a godless nation") will not hear (though they think they do). Thus, God will speak through the Assyrians. What makes the Assyrians such a powerful witness, moreover, is precisely their unbelief. Isaiah recognizes that they do not realize they are being used as God's mouthpiece: "But this is not what he intends, nor does he have this in mind" (Isa. 10:7). It does not matter; pagan Assyria is to be the expression of God's revelation to "believing" Israel.

The analogy should not be overdrawn, but its point is clear. Christians need not claim that non-Christian filmmakers are covert Christians or simply appropriate from their movies what is congenial to or congruent with their understanding of the Christian faith. Rather, if viewers will join in community with a film's storyteller, letting the movie's images speak with their full integrity, they might be surprised to discover that they are hearing God as well. If this sounds surprising, it is no more so that Assyria was once God's spokesperson to Israel.[47]

While such theologizing will sound preposterous to many, not least of all to many filmmakers, I find it (1) not only consistent with Christian theology and (2) supportive of the integrity of the film itself, but also (3) liberating to the human spirit of the viewer. In this context I am reminded of the words of Dietrich Bonhoeffer, written from a Nazi prison:

> I wonder whether it is possible (it almost seems so today) to regain the idea of the Church as providing an understanding of the area of freedom (art, education, friendship, play), so that Kirkegaard's "aesthetic existence" would not be banished from the Church's sphere, but would be reestablished within it? . . . Who is there, for instance, in our times, who can devote himself with an easy mind to music, friendship, games or happiness? Surely not the "ethical" man [person], but only the Christian.[48]

What Bonhoeffer is suggesting is that such attempts as Brown's to reestablish a creative (playful) place for film within an explicitly theological framework might well provide an optimal context in which community can be actualized, in which filmmaker and viewer can truly and freely meet, in which film can be experienced for what it is. To come "ethically" to a work of art with truth in hand is to destroy its ability to speak freely and powerfully. It is true that all viewers watch movies "presuppositionally," that is, with a hidden or stated agenda that is theirs by virtue of their humanity. But it is only the viewers whose presuppositions enable and encourage them freely to engage the center of power and meaning of a movie on its own ground who are able to be critically free and freely critical.

One such experience for me was the viewing of the award-winning movie *American Beauty* (1999).[49] The movie is a dark comedy and not for the easily offended. It portrays the hollowness of suburbia's chase after the American dream—after money, status, youth, and, of course, beauty. The story is gorgeously bleak, the filmic equivalent of a John Updike novel about a hero's midlife crisis. It is also laced with profanity and nudity, adultery and drug use.

Lester Burnham (Kevin Spacey) exasperates his wife, Carolyn (Annette Bening), by dropping out of life. *American Beauty* (d. Mendes, 1999). Photo by Lorey Sebastian. ©1999 DreamWorks LLC. All rights reserved.

As the story unfolds, we might think that the theme of *American Beauty* is going to be, "Eat, drink, and be merry, for tomorrow we die." But the movie is anything but sensational. Its iconoclasm mocks our media-generated illusions without resorting to either a simple fatalism or a perverse cynicism. Lester Burnham, the film's hero, is ignored by his wife, bored by his work, and unloved by his daughter. He is shriveled of soul until an infatuation with his daughter's cheerleader friend shocks him alive. He literally begins to smell the roses. Despite being a near caricature of middle-class life today, the movie's portrayal of a man who does not know what his role in life is and fears growing old is all too real. "I'll be dead in a year," Lester tells us as the movie opens. "In a way, I'm dead already."

But much like the book of Ecclesiastes, despair does not have the final word.[50] There is a hard-won serenity that Lester discovers at life's core. Lester is therefore able, even in death, to embrace his life. And through him, so do we. Ultimately, sadness does not have the last word, but compassion and joy. In the fourth century, Evagrius listed sadness as one of the eight chief sins. Under pressure to use the symbolic number seven, Pope Gregory the Great later dropped sadness from the list to make the deadly sins seven. But Evagrius's recognition is an important one for our own day. At its core, and despite its fragility—its mystery, its amorality, and death itself—life has a beauty that is to be cherished. *American Beauty* understands this. The movie can shock us alive to such beauty, however transient. It can overcome our sadness. It did for me.

Encountering God through Image

> Art does not reproduce the visible;
> Rather it makes visible.
>
> Paul Klee

As we have already noted, film gives story a unique shape. It is not enough to understand a movie according to the canons of storytelling that we might apply to a novel. Movies also have to do with image. This presents yet another challenge for the Christian who would engage in dialogue with Hollywood. For Christianity—or more particularly, Protestant Christianity—has not always looked kindly on the use of image, which has typically been associated with idolatry. For example, under the heading "Image," both the *International Standard Bible Encyclopedia* (revised edition, 1982) and the *Harper's Bible Dictionary* (1985) have "See Idol." These dictionaries echo the bias of the Protestant Reformer John Calvin, who wrote: "Whatever men learn of God in images is futile, indeed false, the prophets totally condemn the notion that images stand in the place of books." Instead, it is "in the preaching of his Word and sacred mysteries . . . [that] a common doctrine [is] set forth for all. But those whose eyes rove about in contemplating idols betray that their minds are not diligently intent upon this doctrine."[51]

In an otherwise helpful book that has been a perennial best-seller, James Packer's *Knowing God* (1973) warns similarly against the use of any image as an aid to worship.[52] For Packer, idolatry consists not only in the worship of false gods but in the worship of the true God through the use of images. As the second commandment states, "Thou shalt not make unto thee any graven image . . . thou shalt not bow down thyself to them, nor serve them." Packer believes this commandment to be categorical. It is not just talking about degrading representations of God, but even pictures and statues of Jesus Christ as a man that are made and viewed with reverence.

According to Packer, images obscure God's glory and convey false ideas about God. If we are to know God, it can only come from God's revelation of himself through his holy Word "and from no other source whatsoever." Why would God make such a generalized prohibition?

> Surely this is in order to make us realize that those who make images and use them in worship, and thus inevitably take their theology from them, will in fact tend to neglect God's revealed will at every point. The mind that takes up with images is a mind that has not yet learned to love and attend to God's Word. Those who look to man-made images, material or mental, to lead them to God are not likely to take any part of His revelation as seriously as they should.[53]

Extrapolating outward from warnings about false worship, Packer concludes that God communicates best through word, not symbols. We have already encountered his conclusion in this chapter with Noll, Wells, and Plantinga, who spoke of the need to avoid the entertainment culture in order to get back to the more important tasks of reading and thinking. Again, word is judged to be paramount over image.

Such rhetoric, typical of some Calvinists, is softened within other branches of Protestantism. Luther, for example, was not against the use of even such religious images as the crucifix so long as they were used not for worship but only as memorials. He wrote:

> It is possible for me to hear and bear in mind the story of the Passion of our Lord. But it is impossible for me to hear and bear it in mind without forming mental images of it in my heart. For whether I will or not when I hear of Christ, an image of a man hanging on a cross takes form in my heart just as the reflection of my face naturally appears in the water when I look into it. If it is not a sin, but good to have the image of Christ in my heart, why should it be a sin to have it in my eyes?[54]

Luther thus felt free to publish his New Testament in 1522 with twenty-two woodcuts as illustrations, though Luther's theology of images was still a cautious one. More in keeping with Augustine's thought perhaps, Luther believed images could "engage reason about revelation. They are icons for the mind, didactic proclamation."[55]

Turning to Protestant filmmakers, it is not surprising to discover similarly that movies often remain icons of the mind, where the primary message is conveyed through words. In the works of two of the best—Ron Shelton, who grew up a Baptist and went to Westmont College, an evangelical school in Santa Barbara, and Paul Schrader, who went to Calvin College, a Dutch Reformed institution in Grand Rapids, Michigan—the movie's message often is communicated through voice-overs. Recall, for example, the opening of *Bull Durham* (1988), where Annie Savoy's monologue begins, "I believe in the church of baseball." What follows is Shelton's "theology," enfleshed in a story about minor league baseball, where the marks of the church are communal celebration (the joy of the ball game), discipleship (Annie and Crash nurturing the less mature Nuke), and living with an eschatological hope (the hope of one day getting to heaven—the big leagues). But we are first "told" what we are to see.

In a helpful address on the nature of the Protestant aesthetic, my colleague Bill Dyrness contrasted two approaches to life as they are found in the classic texts by the Catholic Dante Alighieri (his *Divine Comedy*) and the Protestant John Bunyan (his *Pilgrim's Progress*). Where Dante has as his guides the poet Virgil and the beautiful Beatrice, Bunyan's guide is the Evangelist and the scroll he gives Pilgrim. Where Dante trusts the images of desire that God puts in his way, Pilgrim needs an interpreter to be sure he has the story right. Dante's world is full of signs; Pilgrim's journey in Bunyan's allegory is beset with temptation. Dante suggests the need for a hermeneutic of discernment; Bunyan fashions a hermeneutic of suspicion. Where Dante is compelled by love, Pilgrim is motivated largely by fear.[56] The differences are clear and suggest that it is not to the Protestant traditions that we should turn if we are to see embodied a robust theology of the image, but to Roman Catholics and their filmmakers.[57]

While such a turn might have been deemed controversial by our Protestant colleagues a decade ago, now even a leading evangelical such as Mark Noll recognizes the contribution Catholic theology can make to his branch of the church: "Catholics offer evangelicals a sense of tradition and centuries of reflection on the bearing of sacramentality on all existence."[58] He sees this as a sign of hope in the emergence of evangelical thought today.

It is in the works of such Catholic directors as Martin Scorsese, Alfred Hitchcock, and Francis Ford Coppola that we see meaning conveyed most forcefully through image.[59] Such directors have both inherited an iconic culture and have helped embody it. In the words of Flannery O'Connor, "The [Catholic] artist penetrates the concrete world in order to find at its depths the image of its source, the image of ultimate reality."[60] Thus, the fight scenes in *Raging Bull* (1980), the shower scene in *Psycho* (1960), and the baptism scene in *The Godfather* (1972) go beyond what words can express, giving viewers a visceral experience of evil's presence.

Taking its lead from Aquinas, Roman Catholicism has valued creation as well as salvation, the natural together with the supernatural. In chapter 3 we noted in our discussion of Andrew Greeley some of the distinctives of Catholicism at this point. Where the Protestant tradition assumes God to be largely absent from creation and human creativity, the Catholic tradition assumes God to be largely present. Where Catholics focus on the sacramentality of the world, Protestants concentrate on the basic sinfulness of the world. Where Protestants recognize an infinite qualitative distinction between the finite and the infinite; Catholics live believing that the transformation of the ordinary into the extraordinary is a regular occurrence. H. Richard Niebuhr, in summarizing the Catholic position, writes that Catholicism (what Niebuhr calls the "synthesist" view) expresses "a principle that no other Christian group seems to assert so well but which all need to share; namely, the principle that the Creator and the Saviour are one, or that whatever salvation means beyond creation it does not mean the destruction of the created."[61]

Recognizing the wisdom of having such a theology of natural life, the Lutheran theologian Dietrich Bonhoeffer argued that it was folly to speak only of the person and work of Jesus Christ (the ultimate) and ignore all that was penultimate. He asked, how could the church recover a christologically informed, but creationally based, understanding of the natural, one that would challenge the perennial heresy of gnosticism? Bonhoeffer concluded, "The concept of the natural must . . . be recovered."[62]

The Protestant suspicion of the image, its reverence for the rational word, and its concentration on redemption theology to the sometimes exclusion of creation theology have all combined to have a major dampening effect on this church's engagement with Hollywood. If a full-orbed conversation between theology and film is to go forward, it will be necessary for the Protestant church to recover a more adequate theology of image, one rooted in experience and grounded in creation itself. As David Harned colorfully expressed it, we must "prevent the reduction of the Genesis account (of creation) to a sort of dubious archeological appendage to Christian faith."[63]

The biblical creation account shows more than God's omnipotence and humankind's fallenness. It also reveals God's gracious desire to enter into relationship with human beings and to bless them. Though Barth is certainly correct to stress the infinite qualitative distinction between humankind and God, this does not deny the goodness of God's creation of us, his creatures. We have, in fact, been created "in his image, in the image of God he created them; male and female he created them" (Gen. 1:27). The meaning of this reference to image is debated by theologians, though it surely has something to do with the way we relate together. We are created male and female and called to live together in community with one another and with God. But God's image in us has also something to do with our participation in life, as the next verse in the Genesis text makes clear: "God blessed them, and God said to them, 'Be fruitful and multiply, and fill the earth and subdue it; and have dominion over the fish of the sea and over the birds of the air and over every living thing that moves upon the earth'" (Gen. 1:28). All that we do, we do in the power of the God who created us. This includes the making of images. Images are one means of responding to the divine call to fulfill life. The Image-maker has blessed us, his creation, with the freedom to be image-makers too.

Moreover, there is no single form of image making that is theologically more significant than others. An image doesn't have to be explicitly religious, for example, to be theologically helpful, though it might be. I have found the theology of Paul Tillich useful at this point. We have noted above how Tillich himself experienced divine revelation through his experience of seeing Botticelli's *Madonna and Child with Singing Angels* at the Kaiser Friedrich Museum in Berlin at the end of World War I. Images, thus, became for him a means to "penetrate to the level where an ultimate concern exercises its driving power."[64]

Tillich identified five types of images, each with its own possibility of expressing human beings' relationship to ultimate reality. The first is the *sacramental*, a numinous realism that "depicts ordinary things, ordinary persons, ordinary events . . . in a way which makes them strange, mysterious, laden with an ambiguous power." The second is the *mystical*, which reaches out for ultimacy without dependence on concrete things or persons, using "basic structural elements of reality like lines, cubes, planes, colors, as symbols for that which transcends all reality." The third type is *critical realism*, where "sober, objective, quasi-scientifically observed reality is a manifestation of ultimate reality, although it is lacking in directly numinous character. It is the humility of accepting the given which provides it with religious power." Fourth is *idealism*, which "sees in the present the anticipation of future perfection" and produces images either of remembrances of the lost or anticipations of the regained. Last, Tillich describes what he labels *expressionism*, which is realistic and, at the same time, mystical; it both criticizes and anticipates, disrupting the given appearance of things. There is in expressionism an element of depth, which is conveyed in and through the encountered image.[65]

Tillich's typology of image was formulated with reference to paintings like Picasso's *Guernica*, and its particulars need not concern us here, other than to say that what is common to the above types of images is their ability to become mediators of ultimate reality. None need be what we have traditionally labeled "religious images," although religious images can be used. The key, instead, is the image's ability to transport the viewer to some more central place, to provide the viewer that experience of "Joy" of which C. S. Lewis speaks. It was just such an experience through the movie *Becket* that was transformative for me.

Theology's Narrative Shape

Biblical truth has a definite narrative shape. Jesus used parables, not treatises. Nathan spoke to David in stories. The Israelites used narrative to speak of the God of Abraham, Isaac, and Jacob and to recount the mighty acts of God in shaping their history. The sermons of Peter and Stephen, which are recalled in the opening chapters of the book of Acts, recite these same stories of Israel and recall the Christ event. Even Paul's more systematic theology is far removed from the abstract reasoning that goes by that term today. His is a missional theology. His argument is never separated from the passion narrative, from his own life story, or from the particular context and stories of those he addresses. To the Corinthians he wrote,

> Now I would remind you, brothers and sisters, of the good news that I proclaimed to you, which you in turn received, in which also you stand, through which also you are being saved. . . .
>
> For I handed on to you as of first importance what I in turn had received: that Christ died for our sins in accordance with the scriptures, and that he was buried, and that he was raised on the third day in accordance with the scriptures, and that he appeared to Cephas, then to the twelve. Then he appeared to more than five hundred brothers and sisters at one time. . . . Last of all, as to one untimely born, he appeared also to me. For I am the least of the apostles, unfit to be called an apostle, because I persecuted the church of God. But by the grace of God I am what I am, and his grace toward me has not been in vain.
>
> 1 Corinthians 15:1–10

Christianity is, at core, not an abstract philosophy, but a story; not pure factual reportage, but a recounting of one life in order that other lives might be transformed. Christian theology is rooted in the testimony of what has been both seen and lived—what is both real in its own right and redemptive in those who experience the story and respond to it. When preachers testify to the death and resurrection of Jesus and its efficacy for Christians, they are speaking of both past event and present reality. And story provides this bridge.

Theologians have not always recognized the importance of story—or, at least, have let it become submerged under a welter of abstract analysis. John Macquarrie, for example, defines systematic theology as "the intellectual discipline that seeks to express the content of a religious faith as a coherent body of propositions."[66] But systematic theology's analytical rigor is also its limitation. It "has difficulty in maintaining touch with the narrative nature of the faith upon which it seeks to reflect, and therefore with the object of its concern."[67] Noting this fact, Old Testament scholar John Goldingay wonders about the preeminence of systematic theology in some circles. Even if we are rational creatures, disciplined reflection need not take the form of systematic theology, he suggests.[68] In Judaism, for example, reflection has for centuries taken the form of the retelling of biblical narrative so as to answer contemporary questions and clarify difficulties. We can think sharply and coherently on our faith using narrative as well.

In his introduction to the Hassidic stories, Martin Buber writes of the importance of the narrative form:

> The story is itself an event and has the quality of a sacred action. . . . It is more than a reflection—the sacred essence to which it bears witness continues to live in it. The

wonder that is narrated becomes powerful once more. . . . A rabbi, whose grandfather had been a pupil of Baal Shem Tov, was once asked to tell a story. "A story ought to be told," he said, "so that it is itself a help," and his story was this. "My grandfather was paralyzed. Once he was asked to tell a story about his teacher and he told how the holy Baal Shem Tov used to jump and dance when he was praying. My grandfather stood up while he was telling the story and the story carried him away so much that he had to jump and dance to show how the master had done it. From that moment, he was healed. This is how stories ought to be told."[69]

Stories are performative; they give meaning to facts. In the process they help answer questions concerning who we are and point us to that larger truth which lies beyond our grasp. But what has this to do with theology and film? A growing number of persons are finding that movies as story provide their viewers a means of recapturing the meaning and power of our story-shaped gospel, something we have all too often abstracted. Robert Jewett, for example, entertains what he calls the "seemingly preposterous proposition" that "certain movies afford deeper access to the hidden heart of Paul's theology than mainstream theologians like myself have been able to penetrate."[70] He argues that Pauline scholarship in the West has centered in issues of guilt rather than shame and has understood grace chiefly in terms of individual forgiveness. But he asks, could it be that shame is the deeper and more problematic dilemma that Paul deals with in his description of salvation? And are there not corporate as well as individual dimensions to the gospel? As Jewett, a New Testament scholar, has explored this interpretive possibility with regard to the book of Romans, he has found contemporary film to provide greater insight into Paul's references to honor, shame, and grace than many of his colleagues' scholarly essays. Conversely, he is convinced that the New Testament can also shed light on the deeper dimensions of films like *Babe* (1995), *The Shawshank Redemption* (1994), and *Mr. Holland's Opus* (1995). The conversation is two-directional.

Jewett is not alone in believing that we need at times to reverse the hermeneutical flow between theology and film. Film's story can affect our understanding of the Christian story, not just the reverse. In five volumes published over the last fifteen years, Larry Kreitzer shows that the meaning modern people have attached to biblical incidents and concepts, as these are evident through film (and the novel), can suggest fresh interpretations of the original meaning of the biblical text.[71] Modern versions of biblical truth as they are enfleshed in film can send us back to the originals with new insight. A popular example of this reversal of the typical hermeneutical flow between Scripture and film is Philip Yancey's *The Jesus I Never Knew* (1995), a book that sold by the tens of thousands in the 1990s.[72] Yancey narrates how it was through watching a dozen or so Jesus movies, which had come out of Hollywood over the years, that he discovered a new sense of Jesus' true humanity. Yancey had been so heavenly-minded that his Christology was of little earthly good until such movies as *Jesus*

Christ Superstar (1973), *The Gospel according to Saint Matthew* (1964), *Jesus of Nazareth* (1977), and *The Last Temptation of Christ* (1988) showed him new ways of seeing the Messiah.

If the church has forgotten that the heart of its theology is story (God's story, which begins in Genesis, "Once upon a time," and ends in Revelation, "They live happily ever after"), if the church has concentrated too often on structure and ethics and dogma, then God's story will be heard in other venues, such as the movie theater. In 1999 alone, movies like *The Matrix*, *The End of the Affair*, *Dogma*, *The Third Miracle*, *The Green Mile*, *The Straight Story*, *The Iron Giant*, *Magnolia*, *The Hurricane*, and *American Beauty* all became the context for theology to be given narrative shape. Each invited a subsequent theological conversation. Similarly, in 2004, it was not just *The Passion of the Christ* that invited theological conversation, but *Eternal Sunshine of the Spotless Mind*; *Hotel Rwanda*; *Ray*; *Mar Adentro* (*The Sea Inside*); *The Incredibles*; *Million Dollar Baby*; *Dogville*; *The Story of the Weeping Camel*; *Woman, Thou Art Loosed*; *Friday Night Lights*; *Finding Neverland*; *Saved!*; *Les Choristes* (*The Chorus*); and even *Spider-Man 2*.

The Spitfire Grill (1996)

A good example of film's potential to engender theological conversation through story is *The Spitfire Grill*. Made on a modest budget ($6+ million) by a Roman Catholic organization in Mississippi, it was the surprise hit at Robert Redford's Sundance Film Festival before playing to general release. The movie tells the story of Percy Talbott, who comes to Gilead, Maine, to find a job after finishing her prison term. Percy is given work by Hannah, the owner of the Spitfire Grill, and is befriended by Shelby, Hannah's niece by marriage. A rocky but genuine friendship ensues between the three women, and their relationship forms the core of the film. Early in the story, when Hannah falls and breaks her leg, Percy takes over the diner with the help of Shelby. Percy cannot cook, but she is willing to learn, and the two younger women keep the restaurant in business. One evening, as she rubs lotion on Hannah's tender leg, Percy asks: "You suppose if a wound goes so deep, the healing of it might hurt as bad as what caused it?"

Here, in microcosm, is the question of the film. For Gilead, too, is suffering from a wound. All the citizens of this small hamlet have been deeply hurt. Their hopes have been shattered by the disappearance of Hannah's talented son, Eli, who represented their future. He has failed to "return" from Vietnam. Their "dis-ease" needs treatment, but the healing will prove painful. It is Percy who acts as a balm to bring spiritual healing and new possibility to Gilead. At first, Percy simply substitutes for Hannah in running the café and in providing food for a mysterious and needy recluse who lives in the hills. But the wound is deep. Healing can come only as it is pierced ("Perced") through sacrificial love. Reconciliation does take place and a son comes home, but not without a heavy price. Percy's death brings hope to Gilead.

When the movie's sponsorship became known, this film was criticized by some as "hidden propaganda" (Percy is a "Christ-figure"), though there is no explicit religiosity in the film. Not all people in the larger society were willing to accept the film's indirect spiritual gift, however, for it had come from a Christian organization. Yet most viewers were taken by the film's story. Perhaps we can understand the value of *The Spitfire Grill* by recalling the fiction of another indirect storyteller. Almost fifty years ago, C. S. Lewis sought to overcome the narrow secularity of our modern age, not by producing movies, but by writing children's stories that also had a Christ-figure. He was concerned that modern women and men were in danger of becoming little more than "trousered apes." It was not enough to have "just the facts," as Joe Friday wanted on *Dragnet*, a television series of the time. Lewis was convinced that we were being cut off from our roots and destiny. Story could help heal our malady.

The purpose of Lewis's series for children, *The Chronicles of Narnia*, was to give a new generation of readers the taste and feel of truth—to baptize their imagination. (This was also Tolkien's goal with his *Lord of the Rings* trilogy, a goal, like Lewis's, that has more recently been achieved through filmic adaptations of their stories.) In this way, Lewis hoped to assist others in getting beyond the tiny, windowless universe they had mistaken for reality. A good story, thought Lewis, should do more than offer an engaging plot or produce excitement. In a good story, plot is important, but only as a net to catch something else. The story should mediate something more, or other, than what we are conscious of in our day-to-day existence. In *The Chronicles of Narnia*, Aslan, the lion (the Christ-figure), explains to the children that he has brought them to Narnia so that, having experienced him there, they might be able to recognize him in another guise where they live. Here is a "theology" of story every bit as applicable to movies as to children's literature.[73]

What Lewis did for his generation through children's fiction—the reinvigorating of our imaginations—others are attempting in our day through film (and not just with adaptations of Lewis, Tolkien, and others like them). Such films need not be created by Christians. In fact, the director of *The Spitfire Grill* was Jewish. It is enough that life be portrayed at some more central region. The shame that a town feels over the "loss" of its son needs healing. And Percy Talbott, unlikely Christ-figure that she is, nonetheless comes with her balm to Gilead to make the wounded whole. Though she comes into the town from the outside, has a questionable reputation, and experiences rejection, Percy is able to expose the hurts of this small town and bring healing (salvation) both to a family and to a town.

Theology's Dialogical Character

Karl Barth once described the theologian as having a Bible in one hand and the newspaper in the other. That is, the theologian's task is a dialogical one. We can observe theology's interactive nature, for example, by reflecting on one expression of it, preaching. How do ministers develop a sermon for a worship service? They might rely on the lectionary that church tradition has provided. Or it might be Christmas or one of the other major holidays of the church year. They might seek to address a crisis in the congregation or in the wider society. They might choose to preach a series of sermons on a particular section of Scripture, perhaps one of its books. They might want to comment on a personal area of growth, meaningful to them, which they hope will prove significant to others. All of these are valid and typical ways ministers begin sermon preparation. But unless the sermon is both rooted in the "Bible" (both directly and as mediated through tradition and the worshiping community) and sensitive to the congregation's personal and social context (the "newspaper"), it will remain stillborn.

Paul Tillich, perhaps more than any other theologian, recognized the importance for theology of such a dialogue between culture and the Christian faith. Writing some fifty years ago, Tillich understood the task of theology as providing Christian responses to the concerns being raised by contemporary experience.[74] Theology, that is, must seek to correlate Christian answers with contemporary questions. Such an approach to culture is still used by many in the field of theology and film, film now being seen as providing the "questions" to which the Christian faith provides the "answers." There are, to be sure, problems with such a unidirectional understanding of theology's necessary dialogue. Contemporary culture, for example, is wrongly seen as alone setting the theological agenda through the questions it asks, while the questions the Christian faith also might pose are denied. Moreover, any answers culture might suggest are similarly denied. Better for the dialogue to truly be two-way, but Tillich's contribution has nonetheless proven significant. One such influence has been on the work of Don Browning, who does give voice to theology's need for two-way dialogue. In his *A Fundamental Practical Theology* (1991), Browning says he "envisions theology as a mutually critical dialogue between interpretations of the Christian message and interpretations of contemporary cultural experiences and practices. Stated more explicitly, Christian theology becomes a critical dialogue between the implicit questions and the explicit answers of the Christian classics and the explicit questions and implicit answers of contemporary cultural experiences and practices."[75]

The co-editor of this book's *Engaging Culture* series, William Dyrness, describes the theological task in similar terms, as seeking to bring together in reflective obedience the telling of our stories and the hearing of God's story.[76]

Again, the basic two-way, dialogical nature of theology is evident. We can diagram theology's constructive task as in figure 4.1.

Figure 4.1 The Nature of the Theological Task

Theologians have often added components to this simple schematic for doing theology, altering its shape in the process. But theology's basic two-way conversation remains. For example, it can be helpful to distinguish some of the different ways in which we hear God's story, for theologians have recognized the unique authority of Scripture over tradition. Thus many theologians use a triangle (fig. 4.2 A) to diagram their theological sources.

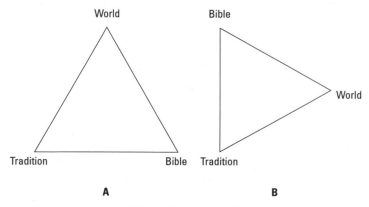

Figure 4.2 Threefold Source of Theology

If we set this triangle on its side (fig. 4.2 B), we can again note the basic interactive nature of the theological task. The dialogue cannot be simply between Scripture and tradition; our position in the world is also significant for our theological reflection. At a minimum, the world (culture) must be seen as theology's setting (it is the form in which we think and learn) and application (theology rethinks God's thoughts in every generation).

Others have recognized the need not only to differentiate resources in hearing God's story, but also in telling our stories. John Wesley, for example, posited a quadrilateral of theological resources that in addition to Bible and tradition included reason (what within your culture you consider reasonable) and personal experience.

Personal experience matters theologically. Varied experiences, for example, sometimes cause women to read Scripture differently than men. If you have had a child die, you will read the book of Job differently. What is thought reasonable also varies culturally. If you think about life from within the thought structures of Asian culture, you will view it differently than in the West. Latin America, which spent centuries under the yoke of the few, was particularly sensitive to the biblical logic of liberation during the seventies, when opportunity for new forms of government presented itself. Such variations in how people reason are significant for how they do theology. Both reason and experience help give shape to our theological reflections. But Wesley's quadrilateral (fig. 4.3) can also be understood as simply a variation of our twofold conversational paradigm. We hear God's story through Bible and tradition. We tell our stories through reason and experience.

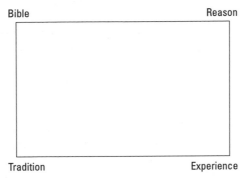

Figure 4.3 Fourfold Source of Theology

My own model for doing constructive theology (fig. 4.4) has five components:

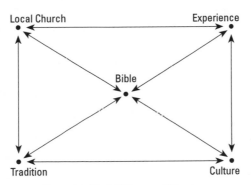

Figure 4.4 Fivefold Source of Theology

Hearing God's story now has three of these components (one's particular worshiping community; the larger Christian community of witnesses, past and present; and the Bible). Our interaction in the world includes both our individual experience and our participation in a larger culture, a shared meaning system. In the diagram (fig. 4.4), the Bible is at the center of the scheme in part to emphasize its primacy of place; the Bible is theology's authority for faith and practice. But it is also located in the center because our access to biblical truth is mediated through one or more of the other sources. We read the authoritative biblical text from out of a worshiping community, in light of centuries of Christian thought and practice, as people embedded in a particular culture, who have a unique set of experiences. Here is the theological process.

Seen in this light, cultural expressions (including movies) function as important resources for theological reflection. Movies need not be explicitly "Christian" in their theme to be theologically significant. As a means of telling our stories (and even hearing God's story pseudonymously), movies have the potential of helping us to hear God as God's story and our stories intersect. God is present in all of life and communicates with us through all of these theological resources. Film, as an expression of the broader culture and as the occasion for our own personal experiences and growth, can serve as a theological resource, providing both insight and conviction to its viewers. For when the dialogue comes together between viewers and a film, we may glimpse something hidden, either in ourselves, another, or even the Other.

An example from my own experience of the two-way, dialogical nature of theology and film might add clarity. I remember seeing David Lynch's *The Elephant Man* (1980), a movie based loosely on the true story of John Merrick, a grotesquely deformed young man who lived during the last part of the nineteenth century in England. Reduced to making a living in the sideshow of the circus, Merrick was thought incapable of either feeling or speech. That is, until he was rescued by Sir Frederick Treves of the London Hospital. Treves had wanted a "specimen" to analyze as he gave his anatomy lectures, but his compassion for John grew daily. Hiding him in an isolated ward of the hospital, Treves sought to give John a life. But hospital policy did not allow "incurables" to permanently take up scarce beds, so the chief administrator asked Treves to show him John in order that he might assess whether Merrick might be helped. Central to the decision of whether John Merrick would be forced onto the streets again was whether he was capable of thought and speech.

In the movie, Treves pleads with John to show the administrator that he can speak. "I can't help you unless you help me. I believe that there is something you want to say to me. . . . We must show them that you're not a wall." And John responds; he tentatively tries to speak. Excited, Treves tries to prepare him for the impending interview by having him repeat the first verses of the twenty-third Psalm. These would be his elocution lessons. But when Carr Gomm, the hospital administrator, comes the next afternoon, John is too frightened to say anything other than a few words that seem almost rote. Frustrated, Gomm asks John cynically, "How long did you and Mr. Treves prepare for this interview?" John has failed, and the two doctors leave him.

As they stand outside John's room discussing the case quietly, the doctors hear John speak again. He is again quoting the twenty-third Psalm. This time, however, he is reciting not only the first three verses, but the remaining ones as well: "Yea though I walk through the valley of the shadow of death, I will fear no evil; for Thou art with me." Hearing John articulate as his own this radical affirmation of trust in God, Treves realizes that he has not taught that part of the psalm to Merrick. The doctors return to John's room, where they learn from him (he is now relaxed enough to speak) that his mother had taught him the psalm when he was a child. John is spared, and he becomes a model to all who later meet him of what true humanity is.

As I saw *The Elephant Man*, I understood one of the most frequently quoted texts in the Bible in a new light. This psalm was not simply a general affirmation of faith by someone reflecting on life. It is not a psalm written when all is well. Rather here is a cry of one in crisis; though all else fail, God's extravagant care will provide. No wonder the psalm is used in hospital settings and at funerals worldwide. But that night at the theater, I also experienced more. My theology was enlarged, as I understood better what it was to be a human. I experienced this both as I watched the contrast between Carr Gomm's legalism and Frederick Treves's grace and as John's compelling personage filled the screen with life. My Christian understanding of what it is to be human took on a new depth it had previously not had. I would not only read Psalm 23 differently, but also Psalm 8:

> What are human beings that you are mindful of them,
>   mortals that you care for them?
> Yet you have made them a little lower than God,
>   and crowned them with glory and honor.
>
> Psalm 8:4–5

My conversation between God's story and our stories took on a new richness and depth that night. John Merrick had taught me about theology.

God can be experienced through film's stories and images in myriad ways, and these experiences both invite theological dialogue and feed into our constructive theology. But in order to make use of the resources that movies provide the Christian believer, in order to hear God speak pseudonymously as spirit encounters Spirit, it is helpful to know better how to view movies on their own terms. It is to this task that we now turn.

are movies art?

Aren't Movies Too Commercial?

Movies are often not viewed as legitimate art. Many reasons are given for this common perception, but chief among them perhaps is film's commercialism. Consider the viewpoint of Max Horkheimer and Theodor W. Adorno, well-known philosophers and social critics of the Frankfurt School, who expressed the following in 1947: "Movies and radio need no longer pretend to be art. The truth that they are just business is made into an ideology in order to justify the rubbish they deliberately produce."[1] All too frequently, so the argument goes, movies are controlled by crass commercial interests. They merely provide escape or indulge our prejudices and fantasies, over-simplifying life in the process. Movies are geared to the masses through their marketing techniques and star system. Hollywood seems fixed on the lucrative subjects of sex and violence and is prone to create spectacular special effects in order to generate a crowd rather than to portray the nuances of everyday life.[2] Where is the art in this?

Criticism of Hollywood's commercialism must be taken seriously. Too much in Hollywood is formulaic and indulgent. But the basic presupposition that art and business cannot mix is erroneous. Michelangelo painted the Sistine Chapel's ceiling on commission; Charles Eames designed for the Herman Miller Corporation his award-winning chairs, which are now shown in leading museums around the world.[3] We might not typically speak of the opera business or the symphony business, but these too are highly sophisticated enterprises. When Esa-Pekka Salonen, the music director and conductor of the Los Angeles Philharmonic, plays Brahms or Beethoven for the sake of pleasing his audience, instead of a steady diet of the twentieth-century composers that he favors, this does not result in the dismissal of these past masters. The Philharmonic's music is often glorious despite its commercial intention. How many ballet companies perform *The Nutcracker Suite* at Christmastime in order to help finance the rest of the year's activity? Yet how many audiences are captivated by the magic of that story in dance? When the Los Angeles County Museum of Art mounted its exhibit on Van Gogh in the winter of 1999, it was for the express purpose of drawing large crowds to buy high-priced tickets. That did not prevent thousands from being transfixed by the paintings they saw.

Marketing need not negate art. Though it is a business, the motion picture industry produces films that similarly have the power to enlighten and to disturb, to make us more aware of who we are and what our relationship with others could be. They can even usher us into the presence of the holy.

Aren't Movies Mere Entertainment?

Others condemn Hollywood for producing mere entertainment. They believe movies allow viewers to immerse themselves in images, in the process becoming anesthetized to life. It took European film critics in the fifties and sixties to discover the value of American Westerns or of a Hitchcock thriller. Americans who had seen them earlier thought these movies to be simply escapist fare, the equivalent of pulp fiction. More recently, when Horton Foote, the Academy Award–winning screenwriter (*To Kill a Mockingbird* [1962]; *Tender Mercies* [1983]; *The Trip to Bountiful*, nominated [1985]), was asked for his opinion of the American film industry today, he said,

> Oh I don't like to knock things. . . . You know, I'm sure there's a lot of sincere, wonderful work out there, but a lot of it just doesn't appeal to me. . . . I just feel that whatever it is, whatever's driving films right now, I feel they're just trying to "out-sensationalize" each other. I think it's superficial and I think it's gotten to be dominated by an MTV mentality. A lot of the photography looks like advertisements.[4]

Those younger than Foote will surely question why advertising-like photography or MTV-like editing is necessarily superficial. But even if his assumption is granted, what of *Hotel Rwanda* (2004), *The Incredibles* (2004), *Monster's Ball* (2001), or *The Lord of the Rings* (2001, 2002, 2003)? Popular movies need not be trivial or tabloid in their storytelling. They need not be—in fact, often are not—mindless entertainment. It is perhaps helpful to recall that much of what we might now consider high art began as more popular ventures. Consider Shakespeare, for example, or Dickens.

For millennia, critics have argued whether art entertains or educates. Horace argued that narrative poetry should be both "sweet" (*dulce*) and "useful" (*utile*).

That is, it is both amusing and enlightening. More pedestrian is a Calvin and Hobbes cartoon that captures something of the debate. In the first frame, Calvin is seen walking down the stairs, yelling at his mom: "Mom, can Hobbes and I rent a VCR and a tape tonight?" His mom, sitting in a chair knitting, responds, "I don't think so, Calvin. It's a school night." "What if we got an *educational* tape?" he responds. "Like what?" is his mom's inquiry. Hobbes replies, "Cannibal Stewardess Vixens Unchained"! In the last frame, Calvin is back in his room with Hobbes, sitting on his bed and saying to Hobbes in frustration: "Now, she won't even let us go into the store." Adds Hobbes, "I think we'd learn a *lot* by watching that."[5]

A matrix can be used to help us understand the range of cinema, both with regard to the education/entertainment polarity and with regard to the issue of realism versus fantasy:

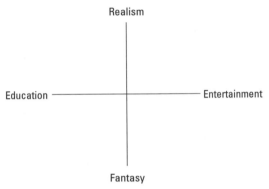

Figure 5.1 Cinema's Communication Matrix

Film is a hybrid, along with the other creative and performing arts. Each movie can be placed at a particular location on this matrix, whose vertical axis runs from realism to fantasy, and whose horizontal axis is a continuum between education and entertainment.

Historically, some critical approaches to film have considered movies to be a "window to reality."[6] They have prized realistic costumes, nonprofessional actors, and themes and stories taken from everyday life. A film like Robert Duvall's *The Apostle* (1997) would fit near the realistic end of the fantasy/realism continuum, as would Thomas Vinterberg's *The Celebration* (1998). The latter was the first to use the precepts laid down by the *Dogme 95* manifesto.[7] On 20 March 1995, Lars von Trier, a Danish filmmaker, stood in front of an audience in Paris on the one hundredth anniversary of movies and tossed out to his listeners pamphlets with bright red covers. With mock religiosity (perhaps alluding to Luther's ninety-five theses or the Ten Commandments), he presented a dictum signed by himself, Vinterberg, and two other Danish filmmakers in which they vowed to eschew technical manipulation in film and seek instead to return to a more fundamental honesty with regard to the moving image. Their goal was to rescue film by producing something that was genuine. They pledged to shoot only on location without props, to produce sound and images together rather than rely on later dubbing, to have a handheld camera and use color film without filters or artificial light, to center the story in the here and now, to reject genre movies, to not credit the director, and so on. In short, their pledge was "I am no longer an artist."[8] Von Trier's *Breaking the Waves* (1996) and Lone Scherfig's *Italian for Beginners* (2002) are examples of movies that have successfully made use of these principles.

At the opposite end of the spectrum, other moviemakers and critics—sometimes called "formalists"—have emphasized the ability of film's formal techniques, such as editing and camera position, to transform reality into a fantastic universe.[9] *Thelma & Louise* (1991) was surely intended to be given a formalist viewing, for example. It was meant to be seen as a fable, a fictional universe created to communicate meaning. How else are we to understand the backlit mountains and the dust-free trucks? The DVD of *Thelma & Louise* includes an alternate ending, where viewers watch as the Thunderbird convertible the women are driving not only soars off the cliff but crashes on the rocks below. This dose of realism destroys the movie, denying the two women their hard-earned freedom. Better the stop-action ending that helps transport the story to the mythic. Some movies are more realistic in their perspective; others, more fanciful. Most are a combination of reality and fantasy.

Similarly, while some movies might best be classified as escapism, as mere entertainment—one thinks of Tom Shadyac's *Ace Ventura: Pet Detective* (1994) or the comic-book adaptation *Fantastic Four* (2005)—most seek something more. J. R. R. Tolkien once commented that *The Lord of the Rings* was indeed escapist, but only because when people are in a prison, of course they need to escape. Here, escapism is a far cry from mindlessness. It was Iris Murdoch who wrote: "Art is far and away the most educational thing we have, far more so than its rivals, philosophy and theology and science."[10] Or recall my earlier reference to the poet Carl Sandburg. Entertainment need not be mindless (the word *amusement* literally means "without thought"); in fact, it usually is not.[11] At the other end of the spectrum, a driver-education "movie" is meant to inform viewers (perhaps after a speeding ticket) of the dangers of reckless driving, but if it is not also to some degree entertaining, viewers will simply put their minds in neutral during the screening. The majority of movies shown are thus a combination of education and entertainment.

Consider another of Tom Shadyac's movies, *Liar, Liar* (1997), whose simple plot reminds viewers of their own manipulation of the truth. Or consider his more recent and theologically complex *Bruce Almighty* (2003), which wrestles with some sophistication (and lots of humor) with the interface of divine power and human freedom. Both movies are highly entertaining, particularly given their common star, Jim Carrey. To the degree that a movie appeals to popular culture, it entertains. To the degree that it seeks to portray some aspect of truth, beauty, and/or goodness, it educates. Again, the vast majority of movies will be located somewhere between the extremes on the education/entertainment axis, for they accomplish both to varying degrees.

Using this matrix, it is possible to locate individual films within particular quadrants. A James Bond thriller will be located near the bottom, right corner of the entertainment/fantasy quadrant; *Left Behind* (2000), near the bottom left corner of the education/fantasy quadrant. *The Incredibles* (2004) or *The Iron Giant* (1999) might be placed closer to the intersection of the two continuums but will be on the fantasy side of the line. *Saving Private Ryan* (1998) fits strongly into the realism/education quadrant; *Million Dollar Baby* (2004), less so. Some people criticized the Academy Award–winning *Life Is Beautiful* (1998) for "joking about the Holocaust," not realizing that the movie is a fable, as the film itself states at the beginning, and should be put in the fantasy/education quadrant. Though here too the film is not pure fantasy, for the Holocaust is all too frighteningly real, and the education is wrapped in entertaining humor and romance. Examples are easily multiplied.

Few movies are pure entertainment or pure art, nor were they meant to be. Good art will always be both entertaining and educational. To the degree that a film is simply escapist—mere entertainment—it should be viewed as such, and there will be little, if any, need for theological dialogue with it. Here is the equivalent of pulp fiction, fare created simply to divert attention from life's ongoingness. On the other hand, to the degree a film is purely didactic—mere propaganda, educating while failing to entertain—it will fail to gain an audience beyond, perhaps, the forced confines of the classroom. Some movies seem to offer little to which the theological critic can respond, because of the seeming smallness of their vision and/or the confusion of their craft. Others seem too preachy. But since movies are experienced differently by various viewers, what seems mindless entertainment to one will be engaging for another. What one person considers didacticism another will view as an honest portrayal of truth. To the degree that a film, whether through fantasy or realism, and even when it is primarily entertainment or didacticism, succeeds artistically in depicting life, it engages our lives. As it does, it educates and entertains, inviting our response as whole persons, including our religious convictions.

The truth is, art cannot be easily dismissed, even when it is commercialized or created for mass entertainment. We must not confuse film's technology with its technique of storytelling, nor its marketing with the portrayal of life that it offers. Roy Anker, in his perceptive book on the religious dimensions of film *Catching Light: Looking for God in the Movies*, writes:

> [M]ost movies have a lot more going on than mere diversion or distraction. Like all the arts . . . movies sometimes offer a way of exploring life's larger riddles and testing out possible solutions to them. On the one hand, the light the movies throw up on

the screen can clarify or illumine the conditions of living, can tell what human life was like, or is like, or will be like . . . filmmakers also provide their hungry audiences with some "take" on what the task of survival requires, "showing" on the big screen or in the flickering home video box some emotion or truth that might help people better understand and survive their real world. That, to be sure, has always been one of the chief attractions—and promises—of any kind of art.[12]

In his "Nobel Lecture on Literature," Aleksandr Solzhenitsyn expressed the possibility of all art transcending its limitations, whether those be commercialism or amusement or politics:

So we also, holding Art in our hands, confidently deem ourselves its masters; we boldly give it direction, bring it up to date, reform it, proclaim it, sell it for money, use it to please the powerful, divert it for amusement—all the way down to vaudeville songs and nightclub acts—or else adapt it (with a muzzle or stick, whatever is handy) toward transient political or limited social needs. But art remains undefiled by our endeavors and the stamp of its origin remains unaffected: each time and in every usage it bestows upon us a portion of its mysterious inner light.[13]

Here is the power of movies!

Film as the World's Art Form

Movies are perhaps singular in their ability to reveal American culture, whether for good or ill. We might study Greek tragedies and epics to know ancient Greek culture, the theater to understand Elizabethan England, or the novel to discover the core of the Victorian period. "Similarly," writes Richard Blake, "if one wants to gather some sensitivity to the United States in the twentieth [and twenty-first] century, then go to the movies."[14] While this is no doubt true, film is increasingly an international phenomenon. Whom we encounter at the movies and how such movies are encountered is as diverse as life itself.

Robert Sklar writes, "Are we not all members or offspring of that first rising generation of movie-made children whose critical emotional and cognitive experience did in fact occur in movie theatres?"[15] I am writing these sentences just as the final installment of *Star Wars* has been released simultaneously worldwide. During its opening four days, *Star Wars: Episode III—Revenge of the Sith* (2005) earned over $300 million in the United States, a record, and the box-office take beyond U.S. borders almost matched what was earned at home. A whole generation of people worldwide have come to understand good and evil, and all shades in between, through this six-part saga since the first installment opened in 1977. In Spain, fans lined up on opening day hoping to get in, just as in Omaha. Two fans in Madrid even wore full Jedi garb, hoping to attend a sold-out showing. And when they somehow got tickets, they said they knew that the Force was surely with them! But these two men in their twenties also commented on suffering a tremendous letdown as the credits ended, realizing that they would never be able again to go through the expectation and wonder of waiting for the next installment. Their sense of loss was similar to that expressed by American viewer Chris Bergoch: "All my life there has been a *Star Wars* film on the horizon, a dream about which I could speculate and wonder. It's strange to think that that sensation is over."[16] Thus, while movies are in one sense dominated by Hollywood, it would be wrongheaded to narrowly interpret this fact, in terms of either their production or their viewers.

It is film, just as it once was the epic or the theater or the novel, that now dominates and best expresses our particular historical moment. Problems notwithstanding, Hollywood, like its counterparts worldwide, continues to do what film as an art form does best: tell our stories. The American movie industry has become internationally the single most dominant cultural force of our times. But India and Spain, Iran and Korea, Argentina and France similarly contribute to this worldwide art form. Through movies, the hopes and fears of our contemporary age find expression. And these hopes, at their best, transcend borders.

Film as Probing Life

Over the centuries, the characterizing elements of art have changed, but its center continues to be its exploration of the meaning of life. Art seeks to initiate a dialogue as it shares the vision of its creator with its audience. It is through this sharing that life takes on added meaning and wholeness. For as Kierkegaard suggests, art recreates experience and awakens it to life.[17] Filmmakers use images and story to probe hypothetically life's possibilities. In a movie, every camera angle has a meaning, every costume a significance. After all, filmmakers have only two hours, more or less, to tell their stories convincingly. A movie implicitly says to us, If you will just suspend judgment and enter into my world for the duration of this film—if you will grant me my initial sketch of life's conditions—then such and such would, or at least might, follow.[18]

In making a similar case for works of literature, Giles Gunn quotes approvingly Roy Harvey Pearce, who argues that a work of art is not literally "true," but

consists instead of a series of hypothetical situations, imaged and motivated in such a way that, within their confines, we can accept as necessary the actions and responses into which the situations—and the imagined human beings in them—are made to issue. What primarily interests us in "created" situations of this sort is, of course, not their inevitable relevance to factuality, but their possibility: their resonance with our deepest sense of ourselves.[19]

Like the novel, film reveals life at a more central region than we are often aware of otherwise. In the everyday or the fantastic, it sees hidden possibilities, which if not "natural" in a literal sense, are nonetheless compelling to our deeper sense of reality. Movies show us what our unaided eye doesn't see.

Movies, like all art, prove self-authenticating. If artificial or forced in their portrayal of the human situation, they are judged harshly. If their images, whether real or fantasy, are beyond the viewer's plausibility, they will remain inert and unconvincing. Here was the problem both in *Star Wars: Episode II—Attack of the Clones* (2002), with its wooden and lifeless portrayals of two young lovers, and in *Left Behind* (2000), with its manipulated script and music and its preachy tone. As Aleksandr Solzhenitsyn said of all true art: "[W]orks which have drawn on the truth and which have presented it to us in concentrated and vibrant form seize us, attract us to themselves powerfully, and no one ever—even centuries later—will step forth to deny them."[20]

Consider the two silent film classics, Victor Sjöström's *The Wind* (1928) and Carl Dreyer's *La Passion de Jeanne d'Arc* (*The Passion of Joan of Arc* [1928]).[21] Their ability to evoke empathy and provide insight remains undiminished over time, for their probings of the human situation reveal themselves to be based in life at its deepest level. *The Wind* has influenced countless filmmakers, not the least of whom was Sjöström's fellow Swede Ingmar Bergman. It stars Lillian Gish as Letty, an innocent girl from Virginia who after moving to the Wild West is forced into a loveless marriage in order to survive. The brutality and isolation of the West in the nineteenth century is portrayed symbolically by the ever-present wind that stirs up dirt and dust, both literally and metaphorically. And it is this wind that eventually causes Letty to go crazy.

When Wirt Roddy, a traveling salesman, forces himself on Letty during a period of isolation caused by a fierce windstorm (a "Norther"), the now-crazed woman is able in one final act of courage to shoot him as the wind and dust blow unmercifully. When her husband, Lige, returns, he sees her really for the first time. As a result, Letty's head clears, and there is finally a recognition of each other's humanity. For both of them, a future now seems possible. Hollywood forced Sjöström to adapt the story in such a way as to have this "happy" ending. Perhaps the movie, therefore, is not "natural" in a literal sense (after all, Letty had become deranged); but its "resonance with our deepest sense of ourselves" is profound. The audience can feel her pain and is rooting for some sense of basic justice, not to mention compassion. It gets both.

La Passion de Jeanne d'Arc tells a parallel story of a woman's fight to remain true to herself despite all odds. The story centers on the historical trial of Joan for heresy. In one of the most riveting performances in cinematic history, Maria Falconetti plays an illiterate nineteen-year-old girl who is pitted against a committee of stern male theologians and lawyers. Her vulnerability before her accusers arouses empathy as it forces upon the viewers issues of power and gender, and ultimately of what it means to be human. Though her fate seems sealed from the beginning, having heard God's inner voice, Joan proves the match of officialdom, even through her martyrdom. As the movie title suggests, it is Joan's passion that is the film's center, and she remains true to herself.

In framing the movie, Dreyer shows us little of the wider landscape. Repeatedly, the camera moves from close-up to close-up, first to Joan's face and then to the judges' faces. The contrast between innocence and craftiness, sincerity and hypocrisy is riveting. Sometimes we are almost too close to the characters for comfort. The chief inquisitor's moles and nose hair seem sinister, just as Joan's shaven head seems saintly. Joan is a sacrificial lamb. As she is led to her death at the stake, the camera moves from a flock of birds soaring away, to a priest holding a cross, to the bonfire itself, to the villagers' passive faces, and, of course, to Joan herself. We as viewers are given the choice of how we will respond to Joan's martyrdom—as the evil establishment, the uncommitted townspeople, or perhaps in terms of the symbol of the soaring birds. The closing images are left open-ended, an invitation for further reflection.

Screenwriter and director Paul Schrader begins his study of the transcendental style of three filmmakers (including Dreyer) by using as an epigraph a quote from Gerardus van der Leeuw: "Religion and art are parallel lines which intersect only at infinity, and meet in God."[22] Schrader would have us understand that film has its own integrity as it probes life in its fullness. It is not a replacement for religion and cannot be conflated with it. But because art (in this case film) images forth life, its parallels with religion invite reflection and dialogue.

Martin Scorsese, who has used Schrader as his screenwriter in the movies *Taxi Driver* (1976), *Raging Bull* (1980), and *The Last Temptation of Christ* (1988), has a complementary perspective as he reflects on his experience as a film director vis-à-vis the church. He comments that when he was younger, he wanted to be a priest. However, he says, "I soon realized that my real vocation, my real calling, was the movies." But rather than portraying these as in conflict, Scorsese goes on to remark much like Schrader on the formal and material similarities between these two callings:

> I don't really see a conflict between the church and the movies, the sacred and the profane. Obviously, there are major differences, but I can also see great similarities between a church and a movie house. Both are places for people to come together and share a common experience. I believe there is a spirituality in films, even if it's not one which can supplant faith. . . . It is as though movies answered an ancient quest for the common unconscious. They fulfill a spiritual need that people have to share a common memory.[23]

In their concreteness, movies nevertheless have the capacity to grasp something general, something universal, about life and to portray that convincingly to their viewers. Movies might seem to portray reality in a superficial sense, but they have the capacity to reveal life at a more central region—to show us our deepest selves. In his Nobel speech, Solzhenitsyn recognized that

> [n]ot everything can be named. Some things draw us beyond words. Art can warm even a chilled and sunless soul to an exalted spiritual experience. Through art we occasionally receive—indistinctly, briefly—revelations the likes of which cannot be achieved by rational thought.
> It is like that small mirror of legend: you look into it but instead of yourself you glimpse for a moment the Inaccessible, a realm forever beyond reach. And your soul begins to ache.[24]

For some this transcendent experience will be a glimpse of what it is to be truly human, even in our fractured and fallen world. I sometimes tell my students that it is seeing Humpty-Dumpty put back together again, if only for a moment, that is revelatory. For others it will be an encounter with the holy, with that which lies outside the human but which nevertheless invests the human with meaning and dignity. But whether a this-worldly or otherworldly transcendence, this experience through film awakens us to life.

Film as Communicative

It is popular today to define art almost solely in terms of the artist's self-expression and to minimize the communicative aspects of art, as if the artistic act had no intended audience. But while this might seem a plausible, if limited, explanation for a poet such as Emily Dickinson, who wrote much of her poetry in private (though it flies in the face of centuries of art criticism), such solipsism is surely foreign to Hollywood.

While a poem can remain unread, a movie, like drama, is a performance piece. A movie is not simply for itself. Moviemakers are seeking to make contact with others through their work. And the success of their work depends on audience response.

When conceiving a film, Paul Thomas Anderson (*Magnolia*, 1999; *Punch-Drunk Love*, 2002), for example, says he always keeps his audience in mind:

> It's nice to always think about audience. Some directors say, "I made this movie for myself." I wouldn't want to see that—like watching home videos, that would be boring. I think, "Is this gonna get them, is this gonna make them laugh?" You always have to be aware of it, how is this gonna go down, in the momentum of an emotional response.[25]

Anderson says that while writing the screenplay for *Punch-Drunk Love*, he made multiple trips to the multiplex. "It was just fun to go to a packed theater in the mall in Hawaii on a Friday night and just try to think about how to try and communicate to this audience that you're sitting in front of. I wanna write a movie that will play well here."[26] Movies help us to learn from the experiences and imaginative insight of others who are trying to communicate their vision to the viewer. In the words of the early filmmaker D. W. Griffith, "The task I'm trying to achieve is above all to make you see."[27]

Film has the power to grip the viewer's emotion, even while it engages the mind. It is not only an appearance, that is, *something* to be seen, but also an experience, something to be *seen*. Movies are not just "discursive," providing information to be digested, but also "presentational," says James Wall.[28] We do not just focus voyeuristically on the material before us in an audiovisual sense, allowing the movie to show us a slice of life or inform us about a "truth." We also focus on the vision of the movie and become vicariously engaged with it depending on whether we, as its viewer, can relate the film's understanding of life to our own. A film dealing only discursively with the sex act, for example, might be used clinically (or perhaps pornographically). But there is a detachment in the viewer. We are seeing something happening out there. A similar action, however, when presented in an engaging narrative, captures our imagination by illuminating the film's vision, drawing us into the event, even if it is a perspective we do not share. It is not enough for a movie to illustrate; it must also involve.

Film as a Complex Art Form

Filmmakers seek to make contact with the audience through a complex art form that includes images, music, and words. Critics have at times debated this point. Wanting rightly to understand movies as primarily about images—as visual—and reacting against interpreted, second-order experience that has sought to dismiss imagistic thinking as less profound than abstract, word-oriented thought, some have swung the pendulum too far. They have wanted to reduce film solely to its images. With the internationalization of movies and the difficulty of adequate translation of text, the minimization of dialogue has also been encouraged by some studios for economic reasons. But movies are interpreted art that includes not only editing, camera angle, and the like, but words and sounds/music.

Be that as it may, movies, like all art, even literature, are about images. Art is not simply imitation; it is the creation of images, the incarnation of creative insight and/or ideas that outpace even the artist's awareness or ability to articulate. A film is not a mere copy or representation of something else, certainly not of an idea. It is something new. In the process of its creation, something will be re-presented, but that is not what makes it a good film. As Dorothy Sayers writes concerning Aeschylus's play *Agamemnon*, its images present "something bigger and more real than itself. It is bigger and more real than the real-life action it represents. . . . When it is shown to us like this, by a great poet, it is as though we went behind the triviality of the actual event to the cosmic significance behind it. . . . [H]is art was that point of truth in him which was true to the eternal truth, and only to be interpreted in terms of eternal truth."[29] So, too, for the moviemaker.

More needs to be said about images. It is not enough to compare film to literature or even drama. For while both literature and film are narrative arts, they portray their stories through different means. In written narrative, it is the consciousness of the hero that is presented as readers attempt to construct his or her social and physical world. With movies, it is the reverse. Viewers see the world of the hero and try to construct his or her person. Moreover, as Joseph O'Neill has helpfully observed, a novel moves from language rather than toward language.[30] Not so with film. Literature and drama use words to penetrate beneath surface phenomena and to connect the reader with a larger reality—a law to be learned or an essence to be understood. Movies, on the other hand, begin with images, and the words follow.

Consider the movie *Breakfast at Tiffany's* (1961). It begins with the camera showing us a deserted Fifth Avenue in New York City. There are oddly no pedestrians and no traffic. A cab drives up and out steps Holly Golightly (Audrey Hepburn) in front of Tiffany's. She is dressed in a designer evening gown, wears large, owl-like sunglasses, and is holding a paper bag containing a coffee and a danish. The clock above Tiffany's shows that it is 5:45 a.m. The image in the early morning light is lush yet mysterious. Shots of this woman are cut so that we see her both straight on and in the reflection of Tiffany's windows, with viewers not always sure which is which. We sense that there is more to Holly's person than what we can outwardly see. Are we getting only a reflection? There is a loneliness and a longing, a sophistication and yet a sadness. Why has this woman come to eat her take-out breakfast alone while staring at the jewelry? Why doesn't she even bother to remove her satin gloves before she eats? Why is she staring at the windows? Why is this store hallowed to her? Is it? Holly's studied mannerisms and slow pace and the fact that we see her strolling down the avenue as soon as she is finished eating suggests this breakfast might be a regular occurrence, a routine.

Music adds to the melancholy and mystery of the opening scene as the movie's theme song, "Moon River," begins with a single harmonica. Sounding both tension and release through the use of major and minor chords, the strings take over the music and then a chorus of voices. What is it that is "waiting 'round the bend"? What is the nature of this dissonance and harmony? Holly seems to be filled with sadness, desire, and innocence all at once. The ambiguity of the music mirrors the ambiguity we sense as we watch this person. We are three minutes into the movie and nary a word has been spoken, but much has been communicated—in fact, more than words could convey. The movie's meaning has been carried by the action and the music.

As we enter the twenty-first century, we are at the beginning of what many think will be a communication revolution. Just as in earlier centuries people made the transition from an oral to a written culture, and again from a written to a print culture, so we are now moving "from a culture dominated by the printed word to one dominated by moving images." We are just at the beginning of this shift, argues Mitchell Stephens, but a new set of intellectual and artistic tools are being forged. Moving images use our senses more effectively; there is more to see and hear:

> Moving images can cut in, cut away, dance around, superimpose, switch tone or otherwise change perspective, without losing their audience's attention; they can encompass computerized graphics, even words. Seeing, consequently, can become a more complex activity; we might see from more perspectives. For when video is cut fast, it allows the interchanging and juxtaposition not just of actions within a scene, not just of angles upon a scene, but of entire scenes themselves—dozens of them. Printed words risk their believability and entertainment value when they attempt such maneuvers.[31]

A movie's images help us gain a new slant on the world. They can capture the chaos and ambiguity of life; they can step back and cut in as never before; they can help the viewer focus. Several examples might prove helpful at this point.

Good Will Hunting (1997) was awarded seven Academy Award nominations, including Best Picture.[32] The movie begins with contrasting "establishing shots" of the working-class neighborhood of South Boston, where Will Hunting (Matt Damon) lives (the tones are muted on this overcast morning) and of the "Great Hall" at MIT in uptown Cambridge, where he works (we are given a colorful shot of the panorama). The music playing in the background of the scenes in South Boston is a melancholic ballad, while at MIT we hear birds chirping and nature coming alive. The contrast of cultures continues as we hear the crude language of the "Southies" and the mathematical language of the university. The bridge for the viewer between these two worlds is Will Hunting, who inhabits both worlds, as a night janitor in the brightly lit hallways at MIT and as a drinking buddy of Chuckie in the dim light of the local bar. The movie thus establishes its premise early: we are to see good Will Hunting attempt to break out of his imprisonment physically, psychologically, and emotionally and establish a new life. His guides from the darkness into light will be MIT mathematics Professor Lambeau, the therapist Sean McGuire, and Will's girlfriend, Skyler. The dialogue in the movie will prove key, but it is set up by the visual and musical contrasts that introduce the story and continue to play throughout.

Garden State (2004) invites comparisons with *The Graduate* (1967), *Donnie Darko* (2001), and even *Fight Club* (1999), giving voice and image to the feelings of a generation, in this case, the twenty-somethings. A comic, coming-of-age movie that was a hit at Sundance, the movie captures something of the angst of a generation. It begins with a picture of Andrew (Zach Braff) lying flat on his back under a white sheet on a white bed in a white room with no other furnishings except an answering machine that is playing back a message from his father saying that his mother has drowned in the bathtub. We follow our "hero" as he gets up, goes into the bathroom, and opens the medicine cabinet, where there are rows of prescription drugs. Thus, viewers are let in on the story's conceit: Andrew is anesthetized from life, both literally and figuratively. He will need to escape his overmedicated, monochrome present if he is to reconnect directly with life. A bit actor reduced to waiting on tables, Andrew is both passive and puzzled by the cards he has been dealt. His mother's death provides Andrew's life a starter, and he leaves his pills behind as he travels back to New Jersey for the funeral. What transpires is filled with both laughter and pain. His new girlfriend, Sam (Natalie Portman), brings color into his life. She will eventually give voice to their reality: "That's life. It's real, and sometimes it fuckin' hurts, but that's all we got." We will also see Sam, Andrew, and a friend stand on the edge of a cliff and scream their lungs out into the abyss, in what constitutes a metaphor for their lives. Such answers don't seem to offer much hope, but surprisingly they do. Reality, rage, and relationship are all better medicine than the pills Andrew's father has provided.

In showing you what an unaided eye would not see, the role of image in movies is key, but it is not singular. Movies use the full variety of artistic media to communicate with their public—image, music, words, dance, drama, pictures, architecture, and more. In his discussion of *The Passion of Joan of Arc* (1928), for example, Paul Schrader refers to the architectural setting as adding to the horror of Joan's situation:

> The receding arches, each with its separate shadow, give the corridors an emotional weight of their own, and as Joan moves unwillingly through them she acquires that weight. The architecture of Joan's world literally conspires against her; like the faces of her inquisitors, the halls, doorways, furniture are on the offensive, striking, swooping at her with oblique angles, attacking her with hard-edged chunks of black and white.[33]

Architecture has largely replaced landscape as background for the film, and this environment adds to the sense of foreboding. And lest we miss its meaning, Dreyer often lets the camera remain focused on a space even after the action has passed. When, for example, Joan walks through a door and it closes behind her, the camera remains focused on the door. And the doom increases.

What Schrader observes with architecture is equally true of music in other movies. The right music can guide viewers to perceive a situation in ways they otherwise would not be able. It can provide comic relief, create tension or a sense of resolution, interpret dialogue, provide a tone, or foreshadow a scene. When studio musicians for Warner Brothers were kept on after the advent of "talkies," they suggested that they play music to interpret the dialogue and action on the screen. The idea was greeted lukewarmly, some believing it would be intrusive. But given their contracts, the musicians had to be used in some way, and so the revolution began. Think of the difference music makes. *Schindler's List* (1993) would not be the same movie without Itzhak Perlman's violin solos. *Life Is Beautiful* (1998) is able to portray the fragility and wonder of life and love through its haunting score, as is *Mar Adentro* (*The Sea Inside*, 2004). The music, in each of these cases, enhances the narrative of the story, communicating a sense of its meaning. Or recall Henry Mancini's score to *The Pink Panther* (1963). Hollywood has reshot the movie with Steve Martin subbing for Peter Sellers. But Mancini's music remains, albeit in a new arrangement. You simply wouldn't have *The Pink Panther* without the music (and the animated title sequences).

Sometimes music can be so central that it actually dictates the structure and shape of the plot. Martin Scorsese's *Kundun* (1997), a film about the Dalai Lama, uses a score by Philip Glass. The music is not narrative in shape with conflict and resolution, that is, with the structural logic of the West. Rather, the music is repetitious and has continuous flow and development. In the words of music critic Mark Swed, "It is expansive, ongoing. It doesn't cadence, because, not going anywhere, it doesn't need to. It is more like the mandala itself, patterned and cyclical, infinite. We feel, as we listen to it, that it could simply go on and on, the way the universe does."[34] Scorsese takes this electronic music and actually builds his film around it. Just as with the music, the movie lacks a clear narrative with a beginning and an ending. The movie was, in fact, criticized for ending so abruptly, but that is to miss its intention. The film and its music, like the message of the Dalai Lama himself, is more attuned to the cadences of nature's ongoingness than to the need for a sense of an ending.[35] It is Eastern, not Western, in its perspective.

Film is a complex art form capable of producing an all-encompassing environment. It has a unique ability to interpret this total experience, for it can include in its form a variety of artistic expressions, expressing itself comprehensively through the use of sounds and shapes, words and images.

Punch-Drunk Love (2002)

Paul Thomas Anderson's slight but winsome movie *Punch-Drunk Love* provides a wonderful example of a movie that tells its story using a variety of artistic expressions. Barry Egan (Adam Sandler), a socially awkward salesman of novelty toilet plungers, is obsessed with buying Healthy Choice pudding so he can collect over a million frequent-flier miles (though he has never flown before). He goes to work one morning at his nondescript warehouse, only to see an SUV careen down his street and flip over, a van mysteriously deposit a broken harmonium on the curb, and Lena, a sweet coworker of one of his abusive sisters, show up at the warehouse and promptly fall in love with him. What carries forward

Lena Leonard (Emily Watson) and Barry Egan (Adam Sandler) connect over dinner. *Punch-Drunk Love* (d. Anderson, 2002). © Revolution Studios and New Line Cinema. All rights reserved.

this simple, offbeat story of unconditional love overcoming weirdness is not the dialogue or the plot, however, but the visuals and the music.

Take the music, for instance. The primary metaphor in the movie is the broken harmonium, which Barry pecks at throughout the story. Its presence seems so random, and his plucked notes lacking in meaning. And why does he carry the harmonium to Lena's place? It isn't until the very end that we are given answers, when the melody that he is again playing on this little organ harmonizes perfectly with Jon Brion's score as it swells to a crescendo. This movie, says Anderson, is "a love story between Adam and Lena . . . [it is about] getting in tune and finding your music."[36] The score itself is alternately romantic and percussive, ferocious and sweet, like Barry himself. It even includes the song from the movie *Popeye*, "He Needs Me," sung by Shelly Duvall. It is a cheesy number, but it works. Overall, the music of *Punch-Drunk Love* has the feel of a 1950s musical, with bright coloration and overblown emotion. Anderson even gives many of the scenes the feel of numbers in a musical with swirls of sound, spectacle, and crescendo that leave the audience . . . well, a little punch-drunk. Music, more than dialogue, cues this movie.

There are other interpretive signals in this movie as well. In a wonderfully perceptive article, Cubie King points out how Anderson has used color, costume, locations, sound, objects, and abstract artwork in order to offer viewers "a purely subjective experience seen through the eyes and emotions of his protagonist Barry Egan."[37] The major sections of this movie, for example, are introduced by abstract artworks that were painted for the movie by Jeremy Blake. They function not only as section breaks in the movie but also as the daydreams of the main characters. The artist describes the first of these as "an orchestral valentine," showing the "scary parts of falling in love." The second is a changing landscape hinting at Barry's need to travel, and the third expresses "an explosion of anger and passion," as Barry starts "removing obstacles that prevent him from falling in love."[38] Viewers of Blake's colorful abstractions would be unable to voice such sentiments so precisely, but the presence of these "lines of color" provides a tonal background and adds to the sense of the movie's off-kilterness.

Anderson's use of color provides still other cues. Barry's blue suit will remind musical aficionados of such MGM movies as *Singin' in the Rain* (1952). Red and white are the other primary colors in the film and might be viewed as in opposition to each other. White is the color of the barren rooms Barry inhabits. An oppressive white light, for example, floods into Barry's workplace, increasing its oppressiveness. Later, as he seeks to escape the blond ("light/white-haired") brothers who have been sent to rough him up, Barry runs through a series of white mazes. In the movie, white represents all that is isolating and cold. Red, on the other hand, is vibrant and alluring. It is the color that points to Barry's future and fills him with hope. Barry is intrigued by a woman seen in the back aisle of a supermarket who is wearing a red dress, for example. Lena often wears a red dress, as well. Signs that point Barry forward are painted in red; the dresses of the flight attendant on his flight to Hawaii are red; and so on.

More daring than these markers of color is Anderson's use of colorful lens flares that he allows to intrude into the sides of the frames at key moments. They function to make objective the inner emotion that Barry is feeling. In an attempt to capture something of Barry's love for Lena, for example, the movie uses a pinkish-blue lens flare to objectify the sparks that he is feeling internally. When Barry has the courage to confront over the phone the operative who is harassing him, a similar lens flare is used.

King labels Anderson a "cinematic painter."[39] He has presented through image, metaphor, and music a small, sweet fable that is both human and mysterious. Through color and sound, viewers are helped to feel with Barry his longing, anger, and love. As he repairs the broken harmonium and learns to play it, its harmony, like the love Lena offers, proves transcendent.

Film as Art and Theology

The theological implications of drama, architecture, music, literature, and painting have long been recognized. Michelangelo's *David* is inspired art. Theater had its origins in religious ceremony and still has the power to make the spirit soar. Gorecki's Symphony no. 3 was composed in 1976 for a performance at St. Magnus Church near Auschwitz. Its haunting laments carry the listener beyond sorrow into an experience of hope. We have little trouble making such connections. Such is the nature of art. But few, until recently, have believed the filmmaker to be a sacrament maker of the same caliber. In this book, I am arguing otherwise. Film has unique possibilities for conveying spiritual truth.

Andrew Greeley argues that God's self-disclosure happens through objects, events, and people. There is, he suggests, a "sacramentality of ordinary folk, their hopes, their fears, their loves, their aspirations."[40] This is what movies can capture and create. In the experiences, images, and stories of life, God can be heard. In his typical sarcastic style, Greeley says it is perhaps asking too much to expect the church's hierarchy to "be as sensitive to sacramentality in films as the laity." Writing in the eighties, he mentions six films—*Places in the Heart* (1984), *The Purple Rose of Cairo* (1985), *A Sunday in the Country* (1984), *Lady-hawke* (1985), *The Breakfast Club* (1985), and *The Gods Must Be Crazy* (1980)—as movies he had recently seen that provided "hints that are obvious and even easy to comprehend of the Being who lurks in beings." He continues, "If the rich sacramental power of films that are currently being made is not being disclosed reflectively and explicitly to the Sunday congregations, the reason is that those who preach to those congregations have not themselves been sensitized to the enormous sacramental power of film."[41]

More recently, Craig Detweiler and Barry Taylor have argued similarly. In their book *A Matrix of Meanings: Finding God in Pop Culture*, they write of 1999 as "The Year That Changed Movies." Their heading is borrowed from an article in *Entertainment Weekly* that noted the new visual style of *The Matrix*, *Fight Club*, *The Blair Witch Project*, *Being John Malkovich*, *The Limey*, *Go*, *Run Lola Run*, *American Beauty*, *The Sixth Sense*, *Dogma*, and *Magnolia*. They add their own choices to the list—*The Third Miracle* (for which Barry was the music director); *Stigmata*; *The Green Mile*; *Jesus' Son*; *The Straight Story*; *The Big Kahuna*; *Keeping the Faith*; *The End of the Affair*; *Dracula 2000*; *Bringing Out the Dead*; *South Park: Bigger, Longer, and Uncut*; *Stir of Echoes*; *After Life*—and conclude: "For all its prescience, *Entertainment Weekly* missed one obvious common bond linking these films: their edgy exploration of ultimate questions. Each of these movies reveals a belief in the transcendent, in unexplainable phenomena, in the random, the unknown, the wholly Other. '1999: The Year That Changed Movies' was the most spiritually charged era in Hollywood history."[42]

If theology is boring to many (and that seems hardly controvertible), if one of the church's primary tasks is to somehow reconnect the church and contemporary life (one thinks of Schleiermacher's *On Religion: Speeches to Its Cultured Despisers*), if theology is wrongly absent from too much of public discourse—then movies might provide a means of reconnection.

6

in film, story
reigns supreme

Our (post)modern art form is the movie. Like all art, it is rooted in dialogue—not the dialogue within the movie, but that between the moviemaker and the audience. Movies address a public and invite a response. They do so, in large part, because the nature of film is story. Storytellers are always aware of their audience, and filmmakers are no different. Moviegoers are also aware that they are seeing a story, and they respond accordingly; they actively engage the film at many levels, some of which they are scarcely aware. We have been watching movies and television for so long that our brains take in and translate the visual and auditory stimuli as easily as the air we breathe. We respond naturally to spatial, vocal, musical, and photographic codes, or "languages." But as Louis Giannetti states, "[I]n the American cinema especially, the story reigns supreme. All the other language systems are subordinated to the plot, the structural spine of virtually all American fiction films, and most foreign movies, as well."[1] Both the filmmaker and the film-viewer are in the storytelling business.

At its best, Hollywood tells memorable stories, for that is what this art medium is set up to do. We go to movies to see stories. We go to experience engaging plots and compelling atmospheres and to respond to memorable characters and themes. Here is the secret of Pixar's recent success, a secret Disney paid billions for when it acquired this studio in 2006. Disney's *Mulan* (1998), *The Emperor's New Groove* (2000), *Atlantis: The Lost Empire* (2001), *The Road to Eldorado* (2000), *Treasure Planet* (2002), and *Home on the Range* (2004) simply could not compete with Pixar's *Toy Story* and *Toy Story 2* (1995, 1999), *Monsters, Inc.* (2001), *Finding Nemo* (2003), or *The Incredibles* (2004). The contest was not even close as both word of mouth and box-office results confirm. The differ-

135

ence between the two studios was not in their contrasting styles of animation, as some have suggested; it was the story. As Jeffrey Katzenberg, co-founder of DreamWorks and head of Disney animation during its golden days, confessed about those still using 2-D, "We haven't done a very good job of picking stories and we've told the stories in ways we've used before. It's not the technique that is flawed."[2] We need to go back to the late eighties and early nineties to find at Disney's in-house studio those creative stories that captured the imagination of young and old alike: *The Little Mermaid* (1989), *Beauty and the Beast* (1991), *Aladdin* (1992), and *The Lion King* (1994). Creative drawing, sumptuous color, celebrity voices, and high-priced sound tracks are not enough by themselves. Without a story, there really is no movie. So Disney paid $7.5 billion in the hope of capturing something of the magic of Pixar's success through its story-telling genius John Lasseter.

The summer of 2003 featured not only *Finding Nemo*, *Bruce Almighty*, and *X2: X-Men United*, but a deluge of high-priced movie sequels and much-hyped blockbusters whose stories lacked both individuality and coherence. *Charlie's Angels: Full Throttle*; *Terminator 3: Rise of the Machines*; *Legally Blonde 2: Red, White & Blonde*; *The Hulk*; *Dumb and Dumberer: When Harry Met Lloyd*; *Sinbad: Legend of the Seven Seas*—the common denominator in all these forgettable movies was their lack of story. That summer, my wife and I taught thirty high school juniors from across the United States a three-week intensive leadership course. One evening we went to the local multiplex and let the students choose the movie they would view. Half of the guys chose *Finding Nemo* over Schwarzenegger's *Terminator 3*! Even teenagers "crave more than pure sensation. They want heroes who have an emotional vulnerability to accompany their special-effects swagger."[3] As Baz Luhrmann's and Robert Rodriguez's agent, Robert Newman, commented:

> It's not about the blue-screen spectacle. Kids are going to see *Finding Nemo* for the same reason they went to see *Spider-Man* or *Titanic*. They relate to the unabashed romance and emotion and the complexity of the characters. That's what makes you want to go see a movie again and again.[4]

We also go to the movies to find ourselves in the stories. As Frederick Buechner has written, "My assumption is that the story of any one of us is in some measure the story of us all. . . . I suppose, it is like looking through someone else's photograph album. What holds you, if nothing else, is the possibility that somewhere among all those shots of people you never knew and places you never saw, you may come across something or someone you recognize."[5]

To be sure, Hollywood has its own unique style of storytelling—framing, editing, sound, photography, light, and the like. Moreover, film's character development is largely through action, for movies find it difficult to probe the inner workings of the mind in the same way a novel can. And a movie's plot has a typical shape to it, as we will discuss later. On top of this, the traditional elements of story—character, plot, narration, and setting—are intensified in film through the actor's portrayals, the freedom of film time to move nonsequentially, and the use of images and special effects, to say nothing of soundtracks and sound effects.[6] Movies do not merely describe; they depict. Film stories can be told with grandeur, as with Ridley Scott's *Gladiator* (2000) or *Kingdom of Heaven* (2005). They can also be more intimate, as in the Japanese film *Shall We Dance?* (1996) or the German/Mongolian fable *The Story of the Weeping Camel* (2003). They can be fast paced, as in *Requiem for a Dream* (2000), or move at a slower speed, as with *Ulee's Gold* (1997) and *Girl with a Pearl Earring* (2003). But basic to everything else, both for the creator and the viewer, is the story.

Garrison Keillor once remarked: "If you can't go to church and, for at least a moment, be given transcendence; if you can't go to church and pass briefly from this life into the next; then I can't see why anyone should go. Just a brief moment of transcendence causes you to come out of church a changed person."[7] Commenting on this observation, Ken Gire writes, "I have experienced what Garrison Keillor described more in movie theaters than I have in churches. Why? I can't say for sure . . . movies don't always tell the truth, don't always enlighten, don't always inspire. What they do on a fairly consistent basis is give you an experience of transcendence. They let you lose yourself in somebody else's story."[8] What many churches have forgotten and preachers ignore, the movie theater recognizes: "story reigns supreme."

Film's Story

There are multiple ways to consider film's story. Some commentators concentrate on its plot, recognizing the importance of pace, and note that particularly in the American context, things must keep happening—the plot must keep moving along. This is as true for Disney's *Tarzan* (1999) as for *The Manchurian Candidate* (2004). *Run Lola Run* (1998), the German cult favorite and a Sundance Film Festival winner provides a particularly good example of the importance of pace, with its three retellings of the same story of a young woman who has twenty minutes to get her hands on one hundred thousand Deutsche marks in order to save her boyfriend's life. The pace is frenetic as Lola literally runs through the streets racing the clock. But just as interesting is the way the filmmakers have built onto the story as they tell the second and third alternate endings so as to keep the plot lively and engaging. But with other movies that have very little plot, to focus on the action is unhelpful. Consider the road movie *Sideways* (2004), which we have already discussed, or *The Straight Story* (1999), where the whole action is a 375-mile trip across the state of Iowa on a John Deere lawn mower!

A film story's style might be realistic, so that the storyteller is almost invisible as the plot unfolds. It can be classical in its structure, combining both "showing" and "telling" as editing shapes the action so that viewers can be brought forward to the intended resolution of the story. Or again, the story can be formalistic, the filmmakers telling their story by overtly restructuring the plot or emphasizing events to better present a theme. Indeed, stories can be told in a variety of ways, but there must be a story!

Movies are criticized by some today for neglecting story for action. In too many current Hollywood movies, the plot is thought to be both confused and confusing. And small wonder: thirty-two different writers, for example, worked on *The Flintstones* (1994)! The story for *Independence Day* (1996) was written in one month, and it shows. Benjamin Svetkey, in a popular article in *Entertainment Weekly*, castigated *Mission: Impossible* (1996), the Tom Cruise blockbuster, for "such a tangled mess of mixed-up plot points you'd need a machete and pith helmet to hack your way to the third act."[9] Though it was rewritten by various screenwriters (or perhaps, because it was rewritten by various "script doctors"), the plot remains incoherent. Moviegoers flocked to see the film (it grossed close to $200 million), but it was for the action and the star, not the story line. Svetkey acerbically comments: "The fact is, pretty much all of the big commercial films being released by major studios these days have a certain written-by-chimps-locked-in-a-room-with-a-laptop quality. Story lines veer in nonsensical directions, dialogue is dim or dopey, characters have the heft of balsa wood."[10] The studios are partly to blame, he thinks, given their unwillingness to take chances with a product that costs so much. But actors and screenwriters themselves share in the problem. Every script must have a script doctor, and stars often demand the privilege of rewriting their lines. The result is that Hollywood stories become little more than a collection of choppy scenes. Of course, there are exceptions. But many critics believe that the story is under attack in Hollywood—spectacle seems to be supplanting drama based in storytelling.

Or is it? True, there are action movies that demand little of the viewer. There are also romances and dime-store mysteries, but these do not negate the power of fiction. Recall a recent movie you enjoyed. When you discussed the movie with friends over coffee, along with the actors and perhaps the special effects, was it not the story with its plot and characters, its situation and point of view that was a focus of your conversation?[11] Each year in Hollywood, scores of good stories are produced. My wife, Catherine Barsotti, and I write film reviews for *The Covenant Companion*, a periodical of the Evangelical Covenant Church. Here are three of our reviews, one of a children's fable, another of an adult drama, and the third, of an adult fable.[12] All three are typical fare. And for each, story is central—central for the filmmakers and for their audience. There is no other way to discuss these films adequately.

Three Examples

Fly Away Home (1996)

C. S. Lewis, in writing about children's stories, commented that any story worth reading as a child should be worth rereading as an adult. The same is true of film. Unfortunately, anyone with children knows that such a standard is rarely realized. Now out on video and DVD, *Fly Away Home* is one of those wonderful exceptions—a children's movie the whole family will enjoy.

Fly Away Home is "about" parenting. Amy, a thirteen-year-old New Zealander played by Oscar winner Anna Paquin, loses her mother in a car crash as the film opens (the scene is not gruesome) and must go to live with her father on a small farm in Ontario. Thomas Alden, an eccentric artist and inventor who creates strange metal sculptures and constantly tinkers with the latest glider or ultralight plane, largely ignores his daughter out of guilt for the divorce and because of his preoccupation as an artist. For her part, Amy disengages from life at her new home out of pain and confusion. Does he care? Can she trust him?

Amy's isolation and her father's bewilderment begin to change only when Amy finds sixteen goose eggs, their mother a victim of a land developer's bulldozer. Amy rescues the eggs and helps them hatch in a drawer of her mother's old scarves. These goslings literally become her new family. The chicks begin to follow Amy, now their "mother," anywhere and everywhere. As the new family develops, so too a bond begins to form between father and daughter. We follow them as they first teach the young geese to fly and then to migrate south for the winter, their only hope of survival. The unwavering trust of the geese in Amy becomes mirrored in the growing trust between Amy and Thomas. Father and daughter soar in their ultralight planes with the geese in formation behind their "mother." And the movie soars too. Even a contrived deadline set by evil real-estate developers in North Carolina cannot derail the movie. The message of "garden over machine" is too simplistic for real life, but in this fable, it works. You will cheer for Amy and her geese.

The movie is based very loosely on the experiments of Bill Lishman. During the mid-eighties, he showed that newly hatched geese identified with humans and followed them in flight as they guided the geese southward using small planes. But this film is not meant to be a biography; it is a fable to inspire. Stunningly photographed by Caleb Deschanel and lyrically directed by Carroll Ballard, *Fly Away Home* was made by the same team who created the children's classic *The Black Stallion* (1979).

There are some magical moments, as when Amy and a newly hatched gosling just look each other in the eye, or when Amy and her father emerge from the fog to find themselves among the skyscrapers of Baltimore. But equally awe-inspiring is the growth of a new love between father and daughter. When Amy asks her dad why he never came to see her, Thomas answers, "New Zealand's really far away." To which Amy replies, "That's a really lame excuse, Dad." And Thomas is able finally to say, "I was afraid, Amy. Angry. I'm really sorry." Not only have the geese found their way to a new home in North Carolina, but Amy and Thomas have come home too.

There are several themes in this film worth discussing with family or friends: the sanctity of life, all life; the rewards of perseverance; the wonder of human inventiveness; and the importance of keeping promises. But first and foremost, the film portrays the rebirth of a family—families can have second chances too.

Amistad (1997)

Steven Spielberg is known for such blockbuster movies as *Jaws* (1975), *E.T.* (1982), and *Jurassic Park* (1993). He has been most honored, however, for *Schindler's List* (1993), his retelling of the story of one man's resistance to the Holocaust. Now with *Amistad*, Spielberg has again dramatized a historical event of resistance to corporate evil. The film has such symbolic importance for one ethnic group—African Americans—that some have questioned Spielberg's right to tell their story. After all, isn't he Jewish? But tell it he does, and the film has moral implications for us all.

Cinque (Djimon Hounsou) cries out in the courtroom, "Give us free!" *Amistad* (d. Spielberg, 1997). Photo by Andrew Cooper. ©1997 DreamWorks LLC. All rights reserved.

The movie dramatizes the story of a group of Africans who rise up against their slave-trading captors and are, as a result, brought to trial in a New England court. But this is only one of the stories that this film tells so well. There is the story of slavery, the story of an African named Cinque, the story of Christian abolitionists, the story of two presidents and their own struggles with a nation divided, and even the gospel story. The importance of the historical event may have been the initial reason the movie was made, but the interplay of its various stories is the reason you should see it.

Let's take one story at a time. In 1839, fifty-three Africans threw off their chains on board the Spanish slave ship Amistad, killed most of the crew, and tried forcing two of the survivors to sail them home to Africa. Eventually captured by the U.S. Navy because their guides had instead sailed them along America's eastern seaboard, the Africans and their charismatic leader, Cinque, were forced to go through a series of complicated legal proceedings as their fate became a focal point for the antislavery movement. Former President John Quincy Adams ultimately pleaded the case for their freedom before the U.S. Supreme Court. Yes, Spielberg has certainly brought the skill (and glitz!) of Hollywood to this historical recreation, and critics may argue minor details (Morgan Freeman's abolitionist character is fictitious; Adams's speech is not the original words). But the power of this story to name our national sin is evident to all who have eyes to see.

While this story based on history shows the inhumanity of humankind (as the Africans are treated as mere property) and the degradation of slavery for both slave and slave owner, it is only when the human story of Cinque unfolds that the movie becomes compelling. John Quincy Adams, when pressed by the black abolitionist to take the case, asks, "But what is their story, Mr. Joadson?" Though the trial is at one level about laws and property, it is in reality about people—Africans who have suffered unjustly. Their story needs telling. The abolitionist and the young lawyer defending the Africans press Cinque to tell his story. And tell it he does. We see Cinque's family in Africa. We see his kidnapping and sale into slavery. We see the horrifying voyage to Cuba and the atrocities inflicted on the prisoners (note: the violence is too graphic for young children). We see the dignity, intellect, passion, and grief of a fellow human being. And then we weep for the shame of slavery; our shame and our country's shame. The power of this human story is the power to convict and to call out for repentance.

Yet a third story is present in the movie—the *gospel* story. Some reviewers have questioned this insertion, but the Christian presence in opposing slavery is historically accurate. We see the Christian abolitionists being portrayed at times humorously, at other times cynically, at still other times kindly. And never has film recorded a more beautiful telling of the gospel story than when one of the Africans tells the story to Cinque using only the illustrations from the Bible an abolitionist has given him. From the slave of Egypt crying out to the God of salvation, to the baby Jesus' birth, to his teaching and healing, to the cross and then the resurrection, we hear the good news in all its simplicity and power. Although the African storyteller is fearful that they will be killed, he can point to Christ rising into the heavens and believe that "where we'll go if we die doesn't look so bad." The power of the story brings hope and freedom.

Like *Schindler's List*, *Amistad* does not simply portray the dehumanization caused by racial bigotry; it also reveals human goodness even within evil systems, hope within horror. How is such hope possible? Partly, it rises up from out of the indomitable human spirit. At his trial, Cinque cries out for us all, "Give us free!" But Spielberg hints at something more. There is also God's Spirit at work in and through us.

Chocolat (2000)

When cacao beans, the basis for chocolate, were brought to Europe for the first time, their magical taste so impressed Swedish naturalist Linnaeus that he gave it the botanical name *Theobroma cacao*, or "food of the gods." It should come as little surprise, then, that fellow countryman Lasse Hallström, in his movie *Chocolat*, has used chocolate as both metaphor and occasion for a town's redemption. In a story reminiscent of *Babette's Feast* (1987), another Scandinavian film, Hallström has created a fable about the transformative power of food in the life of a village.

Vianne Rocher (Juliette Binoche) in her chocolate shop. *Chocolat* (d. Hallström, 2000). © Miramax Films. All rights reserved.

Set in a small town in France in the 1950s, the movie tells the story of Vianne Rocher (Juliette Binoche), a free-spirited mother wandering the world with her daughter, Anouk, and the legacy of her Latina grandmother: a passion to bring healing and life to people through her chocolate treats. The ancient recipes contain a special chili, which ignites a passion for life—thick hot chocolate, chocolate bonbons, chocolate-covered nuts and coffee beans, chocolate cake. . . . The M&Ms and Milk Duds offered for purchase at the movie snack bar had little appeal when I saw the movie. It seemed like sacrilege.

Vianne arrives in the village to open her *chocolaterie.* In a town shaped by rules enforced by the church and the mayor, her mission is not an easy one. It is the beginning of the season of Lent, and the townspeople have been admonished to forsake any pleasure during the forty days leading up to Easter. Though Christian on the surface, the town is hurting and lonely from its severe denial of the goodness of life. One woman is beaten by her drunken husband and survives the pain by acting crazed before her neighbors. A lonely widower is afraid to speak to the widow he admires in town. A young boy with a gift for drawing is almost crushed under the weight of a controlling mother. Even the young parish priest is forced to carry out his predecessor's long-standing penchant for religious conformity and the mayor's pain-denying personal discipline. All of them must, above all, conform to the rules of the church and the village. As Easter approaches, it is apparent that life is hardly lived out in the light of the resurrection. The religiosity of the town is all law rather than grace.

Through Vianne's patient persistence and care for the townsfolk, however, several individuals experience "new life"—through her chocolate, yes, but also through her belief in them and their unique value. Vianne revels in who they are and affirms their gifts. She teaches, encourages, disciples, and loves each one of them, and of course dispenses her chocolate. When gypsies float into town on river barges, she even embraces them. (Johnny Depp plays the leader of these traveling "river rats.") This is the last straw for the mayor, who proclaims a war on immorality. Almost broken by the mayor's constant attacks, Vianne decides to leave town before Easter. However, her small group of "disciples" comes together to create chocolate treats in her stead. The moment she discovers them in her kitchen—expressing their love not only for her but for each other and enjoying their newfound abilities—is truly an epiphany. The delight of community is always something to behold.

Some might ask, "Why is it that in fables like this, the church so often is portrayed as rigidly harsh?" Roger Ebert asked such a question in his otherwise favorable review of this movie. And viewers can criticize this movie for once again falling prey to caricature. (It should be noted, however, that in the novel on which the film is based, the chief opponent to Vianne is the pastor, not the mayor. Hallström has toned down the story's anticlerical bias.) But such a critique also shields us, disciples of Jesus and churchgoers, from what has been all too often the truth. Many of us can tell our own stories of rigid practices that have continued to be enforced in Christian communities long after they have lost their meaning. The disciplines of Lent can be wonderfully redemptive, for example, but wooden practice kills the abundant life Christ came to bring. Discipline needs wisdom and above all love, if its refining fire is to shape and mold us anew.

This story provides more than a critique of the church, however. More importantly, *Chocolat* portrays the transformative power of something of which we have a long tradition—a shared meal. Jesus and his disciples at their last supper, the agape meal of the early church, and our own celebration of the Eucharist predate any movie. But movies like *Chocolat* and *Babette's Feast* remind us anew of food's importance in creating community.

When our colleague and friend David Augsburger was asked to write an article on chocolate for *The Complete Book of Everyday Christianity*, his friends smiled. He is a lover of chocolate (people line up for invitations to his gourmet dinners) . . . but what could be theological about chocolate? After all, our cakes are called "chocolate decadence" and "devil's food." Tongue in cheek, but with more than a modicum of truth, David put into words what Hallström has portrayed in this movie so winsomely: Chocolate's "essential purpose is the creation of community, of joint experiences of joy, of celebrating the goodness of creation."[13] (After all, who wants to eat a piece of chocolate cake alone?)

These three examples of the centrality of story are not the exception in film, but the rule. We go to movies to see such stories. And even when a movie has a confused or confusing story, that too is noted. We complain about its incoherence or lack of plausibility to our friends, just as Benjamin Svetkey did in his critique of *Mission: Impossible* (1996). The heart of film is story.

Film's Three-Part Structure

Every story, regardless of the medium, will have a beginning, a middle, and an end. ("Once upon a time. . . . And they lived happily ever after.") This is equally true for a movie. Screenwriters often speak of a movie script's three-part structure. During act 1, the protagonist is offered a new challenge, which after some indecision she or he accepts. Then, in act 2, the challenge produces conflict, which escalates throughout the act until a crisis is reached. Finally, in act 3, the protagonist must "fight" to achieve the goal, often against great odds, before achieving (or not achieving) the "prize."[14] Metaphorically, it has been said that the story is a "three-stage journey of courage, heartbreak and redemption."[15] Or as screenwriter Craig Detweiler says more colorfully, a movie shows (1) someone climbing up a tree; (2) then being shot at; and finally (3) climbing down a hero. In a movie, a need or a desire must first be established for the hero or heroine. After the possibility of achieving what he or she wants briefly appears, opposition arises and a test or battle ensues. Finally, after all seems lost, the hero or heroine does something new and things turn around, the heroic act bringing self-revelation or new equilibrium. (Or, in the anti-heroic movie, the leading character fails to act and there is no redemption.)

Paul Woolf, who teaches screenwriting at the University of Southern California's Cinema-TV School, explains how he discusses this pattern in the classroom:

> So I say to my students, take my word that this pattern exists. If you look, you'll find it. Why do you think it exists? Because some screenplay writer invented it? Is it a formula? Finally, someone in my class thinks about it, and says, "It's there . . . because it is life." Movies are life. That's why we go. We're hoping the characters will do teshuvah [i.e., come back to something you once were, return to God, journey homewards] because we want to know it is possible.[16]

Typically, the first and third acts of a movie are each twenty-five to thirty minutes in length. Their transitions are signaled by an event that changes the course of the action. The middle act is approximately an hour in length. There are, of course, exceptions to this pattern, for it is not a rote formula. Robert Altman's *Nashville* (1975) and *Short Cuts* (1993), Paul Thomas Anderson's *Magnolia* (1999), and Paul Haggis's *Crash* (2005) are good examples of an alternate pattern that is more like beads strung on a necklace. Some recent films are also purposely adopting a nonlinear storytelling approach, juggling time in the hopes of keeping their audiences involved. In the hands of a master filmmaker this works, as with Quentin Tarantino in *Pulp Fiction* (1994) or Christopher Nolan in *Memento* (2000). But in the hands of less competent directors, such techniques can seem gimmicky. Moreover, these exceptions only reinforce the existence of the norm by their rarity. And we notice their differences easily, because we are used to the standardized pattern.

Story's General Characteristics

As with storytelling in general, film stories have certain characteristics that help convey their meaning and significance. Wesley Kort, a professor of religion and literature at Duke University, argues that the power and meaning of a story (as well as its relationship to religion) can best be understood by analyzing the story in terms of its constitutive parts: character, plot, atmosphere, and tone (what I will call "point of view").[17] Some stories are more like parables and others like myths, but all share certain structural properties. Moreover, in any given telling of a story, one or another of these four aspects of the narrative will be emphasized or given precedence. It is by reflecting on a story's makeup that the audience can find a key to the heart of the story.

Stories that emphasize *character* portray issues of human need or potential. They deal with the question of human nature by offering paradigms of possibility. What is it to be human? *Italian for Beginners* (2002), *We Were Soldiers* (2002), *About Schmidt* (2002), and *Chronicles of Narnia: The Lion, the Witch and the Wardrobe* (2005)[18] all focus on characterization in the telling of their stories. So too does the movie *Shine* (1996). In this film, we are told the story of an obscure Australian pianist who suffers a breakdown while trying to capture through his fingers the emotion of Rachmaninoff's Piano Concerto no. 3. *Shine* portrays the struggle of David Helfgott's fragile life, but it does more. Despite obstacles, Helfgott is finally able, *through* the compassion offered by another, to again sound forth glorious melodies, and viewers everywhere have found their spirits quickened by his example. The film's story has the power to inspire as it portrays the triumph of the human spirit against overwhelming adversity. *Shine* gives its viewers hope concerning the possibilities for their own—perhaps less-fractured, but nevertheless fragmented—lives. It matters not that Helfgott is not quite in real life the virtuoso pianist the movie claims. In fact, audiences flocked to sold-out concerts by the real-life Helfgott once the movie came out in 1997, despite music critics panning the music in advance. As one concert-goer said at a concert in Pasadena, "I love the music; I love the story; he's a fascinating man." The ascending order of her comments is significant. It is not so much the music as the story that attracts, and the story is compelling for it is about a fascinating character.

There are also movie stories that are *plot* driven. The playwright Lillian Hellman has described the difference between plot and story in this way: "Story is what the characters want to do and plot is what the writer wants the characters to do."[19] Plot is the way the movie constructs and conveys the unfolding of action over time. Movies that portray how our existence in time might be thought significant, how our lives reveal patterns that can take on meaningful shape, have plot as their center. *The Rookie* (2002), *Friday Night Lights* (2004), *Monster's Ball* (2001), *Spider-Man* (2002), and *The Incredibles* (2004) all center their story's power and meaning around their plots.

Do you remember the movie *Sister Act* (1992)? It tells the story of Deloris, a Nevada lounge singer whose life is threatened by mobsters and who must hide out as a "penguin" in a convent attached to a dying urban church. Assigned to direct the off-key and unsuspecting choir, she leads her sisters in a new type of sacred music. Their Sunday choral pieces now include "My God" ("My Guy") and "I Will Follow Him."

Sister Mary Clarence (Deloris) does more than lead the choir, however. She also leads her colleagues out into the neighborhood to a biker's bar, to painting projects and car repair in the neighborhood, to jumping rope and dancing with the youth. There is opposition from the establishment, of course, but the result is the revival of a dead church, which is packed to overflowing once again. Even the pope comes to celebrate the renewal of this parish! This is not a complicated plot, but church leaders can nonetheless learn from this movie. Vital worship and ministry in the neighborhood are basic ingredients for the renewal of any church. Here from the antics of Whoopi Goldberg and her colleagues, we learn good theology, a pattern for the life of the church in other times and places.

Third, movies can find their center of power and meaning in the story's *atmosphere*, the unalterable given(s) against which the story is told and the characters developed. Atmosphere is more than just the prevailing mood, or emotional element, of a story. It is the unchanging backdrop against which the story is played out. *Jurassic Park* (1993) is not just a dinosaur movie, but a story about the existence of lost worlds. In the movie *The Wizard of Oz* (1939), as in *E.T.* (1982), the story is shaped around the notion of "homecoming." *X-Men*, *X2: X-Men United*, and *X-Men: The Last Stand* (2000, 2003, 2006) are not just retellings of a comic-book story about mutants, but their portrayals confront humankind's perennial fears about those different than ourselves. In *Hotel Rwanda* (2004), the quiet, desperate courage of Paul Rusesabagina (Don Cheadle), the hotel manager who rescued more than a thousand from certain death during the genocide of a million people in Rwanda in the mid-nineties, is demonstrated over against the inexplicable, incorrigible evil of tribal hatred. Viewers are left speechless, wondering whether we would have had such courage given the inevitability of the situation. In all these movies, we are not *simply* dealing with interesting and/or compelling characters, though there are these. Rather, the stories find their energy in confronting something larger than characterization alone—a backdrop against which even their plots must be played out.

There is a basic given that characterizes an atmosphere's presence. It is that which is beyond the story's ability to control. In *Schindler's List* (1993), for example, the story is dominated by the specter of anti-Semitism. Its presence is not up for debate—only how characters will respond, given its ghastly reality. We see the commandant force a young Jewish woman into sexual slavery. We see Jews stripped naked and, heads shaved, being led to the "showers." We see fear in the eyes of Jewish people as they are herded into railcars. As Oskar Schindler comes to care for his Jewish workers over the course of the film, we witness his growth as a human being. What is going on is bigger than just Schindler. What is at stake is the very sanctity of human life itself. When his workers give him a gold ring made from the fillings of their teeth on which is engraved "Whoever saves one life, saves the world in time," we sense that Schindler's resistance to Nazi anti-Semitism has a larger meaning than even he knows. To emphasize this fact, the movie ends with streams of people, some actors in the movie and some the Jews Schindler rescued, together with their descendants, walking by his grave. Anti-Semitism will not have the final word. Humankind's very survival depends on our resistance to such tyranny. Here is the power of this story.

Last, stories are told with a certain *point of view*, the implied narrator's attitude toward the story's subject and audience. Achieved at times by voice-overs or by monologues, it can also be conveyed through the movie's language—its editing, photography, composition, music, pace, and lighting (we will discuss these formal aspects of movie's tone below). A movie's point of view is the way a story is given value.

With movies, the concept of a coherent point of view is complicated because most movie stories are created not by a single storyteller but by multiple script-writers. There are also producers, directors, stars, editors—all have their influence on the final product. But if we deal with film as story, then we can locate a storyteller's perspective submerged in the storytelling process itself. A movie's creation and creators have relevance. But there is also an auteur's point of view inherent in the movie itself (an "implied author" if you like), and at times this can be the dominant means of conveying a story's power and meaning.

The 2003 Academy Award winner for Best Foreign Film was *No Man's Land* (2001). It tells the story of three soldiers, two Bosnians and a Serb, who find themselves trapped together in a bunker in no-man's-land. The tragicomedy gets its power and meaning from the ironic posture in which the story is told, that is, from its point of view. Here is an antiwar film like no other, one in which we are forced to laugh at the ludicrous particulars of deeply held hatreds. *Moulin Rouge!* (2001) quite possibly should have won the Academy Award for best picture, even though it did set up *Chicago* (2002) for that same award a year later. The movie is purposely filled with kitsch and spectacle, musicals and MTV. It is a fairy tale told by a poor writer, Christian. His "telling" of Satine's story challenges viewers as to whether in our postmodern cynical age we can still believe in the Bohemian's creed of "Beauty, Truth, Freedom and above all things Love." And most viewers respond, "We can!" At least, I did. Or to give another example where the film's point of view carries its primary meaning, *Dead Man Walking* (1995) tells the story of the rapist-murderer Matthew Poncilet (Sean Penn) from the point of view of Sister Helen Prejean (Susan Sarandon), his spiritual companion and ultimately confessor. It is her presence throughout the movie that provides the film its direction, heart, and suspense. In fact, Sarandon is in the frame continually, until at the very end the guard calls her away so they can manacle Matthew to lead him to his execution—a dead man walking. But by then Sister Helen has gotten Matthew to tell the truth, and her absence is thus all the more telling.

In Woody Allen's movies, point of view is often central. *Broadway Danny Rose* (1984), for example, tells the story of Danny Rose, another of Allen's perennial losers. Danny, played by Allen himself, is a down-on-his-luck Broadway talent agent, who invariably loses any acts worth having just when they start to make it big. His clients include a one-legged tap dancer, a skating penguin, and a blind xylophone player, as well as Lou Canova, a washed-up lounge singer with a drinking problem and a wandering eye. What is important to this story is neither character nor plot. What makes it interesting is how it is narrated. A group of retired stand-up comics (playing themselves) from the 1950s and

1960s tell the story as they sit around a table at New York's Carnegie Delica-
tessen recalling the old days. There is thus a "shaggy dog" quality to their tale;
it is exaggerated and loosely constructed. For these real-life comics, Danny
is a "schlemiel become saint." These retired comics would make losers into
winners, we suspect, if only for personal reasons. As they tell the story, fast-
talking, bighearted Danny gets involved with Lou's hard-as-nails girlfriend, Tina
Vitale, and eventually creates a lifestyle of "acceptance, forgiveness, and love"
so that she becomes a new person. We do not know where reality leaves off
and nostalgia begins, but it doesn't matter. As told by these comics, the story
gives moviegoers a lesson in hope. We are to celebrate the transformational
power of a generous spirit.

To talk of a movie in terms of its characters, plot, atmosphere, and point
of view is of course artificial. It is to risk making abstract the film's concrete
story. We don't go to a movie to see a plot or to sense an atmosphere, but to
experience a story. Moreover, many movie stories are complex, with character,
plot, atmosphere, and point of view all exhibiting a power. It can be artificial
and self-defeating to argue over which narrative element is most important in
a given movie story. While stories tend to concentrate their center of meaning
and power in one or another of these narrative elements, they can also invite
internal dialogue between the various components of a story as the viewer
responds, for example, by playing character off atmosphere (as in *Schindler's
List*), or point of view off plot (as in *Broadway Danny Rose*). Having said this,
however, story assumes an audience and invites a response. Using the above
critical apparatus, the movie-viewer with theological interest is often able to
focus attention where it first belongs—on the film itself—and to respond to the
movie from its own center. All four of these aspects of a movie story are simply
analytical constructs, but as such they can be useful as we seek to appreciate
film on its own terms.

Film's Critical Circle

We go to the cineplex to view a movie—to receive a story. But story implies
both a storyteller and an audience as it embodies a particular vision of reality.
In the words of literary critic Northrop Frye, "There can hardly be a work of
literature [a story] without some kind of relation, implied or expressed, between
its creator and auditors."[20] To speak in this way is to recognize that, as with art
more generally, there is in the telling of a story an impulse toward communion.[21]
I use the word *communion* rather than *communication*, for the latter is reductive
as a word to describe the artistic process. When artists create, they are in constant dialogue, imagining an audience, even if that audience is only the artists
themselves. In the words of T. S. Eliot, "The author of a work of imagination is
trying to affect us [the audience] wholly, as human beings, whether he knows

it or not; and we are affected by it [the work of art], as human beings, whether we intend to be or not."[22] Walter Ong, borrowing the explicitly religious language of Martin Buber, speaks similarly, suggesting that a "[work of art] can never get itself entirely dissociated from this I-Thou situation and the personal involvement which it implies."[23]

In a movie, similarly, meaning is found not only in the story itself and its envisioning of reality, but also in the storyteller and the community of viewers who interact with the story. This relationship can be sketched, as in figure 6.1.

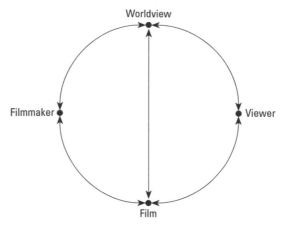

Figure 6.1 Story's Critical Circle

An adequate critical theory of film will take into account not only (1) the movie itself, but also (2) the filmmakers lying behind and expressed through it, (3) the viewers with their own life stories that help interpret it, and (4) the larger universe, or worldview, that shapes the story's presentation.

All four of these critical moments add perspective and meaning to the artistic event—to the story's portrayal. In chapter 8 we will take up the task of film criticism, looking at how auteur criticism (focusing on the filmmakers), genre criticism (focusing on the film's larger worldview), cultural criticism (focusing on the context of the viewers), and thematic criticism (focusing on the internal development of the film's theme) can all assist in helping the Christian viewer understand a film. But here, we will look more generally at the importance of each of these critical perspectives to the film experience.

Occasionally a critic has tried to eliminate from view one of these four critical perspectives, whether for ideological or practical reasons, but there are dangers in doing this. A critic can focus on the filmmaker at the expense of the film, for example. A focus on the internal structure of the movie can produce a new aestheticism that refuses to relate film to meaning. Cultural criticism when practiced univocally can lose the movie in a welter of sociological, political, and economic facts. And genre criticism can reduce a film to formula. What is needed is a well-rounded approach to film; only then can communion with a story be both useful and honest to the artistic process. Let us see how each of these approaches works to affect our critical judgment of film as story.

The Filmmakers

When we view a movie, although we are removed from the filmmakers, we are still participating in dialogue. The movie is not self-contained but exists only as a conversation between artist and audience. The filmmakers present the story from their perspective; it grows out of who they are, what they have experienced, and how they perceive the world. Though this is the case, the usefulness of this observation is complex, since a film's creators are multiple, and their various influences not clearly differentiated.

There are, however, a few almost pure auteurs in the motion picture business who control script, direction, editing, and producing. John Sayles comes to mind, as do Federico Fellini, Spike Lee, Woody Allen, and Jim Jarmasch.

The Apostle (1997), written, produced, directed, acted in, and bankrolled by Robert Duvall, has the stamp of its creator from beginning to end. It thus portrays for its viewers something of Duvall himself and the axiological convictions he holds. The movie brings to the screen the story of a flawed Southern Pentecostal evangelist who flees from the law, only to baptize himself "the apostle E. F.," start a new multiracial church, and in the process of ministry live into that baptism. Duvall had worked on this story for many years. Told with power and acted with aplomb, the movie garnered a 1998 Spirit Award (independent films) for Best Film, and Best Actor Award for Duvall from the Screen Actors Guild, as well as his nomination for an Oscar. But even so, the film in its final form is not totally as Duvall originally envisioned. Just prior to release, the studio asked for a final cut; and thirty minutes were removed. Duvall related in an interview:

> The cuts stung me. We lost ethnic points, the religious differences. Previously, things had added up and it's so easy to mess them up. So it was a tough time for me. I had painted myself into a corner: the shorter the film the more showings you can get and the more money it would make. But some things I didn't want to lose.
>
> So I sat down and addressed sixty things I didn't like about the cuts, explaining them, and so on. Then the final version went to about two hours and fourteen minutes and it was, to my eye, like a trimming process rather than a degutting. . . . But the thing about it, which is really nice, is that people understood the film.[24]

That is, Duvall's point of view was not lost.

As this example illustrates, a movie's creation is often a corporate affair (sometimes almost literally, for the studio executives most often have the final say as to what should be added or deleted). A producer friend finished shooting a family movie for Disney in which the studio heads had said there should be enough action to hold the attention of teenagers. However, after the writers, director, editors, and producers had finished their first cut, these same studio bosses had them go back to the drawing board to tone down the movie (at the additional cost of several million dollars!). The result was so tame that reviewers generally said it was a pleasing story but lacked punch. Unsurprisingly, family box-office results were disappointing. But though, in this case, we must speak of a collective auteur who creates the movie we see in the theater, we still recognize the presence of a storyteller. There is a certain expectation concerning a Disney film, for instance. Executives believed that a too grown-up story would confuse the Disney storytelling persona, even if in this case the result was a movie that failed to capture the viewer's attention.

In cases where one individual (usually the director) is able to exercise sufficient control over the finished product, we can speak of a film's auteur, even if others are involved in the process. Quentin Tarantino, Joel and Ethan Coen, Steven Spielberg, Pedro Almodóvar—the list of auteurs can easily be extended. We can bring into dialogue with the film our understanding of these directors' typical film languages—how they use editing, framing, lights, symbols, and so on—as well as their informing visions and root convictions as portrayed in their other movies.

The Viewers

We might say that there is both a moviemaker's version and a viewer's version of the same movie. That is, the meaning of a film is not found solely within the celluloid frames (though it originates there and must find there its ultimate reference point), but also in the collective viewers' response to it. Norwood Russell Hanson provides an example that illustrates this simple point about the importance of the viewer's perspective in the interpretive process:

> Let us consider Johannes Kepler: imagine him on a hill watching the dawn. With him is Tycho Brahe. Kepler regarded the sun as fixed: it was the earth that moved. But Tycho followed Ptolemy and Aristotle in this much at least: the earth was fixed and all other celestial bodies moved around it. Do Kepler and Tycho see the same thing in the east at dawn?[25]

Given the presence of different life experiences and perspectives, moviegoers will see stories on the screen differently, just as Kepler and Brahe saw different universes. What we bring to the film experience is crucial. What Paul Woolf saw in *Spartacus* that day in downtown New York or what Catherine Sittser discovered in *Beauty and the Beast* was dependent not only on the story in these films but on what these two viewers brought with them when they watched the movies. There is a dialectic present between filmmakers' intentions and viewers' engagement, between viewers' immediate stories and the story flashed before them on the screen. And insight is achieved in the tension between these two stories.

Stories ask their audience to grant their initial premises or sets of conditions. People cannot come to the theater with a "hermeneutic of suspicion" and expect to receive from the film's story something of value. Though the created story need not seem altogether natural or inevitable, it must be judged "at least plausible and compelling to 'our deepest sense of ourselves.'"[26] Otherwise, the story simply fails its viewers.

In his introduction to the art of filmmaking, Jon Boorstin distinguishes three different ways in which an audience watches movies.[27] With each, viewers must give to the movie their "as-if" assent if the film is to work its charm successfully.

Audiences watch some movies, Boorstin first notes, with a voyeur's eye, asking with their *mind* if what they observe is plausible. Movies take us to places, show us situations, put before us dilemmas, move us forward or backward in time, allow us to see people in ways we have yet to experience. And we must be able to put ourselves into these places, times, and situations if the movie is to have its intended effect on the viewer. Such voyeurism can be misplaced, as when abuse or violence are depicted in a way that exploits, or when youth are exposed to the world of adults at too young an age. Nonetheless, a movie's ability to create an alternate, believable world is the sine qua non of successful filmmaking. In the movie *Titanic* (1997), for example, viewers must find the re-creation of Rose's story through set design, costume, and artifacts plausible, or the movie simply does not work. We are asked to accept the depiction of Vietnam that we are shown in *We Were Soldiers* (2002) and *Platoon* (1986), and that of Somalia and Rwanda in *Black Hawk Down* (2001) and *Hotel Rwanda* (2004). If we sense that any of these lacks coherence or verisimilitude, the movie does not work. Or take a movie like *Star Wars* (1977); there is pleasure in simply entering into its alternate universe. Similarly, we enter willingly into the world of *The Story of the Weeping Camel* (2003) with its vast Mongolian panoramas and simple domestic life, for its otherness proves compellingly familiar. With each of these examples, we are invited as viewers to imagine ourselves in(to) these alternate worlds.

Second, audiences watch with a vicarious eye and are asked by the film to give their *hearts* over to the story. We are invited to feel the experiences of others as if they were our own. Lighting and music are important here in guiding the viewer, as are acting and camera placement. In watching Jack Nicholson's characters in *One Flew over the Cuckoo's Nest* (1975) and *About Schmidt* (2002), for example, if we conclude that his character would not have choked Big Nurse, or that his response to the sight of Kathy Bates nude in a hot tub is inauthentic, the film has failed. But most viewers easily feel his anger and angst. Most viewers are similarly able to feel the experiences of the principle characters in Sam

Mendes's *American Beauty* (1999) and Roger Daldry's *Billy Elliott* (2000). Both movies portray their stories with such humor and heart that audiences find themselves identifying with them emotionally. But when given bigger budgets for *Road to Perdition* (2003) and *The Hours* (2002), these directors stumbled, produced technically stunning, thematically important, yet inert dramas that failed to involve us as viewers.[28] These movies had little heart, and as a result, they passed from the scene largely unnoticed. To give a more personal example, I went to see *Life Is Beautiful* (1998) a second time chiefly because I wanted to again identify with the father in the film. Roberto Benigni's character goes to extraordinary lengths to support and protect his son, even after he and his boy are arrested and put into a concentration camp because they are Jewish. The games the father plays for the sake of his young son are deadly serious, and we as viewers do not know whether to laugh or cry. Yet, what is abundantly clear is that he knew what it was to love with a father's heart. Having two daughters myself, I identified with him and wanted to feel that experience again. His extravagant love knew no bounds. Here is what I wished for my relationship with my daughters, as well. With some movies, we identify with characters in the story: their lives touch ours, their stories echo ours, their struggles and hopes become our own. When that happens, the movie has "worked."

Third, audiences see with a visceral eye. The point here is not to understand another universe as believable or to feel someone else's emotion as if it were our own, but to actually be swept up into the movie's experience ourselves. Head, heart, gut! Movies can rivet us to our seats or shock us alive. Special effects are a common means of doing this, as are rapid cuts, compelling music, and graphic depictions. In both *Saving Private Ryan* (1998) and *War of the Worlds* (2005), Steven Spielberg uses handheld cameras, frightening sound effects, graphic violence, and rapid cutting to give viewers a firsthand experience of the horror of war. Similarly, Mel Gibson's *The Passion of the Christ* (2004) repeatedly takes viewers to the edge of their tolerance in order to make Jesus' experience of violent suffering and death our own. For both filmmakers, their goal was to deglamorize events that have become idealized by providing a visceral experience of their horror.

In his reflections on Charles Laughton's *The Night of the Hunter* (1955), novelist Charles Baxter writes of being both "transfixed and transported" by the hallucinatory visual poetry of this tragic-comedy. There was, he said, a "terror and exhilaration" to his adolescent experience.[29] When the villain, Preacher Harry Powell (Robert Mitchum) calls out to the children whom he intends to harm, "Child-ren? Child-ren!" Baxter recalls that he cringed in horror. When the preacher absentmindedly and blasphemously sings "Leaning on the Everlasting Arms," he shuddered. When Powell ritualistically kills his wife over her womanly sexuality, he winced. Laughton is said to have told Mitchum, "I want you to play a diabolical shit," to which Mitchum's reply was, "Present."[30] And his presence continues to grab viewers fifty years later.

Three other comments are relevant here. First, movies encourage audience engagement as perhaps no other artistic expression can. The context of the presentation, the darkened theater with surround sound and high-resolution photography, helps capture our attention. And the full toolbox of storytelling technique—shots and cuts, music, and special effects—allows filmmakers to direct our attention to the meaning of the story, as they would have us understand it. Such was the experience of millions of viewers during the screening of *The Passion of the Christ* (2004). The experience was overwhelming as many were moved to tears, while others cringed at the violence. And after the lights came up, moviegoers simply remained in stunned silence as the credits played. Even as they eventually filed out, there was little conversation, though the sense of a collective experience was palpable. A movie did what bas-relief of the stations of the cross seldom accomplishes. It transfixed the gaze of its viewers.

Second, the community of an engaged audience helps us respond empathetically to the movie. To see a movie on video or DVD is convenient, but it is a poor substitute for the darkened theater. I remember seeing the movie *Das Boot* (1981) in a packed theater in downtown Skokie, Illinois. The film is a sympathetic portrayal of the horror of war for young teenagers who were conscripted for submarine duty by the Germans near the end of World War II when manpower was short. The audience—98 percent Jewish, with many in attendance having been directly affected by the Holocaust—was asked by the movie to empathize with these German teenagers as their submarine was trapped beneath the ocean. The conflict in the audience between anger and pathos was palpable. That evening, I learned the terrible price that forgiveness can demand. As a moviegoer, I not only vicariously experienced the story on film, but also an audience's visceral reaction to it. And it was the community's response that made the more lasting impression.

Third, with movies, a variety of "seeings" are possible, both by the individual viewer and by an audience. Not every opinion is supportable by the film's story, but multiple perspectives on a movie's story are the norm, not the exception. The pleasure of listening to Ebert and Roeper as they review movies on television is in part watching their disagreements. Even these best of critics often have differing perspectives. It is the universal experience of moviegoers to find others who liked a movie we didn't, and vice versa. "Did we see the same movie?" we ask. And the answer, as we know, is both yes and no.

Much is missed on a first viewing, and a "re-seeing" of a movie allows for new insight and perhaps a refocusing of one's interpretive intention. The growth of video and DVD rentals and retailing has allowed viewers this luxury and has forever changed the nature of film criticism. Where earlier viewers were beholden to their memories and to reviews by others, now we can confirm perspective and challenge erroneous viewing by renting the film.

In *St. Paul at the Movies*, Robert Jewett discusses the film *Amadeus* (1984) and concludes the movie is about sin.[31] There is certainly sin present for all to see, and to speak of the movie in this light is not mistaken. But a "re-seeing" might show another focus, perhaps one more primary to the filmmaker's intention. "Amadeus" means "loved by God," and Mozart is just that. It matters not a whit that Mozart is crude and childish in the film. He can write heavenly music. How odd of God to choose Mozart. Yet he does, with the result that Salieri ultimately goes mad from jealousy. For many viewers, the movie's theme is vocation, not sin.

Similarly, *The Shawshank Redemption* (1994) can be seen as a movie about hope, and there is much in the structure of the story itself to suggest such a primary reading. But other "seeings" might bring into the foreground the centrality of friendship, the importance of freedom, the fragility of humanity amid inhuman circumstance, or even the evil of the justice system. Because movies are viewer sensitive, even when the movie's own witness seems clear, the pluralistic nature of the audience means multiple interpretations will prevail.

Film's Worldview

In understanding film as existing within a critical circulation between creator, work, viewer, and worldview, we need to consider the way a movie looks at the world. Any film, as a product of human creativity, contains hints of the worldview of the moviemaker. A movie story when "told" has an informing vision, or axiological perspective. There is a frame of reference embedded in the film that invites our interpretation. In fact, no story can develop without some more-or-less coherent perception of reality, some fundamental opinion about life.

Stories offer meaning to the "facts" of life, even if they are presented as fantasy. Movie stories offer a pattern; they make a claim; they challenge or proclaim; they seek to make a difference in their viewers. In the words of Lillian Hellman, a story is given a plot.

There are surely movies made without such an informing vision. They are presented merely to showcase the latest special effects or piggyback in a formulaic manner on someone else's vision. Pornography is a particularly offensive example of a movie lacking any integrating perspective. Other movies might purposely blur their vision in the hopes of attracting a disparate audience, one with conflicting views of reality. But such movies often prove self-defeating. Without a foundation on which the story is built, the movie falls flat.

It is on first reflection incredible that we can view a story about someone or something else that takes place in a different place and time and still say, "This is important to me." Or, "I agree." Or perhaps, "Wonderful." But such responses by the viewer are fully understandable when it is recognized that a movie is built on someone else's view of reality—on "an irreducible kernel of human nature, a particular case of a fundamental underlying problem we all struggle with in defining ourselves."[32] Part of the power of the film *Titanic*

(1997) was its ability to make its worldview more explicit through the device of a "story within a story." As the movie opens we hear Rose telling her story to Brock Lovett, the undersea adventurer who had discovered the sunken vessel. Then at the end of the film, Rose finishes the narration, giving us to understand that this has been her understanding, not only of the story, but of life itself. The movie is not just a disaster film; it is a love story in which one person sacrificed his life that another might live. And the results proved transformational over a lifetime.

Just as we relate what we do and who we are by telling our own stories, and just as we seek to connect the fragments of our lives by placing them into some greater whole, so a movie provides us alternate narrations on reality. The recognition that movies have an informing vision, or worldview, embedded in the shape of their stories is a natural point of connection for any person wanting to explore the relationship between theology and film. These filmic visions need not be intentionally Christian to be significant for Christians wanting to make theological connections; they need only be rooted authentically in life itself. For example, without themselves being Christian believers, filmmakers have often used the Christ story as a root metaphor concerning reality. Ken Kesey and Milos Forman do this in *One Flew over the Cuckoo's Nest* (1975). Or to give another example, *Kundun* (1997) is shaped around the cyclical patterns of the Dalai Lama's thought, though it was filmed by the Catholic Martin Scorsese. It is enough to recognize that a moviemaker might find in the Christ story, or some other informing vision, a hint of the shape of the authentically human. We need not gratuitously "baptize" the moviemakers.

Narrative Criticism: An Example

Crimes and Misdemeanors (1989)

Woody Allen's *Crimes and Misdemeanors* interweaves two main *plots*. In the first, Cliff, played by Allen himself, is an insecure, struggling documentary filmmaker whose topics include terminal diseases and natural disasters. He falls in love with an attractive producer only to lose her to his materialistic and egocentric brother-in-law, Lester, a TV producer. In the second story, Judah, an ophthalmologist, tries to end an affair with Dolores but cannot; has his brother arrange for her to be killed when she threatens to expose him; is racked with guilt; but comes to realize that he has gotten away with the act and his guilt fades. These two plots are juxtaposed in the movie, with Cliff's comic "misdemeanors" set to jazz, while Judah's dark "crimes" have Schubert as their musical background. Allen says about the film, "There are certain movies of mine that I call 'novels on film,' and *Crimes and Misdemeanors* is one of them,

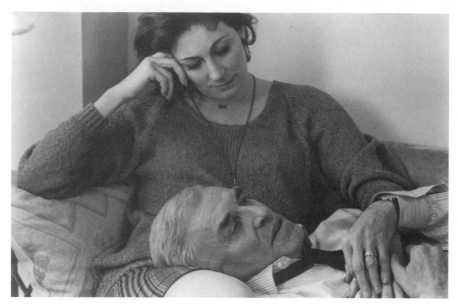

Judah (Martin Landau) tries to end his affair with Dolores (Angelica Huston), before having her killed. *Crimes and Misdemeanors* (d. Allen, 1989). Photo by Brian Hamill. ©1989 Orion Pictures Corporation. All rights reserved.

wherein a number of *characters* are being dissected and a number of stories are going on at the same time."[33]

Underlying these interwoven story lines is the conviction that life is amoral, however we might want it to be otherwise. This is not portrayed as a value judgment; it is simply a given. Here is the movie's *atmosphere*. We might go to the movies in hope of feeling "reel" life, or we might wish that religion could offer real answers, but the reality is what Judah's brother tells him: "This is murder. You paid for it. Engineered it. It's over. Forget it!" As the movie unfolds, we see a killer go on to live a "successful" life; a lonely woman abused through a relationship started through the personal ads; a saintly rabbi go blind; a wise philosopher who speaks of love commit suicide; and the wrong man "get the girl." Ben, a rabbi friend and a patient of Judah's, says to him at one point, "Our entire adult lives, you and I have had this conversation regarding life. You see it as harsh. I see it as having a moral structure with real meaning and forgiveness and some kind of higher power or there's no basis to live." Judah responds sarcastically, "You're talking like you do to your congregation." In this movie "crimes" have no "punishment"; that would take the existence of a moral code. There are only "misdemeanors."

Like one of the movie scripts that is discussed in the film, life seems simply "made-up"—and not very well. Success often goes to the wrong people (e.g.,

Lester). As the philosophy professor Louis Levy recognizes, "The universe is a pretty cold place; we invest it with our feelings." But Levy commits suicide. How then should we live? The characters explore various options, but they boil down to two: "reel life" and "real life." Cliff wants his niece to learn from stories and is always taking her to the movies. But he is a hopeless romantic, out of touch with life. Judah imagines a conversation with the rabbi Ben in which he tells him, "You live in the kingdom of heaven." That is, he is out of touch with reality. But ironically, Ben is content as the movie ends—even if he is both literally and metaphorically blind.

At another point in the movie, Judah recalls a conversation around the table when he was a boy in which his father said, "The eyes of God see all." To which Judah responds, "Do you prefer God to truth?" Is it to be "real-ity" or "reel-ity"? But even Judah is dissatisfied with only a crass realism. He wants more. He wants to project some meaning onto life (to "invest it with our feelings"), so much so that his brother must chide him, "I'm not so high class that I can avoid looking at reality." One option is to live by some higher principles, but that leads to suicide (Levy), blindness (Ben), failure (Cliff), and guilt (Judah). Such "reel life" does not seem to work.

A second option that the characters test is the attempt "to get away with murder," whether figuratively (Lester) or in reality (Judah). Accept reality for what it is. But this is next to impossible, it seems. Cliff's brother-in-law Lester has no principles other than success, and he is a buffoon. But Lester wants a documentary made about his life that will show him as the man that he projects himself to be. Fame and fortune (and women) come easily, but the movie's *point of view* suggests that life must be more than crass materialism. Even Lester rejects such a view of reality. Judah "gets away with murder," but he too is eager to create his own set of values. His choices have consequences, even as he comes to realize that there is no one to punish him for his mistakes if he does not punish himself. Work, family, and friends remain fundamental. Here is his value frame.

In telling *Crimes and Misdemeanors*, Allen uses a variety of techniques to project an understanding of life, given the amorality with which it presents itself. (Here is the story's *point of view*.) He frequently juxtaposes scenes from old movies (the "reel") with the "reality" that is happening in the story. In this way, the two options—the reel and the real—are always before the viewer. Allen also uses eyes as a primary metaphor. The camera often focuses on the eyes of the characters. The movie is about people who see and those who don't. Rabbi Ben is going blind; Judah, an ophthalmologist, helps us see life clearly. Cliff tells his young niece, "Don't listen to . . . your school teacher. . . . Just see what they look like." The movie is full of others making movies about what they see. When Judah drives through the tunnel in his car and comes out into the brilliant light, he is able to again see clearly and recognize that if he does not judge himself, no one else will either. The film would have us believe that if we see life clearly, we will observe that the only meaning there is, is the meaning and values we invent. Reality has no inherent meaning.

Yet this is not all that the audience sees either, for the movie ends on a positive note. Allen is purposefully ambiguous. Despite life's amorality, there are "compensations—friends, family, love, art," and these seem more than arbitrary inventions. Ben might be blind, but he is dancing with his daughter at her wedding as we again hear Levy in a voice-over. "Most human beings seem to have the ability to keep trying and even find joy from simple things like their family, their work . . . future generations." Interestingly, Allen changed his original ending to the movie after seeing the first cut. He first had a scene with Cliff and Jenny, his young niece and only real friend. Cliff is telling her that little girls are the hope of the world. Allen also toyed with juxtaposing cuts from *It's a Wonderful Life* (1946). Allen wants his viewers to feel life's ambiguity and tugs, but to continue to hope. Thus, it is Levy who interprets the movie's final joys—and they are joys, despite Levy's suicide. It is important that people create some meaning, even if we realize that in a larger sense these are merely fictions of consolation.

In ways such as this, the film critic who is using the elements of story—plot, atmosphere, character, and point of view—might analyze this movie. A fuller criticism would surely also take up film's unique storytelling techniques—color, editing, light, special effects, music (jazz vs. classical), camera angle, framing, symbol/metaphor ("eyes"), art direction, opening and closing—that is, on how the story is told. (We will do this in chapter 7.) But to concentrate on the elements of story is a helpful beginning.

With more time and space, we could also profitably compare and contrast *Crimes and Misdemeanors* with Allen's other films. (We will look at auteur criticism in chapter 8.) *Match Point* (2005) comes to mind. We can find similarities in theme and style throughout Allen's body of films, but, here, we will limit ourselves to Allen's own commentary on certain elements of film found in this movie. Consider the following:

[point of view]: I think that at best the universe is indifferent. At best! . . . so we create a fake world for ourselves, and we exist within that fake world . . . a world that, in fact, means nothing at all, when you step back. It's meaningless. But it's important that we create some sense of meaning, because no perceptible meaning exists for anybody.[34]

[character]: My own feeling about Ben is that, on the one hand, he's blind, even before he goes blind. He's blind because he doesn't see the real world. But he's blessed and lucky because he has the single most important lucky attribute anyone could have, the best gift anyone could have. He has genuine religious faith. . . . The worst kind of adversity can be surmounted with faith. But as the author, I think Ben is blind even before he's blind, because he doesn't see what's real in the world. But he's lucky, because he has his naiveté.[35]

Allen's comments both confirm and extend our analysis. Particularly interesting is this statement about the "plot" of the movie:

[plot]: No higher power is going to punish us for our misdeeds if we get away with them. Knowing that, you have to choose a just life or there will be chaos, and so many people don't do that that there is chaos.[36]

Does Judah choose a just life? Perhaps. He has returned to his family and his work, but is justice satisfied with his variation of Lester's definition of comedy: tragedy + time = comedy? We are left to wonder. As Judah tells Cliff what is assumed to be a fictitious "murder story" (but which is actually the story of what has happened), he concludes, "Now he is scot-free; his life is back to normal." Only for Cliff to ask, "Yes, but can he really ever go back?" To which Judah responds, "Well, people carry sins around with them . . . but with time, it all fades."

Here, then, is a narrative approach to unpacking a movie that invites dialogue from a theological perspective.[37] What might such a conversation look like? For this particular Christian viewer, the choice that Allen portrays between faith and truth in *Crimes and Misdemeanors* seems to cast the issue wrongly. It need not be an either/or decision—faith or truth, "reel" or "real." Allen's vantage point is only one that a viewer might adopt. There is another, one also invited from within Allen's own Jewish tradition, even though it is ignored in the film. As the Old Testament writer of Ecclesiastes recognizes, life is amoral, death ubiquitous, and ultimate meaning a mystery. Here is the harsh truth of reality. But even though wrong oftentimes goes unpunished, it is not naive to find meaning in accepting the small joys and fragile spaces of life, for they are God's gift. Like Allen, the writer of Ecclesiastes demolishes the easy optimism of "reel" life—whether that be wealth, fame, wisdom, or pleasure (Eccles. 1–2). At the same time, this observer of life's mysteries also recalls God as his Creator and writes concerning "real" life:

Go, eat your bread with enjoyment, and drink your wine with a merry heart; for God has long ago approved what you do [cf. Gen. 1]. Let your garments always be white; do not let oil be lacking on your head. Enjoy life with the wife whom you love, all the days of your vain [or short] life that are given you under the sun, because this is your portion in life and in your toil at which you toil under the sun.

Ecclesiastes 9:7–9

Allen states that he would like to believe but cannot. His understanding of Judaism is that it is rooted in a moral code, in the reality of a universe with answers. But, like Freud, he rejects such a possibility as wishful thinking. The "reel" (whether religion or cinema) must be critiqued by the "real," even if the "reel" is looked at longingly and with nostalgia. Both Ecclesiastes and Job suggest a different possibility, however: not an answer to life's enigmas, but a divine Answerer who meets us within life's complexity. We cannot comprehend, but we can apprehend the divine presence. We need not jettison faith for truth, or truth for life. There is a fragile but real co-inherence, however paradoxical.

7

image and music

Writing in 1922, flushed with the excitement of seeing Abel Gance's *La Roue*, Fernand Léger tried to define something of the radical possibilities of the cinema. The potential of the new art did not lay in "imitating the movements of nature" or in "the mistaken path" of its resemblance to theater. Its unique power was a "matter of *making images seen.*"

Tom Gunning

I have always felt that visual literacy is just as important as verbal literacy. What the film pioneers were exploring was the medium's specific techniques. In the process, they invented a new language based on images rather than words, a visual grammar you might say: close-ups, irises, dissolves, masking part of the frame for emphasis, dolly shots, tracking shots.

Martin Scorsese

Using a literary model for understanding film's story is helpful, but it has limitations. It is easy to ignore the unique form of the movie, that is, how the movie story is told. For example, movie stories do not have the means or time to explore in depth a given idea or emotion as do novels. The plot must keep moving forward, for there are only a couple of hours to tell the tale. Thus, a story's plot has special demands placed on it by the motion picture medium. Again audience studies suggest that it is a movie's characters who are most easily and forcefully remembered by those coming out of the theater. But characterization must largely be accomplished through action, for movies do not have the novel's means to uncover self-consciousness. The means of characterization available to the filmmaker have implications for how movie stories are shaped and, thus, for any understanding of film as story.

Even more fundamental to a movie than its unique features of plot and character, however, are the formal aspects of atmosphere and point of view that the movie storyteller uses. The meaning of a movie is not simply communicated by the story's explicit narrators (as in *Broadway Danny Rose*), whether present or implied. It is also embedded in the very techniques the filmmaker uses to bring the story to the screen. Film has its own idiom. The artistic creators of a film (writers, director, cameramen, editors, producer, art director, music supervisor) shape a picture every bit as much as painters shape their canvas or writers their novel.

The first movies were brief, straightforward depictions with little if any story—a train coming down the track straight toward the viewer, or perhaps a fistfight. These were exhibitions, amusements. Soon, however, film developed a language of its own. E. S. Porter was one of the early pioneers who discovered that by editing the film, a point of view could be presented and a story told. Cameras could be moved so that there could be close-ups and long shots. In *The Great Train Robbery* (1903), Porter took his cameras offstage to film in the great outdoors and then edited the footage to contrast scenes of the robbers escaping with those of the good guys in pursuit. When D. W. Griffith filmed *The Birth of a Nation* (1915), he used a split screen and included a musical score for full orchestra that was meant to be played as an accompaniment. The movie lasted three hours, an unheard-of length in that day. The art of filmmaking was born.

Lynn Ross-Bryant has written, "One way of defining art is, of course, just this: it is a process of selection and interpretation that gives a work of art a coherence and completeness not found in life."[1] Filmmakers shape their works by several means. But in particular it is helpful to be aware of the role that editing (montage), framing (mise-en-scène), and music can have on how a story is heard and understood. A technical study of the language of film is beyond the focus of this book, and there are a number of good introductory studies already available.[2] However, those interested in the relationship between theology and film must also be concerned with how the story is told, for technique shapes meaning by providing a point of view. We turn, therefore, to a brief description.

Editing

There is a famous experiment by Lev Kuleshov, an early Russian filmmaker, who showed on the screen an actor with an expressive but neutral look. He repeatedly used the same footage of the actor but placed him in different situations in order to trigger different emotions in the audience. Spliced between identical images of Mosjukine, the well-known actor, were scenes of a crying baby, a coffin, and even a bowl of soup. Not knowing that the shots of Mosjukine were identical footage, the audience praised the actor for his performance, noting how well he displayed a father's love, a man who was hungry, and again a person in mourning! What had happened was that through editing, the same expressive face had taken on appropriate connotations to match the context. Members of the audience read into the actor's face what they would have felt if they had been in his place.[3]

Sergei Eisenstein, another famous Russian filmmaker, called such juxtapositions of film images "montage." He wrote that "two film pieces of any kind, placed together, inevitably combine into a new concept, a new quality, arising out of that juxtaposition."[4] Europeans still call this process "montage," the art of constructing, or putting together, a sequence. Americans call the same process "editing," the art of cutting. But whether we speak of building up images or of removing them, the goal is the same: the construction of narrative meaning in a movie.

There are few better examples of the power of montage/editing than the shower scene in Alfred Hitchcock's *Psycho* (1960) and the baptism that ends Francis Ford Coppola's *The Godfather* (1972). Both are repeatedly used as examples in film textbooks. Although in *Psycho*, we never see the knife cut Janet Leigh's flesh, the seventy separate pictures that are spliced together in less than a minute tell the story as slashing knife and screaming face are juxtaposed to create a sense of fear in us. There is no real continuity to the sequence. The knife comes from several directions; Marion is seen struggling; water and blood begin to mix around her feet. All is chaos and panic. The repeated staccato screech of violins—emulating the stabbing motion—adds to the sense of horror.

Andrey Tarkovsky called such editing "sculpting in time." He considered it "the essence of the director's work": "Just as a sculptor takes a lump of marble, and inwardly conscious of the features of his finished piece, removes everything that is not part of it—so the film-maker, from a 'lump of time' made up of an enormous, solid cluster of living facts, cuts off and discards whatever he does not need."[5] Hitchcock was famous for using storyboards to break down a scene into a number of shots he could later edit together. He did this because he wanted full control over the outcome of the scene, something he believed he could best achieve in the editing room. In 1938, he wrote:

[I]f I have to shoot a long scene continuously I always feel I am losing a grip on it, from a cinematic point of view. The camera, I feel, is simply standing there, hoping to catch something with a visual point to it. . . . The screen ought to speak its own language, freshly coined, and it can't do that unless it treats an acted scene as a piece of raw material which must be broken up, taken to bits, before it can be woven into an expressive visual pattern.[6]

Or consider *The Godfather* (1972), a film that uses the Mafia as a metaphor for America itself. In the movie, the church is portrayed as oblivious to the seared consciences of the Corleones. As the film ends, we see a high church baptism going on with all its pomp and formality. Then Michael Corleone is asked by the priest on behalf of his godson, "Do you renounce Satan?" And Michael responds strongly, "I do renounce him," just as the movie cross-cuts to show the first of a number of gangland executions, brutal and effective in establishing Corleone as the new Godfather. (One victim is caught inside a revolving door that is jammed; another in a barbershop as he is being shaved; still another as he is being massaged in a steam room.) In between these murders, we watch the priest repeatedly ask Michael the baptismal questions: "And all his works?" "I do renounce them." "And all his pomps?" "I do renounce them." The baptism is notable for its ritual formality; the slayings, for their gruesome reality. Given its juxtapositions, the scene is breathtaking. Through cut after cut, continually jumping back and forth between the gangland executions and the baptismal vows, both the killings and the sacrament are made all the more riveting to the viewer. The hypocrisy of the scene—the immorality of Michael's orchestrated violence contrasted with the impotent ritual of the church—leaves viewers speechless as they exit the theater.

Framing (mise-en-scène)

Editing is one means of giving the story coherence and perspective; so too is framing (mise-en-scène). If editing (montage) concerns modifying the sequence, or time, of the story, then mise-en-scène (literally, "the world within the frame") involves the movie's staging and shooting, that is, how filmmakers shape the story's space. Where Russian theorists championed montage in the interest of directing a viewer's response, it was a French film critic, Andre Bazin, who embraced mise-en-scène.[7] Bazin wished to allow the audience choice in responding to real life. To give viewers maximum flexibility in creating meaning, he embraced deep-focus photography with its depth of field that reintroduced ambiguity into a picture that was carefully constructed. It was not the "cuts" but the "shots" that fascinated him. Photography could re-present reality.

Mise-en-scène involves both what appears in front of the camera (and what is excluded) and how the camera captures that (though some critics choose to split out cinematography and make it a separate category and others add music's sounds). Setting, lighting, color, props, costume, performance, framing, and composition are some of the elements of the movie's staging. Are the scenes shot on location or on a sound stage? What is the set design? How is the lighting handled and the movement of the characters choreographed? Nothing is accidental. With the clock running and the cost escalating, filmmakers want to maximize the effectiveness of their storytelling.

Illustrations of the importance of various aspects of mise-en-scène to the story's meaning come easily:

Setting. In David Fincher's *Fight Club* (1999), the filmmaker chooses repeatedly to shoot scenes in dark and damp quarters. Whether rusty water or gushing blood, his settings are often wet and poorly lit. This setting is similar to that used in his *Se7en* (1995), as Richard Schickel has noted. In both, the setting "enforces the contrast between the sterilities of his characters' aboveground life and their underground one. Water, even when it's polluted, is the source of life; blood, even when it's carelessly spilled, is the symbol of life being fully lived."[8] In *American Beauty* (1999), the critique of suburban life is suggested in other ways. The movie opens with an establishing shot of Lester Burnham's neighborhood and then zooms in on his yard with manicured roses, a white picket fence, and a house whose front door is painted a bright red. The setting, he says, explains his life—a carefully maintained veneer masking the lack of a soul.

Composition. Places in the Heart (1984) tells the story of a young widow, Edna, and her two children who struggle to save her farm in Texas during the Depression after her husband, Royce, the sheriff, is accidentally killed by Wylie, a drunken youth. With the help of a blind man (Mr. Will) and an African American drifter (Mose), they succeed in harvesting the cotton and thus can pay off the mortgage. The movie ends with a carefully constructed final scene that serves as a surprising postscript—actually a benediction. The setting is once again the small church in town where the congregation is singing the hymn "In the Garden," just as it was at the movie's opening. In a long shot, we see Edna sitting in the third row together with her children, Mr. Will, and, to our surprise, the bank manager who has tried to take her house from her. Then we identify Edna's sister and her philandering husband, whom she has earlier thrown out of the house. But here we see her offering forgiveness as she takes his hand once again. The communion plates are passed, as the camera shifts to a medium shot, taking in only two or three people at a time. Thus, we are allowed to see only gradually the composition of who is in the church. As the camera pans slowly along the rows, they are now inexplicably full. The communion of "saints" now includes a klansman sitting next to Mose, Edna sitting next to Royce, and next to him, Wylie! We watch Wylie receiving the bread and wine from Royce, the man he has accidentally killed, and as is the custom in that Baptist church, Wylie responds to him, "The peace of God." The words of the hymn are heard: "And the joy we share as we tarry there, none other has ever known." What has been up to now a realistic story becomes "fantasy." Or is it? Viewers are in this way invited to share in the Christian hope that this eschatological vision provides—a community that transcends all differences. The future has become present.

Lighting. In *Insomnia* (2002), light is almost a fourth character. The story takes place in Alaska during the height of the summer, when there is the midnight sun. On the DVD, Wally Pfister, the director of photography, talks about the use of light as a metaphor for the guilt that Detective Will Dormer (Al Pacino) feels. Throughout the movie, Will tries to shut out the light of the sun so he can get some sleep, but as the movie progresses, his insomnia becomes all the more revealing. In one scene, as light comes streaming in through the bathroom window, Will tries to hide in the bathroom's shadows to avoid the local police. As he leans forward, he is surprised by the sun's bright, almost melting light and immediately recoils. We watch transfixed as the detective has a "dialogue" with the light. Says Pfister, "We're manipulating them [the audience] emotionally with light, darkness, colors, contrast and composition."[9]

In *K-Pax* (2001), light is used, rather than special effects or computer-generated images, to suggest an alien world. A small kick of light inserted from somewhere offscreen suggests something more, and prismatic light flashes across the face. The idea is to capture the eye of viewers for a brief moment and make them wonder what is happening. The flickering light is a subtle suggestion that something out of the ordinary might be going on.[10]

Color. Color can have both a psychological and a symbolic effect on the story being told. It can be conveyed both through how the story is filmed and by what is filmed. In *Traffic* (2000), for example, Stephen Soderbergh uses different coloration in the film itself to tell his three interwoven stories about drug trafficking. The bureaucratic world of the government's war on drugs has the hue of a cold, sterile blue. The corruption of sunny, suburban San Diego is photographed as overexposed and washed out. And the earthy Mexican world of violence and death is given a golden brown hue. In this way, viewers are predisposed to interpret the scenes in a given way. The martial-arts epic *Hero* (2004) retells the same story three times: how an anonymous assassin in ancient China defeats three rivals. A cameraman turned director, Zhang Yimou is known as a visual stylist, and once again in this movie, the shots are carefully composed. Central to his vision is the use of color to differentiate possibilities. One of the retellings is thus given a red hue; another, blue; and the last, white. Viewers also see a number of flashbacks that are cast in strong greens, and a framing tale is dominated by shades of black. The cinematographer, Christopher Doyle, said about the movie: "Part of the beauty of the film is that it is one story colored by different perceptions. I think that's the point. Every story is colored by personal perception."[11]

One of the best-known uses of color is in *The Wizard of Oz*. The drab gray monochrome of Kansas life becomes Technicolor for Dorothy in *The Wizard of Oz* (1939), as she and her friends travel the bright yellow brick road. The poppy fields are vibrantly red and the Emerald City green, as is the skin of Margaret Hamilton's wicked witch. Dorothy responds to this new splendor with words that have taken on a whole afterlife: "Toto, I have a feeling we're not in Kansas anymore."

In this discussion of visual literacy, we have treated each aspect independently. But obviously color does not operate independently of other variables at the filmmaker's disposal. A good example of the use of color, working together with lighting and composition is the exquisitely filmed movie, *Girl with a Pearl Earring* (2003). The movie's story is slight—a young woman (Scarlett Johansson) whose family has become suddenly poor becomes a maid in the household of the great Dutch painter Johannes Vermeer (1632–1675). Both the painter and his patron are attracted to the maid and persuade her to pose for what became one of Vermeer's most famous paintings of domestic life. That's it! The acting is also subdued. Not a lot of suspense except for a jealous wife. The dialogue is minimal. Nevertheless, the movie soars because it is the cinematic equivalent of one of Vermeer's paintings. Radiant with color, lit with the ethereal light that was Vermeer's trademark, and carefully staged with symmetrical, peaceful backgrounds taken directly from the painter's work, the movie invites our contemplation. The movie's intimate visuals, like Vermeer's paintings, become almost iconic. During the final ninety seconds of the film, viewers are invited simply to stare at the painting. It is breathtaking!

Camera. It is the cinematographer (director of photography) who helps tell the story using lighting, color, and composition. Rodrigo Prieto, who shot *8 Mile* (2002), says,

> I believe shooting a movie is an act of love. My goal is for every scene in each film to move the audience emotionally in the right direction. You have to create a logic that is right for the story. . . . You have to trust your instincts and collaborate with many different people to achieve images that enhance the storytelling.[12]

In telling this story, the director of photography will ask, how does the camera's angle play to the viewer? Sometimes the camera, for example, does not show us a scene so that we remain objective viewers from afar, but we see the world of the film through the eyes of a character in the film. Here is how the audience is moved emotionally in the right direction. Horror films often take this approach so that the audience becomes one with the victim. It is not just camera angle that needs to be considered, however. The camera also suggests the tone of a story. The Coen brothers were brilliant, for example, in their choice of black-and-white for *The Man Who Wasn't There* (2001), a film noir set in 1949 about a California barber (Billy Bob Thornton) filled with dread.

Elvis Mitchell, the insightful film critic for the *New York Times*, reviewed the movies of 2003 in terms of their cinematography.[13] He found much of the imagery impressive. Take the movie *Seabiscuit* (2003). Its photography had the fuzzy warmth of a series of family pictures in your grandmother's album. So too did the photography by John Seale in *Cold Mountain* (2003). With many of that year's best movies focusing on stories of displacement, Mitchell noted that the camera often created "tone poems that suggest(ed) emptiness." He singled out Edward Zwick's work in the movie *The Last Samurai* (2003), "especially in the first battle scene, in which the precise and lethal samurai appear in the midst of a foggy, smoke-shrouded battlefield like a host of apparitions." *Lost in*

Translation (2003), on the other hand, used a handheld camera to follow Bill Murray and Scarlett Johansson, two dislocated Americans, through the streets of Tokyo. The result is a certain intimacy, the visual equivalent of a series of diary entries.

In *American Beauty* (1999), cinematographer Conrad Hall used three distinct looks to help reveal Lester Burnham's world. To show the folly of the Burnhams' misguided attempt to make life work to their advantage, he created through his photography a series of "jail cells" in which this family lives. Shot after shot suggests enclosure, for they are framed through divided windowpanes or drive-in windows, shower cubicles or SUVs. When Lester enters his fantasy world dreaming of a new life, Hall's photography turns lush and the colors vivid. The viewer is thus invited to enter viscerally into his dreams. Finally, there are pictures within the picture—images seen at times in a mirror, or more often through Ricky's handheld camcorder. Often these are portrayed as attempts at remembrance, and their texture remains grainy. Yet their surreal quality invites viewers to look more closely. In *American Beauty*, it is the photography itself that invites viewers to see life's options and to choose between differing images of reality—of beauty. Do we look with melancholy through life's enclosures? Do we self-indulgently imagine a fecund, brightly colored world? Or do we gaze intently through the grainy, commonplace things of life, only to find in them a transcendence?

Special Effects. The explosion of technology's capacity has increased the scene-creating possibilities of the filmmaker. Spectacles like Ridley Scott's Academy Award–winning *Gladiator* (2000) or his more recent *Kingdom of Heaven* (2005) would have been cost prohibitive without computer graphics. George Lucas, whose company Industrial Light and Magic is a leader in the field, comments:

> Nobody can afford to buy three or four thousand extras . . . you have to costume them, you have to transport them, you have to feed them and you move very slowly when you are trying to direct a large group of people live. Doing that today is next to impossible. But doing it digitally, you get a small group of people, say one hundred people, and you replicate them and move them around, and you can have exactly the same effect for one-tenth the cost.[14]

Advances in special effects and in sound have made audiences flock to some movies just to see and hear the thrill. But when used effectively as part of the language of the film's story, such technological wizardry increases the power and meaning of any story. The six episodes of George Lucas's *Star Wars* (1977 to 2005) have almost single-handedly created this artistic revolution. Light sabers, droids, intergalactic space travel, talking monsters, ice planets, and steamy bogs—Lucas's imagination seems endless. Not all of his six episodes have worked. Some think that *Star Wars: Episode I—The Phantom Menace* (1999) failed because the story never engaged the viewer beyond its technology. Certainly, this was the case in *Star Wars: Episode II—The Attack of the Clones* (2002), which never recovered from its stilted dialogue and sterile acting. But *Star Wars: Episode III—Revenge of the Sith* (2005) recovered much of the magic, even as it completed the story by showing the genesis of Darth Vader—revealing in the process how good turns bad.

The *Star Wars* franchise has created one of this generation's most enduring myths. "May the Force be with you," light sabers, C3PO and R2D2, Luke Skywalker, Obi-Wan Kenobi, Han Solo, Princess Leia, Yoda, and, of course, Darth Vader—these characters are burnt into our collective psyches. Listen again to Lucas:

> We have changed the medium in a profound way. It is no longer a photographic medium. It is now a painterly medium and it's very fluid so that things that are in the frame you can take out, move, put them over there. It's almost going from two to three dimensions in the dynamic that has been created at this point.[15]

The studios of George Lucas in northern California have provided Hollywood with state-of-the-art technology for several decades. Their advanced editing equipment, computer-generated special effects, and new sound systems have enhanced scores of movies and theaters. Nonetheless, it is important to hear Lucas himself reflect on his craft: "Technology enhances the tools you have available and expands your vocabulary. But they don't make a picture successful. A film is not about technique. It's about ideas."[16] Or better, story!

Other Filmic Elements

We have only scratched the surface regarding the palette filmmakers use as they "paint" their pictures. Proximity and proportion, costume and props, texture and movement, open framing (where the viewer is subliminally aware of the area outside the frame) and closed frames, close-ups and moving cameras, slow motion and freeze frames—these also might helpfully be considered by the theology and film critic. All of this is part of a movie's mise-en-scène, which together with the film's montage make up its visual language of time and space. Nathaniel Dorsky, a much-honored experimental filmmaker, summarizes the filmmakers' craft thus:

> Shots and cuts are the two elemental opposites that enable film to transform itself. Shots are the accommodation, the connection, the empathy, the view of the subject matter we see on the screen. The cuts are the clarity that continually reawakens the view. When there is a balance of these essential elements, a film blossoms as light in the present tense and gives devotion the space to manifest.[17]

An understanding of these "shots" (of space) and "cuts" (of time), of mise-en-scène and montage, will help viewers who want to engage a movie theologically by providing a visual literacy.

But it is also important to note other filmic elements, ones that derive their potency from a combination of the visual, the aural, and the literary. They too add to the unique expression of a movie's power and meaning and invite our comment. In particular, the theology and film critic will be helped by taking note of a movie's (1) imagery, (2) opening credits and/or sequence, and (3) closing. Let us turn briefly to each of these:

Imagery. Paul Ricoeur understands a symbol to be a sign with multiple meanings, which disclose these hidden meanings in and through their immediate use.[18] Movies often make use of props or other narrative markers in this way. We have already looked at Woody Allen's use of sight imagery in his movie *Crimes and Misdemeanors.* Judah is an ophthalmologist; Ben becomes blind; Sol is told by his sister to open his eyes; Cliff and Lester see life through a camera lens; Delores speaks of the eyes as "the windows of the soul," but after she is murdered, Judah tells his brother, "There was nothing behind her eyes. All you saw was a black void." The movie consistently uses movie reels to comment on the real. In these ways and more, viewers are encouraged to consider how they will "see" life.

Or consider Morpheus's (Lawrence Fishburne) offer of either a blue or a red pill to Neo (Keanu Reeves) in *The Matrix* (1999). "You take the blue pill and the story ends. You wake in your bed and you believe whatever you want to believe." The choice of pills propels the story forward. But the blue pill is more than a plot device, as the viewer knows. It represents our succumbing to the Matrix, the numbing of our minds, a retreat to the comfort of life as usual, our urban/suburban captivity. The red pill, on the other hand, represents the uncharted territory of truth: "Remember, all I'm offering is the truth. Nothing more." But that is not quite "true." It also is the gift of life—of being reborn. Neo, of course, chooses the vitality of the red pill, and as we watch, a new self is (re)born and the old, flushed down the chute. Awakened to life, Neo is no longer desired by the Matrix, which drops him into the sewage. Rescued by Morpheus's ship, the *Nebuchadnezzar,* Neo is welcomed to "the real world." And the story begins.[19]

In the lyrical horror movie *The Night of the Hunter* (1955), we see the serial killer and itinerant preacher Harry Powell (Robert Mitchum) driving his stolen convertible Model T with LOVE tattooed on the knuckles of his right hand and HATE on his left. Here is the central imagery of this classic movie, its plot in a nutshell. As viewers worry over the fate of two young children, we are shown a life-and-death battle between love and hate—good and evil. Not all is as it seems—this "preacher" worms his way into people's lives with his charm, but he means them harm. He sings "Leaning on the Everlasting Arms" but trusts only his own sexually deviant self-righteousness. As the movie moves toward its climax, the children float down the ominous Ohio River with Harry in pursuit of them, only for them to be rescued in the nick of time by Rachel Cooper (Lillian Gish of silent film days). This frail older woman takes in stray children, feeding and clothing them and reading to them from the Bible. Here is the loving servant of God, not the hate-filled hypocritical preacher. The stylized scenes, particularly on the river, are chock full of symbols, but basic to all is this fundamental choice of right hand or left. And, of course, good triumphs, but not without viewers finding their hair standing on end.

The ominous presence of the preacher, Harry Powell (Robert Mitchum). *The Night of the Hunter* (d. Laughton, 1955). © United Artists. All rights reserved.

The Opening Credits or Sequence. The Night of the Hunter opens with children sitting in a circle singing "Dream, Little One, Dream." Rachel Cooper is telling stories to her foster children. Reading from the Bible, she tells them, "Blessed are the pure in heart" and "Beware of false prophets who come to you in sheep's clothing but inside are ravening wolves. Ye shall know them by their fruits." Here, the viewer is provided with the movie's point of view, its moral premise. This scene is soon followed by the discovery of a murdered woman's body in a basement where children are playing, then by Powell driving in his convertible while praying to his Lord, and the horror movie picks up steam. Another famous opening sequence is from Federico Fellini's *La Dolce Vita* (1960), where a huge statue of Christ the Laborer is seen being carried by helicopter across the sky of Rome. Has Christ come to judge this hell on earth (the remaining movie takes place in Rome over nine days, suggesting Dante's nine circles of judgment in hell)? Or is this rather an image of the church's irrelevance to life, its Savior simply floating over the city, disconnected from reality? Or is it both? Viewers are cued from the start that the good life is to be understood in terms of the religious imagination.

Such is also the case in *Bull Durham*, though the opening monologue lacks the grandeur of Fellini's image. Annie Savoy (Susan Sarandon) is sitting at her dressing table, which looks almost like a religious shrine, getting ready to go to the opening baseball game of the Durham Bulls. In a voice-over we hear:

> I believe in the church of baseball. I've tried all the major religions and most of the minor ones. I've worshipped Buddha, Allah, Brahma, Vishnu, Siva, trees, mushrooms and Isadora Duncan. I know things. For instance, there are 108 beads in a Catholic rosary and there are 108 stitches in a baseball. When I heard that, I gave Jesus a chance. But it didn't work out between us. The Lord laid too much guilt on me. . . . You see, there's no guilt in baseball, and it's never boring.

What follows is a movie ostensibly about baseball (celebrative, nurturing, goal oriented), but also a movie about what the church isn't but should be (celebrative, nurturing, goal oriented).

One of the most audacious openings is in Paul Thomas Anderson's *Magnolia* (1999), where we are given three urban legends in the guise of increasingly lengthy newsreels that question whether anything in life is mere chance. The intertwining of the lives of the nine chief characters in the drama that follows convincingly reinforces this theme. Perhaps the most celebrated opening, however, is that of Steven Spielberg's *Raiders of the Lost Ark* (1981), where scary forests, poison darts, spikes that impale, a scream, a whip, and, of course, the giant rumbling ball set up the suspenseful story that is to follow.

All these openings have one thing in common: if you miss them, you might as well have not seen the movie. And this is what any filmgoer will tell you. Last week, we went to our local "second-run" theater to see a movie we had missed when it first came out, only for the sound to be garbled for the first two or three minutes. The problem was fixed, but the projectionist failed to rewind the movie and start it again. Instead, he simply started the movie midstream. As you can imagine, the audience expressed its displeasure. If you are five minutes late to the cineplex, better to go to one of the other movies that are playing. With only two hours to see and hear the story, you must see the opening, which sets the stage, provides the tone, offers the central imagery or symbol, and fast-forwards the spectator into the heart of the story.

The Ending. Filmmakers, like their audiences, realize that endings are crucial to a movie, even if viewers often disagree over whether an ending works. Is the final cemetery scene necessary or sappy in *Saving Private Ryan* (1998)? Does the Thunderbird soaring into the sky in *Thelma & Louise* (1991) express the story's intended revolutionary freedom for these women? Do the frogs work in *Magnolia* (1999)? Though endings might be debated, their importance is not. "All's well that ends well!" The screenwriter of *Chinatown* (1974), Robert Towne, once commented:

> If you don't have a strong finish to a film, you're in serious trouble. It can be muted. It can be explosive. It can be a bang or a whimper, but it better be memorable, or else people will remember very little about the movie.[20]

If a movie's ending grabs an audience, it is often willing to overlook earlier gaffs. Take, for example, *The Sixth Sense* (1999). Its surprising twist at the end caused viewers to want to see the movie again and contributed to such great word of mouth that the film became a summer hit.

Endings are often contested while the movie is being made, creativity (the filmmakers) coming into conflict with commerce (the studio "suits"). After test screenings and focus groups for upcoming movies, it is the ending that is most often reshot in the studio's hope of releasing a box-office success. Sometimes this works; often it does not. Believing, for example, the audience needed a happy ending, the studio tacked onto the original release of *Blade Runner* (1982) a sentimental ending over the objections of its director, Ridley Scott. Only eleven years later did Warner Brothers release Scott's original version, to critical acclaim. In the studio version, consistency in story had been compromised; in the director's cut, the ending seemed to develop out of what had preceded it.

Perhaps the best-known example of a reshooting is *Fatal Attraction* (1987), where producer Sherry Lansing had a bloody and vengeful finale added after test audiences rejected the film's initial ironic conclusion. Instead of Glenn Close's character, Alex Forrest, committing suicide, what audiences now see is her dying at the hands of Dan Gallagher's (Michael Douglas) wife, Beth. Most critics hated the new ending, believing it sold out both characterization and plausibility, though in this case, audiences streamed into the theater to experience the satisfaction of this visceral act. A similar reworking of the movie's conclusion that brought in increased revenue happened with *My Best Friend's Wedding* (1997). Test audiences thought that in the version they saw, Julia Roberts's character had not been adequately chastised for her unrepentant selfishness. Added was a redemption scene in which Roberts cries and expresses remorse.

For an ending to work best, some suggest that it must satisfy two seemingly conflicting demands. It must come as a surprise, and it must nevertheless make sense, growing organically out of the preceding story (both the narrative and its tone) and bringing it to a suitable closure.[21] *The Sixth Sense* had both. So did *The Usual Suspects* (1995) and *The Night of the Hunter* (1955). Consider also the endings of *Magnolia* (1999) and *American Beauty* (1999). The first frog that rains from the sky in *Magnolia* catches everyone by surprise, and the deluge that follows is surreal. But the frogs also allow the various characters to respond in new ways, rounding out the story and bringing a sense of completion that many viewers experience as transcendent. Similarly, the shocking murder of Lester by his neighbor in *American Beauty* cannot adequately be prepared for by the viewer, but the movie has carefully set up the viewer to receive it. It seems right for the story.

Visual Literacy: A Brief Example

Thelma & Louise (1991)

The movie *Thelma & Louise* (1991) is a fable concerning women's freedom from male oppression. The movie tells the story of two women finding their freedom as they light out for the West (a female variation of the American myth, "Go west, young man"; cf. *Huckleberry Finn*). Some viewers consider this road movie antifeminist, for it ends with the women driving off the edge of the Grand Canyon rather than submitting to the law with its male authority. However, this is a misunderstanding of the symbolic intention of the movie. The movie is not meant as a realistic cultural depiction, but as a dream work, an adult fairy tale. Thelma and Louise have refused to submit any longer to male oppression; in the end, they "ride off into the sunset."

As is often the case in a movie, the opening sequence helps us determine the tone of *Thelma & Louise*. The mythic trajectory of the movie is foreshadowed during the credits as the landscape with its road stretching forth into the distance changes from black-and-white into bright color. Like other road movies, we are going to see a story of awakenings. As the movie ends, the dreamlike intention of the movie is reinforced. The car does not crash; the frame is frozen with the car flying off into the heavens. The final image is that of freedom, not disaster.[22]

To give a sense of immensity and grandeur to this tale, a deep-focused camera is used to follow the two women as they are escaping in their convertible along the highways in the Southwest (that is, there is nothing in the frame that is seen out of focus). There is no "realistic" dust on their car nor on the phallic stainless-steel gasoline tanker that the women blow up. Rather, that scene has

Thelma (Geena Davis) and Louise (Susan Sarandon) on their '66 Thunderbird. *Thelma & Louise* (d. Scott, 1991). © Metro-Goldwyn Mayer (MGM).

an intended surreal quality. The audience is ushered into the mythic vastness of the American frontier. The brightness of the sunlight by day and the lighting that illumines the underside of their car at night only reinforce the mythical quality of the scene, as does the floodlit brightness of the mountains even in the evening glow.

The use of such techniques in the filming of *Thelma & Louise* provides interpretive clues about how to view its tale. This is not a realistic story of two women escaping abusive contexts. It is instead a supra-natural fable of liberation, of two women finding themselves as they "go West."

Music

Music is the shortest distance between two points. And it is the only way to touch infinity.

Peter Sellers

(Music) is brimful of meanings which will not translate into logical structures or verbal expression. . . . Music is at once cerebral in the highest degree . . . and it is at the same time somatic, carnal and a searching out of resonances in our bodies at levels deeper than will or consciousness.

George Steiner

Understanding a movie demands both verbal and visual literacy. But there is still more, for movies have always included music, even if it was only played by an organ in the theater. In fact, it can be argued that historically, music predates dialogue in films. Be that as it may, a movie is made up of words, images, and music. A movie's power and meaning is supported by this tripod. Put in the lingo of postmodernity, there is in film a culture of intertextuality. Thus, we need finally to turn from screenplay and image to sound, if we are to have the full complement of tools needed to understand a movie's story.

Though music has most often been ignored or treated casually by interpreters of film (in the first edition of this book, I too was guilty of this), it is increasingly being recognized by those writing in the area of theology and film that film music is more than inaudible Muzak, background filler of dubious artistic merit.[23] Though its role in the early decades of film might have been to drown out the noise of the projector and to alleviate audience unease, given the darkness and otherwise silence of the theater, film music has developed far beyond those beginnings. In particular, it is music's affective ability that should be noted. More than language, more even than imagery, music can bypass our cognitive abilities and impact our emotional centers. Music has a physical impact that possesses its own independent power and presence.

It was the composer Aaron Copeland who in 1940 offered a useful summary of five functions of film music. As outlined by Pauline Reay in her helpful book *Music in Film: Soundtracks and Synergy*, Copeland suggested that

(i) it conveys a convincing atmosphere of time and place; (ii) it underlines the unspoken feelings or psychological states of the characters; (iii) it serves as a kind of neutral background filler to the action; (iv) it gives a sense of continuity to the editing; (v) it accentuates the theatrical build-up of a scene and rounds it off with a feeling of finality.[24]

Copeland was concentrating in his overview on the role of the film composer, that is, on music created in conversation with the images and dialogue on the screen. There is also a second kind of screen music, scores compiled from popular music by music supervisors. While much of what Copeland suggests is equally applicable here, given the lyrics of most popular music, its use in film scores can have additional meaning, which we will discuss below. But first it is helpful to consider the musical score sans lyrics.

My colleague Barry Taylor, himself a film composer, has suggested that the musical score contributes to a film's power and meaning in four principle ways.[25] First, "music gets 'inside the drama': creating atmosphere and coloring the film." That is, music has a collaborative role, unobtrusively making connections between the words and the pictures, engendering meanings of its own. Says Taylor, film music "interpret(s) what we see . . . it allows meaning to happen." John Ottman, composer of *X2: X-Men United* (2003) for Bryan Singer, echoes Taylor as he discusses what he tried to accomplish with that music: "As with any film, the score has to provide the soul of the movie and bring out the emotions beyond a surface level."[26]

Second, "music invests particular scenes with strong emotion." Think of the staccato screams of the violin in the shower scene of *Psycho* (1960) and the soaring orchestration of the John Williams score for *Star Wars* (1977). Third, writes Taylor, the film score creates "rhythm and movement." It is music that will slow down a scene or perhaps shift a film in a new direction. Music's ability to set the pace is quite literally realized in the majestic score of *Chariots of Fire* (1981), which provides both rhythm and meaning to Eric Liddell's running, whether on the beach or in the stadium.

And last, Taylor rightly recognizes that "music is the communicating link between screen and audience." The score both interprets what is shown on the screen and evokes concomitant feelings in the listeners/viewers. As Aristotle recognized, the power of music is in its ability to produce an effect on the character of the soul. In its very structure music evokes in the hearer such feelings as sadness or happiness, which when used effectively match the visual imagery and the narrative on the screen. Here is what John Williams was able to do with brilliance in the latest of his Star Wars scores for *Revenge of the Sith* (2005). Viewer/listener response to scenes with Obi-Wan Kenobi and Anakin, for example, is shaped by the ambivalence, or murkiness, found in Williams's music. We simply feel with Obi-Wan Kenobi his dilemma, wanting to believe in Anakin but sensing the young warrior's rebellion. What the image alone could not do, Williams's score accomplishes. In short, film music both informs listeners/viewers about how the characters in a film are feeling at any moment *and* tells this same audience how it is to feel.

An extended example can help enflesh our discussion, even if, as the composer Camille Saint-Saëns recognized, it remains difficult to talk about music effectively. Few are better at the use of a score than director Stanley Kubrick. As he struggled time and again with depictions of the emptiness of the human spirit or with the ambiguity and contingency of life, it was music that helped give surrealistic and sarcastic meaning to the surface realism on the screen. We think of the final scene in *Dr. Strangelove* (1964), where Vera Lynn sings the original World War II recording of "We'll Meet Again," a song originally recorded as a morale booster for the troops (we'll speak more of lyrics below). But here, the effect is anything but positive, as on screen we see the mushroom cloud of the detonating hydrogen bomb. Or again, in *2001: A Space Odyssey* (1968), Kubrick effectively uses Richard Strauss's *Thus Spoke Zarathustra* to bring home the mysteries of the universe.

In *A Clockwork Orange* (1971), classical music is again used for point and counterpoint, this time played on a Moog synthesizer, giving it an ethereal and even sinister quality. In the first scene, the rhythm and movement of the movie's violent action is organized around a Rossini score, and the violence becomes almost like a dance. We also hear Beethoven's Ninth played while Nazis goosestep and Purcell's "Music for the Funeral of Queen Mary" while Alex is beaten and tortured. Handel's *Sarabande Duel* plays to highlight the actual duels on screen in *Barry Lyndon* (1975), squeezing a mythlike quality out of these otherwise realistic scenes. Similarly, at the beginning of *The Shining* (1980), the theme music has an unearthly quality, like a requiem mass. But all the while the camera is soaring like a bird as it roams over mountain and water. The viewer is led to ask, are we trapped in an endgame, or are we allowed to wander? For Kubrick, the answer is open-ended. Life, like his music, is both ethereal and menacing. In his last film, *Eyes Wide Shut* (1999), Kubrick again turned to music in order to provide an interpretive language for the story. He has a single piano note pound harshly with little thought to melody as much of the wordless action goes on. Life's menacing presence is made palpable.[27]

Film music—created by film composers looking at daily takes and/or screenplays and imagining the scenes musically—informs viewers/listeners of on-screen feelings, emphasizes significant moments, provides pacing for the action, and instills in audiences appropriate feelings. As such, music is integral to the meaning-making function of a movie. If these scores are not only original compositions, but compilations from popular music that usually include lyrics, additional possibilities for the significance of the film music also emerge. If a character, for example, likes a song that you as the viewer also like, you are attracted to that character and believe you understand something about him.

Along with establishing mood and creating emotional connections with the audience, the use of lyrics can evoke both time and place, while allowing the filmmaker to signal his or her attitude toward a character or comment on the action. That is, music can either provide a point of view for the scene or give an authorial take on it. Sometimes, a song will do both. Such was the case in *The Graduate* (1967), which won the Grammy Award for best original score. Its music by Simon and Garfunkel (in particular, "Sounds of Silence," "Scarborough Fair," and "Mrs. Robinson") not only roots the film in the rebelliousness and angst of the sixties, but also gives voice to the movie's mood and themes and provides important comments about Benjamin's character.

A second, more recent example is Paul Thomas Anderson's *Magnolia* (1999).[28] *Magnolia* is organized around three Aimee Mann songs and was inspired by a fourth. Anderson says, "I really set out to write an adaptation of her songs. . . . Her songs become the built-in voice of the movie, tying all the stories together."[29] That is, the major narrative freight of the movie is provided by the music and their lyrics. These are foregrounded in the movie.

Jim Kurring (John C. Reilly) and Claudia Wilson Gater (Melora Walters) find friendship together. *Magnolia* (d. Anderson, 1999).

After its prologue, the movie's opening credits appear, and we are introduced to members of the ensemble cast while an extended version of Mann's song "One" plays alongside the dialogue: "One is the loneliest number / that you'll ever do. / Two can be as bad as one, / It's the loneliest number / Since the number one." The song sets the mood and provides one of the movie's major themes, that everyone is indeed terribly lonely: Frank Mackey, the guru of female seduction; his estranged father, Earl Partridge, a television producer who is dying, and Phil Parma, his nurse; Earl's trophy wife, Linda; former child quiz-show star, Donnie Smith, and current child protégée and quiz-show star, Stanley Spector; game show host, Jimmy Gater, who is dying of cancer, and his drug-addicted daughter, Claudia; and police officer Jim Kurring, who is looking for love.

Two and a half hours into the movie, after the tragedies of the characters' lives have become all too apparent, Anderson introduces another Mann song,

"Wise Up." In an audacious move that serves as the emotional heart of the movie, Anderson weaves together the lives of these characters by having them serially sing lines from this song. As the film cuts to each of their individual settings, we hear them sing along with Mann's vocals. Though they remain isolated, the effect is that of a corporate voice. With the characters at the end of their ropes, with rain falling outside and Earl having been humanely given a lethal dose of morphine by Phil to ease his death, we see Claudia sitting alone in her apartment as she softly joins in with Mann, who is heard singing "Wise Up." Then we cut to Jim Kurring, the bungling, lonely cop, who picks up the lyrics. And on it goes. First Jimmy Gator, then Donnie, then Phil and Earl, then Linda in her car, then Frank, then Stanley—each singing along with Mann in succession. The lyrics we hear the characters sing match their particular situation—Donnie's drinking, Claudia's drugs, Jimmy's cancer, Linda's need to make things right, Stanley's resignation. But the fact that everyone is singing the same song's lyrics ("It's not going to stop / 'Til you wise up") also unites them with one another and with the audience in ways that story structure and dialogue cannot. The music reveals that they are at the same point in their transformation process.

Anderson comments on the song: "Hopefully it unifies everything, calms everything down and feels completely natural. Haven't you ever sung along to a song on the radio? In the simplest way, it's just that. . . . I thought it was going to be something very sweet, sentimental in the best way. I didn't consider it outlandish. And I still don't."[30] Outlandish, no; audacious, yes. Although "one is the loneliest number that you'll ever do," "it's not going to stop / 'til you wise up." The music provides the filmmaker's (auteur's) take on life. The songs and their lyrics provide not only theme, mood, and momentum to the story but also continuity and unity. Here the music is not subordinated to the dialogue; it is the dialogue.

The foregrounding of the music continues with a third Mann song that ends the movie and continues into the credits. We have already commented earlier on the use of this song, "Save Me." Claudia is seen sitting, disconsolate, on the edge of her bed. Jim is talking to her as we hear in the foreground Aimee Mann sing: "You look like the perfect fit, / a girl in need of a tourniquet." And Jim offers just that. "Can you save me / come on and save me," the song pleads, giving words to Claudia's suffering silence. As the song continues, "If you could save me / from the ranks of the freaks / who suspect they could never love anyone," Jim's voice is barely audible over the music, "You are a good and beautiful person." The camera focuses on Claudia and stays there as she struggles to accept his gift of love. Miraculously, she smiles briefly for the first time, and the movie ends.

Rather than being simply a series of vignettes, *Magnolia*'s nine stories ultimately play out with this one voice. Unified by the music that initially inspired it, the story moves painfully from "One Is the Loneliest Number" to a recognition of the need to "Wise Up" to a fragile acceptance of the gift of another's care, "Save Me." The movie thus presents through music, reinforced by image and dialogue, a coherent understanding of life, one rooted in others and quickened by the reality of death. Dark yet hopeful, *Magnolia* helps viewers confront their pasts and live into an uncertain future.

A final footnote to our discussion of music is in order. Any discussion of film music begs also for comment with regard to film silence. Given music's importance to the power and meaning of a movie, the absence of music is also significant. *Chinatown* (1974), for example, has more than a dozen changes of scene in the first forty minutes of the movie, but there is no music after the haunting trumpet solo during the opening credits. The audience is in this way denied any help in interpreting the character of Jake Gittes (Jack Nicholson). The only clue we are given about this private detective (this "snoop") is a visual one, his sliced and bandaged nose. (With a compromised nose, are we to trust any of his judgments?) It is not until the final third of the movie when the bandage finally comes off that music plays an interpretive role, alternatingly suspenseful with its plucked harp and percussive piano, and romantic with violins, strummed harp, and treble piano. With Jake, we are again allowed to sniff for hints and guesses.

The lack of music at a crucial moment in the narrative can also be telling. In *Dead Man Walking* (1995), after an hour and forty minutes, Matthew Poncilet (Sean Penn) finally confesses his crimes to Sister Helen (Susan Sarandon) and takes responsibility for them with his attempted apology to the parents of the young couple who have been raped and murdered. As the guards lead Sister Helen away so they can manacle this "dead man" and walk him to his execution, the camera does not follow, choosing to remain on Matthew instead. In this way, the focus shifts from Sister Helen's pleading to Matthew's remorse and fear. We see him sobbing. Then he stops, swallows, and opens his eyes. There is neither dialogue nor music to indicate his feelings. All we have is the image: a three-quarter profile of him alone, shot through the bars. Spared any melodramatic music, viewers are forced to accept the ambiguity of the moment and make their own judgments about the heart of this man and the rightness of what is to follow.

Filmmakers craft a movie, telling a story for their viewers from a particular point of view. Meaning is conveyed through a well-crafted script, through skillful editing and framing and special effects, as well as by music. While a movie might also have an explicit narrator to interpret the action, it is these implicit "narrative" guides that primarily direct the viewer's interpretation of the tale. When done well, the movie works. If such tools and technologies simply become a source of marvel, or a substitute for a good plot or engaging dialogue, the movie fails, and the story proves inert.

becoming a film critic

Siskel and Ebert became household names in America by using their thumbs to rate movies; now Ebert and Roeper carry on the tradition. Two thumbs up on their weekly television show means a movie is worth seeing; two thumbs down, avoid it like the plague. More elaborate reviewing schemas are used in newspapers across the country, but the goal is similar: to express personal satisfaction or dissatisfaction with a current release. The *San Francisco Chronicle*, for example, uses pictures of a little man sitting on his chair watching the movie. If the movie is judged to be a dog, the little man is snoring; if it is okay, the man is watching; if it is good, the man is clapping; and if it is a "must-see," the man is standing on his chair clapping wildly as his hat comes off. Such judgments by reviewers have become the staple of journalism, and they are repeated informally by moviegoers themselves who share with friends over a cup of coffee their opinion of the latest movie. Such judgments serve an important function in helping potential viewers know which movies to see.

Film criticism, however, has a different goal from simply the negative or positive evaluation of a film. It seeks to initiate a process of inquiry and reflection in order to better understand a movie. It does this by commenting on a movie's style and story, its structure and theme. Moreover, film criticism explores the connection a movie has both to its creators and to its audiences. The best film criticism seeks to ask comprehensively, how is it that the movie is (or is not) a meaningful experience?

If theologians, both amateur and professional, are to avoid reading into movies what is not there, they must learn something of the craft of viewing and reflecting; they must develop their critical skills. It is important to recall, however, that the process of film criticism is not foreign to the church. The church has, in fact, been involved in film criticism throughout the past century and has even helped shape some of its distinct aspects. Richard Blake argues that the church itself initiated film criticism: "[I]t would not be much of an exaggeration to claim that the churches actually invented film criticism, as opposed to the reviewing carried by the daily papers, in the first years of the century."[1] Churches were concerned about the social impact (public morality) of film. They also saw the catechetical (Christian education) function that movies could provide through their interpretation of life, and so film criticism began.

We have already considered in the previous chapters how we might understand a film's power and meaning by concentrating on the narrative shape and unique features of the movie itself. In this chapter, we will look in an analogous way at four particular aspects of film criticism: (1) *genre criticism* examines the common form and mythic shape of film; (2) *auteur criticism* attends to the movie's "author"; (3) *thematic criticism* compares film texts; and (4) *cultural criticism* focuses on a film's social context. We can diagram these four methods by again using an artistic-critical circle:

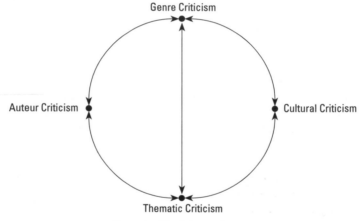

Figure 8.1 Film Criticism Options

It is to these four critical approaches that we now turn.

Genre Criticism: Examining the Common Shape of Film

"My name is John Ford. I make Westerns."

John Ford

When we go to Blockbuster to rent a video and ask our companions whether they would like to see an adventure film, a comedy, a sci-fi, a thriller, or perhaps a romance, we are acknowledging that many movies fit into certain categories—into genres, a system of orientation for both the filmmaker and film-viewer, a means of communicating expectation and convention. These expectations need not exactly reflect real life, but need only correspond to a viewer's previous experience with like movies. *The Bourne Supremacy* (2004), for example, is hardly realistic with regard to its surface story, but it doesn't matter. The movie is a suspense story, a "spy-thriller." The organization of its surface details is like others of the genre (James Bond movies, the *Mission: Impossible* franchise, *The Bourne Identity*), and the fact that it is a spy-thriller allows its audience to identify with the movie at a deeper level. It provides us both the pleasure of the familiar and the pleasure of its originality within that genre.

When movie-viewers fail to recognize a film's genre, their interpretation becomes skewed. This is what happened for some viewers of *Thelma & Louise* (1991), for example. Not recognizing its road-movie genre that centered not on the plot, but on the changing relationship between the two women, the film was judged harshly by some as painting women into a corner in which their only liberation was suicide. That is, the film was taken literally, and its meaning wrongly reduced to its face value. On the other hand, most reviewers recognized the noir comic-book genre of Robert Rodriguez and Frank Miller's *Sin City* (2005). Though it portrayed cannibalism, castration, decapitation, dismemberment, hanging, massacres, slashings, and torture, the movie's stylized and abstract images were seen by both viewers and reviewers as more camp than scary and as being faithful to the original comic books. Devin Gordon, for example, writing for *Newsweek* magazine describes the movie with the oxymoron, "delightfully depraved."[2] In the movie, the blood is not only red, but white and yellow. And the point of it all is not the violence, but the love the three "heroes" have for the women of the city. As Bob Weinstein says, "It's about the lengths they will go for redemption and revenge. That's the core of it, and that's what Robert and Frank got, and that's what every film noir piece has. And people love that."[3]

Each genre—the musical, the comedy, the gangster/crime movie, the war movie, the film noir, the teenpic, the horror movie, the road movie, the action-adventure film—carries with it a characteristic set of conventions. Its subject matter, style, and values are standardized. Thus genre becomes a convenient way of selecting material, determining the narrative's strategy, and organizing the story. If a hero is killed at the end of a Western, for example, the audience feels cheated. If a Disney children's fable is too dark or its values nontraditional, viewers feel betrayed. Genres provide a set of built-in satisfactions by taking on something of a collective ritual or game. Audiences come expecting a certain kind of pleasure (just ask the teenager who attends a slasher movie). Originality is, of course, part of the fun, but only as it intensifies the expected experience.

By organizing and synthesizing vast amounts of material, genres give viewers cues about how to interpret the story. They are not ironclad rules, but rather loose sets of expectations that provide direction. We all know who wears the white hat, for example. But if it is worn by another character, as in a Clint Eastwood film, we immediately take notice—it is an important part of the movie's originality and invites reflection as to its intended meaning.

Mediocre filmmakers merely repeat the formula; serious artists reinterpret. It was Aristotle who noted in *The Poetics* that the conventions of classical tragedy were basically the same whether they were used by a genius or a dolt. It is not genre that determines a movie's excellence, but what is done within a genre. Because filmmakers have only a limited amount of time to portray their story, they often rely on convention to convey meaning and give direction. Genre thus becomes a heuristic device pointing the audience to a film's meaning.

Genre criticism is two-pronged. It is interested both in a movie's text and in its context; that is, it has both an internal and an external focus. With regard to the film itself, genre critics explore those formal and rhetorical patterns that give shape to the movie's meaning. In a musical, for example, the viewer moves back and forth between narrative and musical presentation. The song and dance numbers become a stylized means of portraying the meaning and intention of the larger situation. Aware of this, viewers do not expect the songs to carry the plot further, but look to the production numbers to convey primary meaning. They function something like the soliloquies of Elizabethan drama ("To be, or not to be? That is the question."). It is foolish to judge *The Sound of Music* (1965) for being untrue to the facts or Pollyanna in content; this is to miss the genre's intention. Rather, we must listen to the music in the production numbers. If we do, we too will discover that "the hills are alive with the sound of music."

Genres are a form of contemporary myth, giving expression to the meaning of everyday life. Genres carry an intrinsic worldview. They become stylized conventions to portray universal conflicts whereby viewers can participate ritualistically in the basic beliefs, fears, and anxieties not only of their age, but of all ages. As Orson Welles once remarked, "The camera is much more than a recording apparatus; it is a medium via which messages reach us from another world that is not ours and that brings us to the heart of a great secret. Here magic begins."[4] Genre films become iconic. That is, through repetition, a certain imagery, story line, and characterization become archetypal. Behind their repeated use, we sense some sort of pattern or model that gives shape to, or provides options for, interpreting reality. Here is the way human existence is structured at a central region.

Genre critics do more than note the iconic, however. They also focus on how shifts in the general characteristics of a genre reflect changes in the culture out of which it came. Here is genre criticism's external focus. Martin Scorsese, reflecting on the history of cinema for an American Film Institute documentary, commented:

The most interesting of the classic movie genres to me are the indigenous ones: the Western, which was born on the Frontier, the Gangster Film, which originated in the East Coast cities, and the Musical, which was spawned by Broadway. They remind me of jazz: they allowed for endless, increasingly complex, sometimes perverse variations. When these variations were played by the masters, they reflected the changing times; they gave you fascinating insights into American culture and the American psyche.[5]

Helping to locate the basic structure of a movie, its dramatic pattern, genre criticism also turns its attention to exploring the relationship between that genre and the world surrounding it. For example, a gangster film like *The Godfather* (1972) can be viewed as a way of exploring America's growing social unrest. Or an animated Disney film (e.g., *Pocahontas* [1995], *Tarzan* [1999]) can be interpreted as reinforcing conservative values.

The evolution of the Western on the screen provides a clear illustration of a genre's ability to shed light on the culture in which it was created. The typical plot for a Western prior to World War II centered on the hero as rugged individualist who rode into town from the outside and solved the problem out of a sense of what was right, or perhaps for the love of a girl. In this way the West was won and community achieved (even if the lone hero had to ride off into the sunset). But through the 1950s, the dark side of this morality play was explored. Were Americans so noble? Was this Hollywood myth true to the American experience? In John Ford's *The Searchers* (1956), Ethan Edwards (John Wayne), the hero, is now motivated in his sadistic violence, not by a sense of rightness, but by vengeance, and in Arthur Penn's *The Left-Handed Gun* (1958), Billy the Kid (Paul Newman) is a juvenile delinquent. Again to quote Scorsese, Billy is "a suicidal antihero who sought his own death. Neither a vicious killer nor a sympathetic outlaw, Billy was a rebel without a cause. His rage and confusion had more to do with the malaise of adolescents growing up in the 1950s than with the realities of the old West."[6]

In the 1960s, American culture changed again, becoming more corporate and professional in nature. Thus it should come as no surprise that the typical Western plot changed with it. Now, the hero became heroes, and they often worked for money. They were specialists (typically professionals who are for hire; sometimes even outlaws) who formed a group to solve the problem (consider *True Grit* [1969], *The Wild Bunch* [1969], and *Butch Cassidy and the Sundance Kid* [1969]).[7] American society had changed and with it the Western. This change in the structure of many (not all—genre is fluid) Westerns signaled a change in the attitudes and expectations of the movie audience. And this has continued. There are few Westerns being made today. The disillusionment within American culture has allowed little room for the classic, mythic struggle between good and evil, at least in this form. That Kevin Costner has tried to revive the Western (*Open Range* [2003]) with only mixed success, or a movie like *Witness* (1985) has transposed the structure of a Western into a story of a

Philadelphia cop in Amish country, only confirms the fact that American society has changed since the days of John Wayne. We all know too well the mixed motives for establishing civilization on the frontier and the consequences that resulted. Yet the genre is not completely dead. Clint Eastwood has continued to use it to great effect by again playing a riff on it. *Unforgiven* (1992) explores our society's present ambivalence toward violence and guns. As Eastwood's character, an old gunslinger says to a young kid who is practicing his draw, "You've got to be careful when you talk about killing a man, because you're not only taking his life, you're taking all that he was and all he's gonna be." Even though the story is set in the 1880s, it echoes contemporary concerns. If you commit violence, what does it really accomplish? Does it do something to you, diminish you, as well as the victim?

Genre criticism thus opens out to auteur criticism, on the one hand, and to cultural criticism, on the other. It has its limits, of course. Many have pointed out the problem of classification—isn't there a circularity in definition as a group of movies are chosen to represent a genre and then their characteristics are used to describe the genre? And can't movies have multiple genres? We think of *Titanic* (1997), for example, which is a love story, a disaster movie, and a historical epic all in one. Nevertheless, for many movies, a recognition of their genre allows viewers to appreciate the director's personal vision as they embellish and reinterpret the pattern. It also offers the critic a means of assessing the cultural values and changes expressed through the movies' originality. Tom Ryall writes:

> When we suggest that a certain film is a Western we are really positing that a particular range of meanings will be available in the film, and not others. We are defining the limits of its significance. The master image for genre criticism is a triangle composed of artist/film/audience. Genres may be defined as patterns/forms/styles/structures which transcend individual films, and which supervise their construction by the film maker, and their reading by an audience.[8]

Shane (1953)

The movie *Shane* provides an example of the way genre criticism works. It is one of the great Westerns of all time, largely because of the clarity and simplicity with which it interprets the classic ingredients of the Western genre. Will Wright says simply, "*Shane* is the classic of the classic Westerns."[9] For Wright, the plot of a typical Western will unfold as follows:

1. The hero enters a social group.
2. The hero is unknown to the society.
3. The hero is revealed to have an exceptional ability.

4. The society recognizes a difference between themselves and the hero; the hero is given a special status.
5. The society does not completely accept the hero.
6. There is a conflict of interests between the villains and the society.
7. The villains are stronger than the society; the society is weak.
8. There is a strong friendship or respect between the hero and a villain.
9. The villains threaten the society.
10. The hero avoids involvement in the conflict.
11. The villains endanger a friend of the hero.
12. The hero fights the villains.
13. The hero defeats the villains.
14. The society is safe.
15. The society accepts the hero.
16. The hero loses or gives up his special status.[10]

Shane follows this pattern closely. Filmed against the backdrop of the Grand Teton Mountains and starring Alan Ladd as Shane, the movie begins with the hero wearing spotless buckskin as he rides down from the mountains into an "Eden-like" valley. There he is spotted by young Joey across a still pond, where a deer is peacefully drinking, even though Joey is playing with a toy gun. Shane asks for water at the farm of Joey's parents, Joe and Marian Starrett, who perceive him as a threat and force him to leave at gunpoint. But after the Riker brothers ride up and threaten Starrett in order to get him off his land so their cattle can use it for grazing, Shane returns wearing a gun and announces he is a friend of the Starretts. Scaring off the Rikers, Shane is now invited for dinner and offered a job on the farm.

The next day Shane goes to town for supplies and is harassed by the Rikers' men. Shane avoids a fight, however. Later that evening, when a group of the farmers meet to plan their response to the Rikers, Shane is present, but he is accused of cowardice by one of the farmers. When all the farmers go to town on Sunday, Shane goes along and intentionally returns to the saloon where he had been harassed. This time he fights a cowboy named Chris and defeats him. The Rikers try to neutralize his opposition by offering Shane a job, but Shane refuses. When the cowboys in the saloon attack Shane, Joe Starrett comes to his defense, and together they defeat the cowboys. Realizing something must be done, the Rikers send for a gunfighter, Wilson.

After arriving in town, Wilson soon forces a showdown with one of the farmers and kills him. This is followed the next day by the Rikers setting fire to one of the farms. Dispirited, the farmers get ready to leave the valley, but Starrett persuades them to stay one more day. Trying to take matters into his own hands, Starrett then decides to go to town to kill the Rikers. Marian asks Shane to try to stop him, for her own pleas have failed. Told by Chris that Starrett is heading into a trap, Shane again puts on his gun and tells Joe to stay home. When the

farmer refuses, Shane must knock him out. Saying his good-bye to an adoring
Marian, Shane rides to town, where he outdraws Wilson and kills him and the
two Riker brothers. Shane tells Joey, who has followed him to town, that the
valley will again have peace, but that he must be going. Wounded in the chest,
Shane rides out of town back up the mountain, while Joey calls out after him,
"Come back, Shane! Come back!"

Is this simply a repetition of the formula? After all, it fits almost perfectly
Wright's description of the classical Western plot. But as Jean Renoir, the French
director and critic, once observed, "The marvelous thing about Westerns is
that they're all the same movie. This gives a director unlimited freedom."[11] It
is the freedom that director George Stevens displays that both distinguishes
the movie and heightens the meaning of this story. Stevens wants us to see the
story's mythic qualities. There is more to the film than the slow and stylized
plot. Viewers are struck by the mystical quality of the movie.

In his article "The Drama of Salvation in George Stevens's *Shane*," Robert
Banks points out a number of ways in which the screenplay varied from the
novel from which it was taken.[12] For example, in the book by Jack Schaefer,
there is no opening descent from the mountain by our hero, nor is there a
return back up the mountain at the end. In the book there is no idyllic, Eden-

like opening setting into which evil intrudes. Although according to the book Shane's clothing is dusty, in the movie his buckskin is spotless, in contrast with Wilson's black outfit. In the film, Shane's gun represents his extraordinary ability, but he puts the gun away to work on the farm. Only when forced to defend his friend does he put it back on. It is Shane furthermore who preaches a kind of Sermon on the Mount to the farmers, reminding them of what is at stake. As Shane rides into town for the final time, Stevens frames the scene in such a way that the cemetery crosses seem to follow him for a time as he rides. Again, as he speaks to Joey one last time after the fight in which he is wounded, Shane reaches out and touches Joey on the head, in effect consecrating him to continue in his stead. And then of course, Shane has come into the valley to live with Joe (Joseph) and Marian (Mary), and little Joey calls out to him as he leaves, asking him to return (Christ's second coming). Stevens has cast the confrontation between farmer and rancher, between frontier and civilization, between good and evil, as a variation of the Christ-story. Shane has come into a tarnished Eden to restore it to its rightful self, and his followers will await his return.

Geoffrey Hill sees other mythic archetypes in the movie. In particular, he finds parallels with the Cain and Abel story. The story pits gatherers against hunters, farmers against cattle herders, nesters (homesteaders) against ranchers, vegetarians against meat eaters, matriarchies against patriarchies, domesticators against warriors. Shane rides into the valley wearing buckskin, but he soon changes into clothes made from fiber. He tries to shed his gun but ultimately cannot. And as with the Cain and Abel story, the result is human violence. Like Cain, Shane ends up a wanderer.[13]

In ways such as these, George Stevens, the director, has given us a multilayered story that invites our deeper gaze. An allegorical treatment of either the Christ-story or the Cain and Abel saga is not intended. It would be wrong to overinterpret the film. But allusions abound that add a universality and depth to the portrayal. Moreover, Stevens has done more than this. Not only has he recast this Western to heighten its mythic, quasi-messianic meaning, but also he has done it in a way that ties it into what many in the early 1950s thought of as the American myth. He has sought not only to connect the story to its ancient past but to plant the movie in its present soil. His success is perhaps evident in the fact that hundreds of American babies were named Shane soon after the film came out. Joe and Marian recall not only Joseph and Mary but George and Mary of the classic American film *It's a Wonderful Life* (1946). Quoting John Wiley Nelson, Banks summarizes the American dream:

> Evil intrudes from outside the essentially good society: people are basically good not evil, but some have yielded to their baser instincts; this breaks social relations and threatens social institutions, such as the family, community or nation; the source of deliverance is also external: it comes through a mysterious, celibate individual with

special powers; the outcome is preservation of the family-community-nation, and the future guarantee of schools, churches, law and order.[14]

The similarity with *Shane* is again clear. Though people are weak, they are basically good. Though a community is present, it is the work of a strong individual who preserves order. And the religious is present mainly to preserve family–community–nation. ("In God We Trust" was put on our coins by Congress in the Eisenhower era.) Though in the later fifties, cracks perhaps began to surface in this American dream, it was not until our seemingly invincible hero John F. Kennedy was shot, followed by Martin Luther King Jr. and Robert Kennedy, that this mythic balloon popped. Future generations would come along and question whether there ever really had been a Camelot (cf. the movie *Pleasantville* [1998]). But at the time *Shane* was produced, the American dream reigned supreme.

Shane is a classic American film, not simply because it follows the Western script, but because Stevens creatively used this genre to tie his story into those archetypal biblical stories that provide it depth and texture. He also effectively brought his story forward into the present and expressed it in a way the early Eisenhower era in America could affirm. The result was a movie that spoke with power and meaning about the nature and possibilities of humankind. However, many students in my classes today find the movie quaint at best, for we no longer live in the days of *Leave It to Beaver* and *Father Knows Best*. That innocence was shattered by the 1960s with its three assassinations, to say nothing of the Vietnam War. But though the movie lacks existential and visceral power for some contemporary viewers, *Shane*'s archetypal patterns continue to fascinate other viewers. Its classic confrontation of the forces of good and evil still speaks to people today.

Auteur Criticism: Attending to the Movie's "Author"

Auteur criticism begins with the talent or person behind the work of film and seeks to understand the movie in that light. Such reflection is made more difficult for the film critic by the fact that moviemaking is a collaborative process. There are producers, writers, directors, camera crew, editors, actors, lighting and sound people, composers, costumers, casting agents, and more. Each brings creativity to the project. The credits at the end of a film speak for themselves. Yet there is often an organizing or unifying force behind a film, typically the director, whose creative vision shapes the story.

It is said that the philosopher George Santayana, while teaching at Harvard University, was asked by an undergraduate what courses he would be offering the next semester. He replied: "Santayana I, Santayana II, and a seminar in Santayana III." The creative person, whether philosopher or artist, has a consistency of vision. This holds true for the film world as well. Many moviemakers both return to the same small group of themes time and again and express these in a similar manner. We can describe a typical Van Gogh, a Vermeer, a Miro, or a Winslow Homer. We can also speak of a typical Woody Allen movie, or a Wes Anderson, an Alexander Payne, or an M. Night Shyamalan film. It is not simply marketing that causes the producers to include in a movie's credits "A Peter Weir Film." There is in a Weir film a unique visual style and a worldview that is expressed in recurring themes. And people come to experience this as it is expressed afresh in each new film he makes.

When filming *One Flew over the Cuckoo's Nest* (1975), Milos Forman fired noted cinematographer Haskell Wexler, not because of his lack of competence, even brilliance, but because they were unable to come to a shared vision as to how the story should be portrayed on the screen. It was Forman's vision that needed to prevail. Though painful, such evaluation is necessary for a film's coherence. Lacking this, a movie often flounders, becoming a mere pastiche of competing interests. (Some believe that independent films, or at least, middle-sized movies put out by the specialty divisions of the major studios,[15] are often more successful today than major studio releases because there is less likelihood of the compromise of the creative process by competing interests and personalities.) Not all movies lend themselves to auteur analysis; the creative process is at times so collaborative and even chaotic, not to say corporate, that no clear artistic voice can be heard. But many films do. When the creative effort of a moviemaker is dominant, a recognition of the auteur allows new insight into the power and meaning of the movie itself.

David Bayles and Ted Orland, two working artists, have written a personal reflection on the perils and rewards of making art. Among their other observations is their belief in the constancy of interior issues for the artist: "We tell the stories we have to tell, stories of the things that draw us in—and why should any of us have more than a handful of those? The only work really worth doing—the only work you can do convincingly—is the work that focuses on the things you care about. To not focus on those issues is to deny the constants in your life."[16]

The validity of this neo-romantic notion has been argued over the centuries. Does the work of art express not only an outer surface but an inner emotion, one arising out of the soul of the artist? Michelangelo thought so, as did Wassily Kandinsky, who speaks of the capacity of the inner life of the artist to evoke a similar emotion in the observer: "The inner element, i.e., emotion, must exist," he argues, "otherwise the work of art is a sham. The inner element determines the form of the work of art."[17]

There are, of course, dangers in adopting auteur criticism. We can lose the uniqueness of an individual movie by submerging it in the whole corpus of a director's work; we can reduce film analysis to autobiography; and we can overlook individual brilliant movies that have no parallels in a director's other works. But used with a modicum of common sense, auteur criticism can help us uncover the full significance of an individual film. We can speak of a Bergman film or a Robert Rodriguez film. Charlie Chaplin, D. W. Griffith, Alfred Hitchcock, Akira Kurosawa, Stanley Kubrick, Spike Lee, Luis Buñuel, Steven Spielberg, Tom Tykwer, Robert Altman, Krzysztof Kieslowski, Gillian Armstrong, Terrence Malick, Abbas Kiarostami, Paul Thomas Anderson, Joel and Ethan Coen, Ang Lee, Mike Nichols, Wes Anderson, Pedro Almodóvar, Wim Wenders, David Lynch, Alexander Payne, Clint Eastwood, Hayao Miyazaki, Quentin Tarantino, Lars von Trier, Martin Scorsese—the list of directors with a body of work that invites analysis and intertextuality (a conversation between the movies, or "texts") is rich, even overwhelming. Some of these directors are cinematic multitaskers, not only directing but writing, and/or acting, composing, and editing as well. Robert Rodriguez (*Sin City* [2005], *Once Upon a Time in Mexico* [2003], *Spy Kids 1, 2, 3* [2001, 2002, 2003], *Desperado* [1995], and *El Mariachi* [1992]), for example, not only directs, but at times writes, produces, composes the score, works the camera, re-records the sound, supervises the visual effects, heads production design, edits, and has even supervised the special effects.

Most moviegoers can, for example, identify a typical Woody Allen movie with its thematic stress on the romantic, a large dose of skepticism, a slightly hopeful ending, a nostalgic look at the joys of family, and a repeated return to memories and to youth as holding sacramental meaning. Viewers can also note his self-deprecating humor, his use of film and music from the past, his sight gags, and his humor that does not mask an underlying sadness and tragedy. In fact, English professor Robert Polhemus teaches a Woody Allen course at Stanford University, much like courses he might teach on Jane Austen or Charles Dickens.

Just as there are internal criteria (what are the film's components) and external factors (what does its particular shape reveal about the cultural context in which it was produced) that genre critics consider when analyzing a film, so auteur criticism can have both an inner and an outer focus. On the one hand, it seeks to identify a consistent vision of reality expressed through similar themes and visual style across a range of the director's movies. Critics look for a personal signature attached to the movies themselves that extends across theme, cinematic style, structure, and even worldview—assumptions about the nature of life itself. On the other hand, auteur critics also explore the biographies of directors as well as their own interpretation and commentary on their work, in the hope of uncovering insight into the cultural and ideological context of the films. Movies reflect the social and personal histories of their makers. Some critics have wanted to deny such external referents as intrusive, wanting simply to stay inside the world of the movies themselves. But under pressure from marginalized groups (whether distinguished by race, gender, sexuality, or religion) to recognize their unique contributions within the industry, biography has been increasingly reinserted into the critical process.[18] Consider these examples:

Smoke Signals (1998)

The importance of the auteur's biography for an understanding of a movie can be seen in the movie *Smoke Signals*. Billed in the advertisements as the first feature movie written, directed, and acted entirely by Native Americans, the film's style and meaning are best understood in this light. Adapted from four short stories by Sherman Alexie out of his collection *The Lone Ranger and Tonto Fistfight in Heaven*, the film won two awards at Robert Redford's 1998 Sundance Film Festival. Interestingly, the writer Alexie is quoted as saying, "I love the way movies have more power than books. They continue the oral tradition [of our heritage], the way we all sit around the fire and listen to stories."[19] Chris Eyre, the director, has taken Alexie's short stories and with his help on the screenplay has captured this oral tradition well.

The film opens on the Fourth of July, 1976, the night Thomas Builds-the-Fire is orphaned. It tells the tale of two modern-day Coeur d'Alene Indians, Victor Joseph and Thomas Builds-the-Fire, who leave their Idaho reservation twenty years later to go by bus to retrieve the ashes of Victor's alcoholic father. Arnold Joseph has died in Arizona, years after abandoning his family, and forgiveness does not come easily. Victor is good-looking, self-righteous, and stoic. He has sealed himself off in anger since his father left him as an adolescent. Thomas—geeky, bookish, happy, and forever talkative—is the storyteller trying to understand his friend's pain (and perhaps his own). It is Arnold Joseph who binds these otherwise dissimilar twenty-year-olds together. Not only is he Victor's father, but he is also the one who saved the infant Thomas from a fatal house fire that orphaned him that July Fourth evening.

From such a skeletal plot description, we might presume the movie to be dark and sentimental; it is not. Humor abounds, and this humor is portrayed from a Native American perspective. The weather report on K-REZ always begins, "It's a good day to be indigenous," and its traffic report typically says, "One car went by earlier." Frustrated with Thomas's nonstop talking, Victor tells him to "Get stoic. Look like a warrior." In this movie, we see young Native Americans poking fun at themselves.

Smoke Signals is a "road picture" genre film whose structure needs only a "destination" to work. Otherwise, the story allows for freedom and improvisation along the way. The need to recover the father's ashes is the plot excuse for the bus trip to Arizona, but the real movement occurs as the two men discover life's meaning and possibilities through their growing friendship. Dialogue is the heart of the movie, but it is never preachy. The film uses humor and a fondness for Native American culture to help viewers better understand both today's Native Americans and themselves. Through the use of storytelling so typical of Native American culture, *Smoke Signals* weaves together fantasy and realism in a series of flashbacks and fast-forwards, often narrated by Thomas.

In the process not only are Thomas and Victor able to accept their past and present, but we as viewers are enabled to discover our stories as well.

The director, Chris Eyre, describes the movie as a "universal story about fathers and friends and forgiveness." He has used the tradition he knows best (Native American), but the movie is meant to transcend culture. Its final soliloquy is a moving poem by Dick Lorrie: "How do we forgive our fathers / Maybe in a dream. . . . Do we forgive our fathers in our age or theirs? Or in their deaths? Saying it to them or not saying it?" These are questions for any time or place.

Yet *Smoke Signals* is also a Native American movie. The life history of its collaborators, Chris Eyre and Sherman Alexie, is crucial to the film. *Smoke Signals* is more than just a metaphorical story with universal meaning. The movie is political despite itself; it is about getting to know the Native Americans in our midst. The filmmakers focus on contemporary Native American life—on living on the reservation and on questions of ethnic identity. In the typical Hollywood treatment of Native Americans, there is far too much nostalgia, and the stories are filtered through a white voice, Alexie believes. "We don't need to make another *Dances with Wolves*, because it's not an Indian movie," Eyre says.[20] Based on their own experiences as a Cheyenne-Arapaho (Eyre) and a Spokane-Coeur d'Alene (Alexie), these auteurs seek to break down preconceptions of who they are by showing viewers three typical ways that Native Americans have learned to cope with the largely indifferent if not hostile world around them—quiet anger, ingratiating storytelling, and alcohol. In *Smoke Signals* no answers are presented; the lives of Native Americans do not allow for this; but the viewer achieves insight nonetheless.

Biography is also important in a second way. Some have tried to interpret the movie through a Native American spirituality. But Alexie says that this is a stretch, for he grew up Catholic and went to Gonzaga, a Jesuit university. He says,

> I still am heavily Catholic—and Christian-influenced. I write about what I am, not what I want to be. A lot more [Native Americans] pretend to be more traditional and connected than they are. It's been fun to see people try to understand [the film] through Native American spirituality.[21]

Thus, it is not to Native American spirituality that critics should turn, but to biblical studies. The discussion of fry bread, for example, is rooted in the Christian story.[22] Thomas tells Victor that it is so good it is used for Communion. Victor's mom's fry bread "can walk across water. Fry bread rising from the dead." Thomas recalls how Victor's mom once had only fifty pieces of the fry bread for a feast where one hundred Native Americans came. He says she knew how to feed the one hundred, alluding, of course, to Jesus' miracle of the feeding of the five thousand. But humorously this time, the "miracle" happens through Arlene breaking each piece in half.

The Native Americans in this movie are "fish" people, not buffalo hunters, as Thomas reminds Victor, and the symbol of the fish appears several times in the movie, alluding to the Christian symbol as well. As the movie ends, Victor is tossing the ashes of his father into the Spokane River, where Thomas has told him they will "rise like a salmon. He'll rise." As Alexie says, "Salmon is very Jesus." Thus, though the interpretive context of the movie is Native American, the contemporary context of these particular Native Americans reflects also an assimilation of Christian beliefs, something typical of many reservations today. Again, we are a long way from Tonto (Spanish for "stupid") and the Lone Ranger in this Native American film.

Woody Allen

The movies of Woody Allen provide us a second example. They have often been analyzed in terms of his ethnicity. Lester Friedman, for example, sees Allen's Jewish characters as "bouncing from one trauma to the next with barely a moment to catch their breaths." They are "the schlemiel endlessly and vainly searching for love and respect."[23] While this is true, the Allen stamp on his films is evident in other ways as well. In particular, many of Woody Allen's movies have a common theme—that of the relationship between the "real" and the "reel"—between life and art, between fiction and reality. Complicating this theme are both Allen's own presence as an actor within his movies and the way in which Allen, the writer, deals on screen with issues that seem to parallel his own life and experience. This causes his movies often to be viewed autobiographically, the line blurring between his own life and the movies he directs.

Allen denies any direct parallel between his life and his art, even while continuing to invite such comparisons. What are we to make, for example, of the fact that many of Allen's movie characters seem fascinated with young girls (cf. *Crimes and Misdemeanors* [1989]), given his public affair and subsequent marriage to Mia Farrow's adopted, teenage daughter? Allen has said in an interview,

> Most people . . . can't understand an act of imagination. So every film I make, they feel is an autobiography. . . . They always think that my stories and ideas are based on reality. Therefore I have to explain to them, that *Annie Hall* wasn't, that *Manhattan* wasn't, that *Husbands and Wives* wasn't.[24]

But Allen encourages this confusion. Allen's movies cannot be reduced to autobiography, but a relationship between his art and his life is clearly present. At times his movies imitate life. At other times they provide a commentary on it. Perhaps they even presage it. It is from the stuff of his own life that his imaginative worlds are created.

To explore the common theme present in many of Allen's films, let's turn again to *Crimes and Misdemeanors* (1989), which portrays the constant interplay between reel life and real life. When Cliff is asked to make a documentary of the slick Lester, for example, he does so by comparing Lester first to Mussolini and then to a talking mule. Lester is understandably upset, saying, "The idea was to show the real me!" Yet the "real me" is in fact presented in the "reel" documentary. Lester is a womanizer, someone who can fire a writer with cancer because he is no longer funny; someone who is narcissistic and self-indulgent. Cliff's visual metaphors are closer to the truth, closer to reality than Lester knows. Reality is reel-ality—or is it?

Allen revels in blurring the lines. For example, he often has real-life figures make cameo appearances in his movies. In perhaps his most famous use of a person playing himself, he has Marshall McLuhan suddenly appear in *Annie Hall* (1977) from offscreen to silence an intellectual bore who is pontificating while in line at the movies. Or in *Broadway Danny Rose* (1984), the story is told by real-life, retired, stand-up comics sitting around a table at a New York deli. That they are telling the story of Danny adds both reality and unreality to the narrative, for their shaggy dog story might well say as much about them as about Danny.

Allen also uses edited photographic images to move back and forth between the reel and the real. In *Zelig* (1983), for example, Zelig/Allen is the son of a Yiddish actor who assumes the characteristics of whomever he meets, so much so that he is nicknamed "The Human Chameleon." As a baseball player he meets major sports heroes, and as a Nazi he distracts Hitler during a rally. Zelig hugs Josephine Baker and James Cagney, clowns with Jack Dempsey, and poses by the side of Calvin Coolidge. The scenes are shot in a pseudo-documentary style using old film clips so that the viewer actually suspends judgment and accepts that these are real events. To add to the ambiguity, we hear New York intellectuals and critics, such as Susan Sontag and Irving Howe, together with Saul Bellow and Bruno Bettelheim, discussing Zelig and his significance. They both provide possible interpretations of Zelig and warn us against overinterpretation. Is he the ultimate conformist? Zelig's existence, the narrator says in a voice-over, is "a non-existence. Devoid of personality, his human qualities long since lost in the shuffle of life, he sits alone quietly staring into space, a cipher, a non-person, a performing freak." Do we agree?

In *The Purple Rose of Cairo* (1985), Allen returns to this theme. But this time he uses the technique of a movie-within-a-movie. We see a character in the movie-within-a-movie, Tom Baxter, stepping off the screen in a theater in New Jersey and then competing with the actor who is playing the part, Gil Shepherd, for the affection of Cecilia. Here Allen is making explicit what all art points to—its role in entering into the very lives of its audience. Gil recognizes the absurdity of the situation and argues, "Tell him you can't love him. He's fictional! You want to waste your time with a fictional character? I mean, you're a sweet girl. You deserve an actual human." But Cecilia is addicted to the movies, in part because of the abusive life that she must endure in her marriage. She is addicted as well because "Tom's perfect!" She says, "I . . . I . . . I just met a wonderful new man. He's fictional, but you can't have everything." Here is her escape.

Ultimately, however, it is not perfection that Cecilia chooses, but real life. Or is it? She explains to Tom, "See, I'm a real person. No matter how . . . how tempted I am, I have to choose the real world." And so with Woody Allen's full irony, she chooses the real world . . . not of New Jersey and her abusive husband, but of Hollywood! When Gil says to her, "Come away with me to Hollywood!" she does. When her estranged husband finds out that she is leaving him to go to Hollywood, he yells, "Go, see what it is out there. It ain't the movies! It's real life! It's real life, and you'll be back!" For Monk, her husband, reality is the neighborhood in New Jersey and his wife, who is to serve him. There is reality and there is reel-ality. Which is preferable? We are left unsure. Even the photography itself reinforces the ambiguity of the choice, for the movie-within-a-movie—also called "The Purple Rose of Cairo"—is black and white, while the movie itself is in color.

In one of his short stories, "The Kugelmass Episode," Allen tells the story of a professor who loves *Madame Bovary* so much that he enters into Flaubert's novel.[25] Allen repeatedly retells classic stories in his films. We have "Oedipus Wrecks" from *New York Stories* (1989; cf. *Oedipus Rex*), *Crimes and Misdemeanors* (1989; cf. Dostoyevsky's *Crime and Punishment*), *Love and Death* (1975; cf. Tolstoy's *War and Peace*), *A Midsummer Night's Sex Comedy* (1982; cf. Shakespeare's *A Midsummer Night's Dream*). Again, we have portrayed the real and the reel. By replaying these old stories, by re-entering them (sometimes most literally), Allen provides himself the categories for both seeing and understanding life itself. But can we really replay these stories? In his movie *Play It Again, Sam* (1972), which takes its title from the movie *Casablanca*, Allen has Ilsa ask Rick to "play it," referring to the song "As Time Goes By." But of course time has gone by, and the words of the song become a contrast to the reality of the situation. We can't go back.

Thematic Criticism: Comparing Film and Other Texts

Michael Hauge defines a film's theme as "the universal statement the movie makes about the human condition . . . it applies to any individual in the audience." While a movie's plot provides the story line—what the movie is about—the theme gives viewers what the movie is "really about."[26] *Jaws* (1975) might be about stopping a shark, but what it is actually about is confronting our primal fears—what lurks underneath the surface of life that might harm or defeat us. Thirty years later, we still need only to hear several measures of the famous score for our hearts to beat faster. *I [Heart] Huckabees* (2004) presents the story of a young, idealistic environmentalist who tries to take on the head of a powerful chain of department stores where his girlfriend is the corporate model.

But this plot is given focus by the movie's theme—its critique of our superficial lifestyle that glosses over life, given its pain and contradictions. *Bruce Almighty* (2003) tells the story of a self-centered television news reporter who wants to be the local news anchor and blames God for not producing this miracle. But what the movie is really about is God's (Morgan Freeman) comment to Bruce (Jim Carrey), "You want to see a miracle, son? Be the miracle."

Film analysts speak about a movie's theme using a variety of terms—informing vision, the heart of the story, the executive principle, the moral premise, the emotional through line. Call it what you will, all effective stories have it. Jon Boorstin writes, "Movies can be made without themes. They're made all the time by producers who don't believe they need an emotional line to their film. They think a film can be about the greatest train robbery of all time or about saving the Super Bowl from terrorists. But I can't think of a movie that works that hasn't had a theme."[27] Boorstin illustrates his observation by considering the Western *The Magnificent Seven* (1960). The story needs to be about more than simply seven guys rescuing a town from bandits. Such a concept does not propel the action forward in a meaningful way. However, once the filmmaker decided that the movie was about bravery, then the process of constructing the film could proceed. The seven men then became different examples of bravery or cowardice. There is a cocky beginner who has never been tested; an old pro who is afraid he has lost his nerve; a strong, silent type; someone filled with his own importance; and so on. The gunfights become ways of testing these individuals, and the plot moves the characters toward their final confrontations. There is the same amount of action as in a cowboy movie lacking in theme, but now the audience is drawn into the story. We are not bored by the gunfights, for these confrontations reveal something of the nature of bravery, not only the characters', but ours as well.

The Interpreter (2005) tells the story of a white woman from Africa, Silvia Broome (Nicole Kidman), who is now a UN interpreter. She has accidentally overheard plans (in the African language of her homeland) for an assassination attempt on the president of her country, who will soon be speaking to the General Assembly. Once a revered freedom fighter, the president is now accused of genocide against his own people. The fictitious country, Matobo, has been drenched in the blood of many innocents, including Silvia's parents and sister, whose vehicle was blown up by a land mine. She has participated in the country's violent struggle for justice and freedom and has seen its failure. Now she says she fights only with the "power of words." But Secret Service agent Tobin Keller (Sean Penn) isn't convinced. Called in to protect the visiting leader and to investigate Silvia's claim, he wonders whether she is actually part of the plot to remove President Zuwanie. Tobin's perspective is equally ambiguous, however, for his vision is blurred by the recent death of his wife in a car accident involving a drunk driver. Tobin's grief and desire for revenge seem to be projected onto Silvia. And so the plot of this cerebral, political thriller unfolds.

What unifies the various plot strands and gives heart to the movie—what the movie is really about—can be summarized in a comment of Silvia to Tobin, "Vengeance is a lazy form of grief." Silvia has just told Tobin of a custom among the Ku people of her African homeland. When a killing has been committed and the perpetrator has been caught, she says that the family of the victim is allowed to mourn for a year, while the person is held in prison. When the year is up, the murderer is bound, sent on a boat to the middle of the river, and thrown in as the village and the family watch. It is up to the family to either save the person or let the killer drown. If the person drowns, it is said that the family has had vengeance but will grieve for the rest of their days. If the person is saved, the family will paradoxically be released from their lament. Here is the heart of the movie—vengeance or forgiveness?—not only for the Ku people, or even Silvia and Tobin, but for the viewer as well.

Jimmy Stewart, the actor, writes that he was often stopped on the street by people who would say to him, "You know, there was this movie you were in, I can't remember its name, but you're in the bar, and you're very depressed, and everything's been going wrong for you, and then you look up and start saying this little prayer. I'll always remember that." These short moments in a film are often simple, as in *The Interpreter*, but they are built on a bigger idea, or theme. Stewart references his own work in two of his best known movies, "in Frank Capra's *Mr. Smith Goes to Washington* [1939] . . . where the idea was that you were not born to be a failure. Or, in *It's a Wonderful Life* [1946], which shows that one man can make a difference." Stewart concludes:

> The fact that people remember these tiny moments, when they don't necessarily even remember the name of the picture or the plot, just shows that people remember the abstract idea (theme) through the human moment in film. They don't remember it abstractly, they remember it because it had some sort of emotional effect on them.[28]

These moments of insight—of grace—focus the story for the viewer and provide impetus for its narrative arc. I started this book with the scene from *Smoke* (1995) where Augie Wren (Harvey Keitel) shows Paul Benjamin (William Hurt) his photographs of the same street corner in New York City and tells Paul that if he doesn't slow down as he looks at the photographs, he won't get it. Here, again, in a short scene, the emotional heart of the movie is conveyed. Here is the perspective, the theme, from which the plot unfolds, from which the story is told.

Themes empower the story; they also help the moviemaker decide during editing what to include and what to leave out. Even if a scene works well, if it does not enhance the theme, it should end up on the cutting-room floor. It was Aristotle who suggested that the dramatist should say only what the story demands. Perhaps an action sequence will draw viewers into the theater, but it might also sidetrack the audience from the story. The successful movie will have all the characters facing the same struggle, albeit in different ways. Stan Williams gives the example of *American Beauty* (1999). In that movie, writes Williams, "all the characters are seeking to embrace a beauty that eludes them. And throughout *American Beauty* each of the characters make moral decisions that affect how they are able to perceive and experience that beauty."[29] It is not surprising, therefore, that the director chose to end this movie with Lester's revelation—his embrace of beauty—rather than finish the movie as the screenplay suggested, with the trial of Ricky and Jane. Though the scene was shot, it was left on the cutting-room floor, for it did not enhance or complete the theme.

Thematic criticism is practiced in a variety of academic and professional settings.[30] A growing number of psychologists, for example, use movies with human themes to help clients achieve personal insight into their own situations. Such movie therapy allows the therapist to ask patients about their emotional responses to what they saw. Did a patient see similarities to her own situation? Were the obstacles identical to his own? Are the strategies transferable?[31]

Recognizing the value of movies as a tool for self-awareness, Mary Ann Horenstein has, for example, co-authored *Reel Life/Real Life: A Video Guide for Personal Discovery* (1994). She writes that she realized the power of film to heal after her first husband died when she was just forty-one. When she went to see Jill Clayburgh in *An Unmarried Woman* (1978), she saw on the screen a woman who had gone through everything she was going through. She too was angry and hurt and refused even to speak to men at first. But Clayburgh's character, who had been married for sixteen years before her husband left her, gradually finds help in a support group and from a persistent suitor who is patient with her. From this personal beginning, Horenstein and her three co-authors expanded their list of movies that they believe say something meaningful about a topic to over seven hundred films. Each movie teaches us something about ourselves and the world in which we live. These movies are reviewed and grouped into chapters that address specific topics or interest areas. "Substance abuse," for example, has a list of thirty-four films that are reviewed. Some of the chapters deal more with topics (e.g., "Feisty Women") than with themes, but the intention of the book is clear. Basic to the design of the book is the belief that "a viewer can watch an individual face a similar life situation and vicariously live that experience, with all the attendant emotions."[32]

It is thematic criticism that the church has used most often. Roger Kahle and Robert Lee's *Popcorn and Parable* (1971), for example, grouped movies according to nine theological topics: relationships, faith, reverence for life, sin, evil, freedom of man, nature of life, alienation, and celebration.

A more recent volume by Sara Anson Vaux, *Finding Meaning at the Movies* (1999), concentrates on nineteen movies, organizing them according to their most prominent theological themes—alienation, integrity, authenticity, home, vocation, purity of heart, celebration, and healing. She sees each film as being a deliberate attempt "to communicate a concept of a moral universe—a sense of order and meaning that affects the ways we live on and with our earth; a search to determine right or wrong behavior; and a grasp of how we should behave toward one another."[33] Each film takes its life from its search for a deeper meaning lying behind life's events and encounters. By concentrating on a movie's theme, Vaux believes the viewer can connect with its creator's purpose and organize the complex perceptions a movie provokes.

Other recent books in theology and film that take a similar thematic approach include Tim Cawkwell's *The Filmgoer's Guide to God* (2004), Gareth Higgins's *How Movies Helped Save My Soul* (2003), Bryan Stone's *Faith and Film: Theological Themes at the Cinema* (2000), and my own *Useless Beauty: Ecclesiastes through the Lens of Contemporary Film* (2004). Even when other forms of movie criticism are used by theological critics, thematic criticism often remains central. The excellent collection of essays titled *Explorations in Theology and Film* (1997), edited by Gaye Ortiz and Clive Marsh, addresses several theological themes and suggests the intertextual methodology of the book: mutuality, salvation, Christology, violence, liberation, Jesus, the human condition, spirituality, grace, and hope.

Thematic criticism refers to the content of the movie. Its focus is on the movie itself, rather than on the moviemaker, the audience, or the embedded worldview. The critic looks for a movie's theme and then compares it with how a similar theme plays out in another text. Most often that companion text is another movie, but once we decide that intertextual dialogue has meaning, there is no reason that a film might not also be compared to a philosophical essay, a biblical text, or perhaps, the novel or play from which the movie was adapted.

One Flew over the Cuckoo's Nest (1975)

One Flew over the Cuckoo's Nest (1975), Milos Forman's Academy Award–winning movie, is based on the novel of the same name by Ken Kesey. In both the movie and the novel, the story's theme has to do with individual freedom over against institutional control. Kesey's cult classic tells a mythic tale through the voice of a huge Native American. Big Chief is a schizophrenic who goes in and out of the fog and whose vitality has been reduced to impotence. The reliability of his narration is, thus, left in doubt through most of the novel. It is not until he is challenged and cajoled into wholeness by Randall McMurphy that the fog lifts. McMurphy is portrayed as a TV cowboy, someone larger than life who wears boxer shorts with white whales on them. The narrative has a mythic shape as the garden is contrasted with the machine, freedom with order, masculinity with maternal dominance, individuality with community. Nurse Ratched, who runs the ward, is both controlling and controlled. When her femininity is literally exposed at the end of the novel, she is shown to be the woman that she is. Similarly, McMurphy's sacrificial death on behalf of the self-referrals in the mental asylum is told as a secularized Christ-story in which McMurphy offers his life so that the men on the ward might live. Kesey wants his readers to take control of their lives, to tell their own story. The message is that we cannot let the "Combine" control our lives.

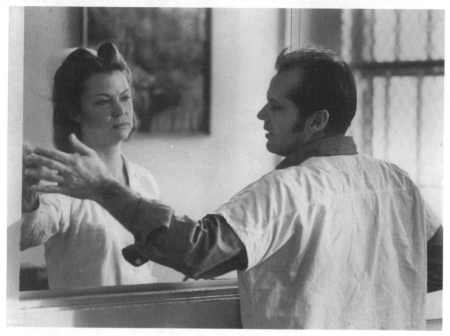

Randall McMurphy (Jack Nicholson) challenges Nurse Ratched's (Louise Fletcher) control of a ward of the mental hospital. *One Flew over the Cuckoo's Nest* (d. Forman, 1975). ©1975 Fantasy Films and United Artists. All rights reserved.

Milos Forman's film adaptation has much in common with the novel. In both we see the mythic struggle between Randall Patrick McMurphy and Nurse Ratched, a struggle between masculine freedom and maternal power. While the opening credits roll, we are given through music and image the fundamental metaphor that will unite the film. We hear the simple music of the Native American culture as images of nature move across the screen. Then we enter into the highly artificial environs of the mental hospital, where baroque music is playing in the background to help keep the inmates calm. The struggle will be between garden and machine, the natural and the artificial, the simple and the ornate. The oppressive structures of the hospital establishment are much like the "Combine" that Kesey describes. It thrashes the men it controls. Into this world McMurphy inserts himself, and by the movie's end, the result is the liberation of "Big Chief" Bromden, a Native American healed in spirit and emboldened bodily through the antics and friendship of McMurphy. Bromden has the courage to break free as he throws a water fountain through the window and escapes into the night.

In telling his story, Forman discards the surrealistic for the real, the mythic for the political. The narrator is no longer the "crazy" Native American. Rather it is now the system itself that is judged insane as the realistic story unfolds. And McMurphy is no longer a mythic cowboy figure and certainly not a very developed Christ-figure. Rather he is a con man who nevertheless comes to care about those in the ward with him and chooses to stand up to the evil system as incarnate in Nurse Ratched. As in other Forman movies, this all too human hero dies for his efforts. (Cf. Coalhouse Walker in *Ragtime* [1981]; Mozart in *Amadeus* [1984]; and Berger in *Hair* [1979]. In *The People vs. Larry Flynt* (1996), Flynt does not die but is paralyzed.) But rather than his death being the salvation of all fifteen of the "self-referrals" as in the novel, only Big Chief leaves. The movie ends with the system of the hospital reasserting its control over the others. It is only Big Chief who takes his destiny into his own hands.

For Forman, the head nurse is not to be considered as evil herself. She believes that what she is doing is in the best interests of her patients. That is what makes her character so chilling. In an interview, Forman has said,

> I have never met anyone who walked up to me and said, "Watch out. I'm a very bad person. . . ." So [in making this film], I start with the assumption that everyone is good and then say, "Ok, now let's watch everybody." When the film is over, the audience can judge who was right and who was wrong. Nixon, Stalin—I'm sure these men were convinced that they were doing the best from all points of view, including the moral point of view, and that is always the main subject of art.
>
> For instance Nurse Ratched. She believes deeply that she is doing right. And that is where the real drama begins for me. That's much more frightening than if you have an evil person who knows he's doing wrong.[34]

Though Forman has called the movie a political film about America, few will fail to see it also as a Czechoslovakian critique of Stalin. Forman, a Czech who began his film career in his homeland, has captured well the horror of a system that hides its conforming power under the guise of concern for the well-being of others. Perhaps Forman would respond that though his life story has sensitized him to the issue in unique ways, it is fanaticism and conformity in any guise that is his enemy. As he commented in his memoirs:

> We invent institutions to help make the world more just, more rational. Life in society would not be possible without orphanages, schools, courts, government offices, and mental hospitals, yet no sooner do they spring into being than they start to control us, regiment us, run our lives. They encourage dependency to perpetuate themselves and are threatened by strong personalities.[35]

It is the hospital system that ultimately is responsible for McMurphy's death. The rebel has no place. Institutionalism and conformism are continuing threats. Here is the theme that drives the movie forward.

Chasing the Sacred

The City of Angels Film Festival in Hollywood organizes its retrospective screenings of significant films around yearly themes. In 1998, the theme was "Chasing the Sacred." Among the films screened were *Jesus of Montreal* (1989) and *The Apostle* (1997). On the surface these were very different movies. One was set in a large Canadian city in the North; the other in the rural South. The one dealt with a particular religious subculture, the Pentecostal church; the other looked at a secularized society in which religious values and beliefs had become largely irrelevant. Both dealt with the formation of a community, although the one was ecclesial while the other was artistic. But beneath the narrative differences there exists in these two films a common thematic concern, the mystery of vocation.

In *Jesus of Montreal*, Daniel Coulombe is hired by the priest of a local shrine to update the text of a passion play that is presented each summer in its gardens and then to produce it. Given a job to do, Daniel hires four actors who are called out from other professions, researches the historical Jesus, and then rewrites the story. He finally produces a new passion play emphasizing a very human Jesus. But Daniel's job becomes a vocation, as he lives into his role. The very events of his life become a mirror image of the Christ-figure he plays. He is forced to oppose the religious authorities at the shrine, for example. Reacting to the sexist abuse that Mireille (Mary) must endure during an audition for an advertisement, Daniel also overturns the tables of equipment in the studio temple. Having captured the attention of the city with his performance, he is taken by a media lawyer (Satan) up to the top of a tall skyscraper and tempted with an alternate career. "This city is yours, if you want it." After a final supper of wine and pizza (bread), the actors put on their last performance. When the authorities try to close down the play, there is a scuffle; and in the free-for-all, the cross on which Daniel is hanging as he portrays Jesus is knocked over, and Daniel's head is crushed. After his death, his organs are transplanted in order that others might live, and a theater is established in his memory. Daniel has lived into his calling to be like Christ. And as a result the lives of his "disciples" (the four actors who are part of his ensemble) are transformed. Montreal is in need of spiritual renewal; its worship of mammon has proven destructive to the human spirit. Not all respond to the "savior" who arrives, but for those who do, there is hope and newness of life.

The Apostle tells a similar tale of vocation, of someone called to be an unlikely savior. From the opening sequences of the movie where we first see a boy evangelist of twelve and then follow him into adulthood as he stops his car at a roadside crash to witness to a couple of teenagers who are dying, Sonny knows he is called to preach. His license plate—SONNY—and his white suit suggest, however, something of his personal vanity in being God's chosen servant. It is only after his temper has caused him to kill his wife's lover with the swing of a baseball bat that his calling takes on fresh meaning. Now he must flee town. Baptizing himself the "Apostle E. F.," the old Sonny seeks to live into his calling as a chastened man. His transformation is not immediate; he continues to flirt with women, and he fights with a heavy-equipment operator who tries to interfere with his new church. But E. F. knows he "has done a lot more zigging than zagging" and is repentant. By the end of the film, he has confessed his past to his co-pastor, is giving baskets of food to the poor anonymously, has turned from his womanizing, and is peaceful when the cops finally arrive to arrest him. Not only does Sammy, the mechanic with whom he is living, come to faith through his witness, but as the credits roll, we see E. F. on a prison work detail by the side of the road, witnessing again to his fellow inmates. He is at peace with his calling.

Sonny (Robert Duvall) knows he is called to preach. *The Apostle* (d. Duvall, 1997). Photo by Van Redin.

These two movies invite dialogue and comparison. Both have as their theme the "redemption" of a person as that individual lives into his calling. E. F. is baptized "the Apostle" and he proves to be just that; Daniel, like his apocalyptic prophet namesake, preaches a message of judgment to his society, as he too lives into his role as the Christ. The salvation that both preach, moreover, is social in character. The needy are given food, whether through soup kitchens or Thanksgiving baskets. The emerging church must function outside the normal religious circles—their leaders having been kicked out of the established church. Yet Daniel's and E. F.'s testimony and life-witness produce disciples, and new faith and life are the result. Throughout the process of their growth into wholeness, there is an incarnational mystery about these leaders. It is almost as if the "hound of heaven" is chasing them. They might have "sought the Lord, but afterward they knew, they were found by thee." Such is the nature of "vocation."

Cultural Criticism: Focusing on a Movie's Social Context

Movies help shape their audience's view of reality. Why else would advertisers continue to buy time on television? By offering viewers a slant on life, they both reflect the reality of an age and help define it. Because movies provide such a powerful representation of reality, their effect on the audience is profound (whether it eventuates in demonstrable change or not). It is also true that people see film differently depending on what they bring to the experience. Gender, education, age, race, and social location all matter. So does the composition of the audience in which we view a movie. Moviegoing is, after all, a community event.

No one today disputes that a movie's story has a powerful impact on its audience. On complex issues, however, it is difficult to isolate the influences. Take, for example, the shooting rampage at Columbine High School in Littleton, Colorado, in 1999. Soon after the killings, John Broder and Katharine Seelye reported on a meeting President Clinton convened in Washington to study the growing problem of teen rage. Gathered at the White House were entertainment executives, representatives of hunting groups and gun manufacturers, clergy, educational officials, nonprofit organizational leaders, law-enforcement officials, and students. Broder and Seelye began their article by saying, "When violence strikes yet again in the school yard, Washington's search for villains is never far behind. Democrats tend to finger guns and their powerful lobby, the National Rifle Association. Republicans are more inclined to blame Hollywood and the glorification of natural born killers in movies, music and video."[36] In reality, it is both of these and more, for the cultural messages about violence are mixed. Though most would decry violence on the streets, there is a continuing openness to certain stories where violence is central, particularly when it is shown in a larger context or given a comic-book veneer as in many action movies. Consider the popularity of wrestling on television, for example, or the success of the movie *Sin City* (2005). *The Matrix* (1999), an action movie filled with violence but clever in its visuals and thoughtful as a cyber-thriller story, made $171 million at the domestic box office soon after the Columbine shootings. *Three Kings* (1999), a movie rooted in the violence of the Gulf War, nevertheless showed the consequence of violence, and escaped strong censure. So too did the graphic violence of the electrocution scene in *The Green Mile* (1999), where violence is implicitly critiqued.

Fight Club (1999), however, even with the drawing power of Brad Pitt, suffered from its release date being too close to Columbine. Despite massive publicity, it could not transcend its violent premise and graphic visuals, and viewers stayed away.[37] Its box-office take was less than $40 million, though the movie has now achieved cult status as speaking for an entire generation in their twenties and thirties. Its biting sarcasm and ferocious energy expose the spiritual bankruptcy of a consumer society bent on happiness to a degree that has rendered many of an older generation sterile. It is a powerful film. But initially people stayed away. For a season, people wanted violence to be toned down. Full-page newspaper ads were taken out, and some studios seemed to heed the calls for voluntary restraint. Amy Wallace reported in the *Los Angeles Times* that Disney would no longer use guns in movie ads. Warner Brothers eliminated all gunplay from the trailers of *The Matrix* (1999) for its international release. And early drafts of *Big Momma's House* (2000), starring Martin Lawrence, were altered to get rid of a violent motorcycle chase that was to open the movie. The producer, David Friendly, said, "We talked about it, post-Columbine, and decided the scene was inappropriate to the movie and inappropriate for the time. We said, 'This movie doesn't need it, we don't want it, let's take it out.' And it cost too much, anyway."[38]

However, with time, memory fades. It was not long before violence was again a staple in many films. Perhaps the most notable was Quentin Tarantino's *Kill Bill: Vol. 1* and *Vol. 2* (2003, 2004). The first part of this single story opened at number 1 the weekend after "the Terminator," Arnold Schwarzenegger, was elected governor of California. *Vol. 1* is the extended setup, telling the tale of a nameless bride (Uma Thurman) who is a member of a female-focused assassin squad. The Bride quits the squad in order to give her unborn child a new life, only to have Bill (David Carradine) and his team of killers seek her out. At the Bride's wedding, Bill and his henchmen kill her fiancé, friends, and pastor and leave her for dead. When she awakens from a coma several years later, the Bride is consumed by the need for revenge—otherwise the world is without morality—and she goes on a murderous, blood-letting quest, hunting down each of the killers. There is little emotional connection in *Vol. 1*, just blood lust, though the choreography, photography, and music are stunning. *Vol. 2* completes the story of the Bride's rampage of vengeance, providing more heart and dialogue in the process. We learn more of the backstory, the pace slackens somewhat, and viewers are given more dialogue and the chance to connect with the determination of the hero.

Inspired by comic books, gangster and slasher movies, Chinese kung-fu movies, Japanese anime, and European spaghetti Westerns, the fountains of blood and severed parts are not to be taken seriously. There is a certain tongue-in-cheek quality to the choreographed combat scenes, more style than substance. The hyperviolence is filmed masterfully, with music and image fused brilliantly in clever pastiche. Seen as such, the movie is Tarantino's homage to the movies of his youth. We can also argue that the movie is, in a sense, a morality play—like a Batman or Spider-Man story. The Bride must focus single-mindedly on stopping Bill both to reestablish the viewers' sense of good over evil and to allow her to leave crime behind and live a new life apart from carnage. But though the movie might embody the biblical theme of an eye for an eye, and its story is about someone trying to leave behind her life as an assassin, its primal suffering, unrelenting violence, blood spurting, carnage, and sadism is nonetheless shocking, as well as troubling ethically—something reviewers all too often ignored, given its visual brilliance. How should we respond to the "vigilante" character of the Bride's revenge? "Vengeance is mine, saith the Lord," has been reduced to "vengeance is mine." We seem as a culture to be accepting the role of morality's guardian, whatever the price, and whatever the carnage. We are being told both in movies like *Kill Bill* and in newspapers by our politicians that freedom is worth the price, and for a season, our culture seemed to collectively agree.

Certainly 9/11 was an unconscious contributor to our fascination with violence. Cultural commentators note that although 9/11 did not fundamentally change American attitudes or practices (despite some early rhetoric), it did strengthen certain cultural attitudes that were already present or developing. A growing sense of resentment toward the social changes that were taking place had already found its way onto the screen in movies like *As Good as It Gets* (1997), *Fight Club* (1999), *American Beauty* (1999), and *Magnolia* (1999). But a heightening of this attitude found expression by 2003 in a spate of movies—*Mystic River*, *House of Sand and Fog*, *Anger Management*, *Anything Else*, *The Hulk*, *28 Days Later*, *The Human Stain*, *The Barbarian Invasions*, *Runaway Jury*, *Monster*, *21 Grams*. All had characters consumed by their resentments toward others and toward life, and many found violence a solution. Again, our belief that war or combat might prove a final solution, however horrible, had already made its way to the screen in movies like *Saving Private Ryan* (1998). But war as an answer to our present problems not only played out on the sand of Iraq; it was also given added currency through movies like *Cold Mountain* (2003), *The Last Samurai* (2003), *Master and Commander: The Far Side of the World* (2003), and even *Lord of the Rings: The Return of the King* (2003).

Similarly, though amnesia was a theme beginning to be explored in movies like Christopher Nolan's *Memento* (2000) and David Lynch's *Mulholland Drive* (2001), many more such movies were to follow 9/11—*The Man without a Past* (2002), *The Bourne Identity* (2002), *Finding Nemo* (2003), *The Bourne Supremacy* (2004), *Gothika* (2003), *Paycheck* (2003), *The Notebook* (2004), *Eternal Sunshine of the Spotless Mind* (2004), *Vanilla Sky* (2001), *50 First Dates* (2004), the remake of *The Manchurian Candidate* (2004). While the initial fascination with memory loss may have been triggered by a vague sense that something was missing in our constructed lives and we should just begin again (that, like a video game, everyone deserves a second chance, or like a computer, perhaps our hard drive can be wiped clean), surely the desire to escape, to wipe the slate clean and begin again, resonated in new ways with many who found the terror and anxiety of contemporary life following 9/11 to be without answers. In each of these examples—rage, war, amnesia—the current cultural context contributed to the positive reception of these movies by giving urgency and power to their stories. A film is only successful if it finds an audience with whom it resonates.

Cultural criticism looks at film in terms of its social and psychological contexts. It studies the life cycle of a film from production to distribution to reception. With regard to a movie's reception, for example, it desires to know what effect a movie has on its viewers, its impact on their attitude, emotions, or behavior. It also considers how the viewers' social situations or competencies influence their experience of a movie. This process can be illustrated with reference to the Japanese movie *Shall We Dance?* (1996). I saw the movie twice—once in a largely Anglo audience and once with a predominantly Asian audience. The difference was startling. While Anglos enjoyed the simple yet elegant parable of a decent, hardworking middle manager in a Japanese company who discovers a new joie de vivre through ballroom dancing, the Japanese American audience laughed uproariously through much of the movie at the incongruity of such a situation. It was almost inconceivable to them. For the Anglo audience, the opening subtitles told us that in Japan ballroom dancing is regarded with great suspicion and dancing before others is embarrassing. But for the Japanese audience, such instruction was unnecessary. They knew this existentially, and their knowledge added greatly to the enjoyment of the movie.

Although there is an increase in "niche" marketing of movies—for women, for African Americans, for families—most movies are still made for the majority population. After all, the purpose of the movie industry is to make money. It is perhaps not surprising, then, that many movies stereotype various minority groups. The results, however explainable, are unfortunate. Cultural criticism studies these effects on the population. To give but one example, Native Americans have been subject to consistent caricature in the movies. *Smoke Signals* is the rare exception. More typical is a film like John Ford's *The Searchers* (1956), which presents Native Americans as brutal killers, perhaps even subhuman. They are portrayed as deserving all the vengeance that Ethan Edwards (John Wayne) can muster. In the film, Edwards even shoots out the eyes of a dead Comanche in order to prevent him from entering his spirit world.

As part Cherokee, I never wanted to play "cowboys and Indians" when I was a child, because I knew from television and the movies what my role was supposed to be. A leading newsman in my youth, Edward R. Murrow, in a speech to the Radio and Television News Directors' Convention, expressed my frustration well:

If there were to be a competition in indifference or perhaps in insulation from reality, then Nero and his fiddle, Chamberlain and his umbrella, could not find a place on an early afternoon sustaining show. If Hollywood were to run out of Indians, the program schedules would be mangled beyond all recognition. Then some courageous soul with a small budget might be able to do a documentary telling what, in fact, we have done and are still doing to the Indians in this country. But that would be unpleasant. And we must at all costs shield the sensitive citizens from anything that is unpleasant.[39]

Feminist criticism has grown up around a similar awareness with regard to how women are portrayed in the movies. Laura Mulvey, in one of the most frequently reprinted essays in film criticism, argues that a person's pleasure at the movies is related to issues of gender. In particular, the viewer's gaze (like the camera's) is fixed on the female characters as a male might watch the action, since males often dictate the choices of moviegoers. While the male star is an object of identification for the audience, the female star is most often defined as a passive sexual spectacle.[40]

How spectators view movies might be more complex than Mulvey's 1975 study indicated. It is possible, for example, to bring an oppositional gaze to the cinema, something the African American critic bell hooks has pointed out insightfully.[41] But Mulvey was certainly right to identify gender representations as a problem in Hollywood. I heard a leading director speak of his current movie that once again romantically linked an older man with a younger woman. When asked why he was interested in making movies that elevated the human spirit and yet continued to treat women as sexual objects who could be discarded as they grew older, his only response was to say that this was the industry norm. He felt he could do certain things to challenge the studios, but this was one area he felt he was helpless to fix. (And this from a director who had grossed over one billion dollars on his last four films!)

Working Girl (1988)

The movie *Working Girl* provides an instructive example of cultural criticism. It tells the story of Tess McGill (Melanie Griffith), a secretary on Wall Street who longs to move up the ladder. Smart and ambitious, she has gone to night school. However, it is not only her brains but also her chutzpah and down-to-earth sensuality that allow Tess to escape her Staten Island digs. Afraid she is stuck at the bottom of the ladder, she gets her break (so to speak!) when her boss is laid up out of town with a broken leg. Asked to watch over her apartment, Tess discovers that her boss (played wonderfully by Sigourney Weaver) has stolen her idea for a proposal to one of their major clients. Furious, Tess takes over for her boss, even wearing her dresses and ultimately stealing her boyfriend. She crashes a wedding reception in order to pitch her idea to the client and succeeds in getting a hearing. When her boss storms into a subsequent meeting claiming the idea was hers, Tess is rescued by Jack Trainer (Harrison Ford), the boyfriend. Everyone realizes it was Tess's original idea; she is hired by the executive she has helped; and as the movie ends, Tess is set up in her own executive office.

When it was first shown in the late 1980s, the movie was meant to be a progressive portrayal of women in the workplace. When Tess is asked by her new secretary what is expected of her, she responds, "I expect you to call me Tess. I don't expect you to fetch me coffee unless you're getting some for yourself. And . . . the rest we'll just make up as we go along." But today many students in my classes find the movie's depictions stereotypical and demeaning to women. The egalitarian ending seems like sugarcoating on a movie that stereotypes gender and class.

Why is it, some ask, that Melanie Griffith must appear partly undressed (she is described as having "a mind for business and a bod for sin")? Why is it that the only way portrayed for a woman to compete in a man's world is to become a masculine shrew or an immoral seductress? And why must Tess become a damsel in distress, rescued in the end by Jack Trainer (note his last name)? Is this movie little more than a throwback to the 1940s secretary movies where a stenographer takes off her glasses, lets down her hair, and gets her man? The newspaper ads for the movie, for example, showed Melanie Griffith peeking out coyly from behind Harrison Ford and Sigourney Weaver. Perhaps nothing more needs to be said than to note the double entendre of the movie's title, *Working Girl*.

As one critic noted, we have in this movie a film of the Reagan-Bush era where there is a kinder "inside trading" and a gentler sexual discrimination. Many of my students would agree. Rather than a thoughtful treatment of women's rights, we are given a "Cinderella," rags-to-riches story in which the heroine uses deceit and seduction to accomplish her goals. Here is hardly a model for the career woman of the new millennium.

Mike Nichols, the director, has made a career of being sensitive to audience attitudes and changing mores. His *The Graduate* (1967) spoke for a generation. *Catch-22* (1970) and *Silkwood* (1983) were also strongly influenced by their cultural context as they sought to give expression to the hopes and fears of the audience. With *Working Girl* (1988), Nichols captured something of the 1980s with its crass materialism, its increasing class differentiation, and its continuing chauvinism. His yuppie fable of the American dream has the feel of the Reagan era. The goal is for the rich to get richer; and, if others must be left behind, it is because some are more deserving. And it is okay to bend the rules and use your feminine wiles; sometimes nothing else will work. Many viewers at the time found such depictions acceptable. The 1990s would prove to have their own ethical challenges, but they would not be framed in the same way.

Nichols's gender and class stereotypes are, in part, a product of his casting the story as a "Cinderella" fable, but whereas his reinforcement of materialistic and sexist attitudes still worked in the 1980s (the movie was very successful), they seem dated—if not demeaning—to many today. The culture has not necessarily improved, but it has moved on.

Genre criticism, auteur criticism, thematic criticism, cultural criticism—the toolbox that movie critics have at their disposal is varied and rich. Used alone, such criticism can deceive the viewer. Auteur criticism, for example, when done in romantic isolation can falsely minimize any social determinates, positing an objectivity that is ill-founded. We have seen this in our discussion of the growing effect of violence on our culture. But cultural criticism, similarly, when used too exclusively, can reduce a person's response to a movie to sociology. But together, such approaches help us unpack a movie's power and meaning and prepare the way for honest and constructive theological criticism. Film criticism, then, is the first step toward a total criticism. It is to this completing task that we now turn in the next two chapters.

9

responding to film ethically: moving beyond the rating system

Harvard theologian Harvey Cox has been one of America's most astute observers of faith and culture for over forty years. His most recent best-seller, *When Jesus Came to Harvard: Making Moral Choices Today* (2004), was developed out of a wildly popular course on "Jesus and the Moral Life," which he has taught to Harvard undergraduates for the last twenty years. As in his other books, Cox has again given voice to emerging religious trends in our culture, this time by focusing on the importance of stories in fostering our ethical discourse. The course uses events from the life and the teaching (the parables) of Jesus to encourage discussion of the moral life. Cox has discovered that while students today are repelled by moral self-righteousness, they also sense, "however vaguely, that there [is] something fundamentally inadequate about moral relativism."[1] Though they have trouble speaking coherently about their moral beliefs, such beliefs are not absent.

Cox recognized early in his teaching of the class that stories helped people of all faiths to "locate a common vocabulary." They were important, because they "speak to the inner spirit. They link the moral reasoning we do in our heads to the courage and empathy that must come from the heart." Cox's course began with religious stories and sought to recover the link between the rabbinic storyteller (Jesus), on the one hand, and our human imagination, our stories, on the other. Here, he discovered, was a way to "jog the slumbering imagination

217

of our times."[2] In a decade of teaching courses in theology and film, I have started the conversation between our stories and the Christian story from the other direction—not from a reading of Jesus' parables, but from a viewing of the "reel spirituality" of those stories we experience in the cineplex. In both cases, however, the goal has been similar—a robust two-way dialogue between our stories and the larger stories of our religious traditions that will issue forth in a deepened faith and a renewed action.

For those interested in the moral discourse that can, and indeed should, issue forth from moviegoing, a chief impediment to using film to locate a common vocabulary is, ironically, the "ethical" watchdog system the industry itself created. The problems related to the Rating Board of the Motion Picture Association of America (MPAA) are well documented. But before moving on to consider what might constitute a robust moral dialogue, it will be helpful to address first the false assumption that a movie's moral perspective can be linked to the rating it receives from the Motion Picture Association of America or, in an earlier era, the Legion of Decency.

Over-Rated!

Since the sixties, the Motion Picture Association of America's rating system has been regarded as the moral watchdog for the industry. Every movie advertisement carries with it a rating that prospective viewers see, helping them to make their selections as to what is appropriate for them to watch. Increasingly, however, the MPAA's rating system has come under attack, and not just by religious leaders. *Los Angeles Times* film critic Kenneth Turan concludes that "no one who has taken the trouble to look closely respects the system anymore."[3] For those like movie critic Roger Ebert, the system seems "hypocritical and broken down." Ebert judges former MPAA president Jack Valenti (in his eighties, he has recently been replaced by Dan Glickman), who administered the system through 2004, to be lacking "the slightest understanding of film as an art form." And there seems justification for this charge. Valenti, in explaining the ratings, stated:

> The criteria that go into the mix which becomes a Rating Board judgment are theme, violence, language, nudity, sensuality, drug abuse, and other elements. . . . The Rating Board can make its decisions only by what is seen on the screen, not by what is imagined or thought.[4]

It is not the movie's meaning as communicated to the viewer, in other words, but only the "raw" data that is judged by the Rating Board. Of course by this criterion, unaccompanied teenagers would be banned by the MPAA from viewing much of the Bible if it were translated to the screen, for its stories depict, among other things, graphic sexuality (Song of Songs); adultery and voyeurism (2 Sam. 11); a disgusting murder (Judg. 3); cannibalism (2 Kings 6); ritual dismemberment (Judg. 19); the collection of one hundred foreskins (1 Sam. 18); incest (Gen. 19); rape (2 Sam. 13); and so on.[5] That the Jewish and Christian scriptures put this "raw" data within a larger moral and religious framework would not be taken into account by the Board, or so it would seem.[6]

The ratings issue is complex. Children and their parents need to be given trustworthy guidance as to a film's content, as newspapers and websites alike are increasingly recognizing. With special effects technology now making on-screen violence (un)believably graphic and the spending power of teenagers encouraging the ongoing production of sexually titillating, teen-oriented fluff, parents need help in identifying what is appropriate for their children. At the same time, a filmmaker's freedom to create needs to be preserved, not to mention the need for a movie's story to be received and judged according to its intended meaning, rather than the film being reduced to how many breasts are bared, bloody scenes portrayed, or four-letter words uttered. Unfortunately, the current system appears to be failing on all counts. It seems no longer able to discriminate effectively beyond the somewhat obvious delineation of movies appropriate for children in the younger grades of elementary school (G) and movies that are inappropriate for them (R). At the same time, the system is unable to allow full artistic freedom to those filmmakers wanting to create a truly adult movie without having the prurient label NC-17 attached.[7]

Most agree, however, that the current standard for judging the appropriateness of a movie, which uses the literal depiction of graphic detail as its primary criterion without considering the larger story line and the imagined response of the viewer, has produced both inanity and arbitrariness in the rating system's judgments. Thus, *American Pie* (1999; whose sophomoric yet explicit raunch is intended for teenagers) and *Election* (1999; Alexander Payne's dramatic comedy, based in an Omaha high school, with far less raunch, but whose audience is intended to be adults as well as teenagers), *Calendar Girls* (2003; where Helen Mirren and Julie Walters are middle-aged garden-club members who pose discreetly, but partially nude, for a fund-raising calendar to aid a cancer clinic), and the adult-themed drama *The Cooler* (2003; a hard-edged but authentic love story in which an older William Macy and a younger Maria Bello have an extended nude love scene) are all rated R despite their obvious differences. It is a "one size fits all" system.

The Cooler provides a particularly interesting example of the ratings problem, for though the movie deserves under the present system its R rating given the graphic nature of its depictions of both sexuality and violence, the story is moral in its overall depiction. (It is not like a DeMille epic with an ethical gloss over an amoral focus.) But *The Cooler*'s sexuality is so frank that the movie was judged initially to warrant an NC-17 rating, before cuts were made to keep it from being marginalized at the box office. On the other hand, the brutal violence of other scenes in the movie was completely overlooked by the American-based ratings board (including one sequence in which the casino head takes a tire iron to someone found cheating at the craps table). In Europe and Canada, the sexuality in the movie would most likely not have been commented on, while the violence would have been questioned, if not censored.[8]

A recent study by *Money Magazine* concerning movies that broke even financially in the United States discovered that whereas 59.4 percent of all movies released broke even, only 58 percent of movies with sex turned some profit, while 76.5 percent of movies with extreme violence proved profitable. The data with regard to how the viewing public responds to sex and violence differ depending on what country is under consideration. In the United States, sex is a more questionable depiction than violence both for the Rating Board and, it would seem, for audiences. Geography is, thus, one qualifier to using the ratings system to assist viewers in ethical decision making. What is deemed ethically questionable simply varies from culture to culture.

Ethical judgments differ, as well, depending on the decade under consideration. What year the movie was released is thus a second qualifier.[9] Consider the following movies that were thought to be "scandalous" when they were originally released. In 1939, producer David Selznick used the original dialogue from the book *Gone with the Wind*, rather than have Clark Gable say, "Frankly my dear, I don't give a hoot." He was fined five thousand dollars for this indiscretion. In the 1959 movie *Some Like It Hot*, Jack Lemmon's character, Daphne, admits she's a man, to which Osgood responds, "Nobody's perfect," while in *The Graduate* (1967), Benjamin tells his mother's friend, "Mrs. Robinson, you're trying to seduce me"—and she is. In *Chinatown* (1974), Jack Gittes (Jack Nicholson) keeps slapping Evelyn Mulwray (Faye Dunaway) until she gives in and admits to having her father's child; in *When Harry Met Sally* (1989), Harry (Billy Crystal) tells Sally (Meg Ryan) that no woman has ever faked an orgasm with him; and in *Basic Instinct* (1992), Sharon Stone became a household name by uncrossing her legs. And then *There's Something about Mary* (1998) and *Jackass: The Movie* (2002) and *Team America: World Police* (2004)—each with its increasing grossness. We cannot transpose the accepted level of openness in any one of these movies to an earlier period. Standards are rather a moving target, pegged to current levels of societal tolerance.

Geography, decade . . . implementation. How the system is presently (not) functioning is a third qualifier in using the rating system as an ethical *discrimen*. Increasingly, if a movie might qualify for an NC-17 "adult" classification, filmmakers and distributors are simply choosing to release the movie unrated. Thus, *Requiem for a Dream* (2000) chose to be distributed without a rating, rather than fight the onus of its NC-17 assignment. The R rating is equally problematic. Most any viewer would say that *Fight Club* (1999) and *Billy Elliott* (2000) should not receive the same rating. But they do. And PG-13 is hardly better. If a movie is assigned a PG-13 rating, it seems reasonable that parents should not have to worry about their teenagers seeing it. But *Blue Streak* (1999) was given a PG-13 rating even though it is extremely violent, with the bad guys getting away with the crime, and Mike Myer's *Austin Powers in Goldmember* (2002) is rude and crude with sexual innuendo and scatological references throughout. Parents have grounds for objecting to such movies being given an approval rating for all teenagers. Even the G rating is not without its pitfalls, as studios insert gratuitous language or action into their "family" films to make them seem a little "racy," fearing that older preteens, as well as teenagers, might otherwise be put off if the movie is given a "children's" tag (a G rating).

Geography, decade, implementation . . . DVDs. Ratings battles over films like Trey Parker's *South Park: Bigger, Longer and Uncut* (1999) and *Team America: World Police* (2004), as well as Stanley Kubrick's *Eyes Wide Shut* (1999) forced artistic cuts and computer-generated insertions in order for the movies to qualify for even an R rating. At the same time, these changes do not really protect teenagers from seeing the final versions. Almost half of theaters still allow teenagers into R-rated movies; multiplexes create the opportunity for teens to buy tickets for one movie but sneak into another; and DVD copies are ubiquitous. A growing practice, in fact, is to make two versions of a movie—one for the theaters, and then a more risqué version for Blockbuster, which is advertised as the "unrated" version. In this way, viewers who have seen the movie in the theaters are enticed to see it again in their homes in order not to miss the added sex, violence, and foul language. Moreover, many of these viewers are the very youth the system was set up to protect. We were at a remote resort on the west coast of Vancouver Island reading in the game room when two young junior high school girls came in, put in two DVDs, and sat laughing and giggling while they watched *Jackass* (2002) and *Team America* (2004). The crudity, vulgar language, sexual explicitness, and narrative vacuousness of both movies were immediately apparent. Neither movie had a "larger" meaning; both were deliberately offensive throughout. Or perhaps, that was the larger "intended meaning" of both—an attempt at crude humor. My point in narrating this chance occurrence is simply to say, the availability of movies with "adult" ratings to those for whom they should not be intended (though in this case, the movies' sophomoric humor suggests that young teens were part of the "target audience") again calls into question the usefulness of the ratings. An R rating has become almost an invitation.

Given the changing standards of different cultures and different time periods, the arbitrariness of nonartistic standards (sex, violence, language) being applied to an artistic medium, and the continuing accessibility of supposedly restricted movies, the rating system has at best a limited usefulness in our society. Some might say, "Well, isn't something better than nothing?" Perhaps, but since newspapers and Internet sites provide details about every movie, perhaps there are better ways to convey this necessary information. For there is also a cost attached to our present system. Allowing the ethical questions regarding film to be framed in terms of the "raw" data concerning sex, violence, and vulgar language encourages a truncated understanding of a movie's ethical significance. It falsely narrows the ethical field, allowing other depictions with ethical import often to come in under the radar. For example, what about the repeated use of cigarettes by on-screen stars, even as we recognize the deadly implications of smoking elsewhere in our society? The average Hollywood movie in the years 1999 and 2000 had one and one-half minutes of smoking in it, the equivalent of three advertisements. *The Perfect Storm* (2000) had seven minutes! Or again, what of the use of seat belts by characters in movies? In a 2001 study, researchers at Saint Louis University discovered that seat belts were used in approximately 30 percent of the movies studied, while the national usage rate is 70 percent.[10] Here are major societal issues—smoking and seat belts—where millions of dollars are spent annually in an attempt to change public practices. And yet, without real challenge, movies have become a major counter-voice to behavior that the vast majority of Americans would consider ethically correct.

As important as noting what the movie industry isn't doing with regard to its moral responsibility is the need to better recognize what it is portraying. Nudity, violence, and foul language seem to have largely co-opted the present ethical discussion stemming from the movies, given their assigned importance by the current rating system. Little discussion is focused elsewhere, even by churches and educators interested in moral instruction. The list of ethically important issues dealt with in films is as wide as life itself. What, for example, of the plight of immigrants? *Dirty Pretty Things* (2003), *Gangs of New York* (2002), *In America* (2002), *Bend It Like Beckham* (2002), *El Norte* (1983), *Mi Familia* (1995), *Lone Star* (1996), *Maid in Manhattan* (2002), *Spanglish* (2004)—each invites both our appreciative gaze and critical reflection about "the stranger in our midst." Or what should we make of movies about Native-Americans that are told through the eyes of white men, for example, *Little Big Man* (1970), *A Man Called Horse* (1970), *Dances with Wolves* (1990), *The Last of the Mohicans* (1992)? Are they honest portrayals? Are they romanticized? Moreover, might these films have anything to say in our current debate over Native American lands and gambling casinos? Again, what insight might the depictions of the countercultural hero (*Rebel without a Cause* [1955], *Easy Rider* [1969], *Dead Poets Society* [1989], *Patch Adams* [1998]), the antihero (*Taxi Driver* [1976], *Pulp Fiction* [1994], *Fight Club* [1999]), or the mentally challenged (*Rain Man* [1988], *Forrest Gump* [1994], *Shine* [1996], *I Am Sam* [2001]) offer viewers? Can such movies help locate a common vocabulary for discussion of societal values and policies? And what might war movies (*The Deer Hunter* [1978], *The Thin Red Line* [1999], *No Man's Land* [2001], *We Were Soldiers* [2002]) have to say about our present involvement in Iraq? Such questions can easily be multiplied. The point here is not to seek to be comprehensive—to list the full range of ethical issues that have been given a "common language" by the cinema and thus invite our discussion. Rather, it is to point out how little moral discourse is at present actually arising from the movies. What ethical discussion there is tends too often to be focused on the presence or absence of sex, violence, and/or foul language. And even these discussions are rarely linked to a movie's larger ethical tone or intention.

There are exceptions, of course. The courageous story of Sister Helen Prejean that was made known to the world in *Dead Man Walking* (1995) is credited by many with helping the Catholic Church more aggressively challenge the use of the death penalty. Rather than argue statistics or abstract principle, the movie concentrated on the power of a human story. Though the U.S. bishops had voted to oppose capital punishment as early as 1974, Catholic doctrine continued to state that capital punishment could be a just penalty. Discussion surrounding the topic, for this reason, was confined largely to an academic, theological debate regarding remaining "loopholes," that is, until the movie came out and a common moral vocabulary was present in society. Influenced in part by Sister Helen's ability as a storyteller and the moral discourse thus generated, opposition to the death penalty gained momentum in the church. In a speech in St. Louis in 1999, the pope declared, "The dignity of human life must never be taken away even in the case of someone who has done great evil."[11] The world's lone superpower had a moral responsibility, he said, to proclaim the gospel of life by lobbying against the death penalty, which was cruel and unnecessary. How directly the pope was influenced by Sister Helen's story is unknown, though her testimony and the movie it sparked were known to him. But what is clear is that Catholics in the United States were now prepared to respond to the theological discussion. *Dead Man Walking* had given the dialogue an emotional center. Latest polls in the United States (2004) show that support for capital punishment among Catholics is down to 48 percent, with 47 percent now opposed, where as recently as 2001, 68 percent were supporters and only 27 percent opposed the death penalty.

Chuck Colson, head of Prison Fellowship, an organization he founded after being released from prison for his part in Nixon's Watergate scandal, is another opponent of the death penalty as presently practiced in the United States. He too has used stories from Hollywood movies to, in the words of Harvey Cox, "locate a common vocabulary." In a *Breakpoint* radio commentary in 2000, he praised *The Green Mile* (1999) for painting "a powerful picture of the dignity and worth of men on death row. It shows us that God's reach extends even to 'the least of these,' the ones the world would only too-happily forget."[12] He titled his remarks "Walk a Green Mile in Their Shoes," and he encouraged his listeners to use this R-rated film to engage ethically in conversation with their neighbors.

Should Christians View Morally Questionable Stories?

Despite the multiple problems associated with the Rating Code, many will still rightfully ask, aren't there morally objectionable movies that a Christian should not watch? Isn't the issue more than bad rating systems? Here is one of the most frequent questions I am asked both by students and by church people. Aren't Christians instructed by Paul to think about "whatever is true, whatever is noble, whatever is right, whatever is pure, whatever is lovely, whatever is admirable" (Phil. 4:8 NIV)? Shouldn't religious viewers at least self-censor what they see? The simple answer is, of course, "Yes." What we find degrading or troubling, we should avoid. I do not see many horror movies, for example, because the grisly images stay too long in my imagination and give me night-mares. But that is me. In an earlier chapter that discusses differing approaches that the church has taken toward Hollywood, I give other examples of rightful self-discipline. However, the question when asked is usually not nuanced by consideration of the sensitivities of the viewer or by other criteria such as movie genre or theme. Nor does the questioner have in mind the need for many of us to understand and empathize with those unlike us. Instead, what is being asked more narrowly is the "purity" question. If the movie contains scenes of, or language about . . . , shouldn't we stay away? The answer, in this case is, "Maybe yes, but maybe no."

When I used *Bruce Almighty* (2003) in one of my classes, a student was offended by the fact that Jesus' name was used exclamatorily three times and questioned why I had assigned the movie in a seminary context. What was overlooked in the question was the simple story arc, which portrays Bruce as an uncaring cad consumed by his own self-importance through the first two-thirds of the movie. For the movie to work, viewers should be repulsed by Bruce's insensitivity on all fronts—including his insensitivity to God. Further, they must also laugh, as they develop an affection for this flawed protagonist, something Jim Carrey brilliantly facilitates by the strength of his performance. When all the shenanigans are finally over and God (Morgan Freeman) asks Bruce what he cares about, Bruce can respond, "Grace" (his estranged girlfriend). "You want her back?" asks Morgan Freeman. "No, I want her to be happy." The transformation of the self-consumed Bruce is complete, and "grace" returns. A more careful viewing/listening before judging would have allowed this student to recognize *Bruce Almighty* to be as provocative a discussion starter about God as has appeared in recent years.

Similarly, although all would agree that the images of genocide presented in *Hotel Rwanda* (2004) are ghastly and garner for the movie a deserved R rating, few would say Christians should not see this movie, though some individuals might choose not to see it because of the intensity of the story. The courage in the face of internal evil and foreign indifference shown by Paul Rusesabagina, the manager of a posh hotel in Kigali, who rescues over twelve hundred people through bribes and cunning, is inspiring. The movie story simply provokes ethical dialogue, as questions pour forth about Africa's neglect by the West, how such brutality is possible, how good people could close their eyes, and whether "I" would have had the strength to do the same. Interestingly, a question typical of more academic discussions—whether the end (saving lives) justifies the means (deception and bribery)—seems out of place; the evil context simply answers the question for us. Here is a moral story about an immoral event that is fully "seen" only as such second-order moral reflection takes place. Here also is a movie some might not want to see for fear of being disturbed, but for that very reason it is one that should be seen.

Daniel Defoe, the eighteenth-century author of *Moll Flanders*, wrote in the book's preface, "To give the history of a wicked life repented of, necessarily requires that the wicked part should be made as wicked as the real history of it will bear, to illustrate and give beauty to the penitent part, which is certainly the best and brightest, if related with equal spirit and life."[13] The language of men in prison should be coarse. The adulterer should be seen to be a real adulterer. A hit man should be callous. A depiction of war might well need to be horrific. A rapist is . . . a rapist. To sanitize life is to falsify the story and thus to bring it stillborn into the world. *Unfaithful* (2002) presents the story of a happily married woman's "illogical" affair with a younger man. Diane Lane, who stars in the movie and has several graphic sex scenes, says, "You can't tell a story about infidelity without [it] . . . how can you have a hamburger without any meat?"[14] Or as John Henry Cardinal Newman reflects somewhat more elegantly, "It is a contradiction in terms to attempt a sinless literature of sinful men."[15]

A student in one of my classes, Ron Reed, himself a playwright and actor who has run a successful theater company in Vancouver for over twenty years, reflected on Paul's advice to Christians regarding purity in a journal he submitted to my wife (a co-teacher) and me. Though Christians, he suggested, might at first blush think a movie like *American Beauty* is not for them (given its sexuality, nudity, violence, and drug content), this would be a mistake. The movie is actually a meditation on "truth"—the truth of our culture of consumption, the truth of estranged families, of things that can imprison us, of the damage we can do to one another. It is also a movie that portrays "purity." Though the temptation of lust and marital infidelity is present right up to the end of the story, Carolyn's tryst is found lacking even within the movie's story line, while Lester ultimately resists and, in his simple care for Angela and his innocent recollections of family, finds peace. Above all, the movie is about "beauty." It asks what is actually lovely, the hybrid American Beauty rose we can nurture to perfection but which lacks any scent, or a plastic bag floating freely in the wind? Like the writer of the book of Ecclesiastes, the movie portrays much of life's vanity. But also like this ancient sage or the apostle Paul, it also recognizes a fragile alternative, the Spirit's gifting, which brings truth, purity, and beauty.

Given the "raw" content of many movies, should spiritually sensitive people protect their thoughts and imagination from evil? I respond with Cardinal Newman, Paul, and Ron Reed that we need not hide from truth or flee from reality. In fact, we must ground our understanding of life in the real. Movies, by eliciting from their viewers emotional responses to the full range of life, can give us a common moral vocabulary, even while portraying that which is troubling and immoral. By focusing our attention and our emotions on one interpretation of life's meaning, they can assist us in a common dialogue about the good, the true, and the beautiful—or the lack thereof.

Just as with other forms of art, there are movies that are obviously trash. To be open to the full range of human experience is not to baptize any and all movies as worthy of viewing. Movies with little or no redeeming social content should simply be ignored. Here would be my take on such crude and rude films as *Jackass* (2002) and perhaps *Jay and Silent Bob Strike Back* (2001). The first is "successful" in every way in outgrossing TV's *Fear Factor* without letting a story line intrude, while the other uses "f***" at least a hundred times in the first few minutes without the movie ever moving beyond its slovenly attempt to portray two slackers. Both movies seem to have little value beyond their sick humor. In assessing whether a movie should be seen, perhaps we can posit as a rule of thumb a variation of Defoe's "law of proportionality": if there is evil presented, is there a concomitant good that shines through, or is offered and rejected, or suggests itself by its very absence, such that truth, beauty, or goodness may be considered? Picasso's *Guernica* is not a beautiful painting, nor is it about the good. But by the absence of what is good and beautiful, the painting conveys a truthfulness about the horror of war that continues to inspire all who let their spirits be touched by it. Such can also be the case with movies. They need not be pretty. *Dead Man Walking* would never be described as such. But they should, by their ability to generate in viewers an honest emotional response, open us to the truth of life in one of its many dimensions.

Developing Skill in Moral Discourse

I have tried in the preceding discussion to respond to the question that I am perhaps most frequently asked in lecture and class settings: "Should Christians view 'morally questionable' movies?" A second question that I am asked almost as frequently concerns my unbridled enthusiasm for film. Given perhaps the unthinking negative judgments regarding movies by some in the religious community, have I not swung the pendulum too far and adopted an attitude that is "indiscriminately celebrative," to use the helpful phrase of Gordon Lynch. Have I not simply "baptized" all film as "reel spirituality"? It is fine to hear and understand a movie on its own terms before critiquing it; but don't we also need to bring our own religious and ethical perspectives to bear on the story, if the dialogue is to truly be a two-way conversation? The answer, of course, is "Yes." I hope the discussion in this book has made this clear. Having said this, however, let me stress once again the need for "ethical patience,"[16] as we first seek to perceive and enjoy, before turning to judge.

I recently heard a lecture by a prominent Christian who is interested in theology and film. He advised his audience that while watching a movie to always be critically evaluating how the filmmaker might be trying to manipulate your emotions through film technique, script, and music. In this way, you can protect yourself from any experience of evil. While such a strategy might accomplish its purpose, it will unfortunately also shield viewers from fully experiencing the truth, goodness, and beauty a movie conveys. Such shielding will ensure that the film experience remains stillborn. Felt emotion is of the essence of the movie experience, as the philosopher Mitch Avila argues effectively.[17] We need first to appreciate before we appraise.[18] We must experience the sense and taste of life if we hope also to sense and taste something of the Infinite. When we go to a movie, we should not first think about what makes the movie religious or moral, or whether a movie is religious or moral, but should rather let the movie itself focus our attention. This of course might indeed include religious and ethical dimensions, but they will be integral to, and flow out of, the movie itself. That is, the process of discernment and dialogue should be inductive, not deductive.

An adequate theological ethic of moviegoing will thus involve an initial, careful "seeing/hearing" before a subsequent "responding" is attempted, even while the viewers recognize that they bring to their viewing a wider life experience and cultural knowledge that inform even their initial viewing. To quote once again the German theologian Dietrich Bonhoeffer, who wrote this while sitting in a Nazi prison awaiting his execution for his involvement in a conspiracy against Hitler: "Who is there . . . in our times, who can devote himself with an easy mind to music, friendship, games or happiness? Surely not the 'ethical' [person], but only the Christian." It is not that ethics were unimportant to Bonhoeffer. He gave his life for a just cause. But there is also the place for the aesthetic joys of "art, education, friendship, play."[19] It is the understanding that God has "the whole world in his hands" that encourages Christians to first perceive and seek to enjoy before seeking to judge or evaluate. What will this mean concretely? An extended example can perhaps best convey the moral discourse that movies encourage.

Two Movies about Euthanasia: *The Sea Inside* and *Million Dollar Baby*

When Terry Schiavo died on March 31, 2005, nearly fifteen years after she entered what doctors described as a "persistent vegetative state," and nearly two weeks after her feeding tube was removed, it closed one phase of a heated debate over the meaning of the sanctity of life—a debate that filled the airwaves and newspapers around the world and extended to include stem-cell research, abortion, the make-up of the judiciary, and even Medicaid. Was there the forcible taking of an innocent life? When is someone dead? Was Mel Martinez, the conservative senator from Florida, right to introduce a bill allowing the federal court to review the Schiavo case? Was President Bush's late-night return to Washington from his Texas ranch in order to sign the bill political posturing or moral courage? Shouldn't we also look at Oregon's Death with Dignity Act, which allows doctors to write lethal prescriptions for terminally ill patients who want to die? And what of Switzerland's legalization of euthanasia? The questions flew easily, or perhaps more accurately, the accusations flew easily. Everyone tended to be either right or a numbskull. Partisan rhetoric prevailed.

The removal of Schiavo's feeding tube was called by Pat Robertson "judicial murder." House majority leader Tom DeLay described it as an "act of medical terrorism."[20] The rhetoric and opportunism on both sides of the debate sounded almost like the debate over abortion in Alexander Payne's biting, comic satire *Citizen Ruth* (1996), where in the heat of battle, the well-being of Ruth is lost sight of by both sides. Except here, the stakes were real.

How can we as a society best enter into a robust moral dialogue on end-of-life issues? If we are to move beyond the current impasse of moral self-righteousness on both sides of the aisle, if we are going to be able to discuss these issues sensitively and knowingly, we must locate a common vocabulary. Moreover, we must learn to link the moral reasoning of our heads with that empathy that comes from the heart. And here two movies that each won an Academy Award for Best Picture even while the Schiavo debate was winding down can perhaps provide us some small but important assistance. For each has a plot line in which euthanasia figures prominently. As was the case with *Dead Man Walking*, viewers come to these movies with the larger cultural discussion clearly in mind. We do not leave our experiences and reflections at the door. But viewers also come to watch a movie, to enter into another time and space, if only for two hours. If these movies prove helpful, it will be because of their ability to help focus our attention on what is closer at hand and more concrete, two stories of individuals wrestling with death—and life. And as they do, these movies might provide a "common moral vocabulary," while offering "an empathetic heart," assisting us in our public ethical discussion.

The Sea Inside (2004)

The Sea Inside won the Oscar for Best Foreign Language Film in 2004. Based on the true story of Ramon Sampedro, a Spaniard in love with the sea who in a diving accident at age twenty-six becomes a quadriplegic, the plot of this biopic tells the story of his successful fight to be able to die. On the surface, the movie would seem to be an endorsement of euthanasia, something a few critics charged. Yet plot is not the same as theme, as we have earlier noted.[21] *The Sea Inside*, though seemingly about death, turns out to be about the mystery of life. As most who have seen the movie will attest, it is about the vitality and wonder of existence. Here is the movie's real theme.

Rosa (Lola Dueñas) and her two sons enjoy a moment of laughter with Ramon Sampedro (Javier Bardem). *The Sea Inside* (d. Amenábar, 2004). © Sogepaq and Fine Line Features. All rights reserved.

Ramon has wanted to die for years, believing the sea to have taken his life from him. Now after nearly thirty years of confinement in a bed in his brother's home in Galicia, he is the willing "poster" person for a group dedicated to changing Spain's laws concerning one's right to die. "Death with Dignity" is their slogan. This also is Ramon's goal. Yet all who meet Ramon, including the viewing audience, are amazed at the fullness of his life. Here is the movie's paradox, its emotional heart and compelling power. As Ramon Sampedro, Javier Bardem gives the performance of a lifetime. Able to act only from the neck up—with face and voice—he nevertheless embodies on the screen a robust character bursting with life, intelligent, funny, articulate, touching. Vital in all ways, a forceful attractive presence, a mentor to his nephew, a flirt with the ladies (he must juggle two romantic interests—Rosa, a young DJ who lives nearby, and Julia, his lawyer who herself is fighting a degenerative disease), Ramon is a charismatic presence. Though Ramon has decided to give up on the life that has been dealt him, he nonetheless infuses everyone he meets with a sense of life's possibility. Though we might assume that a story based on the will to die would be either maudlin or saccharine, it is neither. Instead it is teeming with life. The tragedy, however, is that Ramon remains largely unaware of the gift of life he still possesses.

The talented director, Alejandro Amenábar, allows two scenes in particular to define the movie. The first is a moment of magical realism that provides the film its heart. Bedridden in his room overlooking the sea, Ramon without warning awkwardly stands to his feet, goes to the window, and then flies to the beach into the passionate embrace of his lawyer Julia (Belén Rueda), with whom he has fallen in love. They embrace as the Puccini aria "Nessun dorma," which has been playing on his phonograph in his bedroom, crescendos. Only then does the camera snap back to the room, exposing the dream as nothing more than a heartbreaking fantasy. After soaring with Ramon to the sea inside, viewers are caught short by the bleakness of his real life. We cry out with Ramon.

The second is a humorous, yet pointed argument between Ramon and a paraplegic priest who travels to Ramon's house to convince him that, as the church teaches, life is indeed worth living. Ramon refuses to be carried down from his upstairs bed to meet the cleric and engage in moral debate, and the priest cannot get his wheelchair upstairs to talk to him directly. Convinced, nevertheless, that he can rescue Ramon, the priest has his young acolyte shuttle up and down the stairs as his emissary, delivering one opposing argument after another. And Ramon has the acolyte deliver his rebuttal each time in return. And so the moral debate continues, until the two men become frustrated with each other and start shouting directly from one floor to the next! The scene works both because of its incongruity and humor (they are literally arguing from different premises), and because the intermediary allows the audience to experience a certain evenhandedness in the presentation of the alternating arguments. Both paralyzed speakers, we come to understand, are concerned with the preciousness of life. Although Ramon has tragically chosen a certain path for himself, the movie is not a "right-to-die" tract. It is rather an exploration of life's meaning and possibilities, given the cruelty of life's circumstance.

That reviewer after reviewer points out this paradox—what on the surface seems to be a movie about death proves instead to be an exploration of life—is not surprising given the clear direction of the movie. What is surprising is that these reviewers seem compelled to do so in an untypical way by sharing their own personal experiences. James Berardinelli, who seldom inserts himself into his helpful, descriptive reviews, nonetheless says here, "As we watch *The Sea Inside*, we become Ramon—bursting with life, humor, and intelligence, yet unable to reach out and bridge even the shortest distance to his loved ones. . . . I can think of few things more frustrating than being unable to touch my wife. I can understand wanting to die in this situation, yet I can admire a man like Christopher Reeve for soldiering on."[22] Kimberley Jones, of the *Austin Chronicle*, concludes, "I did indeed feel good, feel stirred, by *The Sea Inside*. . . . I felt good, in broad strokes, about the human condition, yet looking back on it now, that feels somewhat like a failure. On Amenábar's part or mine, I'm not sure."[23] And again, after but three paragraphs in his longer review of the movie, Roger Ebert turns to speak personally about the story of this quadriplegic who chooses to die. He names a number of his friends and acquaintances who are paraplegic or quadriplegic, explaining that their stories might also be relevant as we consider the movie. These friends, he says, function usefully and by and large happily.

He then says he is reminded of the words of another Spaniard, the director Luis Buñuel. "What made him angriest about dying," he says, "was that he would be unable to read tomorrow's newspaper." Ebert concludes: "I agree with Ramon that, in the last analysis, the decision should be his to make: to be or not to be. But if a man is of sound mind and not in pain, how in the world can he decide he no longer wants to read tomorrow's newspaper?"[24]

What is remarkable about all three of these reviews is *The Sea Inside*'s ability to create both a common language and a shared empathy between film, reviewer, and reader. Rather than provide an "objective" review, each reviewer feels compelled to respond personally, to tell his or her story in response, inviting us in the process to tell ours. Rather than mistakenly dismissing the movie as a political tract supporting mercy killing as some of the explicitly religious reviewers did, and thus shutting down the possibility of any real dialogue that the movie might generate between those who disagree before it can even be started, these reviewers first listened and viewed well. They demonstrated an ethical patience along with a humility when standing before the mystery of life. But each also felt compelled to then enter into dialogue by offering his or her personal perspective in return. And the ethical conversation began.

However vaguely they were able to express it, they sensed there was something fundamentally inadequate about Ramon's position. Even in their role as film reviewer, they felt compelled to also become a film critic. Ebert, a faithful Catholic, turned to the renegade Spanish critic of the church, Luis Buñuel, for support. Raised in a sacramental universe, Buñuel could not imagine anything that might trump the wonder of tomorrow, regardless of one's condition. Here is a theological position the movie itself invites, though not one that Ramon chooses to follow. I do not know the theological commitments of the other two reviewers, but they too sensed a moral ambivalence rooted in the movie itself and chose for themselves the call to embrace life, however gingerly.

Here, surely, is a starting point for a more robust theological conversation about the mystery and wonder of life's gift. Ramon lies in his bed, explaining his position to anyone who will listen: Life is "a right, not an obligation." We can empathize with him, wondering how we would feel in his body. But we also sense that Ramon has tragically, if understandably, cast the options too narrowly—he has seen life only in terms of a false dichotomy—"right" or "obligation." Could there not be a third possibility, one rooted strongly in the Judeo-Christian tradition? Might not life also be viewed as a gift? The movie seems to suggest such, despite Ramon's inability to understand and the priest's inability to articulate. When I saw *The Sea Inside*, my mind turned spontaneously to the psalmist:

> Where can I go from your spirit?
> Or where can I flee from your presence?
> If I ascend to heaven, you are there;

if I make my bed in Sheol, you are there.
If I take the wings of the morning
and settle at the farthest limits of the sea,
even there your hand shall lead me,
and your right hand shall hold me fast.
If I say, "Surely the darkness shall cover me,
and the light around me become night,"
even the darkness is not dark to you;
the night is as bright as the day,
for darkness is as light to you.

Psalm 139:7–12

The pathos of *The Sea Inside* centers in Ramon's inability to understand this mystery and the church's inability to convey it. Nonetheless, the movie's wonder is its ability to portray the sanctity of life. Like Berardinelli, I thought of Christopher Reeve and of Jim MacReynold, a family friend in my youth who lay in an iron lung for years. We prayed for him as a family every evening around the dinner table. Though Ramon was no longer able, I could say for him,

I will praise thee;
For I am fearfully and wonderfully made.

Psalm 139:14 KJV

Million Dollar Baby (2004)

Million Dollar Baby is a boxing movie. *Sports Illustrated* has even suggested it "may be the greatest ever," high praise for a film in a genre that includes *Raging Bull* (1980), *The Boxer* (1997), and *The Hurricane* (1999). Adapted for the screen from two stories in the book *Rope Burns* (2000), by F. X. Toole (whose real name is Jerry Boyd), the movie captured four Oscars: Best Picture, Best Director (Clint Eastwood), Best Actress (Hilary Swank), and Best Supporting Actor (Morgan Freeman). Forty-eight years old when he turned to boxing, Boyd was tutored by Dub Huntley, an African American who was a middleweight contender until he had to retire because of a detached retina. Learning how to be a corner man, a "cut man," and then a manager, Boyd used what he had experienced as raw material for his short stories, which he wrote at night. Huntley remembers that a heart problem had sent Boyd back to the church, that there had been three failed marriages, and that Boyd had led a hard, though adventurous life. All of this and more made it into his stories, although no one in his boxing community knew it. For though he continued to write for several decades, Boyd never found a publisher for any of his work until late in his life.

Maggie Fitzgerald (Hilary Swank) takes to the ring as her manager Frankie Dunn (Clint Eastwood) and her cut-man Eddie "Scrap-Iron" Dupris (Morgan Freeman) root for her. *Million Dollar Baby* (d. Eastwood, 2004). © Warner Brothers. All rights reserved.

On the surface, *Million Dollar Baby* is about boxing, even though Eastwood tried to interest studios in the script by calling it a "love story" (which it also is). Its plot line is familiar—with the encouragement of the gym manager, a broken-down trainer takes one final gamble on a young boxer who proves a success, becoming like his own child even as they move together toward personal and professional vindication in the championship match. Of course, the story has its own wrinkles—the boxer is a woman in her early thirties, Maggie Fitzgerald (Hilary Swank), who is desperate to overcome her "white-trash" family, which has abandoned her; the manager, Frankie Dunn (Clint Eastwood), is estranged from his own daughter, who returns unopened the weekly letter he sends her, and perhaps seeking answers for this and other vagaries of life, goes daily to church for mass, only to argue theology with the priest; and the gym manager, Eddie "Scrap-Iron" Dupris (Morgan Freeman), is the seasoned observer of life who narrates the story with a wry wit. "Everybody's got a particular number of fights in 'em," he opines. "Nobody knows what that number is." Scrap should know; his career was cut short by a punch that cost him his right eye. We could not hope for better performances from any of these three actors. They are simply spot on.

Frankie is both a seasoned corner man and a "cut man," practiced in the arts of protecting and patching up fighters. But there comes a time for any fighter when the unexpected happens and repairs are no longer possible. What then are we to do? Here is the movie's central metaphor. For *Million Dollar Baby* is not really about boxing at all; instead, it uses boxing to explore the human search for meaning, given betrayal, circumstance, and finally death. Filmed magnificently, the harsh lights and deep shadows on screen beautifully reinforce the story's rendering of life's hopes and failures. So too does Eddie's superb narration. His tone captures perfectly the poetic, contemplative feel of this movie, one reinforced by the seventy-five-year-old Eastwood.[25] The audience easily trusts the aged wisdom of this one-eyed seer, who guides viewers through Maggie's rise as a boxer under Frankie's tutelage, until her improbable fall.

And fall she does. Given the genre of the movie and its set up, viewers are expecting a female version of *Rocky* (1976) or perhaps *Cinderella Man* (2005), the story of persevering against all odds and winning at the end. Instead, two-thirds of the way through the movie, Maggie is sucker punched after the bell during her championship bout and falls backward, hitting her head on the stool, which Frankie has just set out for her. She is immediately paralyzed from the neck down. Frankie is stunned, as are we. Part of the strength of the movie's storytelling is the visceral "punch" viewers feel at this turn of events, even while our vicarious love and concern go out to Maggie. The theater audience goes from cheers to stunned silence in a heartbeat. It simply is not supposed to be like this. But it is, and we know all too well, this also is life. Here is the movie's true theme. What can you say about life when time runs out (Eddie)? What happens when you can no longer patch it up (Frankie)? What happens when triumph turns tragic (Maggie)? What happens when life implodes?

Frankie remains devoted to Maggie, who has become like a daughter to him, finding her care, remaining at her side. But as her condition continues, Maggie's depression turns to despair. Finally, to Frankie's horror (and to ours), Maggie asks him to help her end her life. "I got what I needed. I got it all. Don't let them take it all away from me. Don't let me lie here until I can't hear them cheering for me anymore." Frankie seeks the advice of his priest, who tells him this is God's doing, that if he honors Maggie's request, he'll be lost and unable to find himself again. And viewers sense this will in fact be the case for Frankie. Yet Frankie, though he is troubled, is also committed to Maggie. Having abandoned one daughter, he cannot do it again. Not to comply with her request would feel like a sin. So as in *Unforgiven* (1992), Eastwood again plays a character forced to make an ethical decision he knows will cost him his soul. The movie ends with Frankie assisting in Maggie's suicide.

As we might expect, given the film's ending, some Christian reviewers were appalled by *Million Dollar Baby*. Andrew Coffin in *World Magazine* called the movie "morally reprehensible," even if it is well crafted and moving.[26] Similarly, Christopher Lyon at "Plugged In" found the movie to have an "artful delivery" but also to be "a deeply troubling film."[27] Behind their judgments was their belief that the movie is "a social treatise," false propaganda about euthanasia.

Others, like Annabelle Robertson at Crosswalk.com, also found the movie to make "a strong case for euthanasia," but instead of condemning it, she praised the film, believing "anyone with a shred of compassion" will accept the movie's conclusion. "Without a doubt, if there is a case to be made for euthanasia (despite the rarity of these clear-cut circumstances), this is it."[28] What both these extremes share in theological judgment is the mistaken belief that euthanasia is what the movie is about. They fail to see the ambiguity resident in the story itself. Together, they would leave us on the horns of a dilemma. Do we choose "truth" (the movie is wrong) or "compassion" (the movie is right)?

Fortunately, such undialectic responses to the movie have been in the minority, even among religious commentators. If my description of the movie offered above is at all congruent with the movie's own center of power and meaning, it is easy to see why. The moral pull and personal tragedy of the movie is Frankie's choice to act against his conscience out of love. Is this to be seen as against or for euthanasia? It is both. The choice of assisted suicide at the end is Frankie's choice, but it is not as clearly the movie's choice. Here is the ambiguity. Viewers leave the theater asking if Frankie was right. At times, there are simply no happy endings despite our best intentions; bad things happen to good people that sometimes produce only grief. We are required, nevertheless, to act. And such actions have moral consequence. By showing the full horror and pain of life at its extremity, the movie provides viewers both a common vocabulary and an empathetic posture for necessary moral discourse.

In this regard, it is interesting to compare *Million Dollar Baby* with *One Flew over the Cuckoo's Nest* (1975), another Academy Award–winning story about the struggle to become more fully human that similarly ends with a mercy killing. When that movie came out, however, there was little concern over the ending in which Big Chief escapes the confines of the state mental hospital, but only after acting in love by smothering his friend McMurphy, who had been lobotomized by the hospital staff as a result of his antics on behalf of the inmates. Here, the mercy killing betrays no moral dilemma; Big Chief's act is not construed as a threat to his soul. Rather, it is a simple expression of his newly found humanity, a concrete manifestation of love. For this reason, the moral discourse stemming from the movie does not focus there. It is found elsewhere—chiefly in questions about institutional control—about well-meaning (or not so well-meaning), but constricting social policy and action that castrates others; and secondarily about Native Americans, gender differences and battles, and even the importance of play.

As with *The Sea Inside*, the ethical power of *Million Dollar Baby*'s story is its ability to elicit viewers' stories in response. Chuck Colson, in a *BreakPoint Commentary*, referenced his friendship with Joni Eareckson Tada, who was severely disabled in a diving accident but whose "life goes on even after paralysis—and is even richer, perhaps."[29] Michael Medved, writing in the context of the pope's final heroic battle with life, referred to the pope's refusal to surrender to frailty and trauma as a counterexample.[30] However, not all the stories told were used to criticize Frankie. Diane Singer, writing also for Colson's *BreakPoint Commentary*, found the movie's ending problematic but believes that Christians need to face some of those "what if" questions that advanced medical treatment makes possible. She speaks of her dad, who in five short days went permanently blind. His life as he knew it was over. The result is continuing grief, depression, and confusion in his thinking and decision making, a loss of purpose, and a recognition that his life is not normal. She refers to the community of support that is needed in such crises and says she is "less inclined to condemn Maggie and Frankie as I am to weep for them," because there was not a better "supporting cast" to encourage them. She says, "It is not enough to say all life is sacred. We must also seek to understand the ethical dilemmas modern medicine has laid at our feet, to seek counsel of godly friends, to be ready to offer love, grace, and wisdom, and to bring our faith to bear on the one fact none of us can escape—life ends."[31] In all these ways, *Million Dollar Baby* can be instructive.

Million Dollar Baby has elicited both critique and counter-stories from one group of persons in particular: those who are disabled. Many have found the movie troubling, if not offensive, particularly those struggling with similar spinal cord injuries. The film seems to suggest that the injury is worse than death itself. "Any movie that sends a message that having a spinal cord injury is a fate worse than death is a movie that concerns us tremendously," says Marcie Roth, executive director of the National Spinal Cord Injury Association.[32] In response to such protests, Eastwood has said that the film is not about the right to die. "The film is supposed to make you think about the precariousness of life and how we handle it. How the character handles it is certainly different than how I might handle it if I were in that position in real life. Every story is a 'what if.'"[33]

Agreed, but for many who are disabled, the hypothetical "what if" threatens to weaken, not strengthen their resolve. But not all who are disabled agree. Soon after the movie won its Oscars, the *New York Times* ran a front-page article on Katie Dallam, a Missourian born into poverty who turned to boxing in her thirties, only to become the only female professional boxer yet to have suffered a serious brain injury. Katie remains seriously compromised to this day. When the injury happened in 1996, it was widely discussed in the boxing world, where Boyd/Toole no doubt heard of it. Here, in all likelihood, was the starting point for his fictional story. Surprisingly, given the harsh ending, Katie found Hilary Swank's portrayal both accurate and compassionate. It even proved inspirational, she related. "I tend to be pretty hard on myself, when I can't remember things or I get lost. But after the movie I thought, no, I've come a long way. I should focus on what I achieved."[34] Rather than weaken her resolve to live, *Million Dollar Baby* strengthened it, by showing someone who "wrongly" gave up.

I will let Roger Ebert have the last word here. Ebert, when asked about the harmful effect this movie might have on some, questioned the idea that movies are supposed to make choices that will satisfy the concerns of all viewers. "The characters in movies do not always do what we would do. That is their right. It is our right to disagree with them."[35] Here was Katie Dallam's right, which she exercised. *Million Dollar Baby* offers the Christian community an important gift: an honest portrayal of a tragic life, together with a thought-provoking response by someone who cared deeply for Maggie. It is for us, the religious community, to take this story and enter into dialogue with it, letting our stories and the Christian story participate in an open, two-way conversation.

responding to
movies
theologically

Even the most commonplace things are tinged with glory.

W. H. Auden

Every year in my theology and film class, there are students who come to the dialogue with such strong religious commitments that they cannot view a particular movie on its own terms. They are quick to judge its ethics or its images from an imposed point of view. I recall one student, for example, who could not get beyond the fact that Charlie Chaplin's character in *City Lights* (1931) was drunk. She could therefore see nothing of his pathos and compassion, let alone take note of the themes of sacrifice, hope, and providence that were central to the movie. However ultimate one's theology is, it is the penultimate—the movie itself—that demands our initial attention. It is for this reason that I have postponed until now a discussion of theological criticism.

T. S. Eliot cautioned that whether a piece of literature was worthy or not could only be decided on aesthetic grounds. This is ground zero with regard to a person's response to any work of art, including film. Eliot then went on to assert that the subject of literature (and film) was ultimately too important not to be completed from a theological perspective.[1] Personal evaluation, including theological dialogue, has its place as in any human encounter, but it must follow the act of first looking and listening. Having been open to receive the images (the "testimony") of a film, we need to take the cinema with sufficient seriousness to complete the critical act by engaging in dialogue and reflection with it.

Movies seek to affect us wholly, and we are affected whether we admit it or not. What the effect is, together with how the film portrays life's power and meaning, should be the subject of our conversation, reflection, and evaluation.

It is this completing act of criticism that we will focus on in this chapter. Film's informing vision—its root metaphors and axiological perspectives—make claims on us both analytically and experientially and thus invite our theological reflection. We cannot escape responding to film from our own perspective, our own center of power and meaning. Even "objective" critics do this, as we have already noted in previous chapters. The potential use of an outside criterion by the critic (or of the critic as outside criterion) is not unique to the theological enterprise. Feminist criticism and Marxist criticism, for example, also bring an outside standard to bear on a film, and the responses are most typically made by feminists and Marxists. There is a personal dimension to the evaluation.

Theological criticism, similarly, seeks to engage a movie from perspectives that come out of, but move beyond, the movie experience. It seeks a dialogue between filmic elements and convictions and Christian experience and belief. It can include issues of class, politics, and gender, but it is by no means limited to them. Rather, it is the visual story of a movie with its particular narrative elements that invites communion on its own terms through theological dialogue. In the movie *Grand Canyon* (1991), Travis, the Steve Martin character, reflects, "Everything you need to know about life is in the movies." His remark rings true. It is a movie's portrayal of "life" that invites, if not demands, our theological response. In the process, Christians can join the more general conversation about the meaning and significance of a particular movie.

The Theological Critic

As Christians, we can take two basic approaches to movies. We can either reflect analytically on or respond experientially to what we have seen. I have spoken of this in terms of engaging a movie's meaning and power. As with all art, movies both invite discourse and become at times a revelatory event.[2] Theological critics of film speak of movies as being both a medium for "critical analysis of theological ideas" and a medium to "provoke religious experience," as allowing theological questions and as being sacramental.[3] They understand movies as both discursive (being about something) and presentational (being something).[4] Of course, it would be wrong to draw this distinction too starkly, for there are a range of meanings within any film that overlap with a range of experiences (though these are limited by the movie's own portrayal).

We might diagram these possible critical responses by using a matrix:

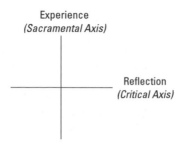

Figure 10.1 Theological Responses to Cinema

Each axis is a continuum suggesting a variety of possible theological responses. We can label the two end points of the sacramental axis "The Holy" and "The Human." Here is a continuum along which we experience revelatory events. For the critical axis, we can describe the two end points as "Staying within the Movie Itself" and "Learning from a Theological Partner." This continuum suggests how we respond to movies analytically:

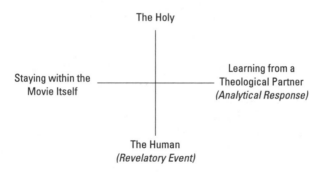

Figure 10.2 Matrix of Theological Responses

Martin Buber's distinction between "I-Thou" and "I-It" relations provides something of an analogy here. He writes, "There is no I taken in itself, but only the I of the primary word I-Thou and the I of the primary word I-It."[5] Buber understands the character of all human existence as being-in-relation. With regard to the world of cinema, the viewer exists in relation to it. But that relationship is of two types—the one analytical and the other experiential. We relate to the living world around us either as subjects ("I-Thou") or as objects ("I-It"). We enter into a shared presence, or we measure and judge. The sphere of relationship that Buber is particularly interested in is that of personal presence, that which ultimately opens us to the eternal. It is the sacramental axis, one rooted in revelatory event, which is his focus. But a critical perspective also has its role. It allows the world of work to function and provides perspective to our experiences.

To use other language, there is first-order and second-order understanding. We can learn as we encounter something or someone directly, and we can understand by reflecting on the experience. In our discussion in chapter 2 of the history of the church's relationship with Hollywood, we noted a general trend during the era of the Code for the church to relate to films critically, assessing their ethical impact. In more recent decades there has been a growing trend to see the human and aesthetic dimensions of film, that is, to seek an encounter with cinema. In our discussion of theology, we noted that the word *theology* could stand for our understanding "of" God or our understanding "about" God. Here, again, the revelatory and the analytical axes are distinguishable.

The Experiential Axis

In our current American climate, the revelatory, that which concerns spirituality, and not the analytical, that which suggests dogma, seems of particular theological interest. The experiential is in ascendancy throughout our culture. Revelatory experience, furthermore, is of two types. The one is an encounter with the sacred itself, with that which lies beyond the natural but which gives meaning to it. For Christians, this is an experience of God, with the divine who is outside of and independent of the world, even if known from within the world. Regardless of the religious tradition, phenomenologists of religion point out that such an encounter is always a mystery that is at one and the same time inviting and yet awe-inspiring, fascinating and yet evoking of dread. Rudolf Otto used the word *numinous* to label this sacred other that is encountered. As he investigated how people worldwide described their experience with the numinous, he noted that it was always a mystery that simultaneously invited and repelled. Think of Moses at the burning bush or Isaiah in the temple. Here was a *"mysterium: fascinans et tremendum."*[6] Transcendence, in this sense (what I have called "Transcendence," with a capital *T*) refers to something independent of and outside ourselves and our cultures, even if it is known from within. It is one pole of the experiential axis, one I have labeled "The Holy."

By its very nature, there is no way to identify which films will be the occasion for experiencing the Transcendent, for encountering such mystery. But stories that dramatize the human search for ultimate meaning seem more often to be the vehicle of divine manifestation than other options. *Dead Man Walking* (1995), for example, is more than a story about Sister Helen Prejean's work as a counselor to inmates on death row. It is also the story of her struggle with the soul of Matthew Poncilet, the condemned murderer who awaits execution. *Babette's Feast* (1987), *Breaking the Waves* (1996), *The Passion of Joan of Arc* (1928), *Andrei Rublev* (1966), *The Green Mile* (1999), and *Becket* (1964) are the kind of movies that seem uniquely able to mediate the holy, to be the occasion for epiphanies. (I say this knowing full well that epiphanies are never coerced.)

Transcendence can also be spoken of in terms of the human possibility of exceeding our limitations, of experiencing wholeness within brokenness, of glimpsing how life was meant to be but is not (I have chosen to call this "transcendence," with a lowercase *t*). In the vernacular, we sometimes get a glimpse of Humpty-Dumpty put back together again. If the first form of Transcendence often uses the imagery of *ascent*, here, we might better speak of "transcending by *descent*, delving more deeply into oneself and one's humanity, and becoming deeper and more spacious as a result," to quote Martha Nussbaum from her wonderful book, *Love's Knowledge*.[7]

T. S. Eliot refers to such transcendence as "the still point of the turning world":

> At the still point of the turning world. Neither flesh nor fleshless;
> Neither from nor towards; at the still point, there the dance is,
> But neither arrest nor movement. And do not call it fixity,
> Where past and future are gathered. Neither movement from nor towards,
> Neither ascent nor decline. Except for the point, the still point,
> There would be no dance, and there is only the dance.
> I can only say, there we have been: but I cannot say where.
> And I cannot say, how long, for that is to place it in time.
>
> T. S. Eliot, "Burnt Norton," *Four Quartets*[8]

Wallace Stevens speaks of the same experience as "a self that touches all edges."[9] Within our fragmented lives, we occasionally rediscover life as a whole, if only for a moment. Here is the other pole of the experiential axis, what I have labeled "The Human" in order to suggest its this-worldly focus.

A number of movies come to mind that seem able to mediate what I am labeling "The Human (lowercase 'transcendence')": *Grand Canyon* (1991), *Tender Mercies* (1983), *Places in the Heart* (1984), *Sling Blade* (1996), *Secrets & Lies* (1996), *Driving Miss Daisy* (1989), *Forrest Gump* (1994), *Awakenings* (1990), and *Life Is Beautiful* (1998). But again, any filmic story that portrays human experience truthfully has this spiritual capacity. Such movies, in the words of writer Anne Lamott, "deepen and widen and expand our sense of life; they feed the soul."[10]

Transcendent human experiences (lowercase "transcendence") are not confined to the traditional religious sphere but occur throughout life's activity. Peter Berger finds such "rumors of angels" in the human activity of play, for example.[11] One of John Updike's characters, David Kern, speaks of these human experiences as "supernatural mail on foreign soil." David's transcendent experience took place as he helped a cat, which had been hit by a car, die. At the time, he was on his way home from the hospital where his wife was giving birth to their daughter. Death and life came together as a moment in time, but out of time. David concludes, "The incident had the signature:

decisive but illegible."[12] Such experiences are transformative, for they convey a sense of the sacramentality of life. Though such encounters are personal in nature, they are never simply subjective or aesthetic. Rather, they are a revelation about Life itself.

What unites these two otherwise disparate understandings of Transcendence/transcendence—what we are labeling The Holy and The Human—is their common recognition of some "Value More that exceeds our current possession."[13] That is, they are revelatory of something beyond ourselves. Both have, in the words of Don Browning, "a hidden domain of ultimacy."[14] David Hay recounts his findings after asking people to describe that "personal experience of the presence or power of whatever is conceived as ultimately real, whether named God, the gods, . . . or anything else."[15] In his surveys over the last twenty years, he has discovered that when given the opportunity and taboos are allowed to be broken down, three out of four individuals recognize that they have had such experiences.[16] For some, these transcendent experiences were what we are labeling "Holy." For others, they were "Human." But however described, they demanded the individual's total involvement, were intensely real, were responses to a perceived "given," and had consequences for their practical lives. Many who were interviewed had not chosen to talk about these experiences before, fearing misunderstanding or rejection. Yet, for most people, transcendence was a known experience.

Hay observes that his findings match the evidence we have from comparative religion, where it can be noted how

> literally anything or any occasion can be associated with a sudden moment of religious awareness. . . .
>
> . . . [T]here are records of such moments during childbirth, at the point of death, during sexual intercourse, at a meal, during fasting, in a cathedral, on a rubbish dump, on a mountain top, in a slum: in association with a particular plant, stone, fish, mammal, bird and so on *ad infinitum*. . . . [T]hough it is worth repeating that there seems to be no way of "switching them on."[17]

It is this experience of a "reality not ourselves" that suggests for Wallace Stevens an affinity between art and religion. Writes Stevens, "And the wonder and mystery of art, as indeed of religion in the last resort, is the revelation of something 'wholly other' by which the inexpressible loneliness of thinking is broken and enriched."[18] Nathan Scott speaks similarly as he writes that "the truth of the matter is that both art and religious faith share a common intention to summon us into the presence of what is other than, and transcendent to, the human mind; and, in this, they provide each other with a kind of mutual confirmation."[19]

Julius Lester, who teaches Judaic studies at the University of Massachusetts at Amherst, tells of his experience while teaching a course on religion and

Western literature. His testimony is true of the power of story more generally. He says that his students are often bristling with cynicism but want to believe. After reading Eliot, Baldwin, Hesse, and Potok, "students who have not been to mass since coming to college are going again. Jewish students who go to synagogue only on Rosh Hashanah start attending Shabbat evening services. Students who do not come from a religious tradition find themselves, like the Psalmist, seeing God in nature." He concludes:

> I harbor no illusions that many of them will be able to sustain their nascent experiences of transcendent meaning. But I respect these new beginnings, regardless of how brief they may be. The students have cared enough about God to suffer the terror of His absence and they are now willing to suffer the terror of His presence.[20]

What is true for the other arts is true also for film. In the opening chapter, I offered my testimony of the power of story, together with the testimonies of Paul Woolf, Rosalind Chao, Christoph Meili, Catherine Sittser, and Gregory Elmer. What these personal witnesses have in common is a transcendent experience. Such revelation cannot simply be reduced to the subjective, however personal its expression. What these witnesses encountered was a "reality not ourselves."

In a special issue of the journal *Image* that was devoted to the topic "Screening Mystery," guest editor Ronald Austin asked a number of writers, filmmakers, and screenwriters to discuss the films that most powerfully influenced their spiritual lives. The testimonials of the contributors included experiences of both forms of transcendence. Cecelia Gonzalez, the former co-chair of the City of Angels Film Festival, recalled a childhood memory when she encountered God while watching a movie under the stars in Havana:

> It was black and white on the screen under a black sky full of white stars. I leaned over the second floor stone balustrade toward the church courtyard. My heart strained at its moorings as the film came alive on a large sheet strung between two pillars. This is indeed a strange tribute, for I don't remember the name of the film, and in my nine-year-old memory only fragments survived, yet I know that the God alive in the film whose holy presence stopped the soldiers from desecrating his church, was the same amazing God who danced with us children in that history-paved patio, the God who made me weep. . . . One summer night in old Havana, the sky, the screen, and the sanctuary were all framed inside the hollow of tiny hands.[21]

Gonzalez had had an experience of "Transcendence."

Arthur Hiller answered the same question by recalling a more this-worldly "transcendence":

> The film *Open City* had a strong effect on me spiritually. Granted, I saw it shortly after returning from flying missions in World War II with the Royal Canadian Air

Force, but it still stays with me by showing me it is still possible to keep your faith and goodness while undergoing one of the most unjust and emotionally wrenching disasters of this century. The scene where Anna Magnani chases after the truck while the fascist troops drag off her friend and priest still haunts me.

It is such an affirmation of the human spirit that it raised my expectations of myself and helped me to realize that doing what is right is essential even in the worst circumstances.[22]

We might distinguish between the experiences of Otto and Gonzalez, on the one hand, and Eliot and Hiller, on the other, by contrasting the miraculous and the marvelous; the supernatural and the truly natural; or perhaps the experience of mystery and the experience of wholeness.

Screenwriter Paul Schrader seems to have distinctions such as these in mind when he distinguishes between (1) movies that either inform the viewer about the Transcendent or reveal the Transcendent in human reflection and (2) movies "which relate the human experience of transcendence, which express not the Transcendent but the human who experiences the Transcendent. . . . The terms 'Transcendent,' 'transcendental,' and 'transcendence' represent a hierarchy of the spiritual from the Other-oriented to the human-oriented."[23]

Schrader argues that such experiences must be kept distinct. I have chosen rather to use the same word, *transcendence*, for the entire range of experiences, but to place them all on a continuum running from the Other-directed ("The Holy") to the human-oriented ("The Human"). I have done this because our experiences of the Transcendent and transcendence often overlap or move back and forth seamlessly. Take Harvey Cox's description of the grotesque characters of Fellini's *Satyricon* (1969), where he speaks of the need to compare Fellini with Hieronymous Bosch: "Both pour on the monstrous and the grotesque first because they want to zap us into an encounter with another reality, and because they want us to see perverts, cripples, idiots, sadists, and weak-kneed pushovers as our brothers and sisters."[24] He would have us encounter the miraculous and the marvelous, the wonder-filled and the fully human. Though these often merge in practice, they can also usefully be described as opposite poles of the same experiential axis. We as viewers will witness to our own experience of the mixture.

The Human (transcendence)

Human portrayals in film have greater theological connotations than we often realize. The human and the theological, in fact, are so intertwined that to speak authentically of the one is to engage the other. Recall the words of Jesus when he was asked what was the greatest commandment. He responded that we should love the Lord our God. But then he immediately added, "And a second is like it: 'You shall love your neighbor as yourself'" (Matt. 22:39).

For Jesus, the supernatural and the natural conjoined. Stories that portray the truly human bind their viewers with the religious expressions of humankind. They awaken a holistic sense in their viewers, providing windows of meaning. Movies are evocative, portraying life's great experiences (e.g., love, birth, work, death) or their opposites, so that the gift of life becomes known by its negation. Here is one pole of the experiential axis.

Ken Gire remembers experiencing such a moment while watching the movie *An Officer and a Gentleman* (1982). The film portrays the story of a Naval Aviation recruit who must make it through boot camp in order to get his wings and fly for the Navy. Though he has done well in flight school (or perhaps because he has done well), he is singled out by the drill sergeant as someone who needs to be broken. While the other recruits are given the weekend off, the Richard Gere character is made to stay on the base and run an obstacle course. The drill sergeant is in his face, yelling at him, taunting him, and trying to make him break. Finally, while Gere is doing sit-ups in the rain, the drill sergeant tells him that he is through, discharged from the Navy. And these words break him. In his tears, Gere pleads, "You can't do it to me. I got nowhere else to go. . . . I got nowhere else to go." The scene had a profound impact on Gire. Here was an expression of his own humanity too. He writes:

> When I was going through my own grueling experiences in the wilderness and being forced to give up what I loved doing most, that scene came back to me in a powerful way. I knew what Richard Gere's character felt. I knew the determination he had to get his wings and the fear he had of not getting them. I knew the rigors of the obstacle course and the agony of endless repetitions of meaningless exercises. I knew because I was the new recruit doing sit-ups in the rain before a stern and unrelenting drill sergeant. "You can't do it to me," I remember crying out to God. "I got nowhere else to go. . . . I got nowhere else to go."[25]

In *An Officer and a Gentleman*, Ken Gire had experienced a concrete story, but he had also been invited to transcend that reality. Through the portrayal of the human, Reality, Life at some more central region, had also been discovered. Because the movie was both particular and universal, it proved to be a source of ongoing inspiration and insight.

For me, it was the Academy Award–winning film *Life Is Beautiful* (1998) that provided such an experience of human transcendence. As a father with one daughter in college and one about to launch her adult career, I was moved deeply by the portrayal of a father's love for his child. Here was a sacrificial and yet joyous love that was boundless. Here is how I should have been more often with my daughters. Here is what it is to be a father. Life is beautiful within the loving embrace of a family; it is worth any sacrifice to love those near to us.

Guido (Roberto Benigni) protects his son, Joshua (Giorgio Cantarini), from anti-Semitic hatred by making a game with him. *Life Is Beautiful* (d. Benigni, 1998). Photo by Sergio Strizzi. ©1998 Miramax Films.

The movie's story is simple and warm, horrific and yet humorous. Using the language of both slapstick and romance, Roberto Benigni, the co-writer, director, and lead actor, tells the story of a young peasant who comes to the city to work. It is 1939 and anti-Semitism is growing. But Guido, a Jew, is oblivious to his danger. He is in love, and life is beautiful. In one of the funniest courtships ever portrayed on film, Guido wins Dora (played by Benigni's real-life wife), a schoolteacher with social standing. The couple's love is genuine and contagious, and their son, Joshua, lives in the wonderful embrace of their love.

Then both Joshua and Guido are arrested and shipped to a concentration camp. The thought of Joshua suffering in fear is more than Guido can bear. The second half of the movie shows the extreme measures that Guido takes to protect his child. (There is an equally moving story of how Dora, who is not a Jew, volunteers to go to the camp in order to be with her family.) Guido plays an elaborate game to protect his son from the horrors of the prison. The extent of Guido's love for his boy brought tears to my eyes, as did the commitment Dora and Guido have to each other. In a scene reminiscent of *The Shawshank Redemption*, Guido risks his life to play music for Dora over the camp's loudspeaker. It was magnificent to watch and to hear. In fact, my wife and I went out and bought the CD so the memory could linger. Guido will do anything for Dora and Joshua, and the compelling power of his affection is reciprocated.

The transition from town to concentration camp is heart-stopping, but the contrast works; the joy and innocence of the opening scenes only make the pathos of the second setting more heartfelt. Some have questioned the appropriateness of linking laughter with the unthinkable. Is not the Holocaust beyond humor? But such a response misses both the genre and the intention of the movie. For this film is not about Italy in 1939 or Germany in 1945. It is, instead, a celebration of a father's love, even in the midst of unspeakable tragedy and pain.

The movie begins by saying that it is going to tell a fable. It thus invites the viewer to see Reality behind, and in, reality. The humor in *Life Is Beautiful* was inviting; the horror of humankind's inhumanity was chilling. But the sacrificial and trusting love between a boy and his father was compelling. Ultimately, in this film the father's love became paradigmatic of what a parent's love should be; it was even analogous to the Father's love (1 John 3:1: "See what love the Father has given us, that we should be called children of God; and that is what we are"). To hold your child in your arms (or to be held in your parent's arms) is transformative. In the words of Joshua as the movie ends, "We won."

The Holy (Transcendence)

The other experiential pole I have labeled "The Holy." Here the Transcendent is disclosed through the material of reality, but in such a way as to manifest a reality that does not only belong to this world.[26] Or, to put the matter more simply, movies are a window through which God speaks. The experience of the Holy cannot be programmed. It is a gift. However, some movies seem to predispose their viewers to receive such an experience. They are sacramental. Some of my students speak, for example, of having a mystical encounter through seeing the baseball movie *Field of Dreams* (1989), though perhaps more experience its transcendence more humanly. Few, if any, speak similarly about *Bull Durham* (1988) in either sense, even though the movie begins with the Susan Sarandon character's monologue about the "church of baseball."

A movie that Andrew Greeley says ushered him into the presence of the Divine was *Places in the Heart* (1984), the film for which Sally Field won an Academy Award in 1985 for Best Actress. The movie ends, as we have seen, in a Baptist church in a small Texas town during the Depression. Writes Greeley, "As the cup and wafers are passed through the congregation and the camera examines the faces of each of the communicants, we become aware that all of the characters in the story are present, the good and the bad, the venal and the heroic, the living and the dead, the killer and the victim." All are brought together as one by Jesus. This portrayal of "the communion of the saints" became the occasion for Greeley to again meet God. Although the meaning of the scene is so blatantly accessible that in the hands of a less-skilled filmmaker it would seem trite, "the sheer, gentle beauty of the scene" rescued it for Greeley from any charge of moralizing. Greeley concludes, "Film in the hands of a skilled sacrament-maker is uniquely able to make 'epiphanies' happen."[27]

Greeley describes Eric Rohmer's *My Night with Maud* (1969) and Bob Fosse's *All That Jazz* (1979) as being similarly sacramental for him.[28] He believes movies to be particularly suitable for the creating of such epiphanies, for they have an inherent power to affect the imagination. I am reminded of C. S. Lewis's book *The Pilgrim's Regress*, when Lewis portrays John hearing words near the Canyon: "For this end I made your senses and for this end your imagination that you might see My face and live."[29] Greeley argues that God discloses himself to us through the experiences, objects, and people we encounter in our lives. He writes, "Grace is everywhere."[30] We must be concerned about the poor, thinks Greeley; but we must also be concerned with the arts, for the artist is a potential sacrament maker, one who can reveal the presence of God within creation itself. Here is the theological basis for our experience of the holy in film.

Greeley's experience with *Places in the Heart* was necessarily unique to him (it was his experience), but others also share it. My colleague and the series co-editor, Bill Dyrness, speaks of this same film as changing his consciousness. He writes, "I doubt I will ever think about the church in the same way after that final scene."[31] Some movies have a sacramental intention that opens viewers repeatedly to experiences of grace. This was my experience as I watched *Becket*; it proved to be similar for Father Gregory Elmer. Similar, that is, and yet distinct, for how God spoke to Father Elmer was different from how I heard my call into ministry.

That movies affect people differently not only has something to do with the varied background and life experiences of the audience. It not only has to do with the mystery of the Holy Spirit's presence. No, movies' effect on their viewers has also to do with the nature of story itself. For stories are not received simply as a string of linear facts. Rather, stories create images; they give us "pictures inside our heads" to which we respond. Joseph Sittler, the Lutheran theologian, recognized something of the unpredictability of story in his comments on the gospel story. He noted that the four Gospels are full of phrases like "and suddenly . . . and on the way he met . . . now it happened that . . . there stood before him a man."[32] It is "in the midst of the many-threaded, wild unsystematic of the actual," he wrote, that "the not-expected was crossed and blessed by the not-possible."[33] It is in the "not-expected" that movie-viewers are often graced by the "not-possible," as God meets us and speaks to us through movies.

The Critical Axis

Movies, like life itself, are first experienced, then reflected on. They affect the heart, then the head. And our gut-level response becomes itself part of what is later reflected on.[34] It is for this reason that we have turned to consider the experiential axis first. It is our encounter with the movie itself that should control all else. Faithfulness to the concrete experience of the movie's story is the first criterion for effective theological criticism. Such movie-centered criticism can be confirmed and extended through the use of genre analysis, auteur criticism, thematic dialogue, and cultural critique. A totally idiosyncratic viewing of the shape or meaning of a film, particularly if it is then used as the basis for theological dialogue, should be thought suspect. The adequacy of any critical response to a movie must be measured by the film itself.

There is also the possibility of saying more, of bringing the engagement with film into conversation with one's second-order theology. To reflect analytically and constructively on a movie's meaning is to treat the film with the seriousness that its creators intend. If the movie is meant to be simply entertainment, mere escapism, theological conversation is of course pointless. But so too is any film criticism. What we have is the equivalent of pulp fiction or dime-store romances. Just as there are bad novels and trite paintings, so there are confused or hackneyed movies. Just as there are mysteries to be read on airplane flights and then discarded, so there is escapist fare at the cineplex. But for any film that seeks to connect with its viewers with regard to the human condition, or to offer a vision of transcendence whether human or divine, theological criticism is both appropriate and even necessary.

As with the experiential axis, we can again view the critical as having two poles, one interior to the movie itself and the other exterior to our experience with a film. These I have labeled "Staying within the Movie Itself" and "Learning from a Theological Partner." The one seeks to find within the movie itself a standard for theological judgment. No outside, or ultimate, ground for critiquing the movie is appealed to. The other uses theological resources from outside the film itself to better understand or judge it, although these outside resources should not be used to skew the first-order experience of movie viewing itself.

Again, in practice these two forms of theological criticism often overlap, with both internal and external theological criteria being brought to bear in analyzing a film's meaning. For example, there is a significant group of movies that have a purely fictional character who has a substantial resemblance to the Christ-figure (e.g., someone who comes into a society from the outside and through suffering love redeems other[s]). *Cool Hand Luke* (1967), *E.T.* (1982), *One Flew over the Cuckoo's Nest* (1975), *Sling Blade* (1996), *Babette's Feast* (1987), *Titanic* (1997), and *The Chronicles of Narnia: The Lion, The Witch and the Wardrobe* (2005) are all such films. Here the theological dialogue needs to take both critical poles into account. That is, the portrayal of the Christ-figure by the movie adds new understanding to who Christ is. It needs to be considered on its own terms. At the same time, because the biblical portrayal of Christ has been used metaphorically, the Christ-story can clarify the character's situation and add depth and authority to the characterization. It too has a place at the critical table.

Perhaps because of the history of heavy-handed theological and moral judgments being levied by the church with regard to Hollywood, there was a time when some theologians were content to limit themselves to internal criticism alone—to only consider film as film and to offer no external theological evaluation. Ernest Ferlita and John May's early work, *Film Odyssey: The Art of Film as*

Search for Meaning (1976), is an example. Having discussed the human search for meaning in a brief opening chapter, they then turn to consider a number of movies that take up this theme. They argue:

> The theological critic of contemporary culture . . . is an eye specialist rather than a painter. The painter gives us an impression of the world as he sees it; the ophthalmologist strives to bring our vision back to the norm so that we can see life as it really is. By exposing the visual structures of a limited number of films, we hope that our reader will sharpen his own capacity for interpreting other films of quest and for discerning in them whatever meaning the form suggests. . . . We go directly to the painting or the film, not of course to stay with the artist's world, but to allow his vision to direct ours to discover anew life's meaning, even if we must in Shakespeare's words "by indirections find directions out" (*Hamlet* 2.1.65).[35]

Though theological dialogue is their ultimate stated goal, the book remains at the level of "ophthalmology." Roy Anker's *Catching Light: Looking for God in the Movies* (2004) is perhaps a second example, though again, the depth of the internal criticism displayed is so exquisite as to muffle any criticism of his approach. Located in the context of a college English department, which has film studies courses as well, he is reluctant to extend his interaction to include the Reformed theological tradition in which he stands.

Theological criticism that "stays within the movie itself" has its place; it can be extremely helpful in focusing the viewer's attention on the center of power and meaning of a movie and suggesting its theological center. Richard Blake's *Screening America* is an excellent example. Written by a Jesuit priest who was for fifteen years the film reviewer for the Catholic journal *America*, the book discusses five classic American films, each representing a particular identifiable genre—the screwball comedy, the gangster film, the Western, the detective story, and the horror film. In the process, Blake not only reveals much about American culture but also much about the nature of the human condition. He does not bring external biblical or theological judgments to bear on the movies in view. But his Catholic sensitivity to a movie's sacramental potential is evident. At a more popular level, the same might be said of Roger Ebert. His film reviewing, thumbs up included, is filled with an implicit Catholic perspective.

While such "autonomous" criticism was perhaps necessary during the period when the church and its theologians tended more often to be artistically insensitive, and though when practiced by a seasoned critic can still be extremely illuminating to the reader, it is less than the total criticism that T. S. Eliot argued for so successfully. Having assisted viewers to better see the religious import of a film, theological critics can go on to engage the film's center of meaning from their own theological perspective. The importance of this final critical step has been increasingly recognized over the last decade or so, in particular by a group of scholars trained in biblical studies. In the preceding chapters, we have had occasion to refer to several of these scholars who are presently engaged in critical conversation with film. Robert Jewett, Bernard Brandon Scott, David Rhoads, Larry Kreitzer, and David Burridge are all New Testament scholars by training. These biblical scholars speak of the needed dialogue between film and Scripture using different metaphors and descriptors. Rhoads argues for a needed critical intertextuality, as does Burridge. Jewett speaks of film as a "conversation partner" with Scripture. Scott seeks a "critical correlation," while Jewett also wants to apply an "interpretive arch" that is rooted on one end in the biblical world and on the other in the world of cinema. Kreitzer argues the need to "reverse the hermeneutical flow" between Bible and culture, letting film and novel inform and instruct Scripture. However it is expressed, for all these biblical scholars, movies need to be brought into conversation with the Bible in order that both Scripture and movies might be illumined.

Again, in their book *Screening the Sacred* (1995), Joel Martin and Conrad Ostwalt define theological criticism as a dialogue between movie themes and Christian categories. Most of John May's more recent writing also fits within this category (cf. *Image and Likeness* [1992], *New Image of Religious Film* [1997], and particularly, *Nourishing Faith through Fiction* [2001]). So, too, does Clive Marsh and Gaye Ortiz's edited volume, *Explorations in Theology and Film* (1997), where Marsh speaks of a needed negotiation between film and theology; and chapter after chapter illustrate the enterprise. In chapter 3, a number of other such books were also referenced. There is possible a fruitful dialogue between movies, on the one hand, and the sources of Christian reflection, on the other.

In order to understand better the nature of theological criticism as practiced analytically, two examples of theological film criticism will prove instructive. Both involve popular Hollywood movies. They were written for a general Christian audience. I wrote the first in 1995. It seeks to put the film *The Shawshank Redemption* (1994) into conversation with the biblical book of Ecclesiastes.[36] In this meditation on friendship, film and Scripture have become conversation partners, each shedding light on the other. Here the model is that of dialogue, or intertextuality. The film's verbal script and visual images are put into dialogue with a thematically similar text from the Bible.

The second example of theological criticism is adapted from a piece I wrote in 1999, as the last year of the old millennium dawned.[37] Here, there is a reverse hermeneutical flow, as the images of a group of Hollywood apocalyptic movies are used to inform and critique the church and its theology of end times (or lack thereof). Both essays are examples of film criticism being completed by its engagement with theology.

A Meditation on Friendship

Two are better than one, because they have a good reward for their toil. For if they fall, one will lift up the other; but woe to one who is alone and falls and does not have another to help. Again, if two lie together, they keep warm; but how can one keep warm alone? And though one might prevail against another, two will withstand one. A threefold cord is not quickly broken.

Ecclesiastes 4:9–12

The Shawshank Redemption (1994) was one of five films up for an Oscar as Best Picture of 1995. Because it lacked the popular appeal of *Forrest Gump*, it lost. But the movie should not be missed. Set in Shawshank Prison, the film portrays human possibility within the impossibility of that impersonal world.

In particular, the movie is a story of human friendship—the friendship of Andrew Dufresne (Andy) and Ellis Redding (Red). Red has been sent to prison for a crime committed in his youth twenty years earlier. Andy, a bank vice president, has been recently and wrongly convicted of the murder of his wife, who was found in the arms of her lover. Red is an African American; Andy is white. Red has little education but lots of street smarts. (He is the guy who can get anything smuggled into the prison.) Andy has lots of education but lacks prison savvy. (He is beaten within an inch of his life by the prison "sisters.")

Red (Morgan Freeman, left) and Andy (Tim Robbins) develop a friendship as inmates of Shawshank Prison. *The Shawshank Redemption* (d. Darabont, 1994). Photo by Michael Weinstein. ©1994 Columbia Pictures Industries, Inc., and Castle Rock Entertainment. All rights reserved.

The movie begins by showing the murder of Andy's wife while the radio plays, "If I didn't care more than words can say. . . . If this isn't love then why do I thrill? . . . Is it love beyond compare?" And the viewer senses the full irony. No, it is not love beyond compare that Andy's wife and her lover have. It is a vulgar, desperate, mutually self-centered affair that ends in a double murder. But the question "Is it love beyond compare?" remains in one's mind and frames the movie. Andy and Red come to care deeply for each other. Their friendship becomes, in fact, a love beyond compare.

At Shawshank, the old prison librarian, Brooks, is let out after fifty years in that jail, so that the government will not have to pay for his final years. Brooks is afraid to leave. He says, "These walls are funny. First you hate them. Then you get used to them. Then you need them." When he is paroled, Brooks tries to live as a free man, but he is lonely and frightened. Finally, he writes a note back to the prison ("I don't like it here. I've decided not to stay.") and then hangs himself in his rooming house. With no friends, he cannot cope.

Woe to the one who is alone and falls and does not have another to help.

As Red becomes older, he too becomes fearful that he has become "institutionalized." He is scared that he will be cast out of the prison when he is too old to readjust to the outside. Wanting to give hope to his friend, Andy shares with him a dream he has. When he gets out of prison, he wants to go to a little town in Mexico on the edge of the Pacific Ocean—Zihuatanejo. He will buy a little hotel and an old boat that needs fixing up.

Andy says to Red, "A place like that could use a man who knew how to get things." Red says he is too old for such dreams, but Andy persists: "Red, if you ever get out of here, do me a favor. Go to a hayfield near Baxton [and Andy describes the place] and look for a black rock and find what is buried there." And Red agrees.

Eventually they do get out. Andy first; Red sometime later. Red, like Brooks, gets a job, but almost despairs of fitting back into society. There is an important difference, however. Red has promised his friend to go to the field in Baxton. So as a final act of desperate courage, Red goes and does, indeed, find what is buried there. Andy has left him some money and a note saying, "Remember, hope is a good thing." The film ends with Red traveling south to Zihuatanejo, where he finds his friend on the beach repairing an old boat.

"If I didn't care, more than words can say. . . . Is it love beyond compare?" The shallow words of the radio song have faded, but they are replaced by the profound actions of two men whose friendship is life giving and life sustaining.

Two are better than one, because they have a good reward for their toil. For if they fall, one will lift up the other.

Human friendship is one of the Creator's great gifts to humankind in helping us deal with life's problems, or so the writer of Ecclesiastes teaches and the director of *The Shawshank Redemption* portrays. For the prisoners, there are issues of injustice, of oppression for those lacking power. The writer of Ecclesiastes outlines similar wrongs, ills typical of ancient Israelite society but which sound jarringly familiar. The Preacher writes of the tears of the oppressed (4:1), of jealous competition as the real fuel of most hard work (4:4), and of the compulsiveness of the rich, who are never satisfied (4:7). What is the antidote for our vain toil? For our work that so often proves little more than a chasing after wind?

Though one might prevail against another, two will withstand one. A threefold cord is not quickly broken.

We need each other. The Lord God once said, "It is not good that the man should be alone; I will make him a helper as his partner" (Gen. 2:18). This simple creational truth is foundational. The Preacher knew nothing of God's ultimate plan of redemption in Christ Jesus, but he was well versed in Genesis (as the text of Ecclesiastes reveals through multiple allusions and references). Reflecting on who we were created to be and therefore on who we are, the writer of Ecclesiastes could thus point beyond the impasse of society's futile work. He could point beyond our vain self-interest to something more primary.

Our habits of the heart so feed our individualistic spirits that a commitment to the common good has flagged in our society. We have asserted our self-sufficiency so uncritically that we have placed our very lives in jeopardy. On the national level, we risk reducing our democracy to single-interest politics. Our own agendas must take priority. At the church level, we feel little compunction against leaving for another congregation that can better meet our needs. Our identification with a body of co-believers has become shallow, if not nonexistent. In the home, marriages are failing as both partners go their separate ways, putting personal fulfillment ahead of other common aspirations. Our collective self-interest is proving meaningless, little more than a chasing after wind.

How can we once again discover the importance of others as Red and Andy did? Dietrich Bonhoeffer, writing from his prison cell in Nazi Germany, penned these words to his friend Eberhard Bethge:

> Who is there . . . in our times, who can devote himself . . . to music, friendship, games, or happiness? . . . I believe that within the sphere of this freedom friendship is by far the rarest and most priceless treasure, for where else does it survive in this world of ours, dominated as it is by [work, marriage, and state]. It cannot be compared with the treasures of the mandates, for in relation to them it is *sui generis*: it belongs to them as the cornflower belongs to the cornfield.[38]

The cornflower to the cornfield—friendship to work. The cornfield requires tilling. The obligation and the opportunity to work is still ours. But alongside the cornfield is the cornflower that sustains.

Thinking about the Millennium

Y2K (year two thousand) brought with it a spate of movies dealing with the end of history. Besides entertaining us with their nonstop adventure and eye-popping special effects, these films challenged the church and its thinking (theology). For the typical, end-of-the-world movie both rejects the established approaches to life and its solutions (including, by implication, the church's) and recasts our apocalyptic dreams and projections in secular terms.

Some of these recent movies are post-apocalyptic, that is, they deal with events after the destruction of the world as we know it. Kevin Costner's *Waterworld* (1995) is a good example of this genre (even if a bust of a film!). Its story plays out amid a world covered in water because of human stupidity and greed.

A second group of films, and perhaps the more prevalent, portray events that threatened to bring about the world's end. Some malevolent force (asteroids in *Armageddon* [1998]; aliens in *Independence Day* [1996]; and dinosaurs in *Godzilla* [1998]) threatens to bring about our destruction. To avoid it, we need the best of both human ingenuity and technology. But humankind is capable, even if barely: we ultimately must take responsibility for ourselves and our posterity. Though there is carnage and loss, life can continue. Or so the scripts suggested.

The 1998 movie *Deep Impact* (1998) is a good example of this genre of doomsday movie. As the film opens, Leo Biderman, a high school student on an astronomy field trip, discovers a comet "the size of Mt. Everest." It is about to collide with the earth—that is, to make a deep impact. What will people do, given this "ELE"—Extinction Level Event? Throughout the rest of the film we observe the response not only of Leo but of Jenny Lerner, an inexperienced but ambitious MSNBC reporter, and ultimately of the president of the United States, Tom Beck (played convincingly by Morgan Freeman). The government

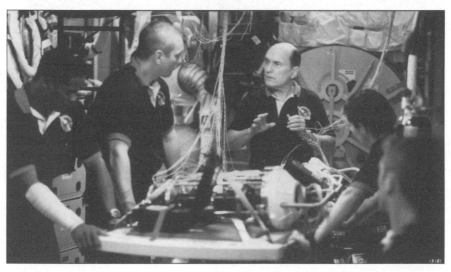

Veteran astronaut Spurgeon Tanner (Robert Duvall, center) confers with the shuttle crew. *Deep Impact* (d. Leder, 1998). Photo by Myles Aronowitz. ©1998 by Paramount Pictures and DreamWorks LLC.

has been secretly working on a survival plan; it is building a spaceship called *Messiah* to intercept the comet, plant nuclear devices beneath its surface, and skillfully blow the comet to smithereens. There are a number of subplots, including one that involves choosing a million people by lottery to re-people the planet (animals "two by two" will also be squirreled away in the underground fallout shelter in Missouri). But without going into the particulars of the ending (we already suspect: "though there is carnage and loss, life will continue!"), a larger pattern with theological significance can be discerned.

Rationality Is Insufficient

First, linear thinking is out. Planning, organization, technology—these are insufficient by themselves. Jenny Lerner uncovers the asteroid threat by mistaking ELE for Elie, a supposed lover of a senator, and she is hailed as an investigative genius. Just as septuagenarian John Glenn joined six younger astronauts aboard *Discovery* in 1998 for a space flight, so Spurgeon Tanner (Robert Duvall) is the older former astronaut involved in accomplishing the Messiah Project (most of these films are not too subtle in their meaning!). Although the younger crewmembers resent him at first, believing he is educationally outdated and along only for PR reasons, Tanner proves indispensable. The others might be better able to handle the necessary technology, but leadership, wisdom, and an aesthetic sense are equally necessary, particularly when plans inevitably fail. A highlight in the film is when Tanner goes to comfort a young colleague in the doomed spacecraft by reading *Moby Dick*.

We are reminded of *The X-Files*, where both Fox Mulder's intuitive, even irrational, grasp of reality (his sister was abducted by aliens when he was a small child, which opened him to believe in anything and everything) and Dana Scully's no-nonsense rationalism (she is the clear thinker, the scientist/medic) must be used if catastrophe is to be avoided. There is no retreat from our technological age, in either the TV or the film episodes of this ongoing saga. But equally sure is the realization that the scientific rationality of our modern age has come to a dead end and must be supplemented. Guidance must come from multiple sources.

In his inaugural lecture as Professor of Practical Theology at Aberdeen University, John Drane points to this need to go beyond rationality and coherence as a major theme in the film *Armageddon*.[39] If there is a way of preserving planet Earth, it will not be through the normal rules of reason and rationality. It is not NASA or the Pentagon that will save us. In fact, at one point in the movie, the NASA director tells his colleagues that if they feel like praying, "now would be the time." It is not the government that will save us, but Harry Stamper, the world's greatest oilfield driller. His strategy will be totally illogical but also ultimately successful.

What are we to make of this? As the millennium approached, *Time* magazine's cover story was about the herbal medicine boom with its so-called alternative remedies. The film *Patch Adams* was about to be released with Robin Williams playing a doctor who dresses in clown outfits in order to assist the healing of his patients (much to the consternation of the chief of the medical staff). Jesse "the Body" Ventura went to Hollywood to celebrate his election victory over Hubert Humphrey Jr. as governor of Minnesota. Was there any doubt about our culture's denial of system and coherence alone? I think of the image of special prosecutor Ken Starr (who was investigating President Bill Clinton) in his grey suit and impassive face, sitting on his briefcase to increase his stature and trying to convince a group of legislators and the wider population that logic should prevail or our system is in trouble. But as the millennium approached, it was logic and mysticism, Prozac and St. John's wort, poetry and physics, a good (successful) president and a bad (sinful) person that together held sway. There was no longer a system to be trusted. Loose ends simply remained. But success could be found in using both the intuitive and the rational.

A SECULARIZED EVIL

There is a second aspect of *Deep Impact*'s apocalyptic vision that is also worth noting. Evil is now secularized. It is not the satanic that is a threat as much as it is a comet (in other movies, you can substitute global warming, viruses, and even aliens). Moreover, it is not a sovereign God who initiates the apocalypse, but natural causes hastened by human blundering and capriciousness. In the biblical vision of the apocalypse, the righteous are raised—they escape the final annihilation. But in this Hollywood version, good and bad people alike are threatened. It is not so important to be among the righteous as it is for human ingenuity and heroism to link with technology in order to save the day.

What are we to make of such a "natural" apocalypse? Conrad Ostwalt, speaking at a conference on religion and film around the turn of the millennium, suggested provocatively that Americans were increasingly substituting Hollywood doomsday films for the more typical Christian apocalyptic vision.[40] With the church part of society's establishment, it has had difficulty portraying world destruction at the hands of a sovereign God. After all, most American Christians like the world they live in. So outside of certain religious groups on the cultural margin, a real apocalyptic consciousness is largely missing from contemporary Christian thought. The church's voice has grown silent (when was the last time you heard a sermon about the world's imminent end at the hand of a righteous God?). Enter Hollywood to deal with millennial fears.

Perhaps Ostwalt has overstated his case. But only slightly. While some theologians predicted one hundred years ago that this century would be the "age of eschatology," few are speaking that way about the next. Typically, we continue to believe that the end times will come, but this is not preached or taught as often as other aspects of the Christian story. A minister friend wrote his master's thesis on "gehenna" (Matt. 18:9) and the "lake of fire" (Rev. 19:20; 20:10). His doctoral dissertation was on angels in the eschaton. But that was in the 1970s, when Hal Lindsey's first book, *The Late Great Planet Earth*, went through multiple printings and the Soviet Union was still the threat from the north. More recently, my minister friend moved to a large evangelical megachurch, and his first lengthy sermon series was on wisdom for life from the book of Proverbs. The focus of his ministry became that of helping people live Christianly. This was what an upper-middle-class congregation needed (and expected). But in the process, the congregation also lost something of the story—God's story. The denouement was absent; the ending, lacking.

Do we as Christians live in the full consciousness that God will bring this age to a close? Do we want to hear an apocalyptic, end-time message? It seems clear that for most Christians, the answer is "No." But the testimony of the Christian church for two thousand years is that God will overcome evil and establish his universal kingdom forever. If this ending of God's story is no longer being heard vibrantly within the church, perhaps God is using Hollywood to challenge Christians to recover a sense of the apocalyptic? Most viewers went to see *Deep Impact* or *Godzilla* with popcorn in hand and then headed for the pizza parlor with their children. These movies were simply escapist fare. But could it be that these futuristic, fantastic images also had the magical capacity to inspire once again our imaginations with regard to the end times? Or speak to our fears about the future? It would not be the first time God has used unconscious agents to accomplish his purposes. Whether a complacent, middle-class church wants to hear such a message, the final act of God's story will happen.

A Medieval Postscript

It is relatively straightforward to note how film can be both a medium to provoke religious experience and the occasion for critical analysis of theological ideas. That is, movies can be theologically important both experientially and analytically. But though it is easy to note the depth and breadth of meaning resident in many movies, it is more difficult to describe and/or delimit what this depth is, let alone define how we might unpack it. Are there guidelines that can be offered? Are there types of theological criticism that can be recognized? Is there a necessary starting point for this theological reflection?

It has seemed to me for some time that help might come for the theology and film critic from a most unlikely source. Could the medieval method of biblical interpretation in which multiple levels of meaning are uncovered from out of a single text help chart a way forward? Medieval biblical exegetes were interested in reading Scripture in order to know God—literally, faithfully, lovingly, hopefully.[41] To facilitate their inquiry they developed a fourfold method (the *quadraga*).[42] They believed that a text must be understood (1) *literally*; before it could be (2) *allegorically* opened up "in faith," producing greater spiritual understanding; which could lead "in love" to further (3) *moral* insight and action (the Latin word "tropologically"); and ultimately "in hope" to (4) a *transcendent* vision that would provide a future perspective for life here and now ("anagogically"). Though this method was used mainly with regard to Scripture, Dante also took such an approach and applied it to a literary text.[43] He was concerned, that is, not just with a reader's understanding of the text, but with that text becoming part of one's experience—one's life—in faith, love, and hope. It was not enough simply to know what a text said; one should know what it meant intellectually, socially, and spiritually as well.

Could such a schema be useful as well to the viewer wanting to engage a movie theologically? And how might this fourfold method of interpretation translate to the screen? Such a viewer would need to first focus on the artistic/ poetic meaning of the movie itself. (If the movie is a biopic, it is not the "literal" history of the person that should be one's initial concern, but the "literal" interpretation of that story on the screen.) Second, as the viewer opens up to the movie story, it might also become by analogy "my story." Though it remains the story of others, we sometimes also see and understand ourselves on the screen. That is, we recognize that there is a "spiritual" connection between what we have experienced on the screen and what we experience in our own lives. Third, it is not enough to say simply that we, as viewers, identify with the story or believe it is true. If we really believe it, we will act on it. The story will stay with viewers and inform how they live. And last, though death will cancel out much, the deeper meaning of a story can speak to that which continues even beyond life. Such a voice is not a mere otherworldly abstraction, but a glimpse of the Transcendent/transcendent within the film that can provide perspective and direction for life here and now.[44]

Is this description, at all, the experience of the filmgoer? It seems to me that it is. There is a thickness to interpretation that is possible when responding to a film's story, a depth that can be discerned, but only as the literal is first focused on. (One should be concerned with determining what a film portrays, before seeking to explore what it might "mean.") Though this interpretation begins with the artistic sense of a film text, this will not prove a final destination for the viewer, however. The movie will open the viewer to an overflow of meaning as the inner meaning of the film and the viewing "self" are grasped together, stimulating faithful belief, right practice, and even divine contemplation.[45]

Titanic (1997)

The movie *Titanic* provides an almost textbook example of the process envisioned. Though some consider it as simple "popcorn" fare, for millions it proved far more. The strength of the film centers in its multiple subplots, each opening out for the viewer onto a different level of meaning. *Titanic* is, at its most basic, an adventure story about the sinking of the Titanic, one of the most written-about events of the twentieth century. Viewers are captured by the verisimilitude of the re-creation. Here is what it would have been like to be on that cruise. Second, the movie is also a love story that draws viewers in—its story becomes our story. Told by the elderly Rose, as she reflects back on her youth, the story invites viewers to identify with her. Here is the "heart" of the movie. (Here, also, is why some teenage girls lined up to see the movie multiple times.) Third, the movie's story has ethical extension; it is a parable of what life is meant to be. The movie challenges us to reject the prejudice of class, to fight materialism, to foster trust, and to find in community our true human-ity. Even if it is only fiction, the story invites our active ascent. We are also to treat all people as equals; this is not just an isolated value of Jack's. Fourth, the story suggests that life has a transcendent core. We see the contrast between the hubris of the ship's invincible builders and crew who tempted the fates, and the "innocence" of Jack, who gives his life that another might live. The movie ends with Rose reflecting on the sacrificial love of Jack (surely intended as a Christ-figure by the filmmakers); she says that he "saved [her] in every way that a person can be saved." As the movie ends, viewers look at photographs on her bedstead that document her rich and full life. Her transformation is more than interior; it has been played out in a life well lived. Here is a love that has transcended all limitations. As a story, *Titanic* opens its viewers out to the Transcendent/transcendent.

Of course, *Titanic* is only one story, not four. Viewers are invited to explore all four levels of meaning simultaneously through the interaction of each of these narrative subplots as part of the larger story. But the emphasis given within each of the subplots also invites a focused gaze on one or another of the story's possible meanings. And the result has proven compelling for many viewers. The success of the movie, both theologically and in terms of the box office, is its ability to open its audience to such a spiritual viewing—one that points outward in faith, love, and hope beyond the movie's story line to the reality of something that transcends our finitude. *Titanic* invites viewers not only to be entertained, but also to be transformed.

March of the Penguins (2005)

A second, and lengthier, example of the use of a fourfold method of theo-logical interpretation can be seen in *March of the Penguins*. The movie was the surprise hit of the summer of 2005. Catching the imagination of millions, it was produced for $8 million and grossed over $100 million worldwide. The movie also spawned illustrated books both for adults and for children and sparked a new interest in travel to Antarctica.[46]

Finding a mate. *March of the Penguins* (d. Jacquet, 2005). © Bonne Pioche, National Geographic, and Warner Independent Pictures.

Instructive for our purposes here was the popularity of the movie with conservative Christians. According to both the *New York Times* and the *Chicago Tribune*, this documentary about the mating ritual and rearing process of emperor penguins was considered by some religious conservatives to be "nothing short of a miraculous allegory about the universality of family values, the value of monogamy, the perversity of gay marriage and the wisdom of intelligent design."[47] Michael Medved is quoted as praising the movie because it "passionately affirms traditional norms like monogamy, sacrifice and child rearing." Medved continues, "This is 'The Passion of the Penguins,'" comparing this documentary to *The Passion of the Christ* (2004). Lennard Davis, in his commentary about Christian responses to the movie, belittled such "theologizing," questioning how intelligent a design it is to leave penguins no pouch in which to put their egg, or what kind of statement it is regarding monogamy when these birds choose a new mate each year. For him, this is yet another example of Judeo-Christian heavy-handedness with regard to film interpretation.[48] And surely it is. Such a reductive miss-viewing of the movie is neither called for nor necessary to a theological response. Yet the question remains, is there not a legitimate spiritual viewing of this movie, one that would take seriously what so many Christians and non-Christians alike reported as they engaged the images, music, and words

responding to movies theologically ————

of this film? Might there not be a Christian reponse to this movie that follows the lead of the medieval interpreters?

On the *literal* level (the poetic meaning of the film text), *March of the Penguins* is a journey into a world most of us have never seen or experienced—the world of the emperor penguin of Antarctica. In a world where the average temperature is 50 degrees below zero, not to mention the gale force winds that blow, only the emperors have survived for centuries. While the film is a visual feast from the opening scenes of ice floes to the textured close-ups of the penguins' coats, it is also the poignant story of their survival (wonderfully narrated by Morgan Freeman).

Every March, the emperors march single file from the sea to their mating area up to seventy miles away. (Actually it's more of a waddle; when they aren't belly sliding on the ice.) There, through elaborate courtship dances and songs, couples unite, and the female subsequently lays one egg. Their communal and individual task is to protect and nurture the future generation. For almost two months the males huddle, with the eggs safely cradled on top of their feet under their warm coats. Meanwhile, the females, having lost one-third of their body weight, return to the sea for food. By the time the mothers return to feed the newly hatched babies, the fathers have endured as much as 120 days without food and have lost half of their body weight! The mothers now become the protectors, while the fathers return to the sea. These journeys are made several times as the chicks grow and become independent, at which time both parents leave their young for a brief period. Finally the summer draws near with the ice floes melting and the ocean waters close enough for the young penguins to enter and begin their life in the sea, until four years later, when they too will return to the place where they were born and continue the life-cycle as their parents did.

What makes the film captivating, besides the natural beauty of these animals and their surroundings, is the depth of meaning that this movie embodies. It is not simply a documentary about the "facts"—eighty minutes of penguin sex, though it is also that. The movie is for many also about the viewers and their lives. Surprisingly, it opens us out as viewers to our own struggles for survival, our own need for family protection and care, and our own need to provide for our children. In the penguins' dance of survival, where timing is everything, we recognize our own dance for survival. We too have our struggles for survival; we too need to give and receive protection; we too must respond at the right time. There is, in short, a spiritual resonance that the film creates. *March of the Penguins* is not an allegory about human life as intended by the Creator (here is the mistake that Lennard Davis ridicules regarding the response of the conservative right). Rather the movie provides an understanding about "life," all life—particularly our own lives. The amazing truth of the movie is this: we can vicariously identify with those penguins!

Third, for many the movie is more than even a narrative inviting reflection on our own lives. It is also an Antarctic ballet where "lovers" and those they "love" are held in the balance. *March of the Penguins* is not simply about their lives, or even our lives. It is about the lives of all creatures big and small. Despite its brutal hardships and unforgiving ways, life in the Antarctic is also wonder filled and precious. The movie opens us up as viewers to the goodness of creation and to our responsibility somehow to work as hard as these penguins do to preserve it. In his critique of conservative Christian reactions to the movie, Davis says that when he went to see the film, he was left thinking: "How could there be a god that would subject the poor penguin to such horrendously difficult reproductive technology?" And as to the notion of loving families, it seemed strange to him that "the mothers and fathers abandon their chick to return to the sea when the chicks seem knee-high to a grasshopper, never to see them again."[49] But surely this is not the point of view of the film. It is wonder, not cynicism, that sets the tone for this movie (helped, of course, by the majestic voice of Morgan Freeman). Though a few females are portrayed trying to steal the eggs of others after the loss of their own due to the clumsiness of their mates, this does not detract from the movie's larger perspective on the sanctity of life—all life. Clearly, we all must do our part to help their world survive. Here is the film's unspoken, but enacted "agenda"; here is the *moral* duty it embodies; here is how we as viewers are to act out in love our commitment to life, all Life.

And finally as religious persons, many of us will find ourselves more open to marvel at the choreography of the Creator.

> "For everything there is a season, and a time for every matter under heaven:
>   a time to be born and a time to die. . . .
> [H]e has put a sense of past and future [i.e., eternity] into their minds, yet they cannot find out what God has done from the beginning to the end. I know there is nothing better for them than to be happy and enjoy themselves as long as they live; moreover, it is God's gift that all should eat and drink and take pleasure in all their toil."
>
> Ecclesiastes 3:1–2a, 11b–13

Even if this sacred "time" remains shrouded in mystery, just as for the writer of Ecclesiastes, the filmmakers and composer imbue the story with such humor, fear, pain, suffering, joy, and love, that for many viewers, its reality is not in doubt. *Penguins* are neither an argument for intelligent design nor propaganda for the anti-gay marriage movement, but it has provided many viewers a *transcendent* experience. We saw the movie with two friends who were struggling with whether they could risk their future by taking a job that would most likely mean struggle and insecurity. After reflecting on their experience in the theater, they told my wife and me the next day that they had decided to risk the unknown: "If God could take care of these 'stupid' penguins, surely God could take care of us as well." Here is the "anagogic" imagination.

Perhaps a comparison will clarify this suggested "thick description" of *March of the Penguins*. *Winged Migration* (2003) is another French-produced nature documentary, also with spectacular photography and portrayals of survival. It is also about birds, though this time those that soar effortlessly. However, lacking a compelling narrative structure—a story—it failed for most viewers to transport them beyond the surface beauty of the images (though the surface beauty is no small feat in itself). The analogical, the moral, and the transcendent dimensions of this movie remained largely absent, despite the stunning visuals. And the box-office receipts reflected this lack: $11 million for birds that flew, versus $100 million for birds that waddled, but a film that soared!

In his essay, "Poetry and the Christian," Karl Rahner, the Catholic theologian described by one writer as "a mystic of everyday life," sets forth a variation of these same four principles—principles first meant for unpacking sacred Scripture, but which invite a broader application to the reception of film. He speaks of being open to recognizing a mystery in the word (film) that is inseparable from the word, but not to be confused with it; of being open to hear (see) that which reaches the heart; of being open to hear (see) that which unites and reconciles; and of being open to experience "the overbright darkness, by which all the brightness of each day is encompassed, in a word: the abiding mystery which we call God."[50] Here is the experience of filmgoers worldwide, who, having been transfixed by what they see on the screen, are transported to a more central region where life takes on a richness and texture not ordinarily experienced. Through film, viewers may understand not only others but themselves more fully, be compelled outward to embrace others in communion, and be invited into the presence of the Other. There is a mystery here that defies codification, but the pattern is nonetheless discernible. It is what happens to many of us at the movies. Here is the basis for our theological exploration.

11

an exercise in dialogue: the movies of peter weir

As the twenty-first century's art form, movies continue to play a prominent role in our lives. In many ways they are our world's *lingua franca*. Just ask your kids! Though some are mere entertainment and diversion, many are not. Movies can widen our exposure to life and provide alternate viewpoints as to its meaning and significance. Movies recreate experience and awaken it to life. They reveal what an unaided eye might otherwise miss. This is why the artistic craft of a film, the means by which it portrays its story, is so crucial. Moviemakers and moviegoers alike ask the question, "Does it work?" And the answer is largely an aesthetic one.

Movies also have an ethical dimension, both by what they do and by what they don't. The discussion about sex and violence on the screen is pertinent, even if at times shrill and misleading. More important, however, is the variety of portrayals that the screen provides as to what it means to be human today. For through the stories they present, movies help shape the lives of their audience. That is, the "real" and the "reel" come together in the experience of the viewer. Perhaps the advertisement that declares "We are what we eat" overstates, but its truth with regard to movies is incontrovertible—"We are what we watch."

While movies are both aesthetically powerful and ethically affecting, they are not often considered a conversation partner for theology. It is this deficiency that *Reel Spirituality* has sought to address. Most of us recognize that we are being shaped emotionally and cognitively by what we see on the screen, but we seldom consider the realm of the spirit. Despite the truth of the spiritual's lyrics

"He's got the whole world in his hands," we seldom notice God's sacramental presence in the ordinary experiences of life, including our moviegoing. We fail to hear God speak. For this reason, we rarely respond theologically, whether critically or experientially. That is, Hollywood and the Christian faith are kept distinct, even if it is occasionally recognized that both help give shape to what we think and feel and to how we act.

Movies image life. Through editing and framing, music and screenplay, they give expression to memorable stories. As an art form, we might even say that they tell our stories. It was C. S. Lewis who recognized that "the story does what no theorem can quite do. It may not be 'like real life' in the superficial sense, but it sets before us an image of what reality may well be like at some more central region."[1] In their particularity, movies have the capacity to portray something universal about life and to convey it convincingly.

Reel Spirituality is about seeing and responding, about encountering stories that both interpret us and are interpreted by us. On the one hand, as John Ruskin put it, "The greatest thing a human soul ever does in this world is to see something and tell what it saw in a plain way."[2] Seeing and telling, however, cannot remain dispassionate if they are to be appropriate to the invitation of the movie story itself. For movie stories provide an interpretation of life, inviting movie-viewers to respond to them from their own perspective concerning life's power and meaning. In other words, our response to a movie (with its governing convictions) needs to be completed from a definite theological perspective. Such communion is called forth by the very artistic shape of the movie.

Movies offer meaning with regard to the facts of life. They make a claim, provide a perspective, and portray a reality. In order to help us see what they see, I have suggested a variety of critical approaches to aid our movie viewing. As stories, movies invite reflection on their formal characteristics—their plot, characterization, atmosphere, and point of view. As visual and aural stories, movies also express meaning and focus our attention through music and image. At one level, a movie story is to be experienced, not analyzed. But by reflecting critically on where and how the power and meaning of a given story is centered, the viewer can often see how best to enter into dialogue with it.

Alternately, a movie can be considered in terms of its theme. All good movies have a theme, an overall perspective, position, or point of view around which the content and images of the movie are chosen. A movie's genre provides it with a system of orientation as well as a means of communicating expectation. As such, genres give viewers cues as to the director's personal vision as well as to cultural values within the society. Auteur criticism explores how a particular movie can be illuminated by the similar themes and visual style that occur across the oeuvre of a director, as well as by the director's biography. And cultural criticism can help us recognize the context of the movie's creation, and the role of the audience as both recipients and active interpreters of a movie.

All of the above critical means help us unpack the power and meaning of a movie on its own terms. In thinking about how we might then complete the critical task by responding theologically to the movie's story, I have suggested that theology includes both the study "of" God (an experiential enterprise) and study "about" God (a critical task). Dialogue between filmic elements and convictions, on the one hand, and Christian experience and belief, on the other, can, therefore, be either experiential or reflective, spirit oriented or word oriented. Ideally it will be both. But in all cases, conversation between Christians and Hollywood should be two-way and open-ended, a dialogue and not a diatribe.

As we bring this study of the interrelationship of Christian theology and contemporary movies to a close, an extended example can be helpful in illustrating how these critical perspectives interact in practice. I have chosen to consider the movies of Peter Weir, and to respond critically and theologically to the stories they present.

Weir as Auteur

At the beginning of most of his films is the caption "A Peter Weir Film." This is not simply a marketing device or an expression of artistic ego. Audiences come to a Peter Weir movie expecting something specific, and their experience is filtered in that light.

Peter Weir came of age during the 1960s, sharing much of the anti-authoritarian and idealistic attitudes of his generation. In all of Weir's movies, the establishment is put on notice. Whether it is the army (*Gallipoli* [1981]) or the police (*Witness* [1985]), journalism (*The Year of Living Dangerously* [1982]) or television (*The Truman Show* [1998]), Appleyard College (*Picnic at Hanging Rock* [1975]) or Welton Academy (*Dead Poets Society* [1989]), New York liberals (*Green Card* [1990]; *Fearless* [1993]) or British sea captains (*Master and Commander* [2003]), Australian lawyers (*The Last Wave* [1977]) or American industrialists (*The Mosquito Coast* [1986]), Weir's movies challenge the power structure. Like other Australians of his era, Weir has been impatient with the enforced conformity of the older generation. He has questioned their alliances and structures and has opposed their intolerance. He has recognized there must be something more than the materialism they have fostered. As an alternative, in a number of his films he has explored the spiritual and the uncanny. Here is our beginning point for understanding Weir's movies.

Peter Weir usually puts his characters into closed situations or hostile environments. *Master and Commander*, where his two lead characters are aboard a warship on the open sea, is paradigmatic. His solutions to the needs of his characters, however, are rarely structural or political. Weir is not a social commentator or ethicist. He has not produced movies to critique the military or challenge the legal system. In fact, though his films are situated in the public world, they are not so much interested in it as in the private world, the shadows that lie behind. His movies deal not as much with his characters' external circumstance as with their internal situation. While society's voyeurism is questioned in *The Truman Show*, for example, the movie is more interested in Truman the person. Can he really be a whole human being in the artificial environment of Seahaven Island? While the political unrest and squalor of Jakarta are portrayed in *The Year of Living Dangerously*, Guy Hamilton's personal growth is the film's focus. *Picnic at Hanging Rock* reveals class issues, and *The Last Wave* brings to light the plight of the Aborigines. But neither film ultimately shows much interest in structural solutions. While *Witness* deals with a shooting within an Amish context and *Gallipoli* and *Master and Commander* show the horrors of war, none of these is really about violence. Viewers will bring their own political agendas to Weir's movies and might even be moved to act politically by what they see, but that is not his movies' primary focus.

Rather, Peter Weir's movies are more mythic than realistic. Their specific contexts simply support a larger, more universal intention. In his stories Weir proves to be a romantic, someone convinced that individuals must take control of their own lives, break free from society's constraints, and create a new vision of what it is to be human. He presents to his audience a take on human liberation, and through it, a portrayal of what it is to be a whole person. Weir's heroes and heroines are not just people who are educated or cultured, but people who are at home in the world, particularly given its mystery. Weir would have us "seize the day," choose our love, go back to our jobs transformed, or else fail trying. It is a vision of life that he seeks to portray, not a solution to life's problems.

Weir began his career in the 1960s, just as the Australian film industry was coming alive after a thirty-year hiatus. An immigrant people who left all behind to come to a new land, Australians have often viewed themselves as largely without an identity, without a story. Weir thus set out in his early films to provide not a commentary on issues facing Australians, but a story by which they might celebrate their identity. He attempted to provide a myth by which Australians could envision themselves. In *The Year of Living Dangerously*, both Billy Kwan and Guy Hamilton are half-Australian, struggling with their identities. Billy says to Guy, "We're divided men. Your father an American, mine Chinese. We're not certain we're Australians. . . . [W]e're not quite at home in the world." Much of Weir's initial work focused on this issue: How could the Australian experience (nature's vast and hostile expanse, "mateship," an indigenous people, a difficult circumstance) be put to the service of something more fundamental, the providing of a sense of identity?

It is not just Australians who feel personal dislocation and dis-ease, however. Even though Peter Weir has shifted his location from Australia to Hollywood, and his style from "art-film" to studio movie, he has continued creating universal stories of human possibility. And new audiences have discovered his movies. Peter Weir has transcended his culture and has filmed stories that challenge and renew the human spirit. He would have us transcend our cultures and "seize the day."

Weir's Thematic Concerns

Peter Weir is a storyteller interested in life's central issues—death, nature, friendship, freedom, spirit, and the like. His films are rooted in particular times and places, but they focus on life's fundamental concerns: "What then must we do?" How can we "seize the day"? Is there a reality beyond our surface existence?

As Weir has portrayed on the screen the shape and possibility of human life, he has focused his individual movies on particular thematic concerns—death, Nature, "dreamtime," Asia, "seize the day," friendship. That is, together with his screenwriters, he has organized and empowered his stories by focusing on a given perspective. *Gallipoli*, for example, is not so much about the massive defeat of Australian and New Zealander troops in 1915 on the Gallipoli Peninsula in Turkey, as about the Australian phenomenon of "mateship." In the isolation of the outback, women stayed home to care for children, and men went off to work. In that context, friendships between men developed that were close and innocent. These bushmen made up the core of the Australian army that fought in World War I. Their camaraderie and mutual support is what Weir tried to capture in his film. In an interview (1984), he said:

> It's often said of male filmmakers that we don't deal effectively with women. I think what's more to the point is that we don't deal effectively with emotion, with feminine aspects of the personality, which are also contained in the male. In a stridently heterosexual, macho society, these are doubly dangerous things to deal with, because they can be easily misconstrued.[3]

The tenderness of friendship is given central importance in *Gallipoli*, but it is an important theme in other of Weir's movies as well. In his romantic portrayal of what it is to be human, Weir would have us let the gentler, more intuitive side of our being surface (cf. *Dead Poets Society*, *The Year of Living Dangerously*, *Fearless*, *Green Card* [where the gender characteristics are reversed], *The Truman Show*, *Master and Commander*). Weir would blur the distinctions between those male and female characteristics that we all possess, something he symbolized brilliantly in casting Linda Hunt as Billy Kwan in *The Year of Living Dangerously*. Although *The Year of Living Dangerously* is on one level an adventure story about the political turmoil in Indonesia that characterized the 1970s and 1980s, it is actually about "Asia."[4] It is about the missing spiritual component that the West needs and which is evident in the East. In "Asia," there are the puppet-masters, those able both to balance left and right and to focus their attention on the shadows that the puppets create rather than on the puppets themselves. Billy Kwan, with one foot in each culture, is the appropriate guide into this culture for Guy Hamilton, a foreign correspondent for the Australian Broadcasting Service. As they explore Jakarta, however, Guy seems incapable of seeing anything but his career opportunities—anything, that is, but the puppets. When Guy betrays the confidence of Jill Bryant and publishes secret information about an arms shipment that she has given him, Billy challenges him, saying, "You abuse your position as journalist." Guy has failed to respond to the spiritual, to the gift of friendship that Jill has offered. He has valued detachment over commitment, career over relationship. In the process, he has failed to see as Asians see. He has failed to look beyond the "puppets" themselves. As the movie ends, Guy, having begun to learn his lesson, risks his external eyesight and his career to pursue his love. He now has eyes to see other realities.

In subsequent movies, Weir returns to this same theme: there is in the West a missing spiritual component. *Witness*, *Dead Poets Society*, *The Mosquito Coast*, *Green Card*, *Fearless*, *The Truman Show*, and *Master and Commander* all explore the life of the spirit (the shadow). There is more than the surface realities of life, something his early movies also portrayed. One can substitute Anzac, Amish, or Aborigine for Asian. The concrete political reality is important but only as the occasion to delve beneath the surface to explore life itself.

Or again, Weir has said that in *Picnic at Hanging Rock*, "The grand theme was Nature, and even the girls' sexuality was as much a part of that as the lizard crawling across the top of the rock. They were part of the same whole; part of larger questions."[5] Hanging Rock is itself a volcanic eruption that has forced itself up from the earth's crust. It represents the untamed forces of nature. It is a symbol for a more ancient knowledge (like the Aboriginal "dreamtime" in *The Last Wave*) that provides the schoolgirls entrance into adulthood. The primitive power of Nature over ongoing life is announced with the credits. On the screen we read, "On Saturday 14 February 1900, a party of schoolgirls from Appleyard College picnicked at Hanging Rock near Mt. Macedon in the state of Victoria. During the afternoon, several members of the party disappeared without a trace. . . ." Nature simply engulfed them. No answers are provided in the movie about what happened or where they went. Not even a coherent story is related. Rather, Weir is content to present the problem. Nature does not always give up her secrets.

"*Picnic at Hanging Rock* presents humankind's total helplessness when confronted with the inexplicable."[6] Weir, once again, makes this his thematic center in *Fearless*. After miraculously surviving a plane crash, Max Klein, a successful architect, must somehow make sense out of the surrealistic nonsense of his life. But there is no sense, no rational solace to be given. Therapists are helpless. The promise of an insurance settlement is a profanity. There is no answer for the horror of death he has experienced. As the audience is allowed into Max's thoughts through a series of flashbacks dramatizing the horrific crash, we hear in the background the music of Henryk Gorecki's Symphony no. 3, a haunting piece composed in 1976 for performance at the magnificent St. Magnus Church near Auschwitz. If there is to be hope in such desperate circumstances, it will only be born of such sorrow.

Weir's Use of Genre

Weir has chosen a new genre for each of his films, though usually to subvert or to cross it with elements of other genres. *Fearless*, for example, is a disaster movie. But in order to emphasize that the real suspense is internal, not external, to his character, the disaster happens at the beginning of the movie, not the end. Weir would have us know that it is not the action of the "puppets" but the "shadows" they produce (cf. the Wayang in *The Year of Living Dangerously*) that is of paramount importance. In both *Picnic at Hanging Rock* and *The Last Wave*, Weir has written and directed a horror film, a fantasy that allows him freedom from the constraints of linear thought. (One might compare it to *The Blair Witch Project* [1999].) He can explore the inexplicable without being forced prematurely toward closure.

The variety of Weir's use of genre is impressive. *Green Card* is in the tradition of the screwball comedy, a romantic farce that creates an expectation in the audience that indeed the "opposites" will eventually come together. *Dead Poets Society* is a coming-of-age movie about male adolescents. The genre allows Weir again to explore the shape of the human and to portray the need for us to "seize the day." Dealing with the influence of an inspiring teacher, it also is able to portray the importance of someone to guide you on your journey (cf. Chris in *The Last Wave* and Billy in *The Year of Living Dangerously*). *Gallipoli* and *Master and Commander* (though the latter is more nuanced) are war movies that qualify the macho, redefining in the process what is appropriately masculine.

The Truman Show is of particular interest in that it confronts the boundaries between illusion and reality. It was one of a number of films surrounding its release that dealt with a story within a story: *Pleasantville* (1998), *Wag the Dog* (1997), *Illuminata* (1998), *Edtv* (1999), and *The Game* (1997) to name a few. In each case, "the real" and "the reel," the actual and the simulation, are blurred. We are no longer sure what is rational and what is irrational. The surface is not always what it seems. In *Pleasantville*, the mysterious Don Knotts character is fairly harmless, even if the closed society of the 1950s to which he leads the teenagers is anything but colorful or fulfilling of the human potential. *The Game* is more sinister. The simulations that are played are actually staged, and Michael Douglas is a pawn. And with the character of Christof in *The Truman Show*, the unknown power turns destructive.[7] In each case the "shadows" behind the "puppets" are hardly spiritual in nature. They are simply human manipulation.

But these movies also hint at something more, as our spirits cry out for a Reality by which to judge the "real."

Perhaps Weir's most successful use of a genre to reflect his larger mythic interests is his film *Witness*. The movie is a Western (!), now transposed into Amish territory. John Book, like his counterpart Shane, enters a new community, a stranger to all in that society. He is given special status in the community, even while he is not fully accepted. There is a clear threat to the Amish society from the corrupt Philadelphia police, who have guns and power while the Amish have nothing. Book is friends with the enemy; in fact, he is one of them. Yet Book has rejected their corrupt ways. When the police threaten the Amish way of life and the safety of one of their children, Book defeats the cops in a scene reminiscent of *High Noon* (1952), bringing safety and peace to the community again. Book is a hero, but he must leave. His violent ways are foreign to the Amish and inappropriate for an ongoing relationship with Rachel Lapp. Book says good-bye and then returns to Philadelphia. Here is an almost "pure" expression of the typical plot of the Western.

As with *Shane*, the shape of the plot allows a spiritual, idealized quality to issue forth. There is something quasi-mystical, for example, in the movie's presentations of the barn-raising episode, in John's wearing the less "manly" clothes of the new community, in the chaste love between Rachel and John, in the contrast between rural safety and urban violence, even in the musical score of Maurice Jarre that echoes *Appalachian Spring* and evokes a past frontier. As with the Aboriginal culture in *The Last Wave*, the Anzac innocence in *Gallipoli*, and the Asian culture of *The Year of Living Dangerously*, and even the naturalist perspective of Stephen Maturin in *Master and Commander*, the Amish community in *Witness* is cognizant of life's "shadow," that spiritual alternative to the corrupt materialism and heightened rationalism that has stifled the modern West. Though the Amish might need the protection of modern society from modern society, it is modern society that is in fact the more needy in this clash of two cultures.

Weir's Cultural Concerns

Peter Weir has portrayed in all of his movies a clash between two cultures, not in order to provide political insight, but to reveal a greater depth of meaning lurking behind and under these surface confrontations. In his early movies, Weir used such cultural conflict in the service of creating an Australian myth. The typical rationality of the West needed to be challenged, whether from Aboriginal alternatives or the outback example. In the confrontation, something of permanence shone through.

Since "moving" to Hollywood, Weir has continued to look for juxtapositions between, or within, cultures that can expose and counter the dehumanizing effects of modernity and allow the wonder of life to resurface. In *Green Card*, for example, we see the romantic immigrant challenging the modern, independent woman. In *Witness*, Rachel Lapp helps John Book see the pretense of Philadelphia, the "city of brotherly love." It is not as clear, however, what Book is to do about it. In *The Mosquito Coast*, Weir portrays the hollowness of the industrial North as Allie Fox, an eccentric inventor, flees the United States, which he says he loves, only to impose his alternative society, a jungle utopia, on the Mosquito Coast's population. In *Dead Poets Society*, it is objectivist and pragmatic educational strategies that encounter the romantic passion of Robin Williams's character, again with mixed results. In *Master and Commander*, Captain Jack Aubrey, the military man and realist, and Dr. Stephen Maturin, the naturalist and intellectual, represent the cultural clash. But each share qualities of the other and their lifelong debate about the nature of human life is more nuanced for this reason. Weir realizes that life is more complex than his romantic vision might long for. We cannot put Humpty-Dumpty back together again. Vietnam ended that dream. But the dream persists.

Like others of his generation, Peter Weir's artistic imagination continues to express the idealistic, anti-institutional, anti-imperialistic, and anti-authoritarian commitments of the sixties. He came of age in the cauldron of nationalistic liberations, the women's movement, civil rights, and the opening of the East. It is not the politics of this period, or even the polemics, however, that has captured his soul, but its largely implicit spirituality. The yearning for wholeness, the vague recognition of Otherness, the desire to "make love, not war," the desire for personal fulfillment, a recognition of the value of the Dionysian and not just the Apollonian, a longing to be one with Nature—just as then, so now, it is this larger spiritual vision that is the goal of Weir's films.

In *The Truman Show*, we perhaps best see Weir's "counterculture" mind-set as he explores the spiritual consequences of virtual reality in our computer age. Soon after the movie was released, I watched a news segment on TV concerning a legal battle in Tampa, Florida, between the city council and a business using the Internet. Voyeurdorm.com was making over $300,000 yearly by broadcasting images from a "dorm" house where six female college students lived. As with Truman Burbank, in every room there were webcams that showed the coeds as they lived together. Voyeuristic Internet viewers paid $35 monthly to see the women taking showers, studying, eating, talking on the telephone, and so on. There was no privacy. The city council argued that "voyeurdorm.com" was an "adult" business in a residential section that was in violation of zoning codes. But the real issue was certainly deeper than zoning codes or even the morality of adult entertainment. As in *The Truman Show*, we were being asked whether we could reduce human life to a commodity. Was there not a sanctity, even a sacredness, to life that was somehow being violated?

Truman Burbank (Jim Carrey) lives his life in front of the TV camera. *The Truman Show* (d. Weir, 1998). Photo by Melinda Sue Gordon. ©1998 by Paramount Pictures. All rights reserved.

Weir as Storyteller

Peter Weir calls himself first of all a storyteller, not a moviemaker. He believes that fiction "can give you a truth within its own set of lies."[8] Weir says,

> I belong to that tradition of entertainer or storyteller. There's this cartoon up on my wall of an old lady at a ticket box window saying, "I want my sense of wonder back." I like that idea. It's a desire to feel the sense of not knowing, that sense of danger and potential interlocked. It's very difficult to achieve, but the screen is one of the few places where it is possible.[9]

While skill in the techniques of filming and a sensitivity to the cultural values of one's audience are important, these are not at the heart of filmmaking for Weir. Weir once gave a lecture in a media course where the instructor emphasized the technical functions of a film crew (hitting their marks with the camera or dressing a set). Weir challenged such an approach, saying:

> Right—let's get all this gear out of the way. This has got nothing to do with it, nothing. Let's just talk, about anything, everything, about stories, experiences. You've got too much of this gear. It's summoning up the ideas that's the hard thing—the inspiration, the passion. Without them, this stuff's useless.[10]

Plot

As he tells his story on the screen, Weir is less concerned with the power of his plots than with what they surface. Weir wants to give back to the lady at the box office her sense of wonder. Over his career, he has shifted the perspective of his plots from European ambiguity and nondisclosure to Hollywood's linear and predictable narrative conventions. But the neat closure is still usually avoided (Keating is fired; Book returns to Philadelphia; Bronte stays in New York; and Aubrey ends up challenging Maturin's absolutism). Ambiguity is simply part of the stuff of life.

In the usual Weir movie, middle-class and WASP characters are driven by forces they do not fully understand and encounter something inexplicable and mysterious, usually from another culture (the Amish, a Frenchman, a near-death experience, a loving embrace from a nonactor, the East, a naturalist, and so on). Through this experience, the inadequacy of dominant, Western culture is made clear. The mysterious confronts the individual, for which the typical, rational patterns of understanding prove ineffective. The otherness that is encountered is not sinister, although it is often perceived as a threat to WASP civilization. Instead, this clash of cultures provides an opportunity for a character's personal growth. Here is the archetypal Weir plot.

Character

Weir's characters are typically newcomers from an outside world who encounter a new culture and struggle to understand it. They are firmly planted in the rational world. They are lawyers, reporters, teachers, policemen, military men, and social activists who encounter something alien. In the process they are offered the opportunity for human growth. In *The Mosquito Coast*, Allie Fox goes into a Central American jungle, while in *The Last Wave*, David Burton explores the underground world of the Aborigines. In *Witness*, similarly, John Book finds himself in the closed religious community of the Amish. But Weir also varies the shape of these cultural confrontations that bring the possibility of growth and insight to the characters. In *Dead Poets Society*, Weir has the more spiritually sensitive character enter a less spiritually open context. John Keating, a poet, teaches at Welton Academy, where discipline and tradition threaten to squeeze out the humanity of his students. In *The Truman Show*, Weir alters the scenario once again by having Truman unaware that his culture is alien, while still longing for another. Still again, in *Fearless*, the alien culture turns out to be Max's own, Max now having survived a near-death experience in a plane crash. And in *Master and Commander* there are two cultural perspectives, each needing the insight of the other. In each case, character development revolves around this clash of two cultures.

In order that a character might achieve insight and personal growth, a mediator is sometimes present. This individual remains outside society's norms and embodies the values and heart of the particular film. Just as the Aborigine Chris Lee serves this role for David Burton in *The Last Wave*, helping him to move between Aboriginal and white Australian cultures, so Billy Kwan, half-Asian and half-Australian, is able to assist Guy Hamilton in *The Year of Living Dangerously*. These individuals are almost Christ figures in their life-giving and sacrificial love. But usually such persons are less all-knowing or spiritually alive, and their lives are not put at stake. Georges, a lovable but oafish Frenchman, is the catalytic figure for Bronte in *Green Card*, while Lauren/Sylvia is an actress with a conscience in *The Truman Show* who causes Truman to want something more. Moreover, while John Keating's charisma proves catalytic for his student John Anderson in *Dead Poets Society*, another student, Neil Perry, commits suicide.

For Weir, while insight is often mediated by another, it remains highly personal, even individualistic, in its achievement. The center of Weir's vision is not on the "savior" figure, but on personal and spiritual growth in his characters, particularly in an individual's own encounter with mystery and otherness. Weir remains strongly individualistic in his vision of life.

Atmosphere

It is not his plot, then, or even his characterizations (though the star power of Richard Chamberlain, Mel Gibson, Harrison Ford, Robin Williams, Jeff Bridges, and Jim Carrey should not be discounted) that propel Weir's movies forward. Rather, the source of power and meaning in his movies is the atmosphere he creates, the sense of otherness that controls the story and drives it ahead. This is more than a mere mood; it is the inalterable backdrop against which his story is played out. There is a spiritual presence—that which produces a sense of wonder, which the old woman in Weir's cartoon desired—that is the real star of his films.

Peter Weir shows us that there is something more out there, something far more powerful than civilization is prone to admit. Both Jack Aubrey and Stephen Maturin must learn to yield before it. This deeper reality is embedded in the meaning of the Wayang in *The Year of Living Dangerously*, in Hanging Rock, poetry, the open sea, barn raisings, and the French. The Amish recognize its presence, as do the Aborigines and the Anzac. Near-death experiences provide access to it, as does the death of a mate. There is something outside the "bubble" of our civilized but routine life, as Truman Burbank is set on discovering. For Weir, even the absence of mystery propels forth a sense of its presence. Here is Weir's romantic portrayal of life, one that is neither naive nor uncritical, but which nevertheless sides with innocence, myth, nature, and the uncanny.[11]

Point of View

Opening. The primal otherness of Weir's movies is conveyed to his viewers primarily through his stories' point of view, the implied narrator's attitude toward the story's subject and audience. Weir often begins to paint a backdrop of mystery and otherness even as the opening credits roll. In *The Last Wave*, for example, the movie opens with an Aborigine artist drawing mysterious symbols on the roof of a cave. The scene changes to a small town in the Australian desert where torrential rain and golf-ball-sized hail fall from a cloudless sky as the grade-school teacher tells her Aborigine children, "We are witnessing nature at work." This linking of Aborigine myth with unusual and violent weather continues to set the tone of the storytelling throughout the remainder of the movie. There is something larger than human life and activity to which we are beholden.

In *Witness*, we are first introduced to the pastoral life of the Amish as waving grain gives way to a small rural settlement. The initial look is of the nineteenth century, complete with horse and buggy and old-fashioned costume. But the title that is superimposed on the screen, "Pennsylvania, 1984," jars its viewers back into the present. There is created in this way a strong dreamlike atmosphere that invites our curiosity. The opening is both evocative and enigmatic. Again, in *Fearless*, Weir sets up the film's perspective through the opening scene. We are shown the nightmarish aftermath of the crash of an airplane. People are wandering through a cornfield in slow motion. From the air, the site of the crash has an almost surreal quality to it. Max is seen wandering aimlessly, holding a baby. The scene is one of devastation beyond belief. The remainder of the movie is Max's (and our) response to what we have seen. It is almost more than we can bear. In ways such as this, Weir uses the movie's point of view to make central in his stories its atmosphere—the spiritual otherness that lies beyond the plot and character development, giving shape to them.

Image. Weir has commented on the influence of painting in helping him capture a perspective. Before many of his shots, Weir will develop a folio of postcards, photographs, advertisements, and paintings to help him with the framing and lighting. For example, Sydney Nolan's paintings of Gallipoli were influential in helping Weir create mythlike figures and a dreamlike effect in *Gallipoli*. For *Picnic at Hanging Rock*, Weir studied the impressionistic paintings of the Heidelberg School in Australia at the turn of the twentieth century with their sunlit landscapes and natural realism. Such landscapes contrasted starkly with the Victorian stereotypes of the period, with their imposed and buttoned-up values. This became the clue for Weir's framing of the movie.

In *Witness*, the influence of the Flemish painters, particularly Vermeer, is evident in certain scenes (for example, when Rachel is taking a sponge bath or when she is nursing John back to health). There the framing of the images through the doorway and the delicate lighting are evocative of something transcendent. Weir has acknowledged this Flemish influence, noting that he went to an exhibition of Dutch masters that opened in Philadelphia during the filming of that movie. It is perhaps not too exaggerated to say that the real story in many of Weir's films is told through images such as these. It is these "landscapes of the soul" that we remember and which provide the viewer a rich source of meaning.

Music. Music also contributes much to the shaping of Weir's movies' perspectives. In fact, Weir has commented,

> Music is the fountainhead, the source of all my inspiration, in a way, if you can generalize. It certainly doesn't have anything to do with words and such. Storytelling is my trade, my craft. But music is my inspiration; and my goal, my metaphor, to affect people like music. The images should float over you like music, and the experience should be beyond words.[12]

Weir first used his music to this effect in *Picnic at Hanging Rock*, with its eerie evocation of the natural and yet mystical through the use of panpipes. Or consider *Witness*. When Rachel and John Book dance in the Amish barn to Sam Cooke's "What a Wonderful World That Would Be," we ache for them and yet feel their otherness. And, as the barn raising proceeds, Maurice Jarre's echoing of Aaron Copeland's *Appalachian Spring* helps rivet its images in our souls, reminding us of another time and place when communal values were cherished and family was judged central.

In *Green Card*, Weir juxtaposes a flute concerto by Mozart, which is heard as Bronte takes care of her apartment's rooftop garden, with the street sounds of the city. Yet it is the absence of any music—just the dripping of water—as Bronte returns to her garden after Georges leaves which signals that there is something missing in her life that Georges has uncovered. Their romance cannot be long in coming. In this comedy of manners, the music of life must again sound forth.

Weir's most powerful use of music to provide a point of view that evokes a sense of wonder, however, is in *Fearless*. Max's dislocation is reinforced by the playing of such popular music as U2's "Where the Streets Have No Name." It is not until the sequence at the end of the movie, though, when a flashback is shown of the inside of the plane during the crash, that a sense of transcendence is achieved. The mystery of death and life is conveyed in part through the use of blue light and slow motion. But it is the music, Henryk Gorecki's Symphony no. 3, sometimes called the *Symphony of Sorrowful Songs*, that transports the viewer. Gorecki chose for the text of his first movement a fifteenth-century Polish lament of Mary, the mother of Jesus ("My son, my chosen and beloved / Share your wounds with your mother. . . . Although you are already leaving me, my cherished hope"). The symphony's text continues with a prayer that was found inscribed on the wall of a cell in the Gestapo's headquarters in Zakopane. And it concludes with a Polish mother's folk song lamenting the loss of her child who "lies in his grave and I do not know where though I keep asking people everywhere." It is this last movement that Weir has chosen to use in the film. But the cumulative power of the three movements is simply overpowering in the context of this story. Who will bear our sorrows? Music critics speak of this symphony as evoking "a hope born of sorrow that is not itself sorrow."[13] Here is the wonder of *Fearless* too. The music and the image have joined to portray a hope beyond sorrow. As Laura pleads with Max not to die, he opens his eyes. "I'm alive," he gasps. And they hug. Life begins anew from out of the ashes.

In ways such as these, Weir's artistic stamp helps provide a point of view for each of his films. We can also note his preference for close-ups of long duration on a character's face to create intimacy or to show contrasts. His use of slow-motion and soft-focus shots to create almost a metaphysical quality. His fascination with water as reflecting primal forces, whether peaceful or chaotic. His choice of blue light to project an atmosphere of mystery. His long visual sequences with little or no dialogue. His fascination with light. His seeing through a window or door. All of these stylistic devices are characteristic of a Peter Weir film and add to the sense of presence that he seeks to evoke.

Beneath the often calm exterior of civilized life, Weir would have us to see lurking a sense of the "other." Even when the superficial presence of life would seem to deny that there is anything other or more (as in *Green Card*, or better in *The Truman Show*), the very absence of mystery suggests a sense of its presence. There must be more to life than the television set of Seahaven Island. Although Georges might be an oaf, he is open to life's rhythms and is willing to accept their surprises. Bronte is slower than her viewers to see the light, but it happens.

Responding Theologically

Having experienced Peter Weir's stories on the screen, having encountered their sense of otherness, of presence, of mystery, how are we to respond? How might we dialogue with these stories? Critique them? Learn from them? In Walter Ong's words, "How might we as viewers enter into communion with [them]?"[14] There are, of course, as many responses as there are viewers, as the sense of presence in Weir's stories encounter our stories. Let me respond from my own understanding of life's center of power and meaning, and through this, invite your own reflection on your response. Perhaps my brief reflections can encourage you to engage in the total criticism that is invited by any serious work of art.

Nathan Scott reminds us:

[T]his normative story [the Christian story] that comes down to us from a time long ago is likely to become something desiccated and moribund, if it is not being kept constantly in a lively interplay with all that issues forth from the important storytellers of the age. For, apart from this kind of confluence, the normative story will have no chance to discover new idioms and narrative stratagems whereby it can be retold in fresh and arresting ways: nor will it have a chance to gather the kind of new vitality that can come only, as it were, by its "proving" itself against those stories that offer some radical challenge to its essential validity.[15]

Christian theology can be made stronger both as it is challenged by and itself challenges Weir's vision of life. Let me, in particular, suggest three different approaches that this theological dialogue might take, each reflecting a different place on our theological/critical matrix:

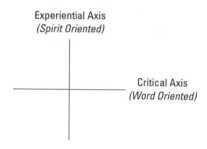

Figure 11.1 Response Matrix for Weir's Films

The Critical Axis

STAYING WITHIN THE MOVIE ITSELF

In the typical Peter Weir film, a clash of cultures is portrayed, in which an outsider finds himself in an alien setting. In the face of a universe that they (we) cannot control (the chief obstacle being death itself), Weir's characters begin to ask, "What then must we do?" They become aware that life has layers of meaning of which they were previously unaware. They begin to see the "shadows" or perhaps to explore the uncanny and the mysterious. They sense life's fundamental ambiguity. They realize that they must get beneath the banality of culture in the West, for life is precious and valued. As Weir's heroes encounter life's terror and joy, they discover their humanity and find the courage to "seize the day." Truman Burbank is perhaps the quintessential example of such a person, but Guy Hamilton in *The Year of Living Dangerously*, John Book in *Witness*, Frank Dunne in *Gallipoli*, Bronte Parrish in *Green Card*, and Max Klein in *Fearless* might also be viewed as examples.

This wider work of "Spirit/spirit" (this is my language; Weir leaves the experience nameless) is problematic for many contemporary Christians. For Christians, particularly Protestants, the experience of spirit is too often limited to a focus on the Holy Spirit's role in the church as the Spirit of redemption and sanctification. It is given, that is, a specific Christological focus. There is too scant mention in Christian theology of the Spirit's presence in nature, in culture's activity, or even in human relationships. And there is little recognition of the human spirit's ability to discern the shape of human life apart from the teaching of the church. Conscience, creation, and creature are too often ignored as spiritual resources. Weir's films can help us recover this creation-based theology. The intimations of Spirit/spirit found in his movies are real expressions of grace, if we would but listen. Moreover, I would suggest, they have strong biblical resonance.

The spiritual center of life as created is the theological heart of the book of Ecclesiastes, for example. Weir's films can help us recover something of this creation-based perspective. For like Weir, the writer of that book, Qoheleth (the Preacher), portrays the vanity of seeking life's meaning and purpose in wisdom, riches, or pleasure. Here is a critique of the West similar to that which Weir portrays. Materialism and rationality make no difference in one's ultimate fate, for death is the great leveler (Eccles. 2:14–16); greed, the real motivator (4:4). Life proves oftentimes amoral (8:9–14), and God's will remains mysterious (3:11; 6:12). And yet, for Qoheleth, life's fragility does not negate its fragrance. As a gift from God, life must be viewed as good (5:18–20). There is nothing better than to enjoy life (2:24–26; 3:12, 22; 8:15), for it is a gift from God (9:7–10; 11:7–10).

Here, too, is the lesson Max Klein learns at great personal cost. So too, John Book, Guy Hamilton, and Truman Burbank. Despite the superficiality and banality of life as it presents itself, life's joys are precious and to be protected. The call of Spirit/spirit is dialectical. Though observable life is often evil and finally incoherent, life is nonetheless sacred and to be valued. The anguish of Weir's characters, as for Qoheleth, is in knowing how to embrace this paradox. At times, Qoheleth's experience causes him to hate life (2:17; 4:2). But he also commends life, for it is God's gift (3:13). The days of our lives, the ability to eat and drink and find enjoyment in our work, even our very spirit are spiritual gifts. Weir shies away from the use of theological language, and his vision of common grace is not Christian in its particulars. But then, neither is "common grace."

Peter Weir's movies can help those of us in the church recover something of life's common mystery and grace. They provide images of the larger life of the Spirit/spirit, with all its terror and attractiveness. In a less overtly religious style, they reflect that paradox of existence that Elizabeth Barrett Browning captures so well.

> Natural things
> And spiritual—who separates those two
> In art, in morals, or the social drift,
> Tears up the bond of nature and brings death,

Paints futile pictures, writes unreal verse,
Leads vulgar days, deals ignorantly with men,
Is wrong, in short, at all points. . . .
. . . .
Earth's crammed with heaven,
And every common bush afire with God:
But only he who sees, takes off his shoes,
The rest sit round it, and pluck blackberries.
. . . .
Not one day, in the artist's ecstasy,
But every day, feast, fast, or working-day,
The spiritual significance burn through
The hieroglyphic of material shows,
Henceforward he would paint the globe with wings,
And reverence fish and fowl, the bull, the tree,
And even his very body as a man.

Elizabeth Barrett Browning, *Aurora Leigh*, book 7[16]

LEARNING FROM A THEOLOGICAL PARTNER

Weir's romantic vision, an expression in part of the 1960s in which he was raised, reminds me of the writings of another student of the same era, Sam Keen. A former professor of theology and popular lecturer and writer in psychology, Keen presents in his first book (and also his best), *Apology for Wonder*, an argument for "wonder." Keen paints a bleak picture of contemporary Western life much like Weir's, and then turns to consider the rediscovery of life's sacredness in the quotidian, the everyday and earthy. By considering Keen's "diagnosis" and "solution" to modern humanity's ills, we might be able better to understand the dialectic at work in Weir's films.

Keen believes the typical Westerner lives under a Promethean illusion, attempting to evade the reality of our transience. He speaks of our "scrubbing compulsion of the mind."[17] Through wealth, competition, politics, and a youthful façade, we seek to hide our "dis-ease" from ourselves. We seek order, reasonableness, and discipline. Yet, we remain impotent. This "masculine" image makes it impossible to appreciate the more "feminine" modes of perceiving and relating to the world. Sterile both in our environment and in our attitudes, Western "man" does not participate sensually so as to create authentic life.[18] Think of Guy Hamilton, John Book, and Max Klein, three of Weir's characters who discover their lives to be hollow. Think, too, of the parents and administration of Welton Academy, or even of Bronte Parrish, a woman who has learned the manipulative lifestyle of a man's world. Perhaps even Captain Jack Aubrey fits here.

Instead of such self-defeating rationalizations, Keen believes we should ask ourselves where we have trembled or been fascinated. Perhaps it is through an experience of nature, at the ocean or on a mountain. Sometimes it is when we are truly in community. Keen recalls when the civil rights protesters sang "We

Shall Overcome" with Martin Luther King Jr. It might happen in our sexuality. Or our panic. Or when somebody tells his or her story and suddenly it is also "my" story. For Keen, such experiences are sacred. They are also often the heart of Weir's portrayals, as we have seen.

Keen believes that we must rediscover our ability to wonder, and we do this through story. Story helps integrate past, present, and future. For Keen this story will not be external to us, but one that focuses on our own experiences. It is one's own biography, one's own experience, which will testify to the holy.[19] Here too is Weir. Truman Burbank is no longer to live the script that others have produced for him. We see him walking through the door into a new life as the movie ends. After his near-death experience, Max must similarly walk through the tunnel into a new light and write a fresh story with Laura, his wife. Bronte realizes that her ordered and scripted life is bankrupt. She has been living another's script. At the end of *Green Card*, she is given the invitation to begin her story anew in France with Georges. Jill gives a similar invitation to Guy in *The Year of Living Dangerously*. Even though John Book will return to Philadelphia to live anew his story, he has become a changed man through his encounter with Rachel and the Amish, someone now committed to making that urban center a "city of brotherly love."

Third, Keen argues that we must become "dis-illusioned," that is, we must shed those illusions that would have us possess rather than admire, exploit rather than enjoy, grasp rather than accept.[20] It is the poet within us that must come forth. We must live with ambiguity and open-endedness. As John Keating illustrates and Keen affirms, even a touch of madness is allowed, but only a touch. Sam Keen writes:

> Dionysus becomes the god of destruction and insanity if he keeps his worshippers in the wilderness with the promise of endless ecstasy rather than sending them back to the quotidian with a renewed vision of what might be possible if the community of man gave up warfare and began dancing together. We must listen to madness to find the seed of wisdom it contains, but we must not make madness an ideal.[21]

Accepting with wonder life's mystery, learning afresh to tell our stories, and forsaking our illusions of dominance and rationality—here is Sam Keen's therapy/theology. Such a romantic vision for life's possibilities is not dissimilar to that provided by the movies of Peter Weir. But can we call this theological? Keen calls himself an ex-theologian, and Peter Weir has certainly not provided his viewers an explicitly Christian vision. It would be dishonest to baptize either one a "Christian." Yet there is a deep spirituality in both. Their phenomenological approach to the mysterious and wonder-filled has much to teach Christians. It harkens back to the seminal description of the sacred in Rudolf Otto's *Idea of the Holy*.[22] In that book, Otto argues there is a *mysterium* due to the presence of the Other that has two defining characteristics: it is *tremendum* (awe-inspiring and frightening) and *fascinans* (compelling and desirable). Described in this way, such experiences can be fostered by nature, or by the puppet world of the East, by the innocence of the faith of the Amish and the "mateship" of the Anzac, and even by the brief encounter with someone who treats you as the person you are (whether a bit actress or a Frenchman needing a green card). There is, in other words, a spirituality of everyday life that should not be ignored. Or in the traditional language of Christian orthodoxy, there is special revelation, but there is also general revelation.

The Experiential Axis

The spiritual path in Weir's movies can be walked with or without a commitment to any organized religion, and certainly independent of any overt Christianity. There is a breadth and an openness to his vision. Here is his strength and his weakness, theologically. On the positive side, as the opening chapters of the Bible portray, humankind is both dust and breath, body and spirit. Weir helps us experience something of the spiritual in an otherwise materialistic age—portraying the life of the Spirit/spirit, giving us, in T. S. Eliot's words, images of

> the waterfall, or music heard so deeply
> That it is not heard at all, but you are the music
> While the music lasts.
>
> T. S. Eliot, "The Dry Salvages," *Four Quartets*[23]

This is an important artistic gift. Weir's filmic vision engenders spirit reaching out to spirit (Spirit?).

While such experiences are central to a spiritual life and thus important theologically, they also remain incomplete. To finish quoting T. S. Eliot's meditation:

> These are only hints and guesses,
> Hints followed by guesses; and the rest
> Is prayer, observance, discipline, thought and action.
> The hint half guessed, the gift half understood, is Incarnation.
>
> T. S. Eliot, "The Dry Salvages," *Four Quartets*[24]

Eliot reminds us of what Weir has ignored: prayer, observance, discipline, thought, and action. In his movies, spirituality rarely moves beyond the level of feeling. Guy Hamilton leaves the poverty of Jakarta for Jill rather than involve himself in the lives of these people. There is little if any discipline in Robin Williams's character. Max, Bronte, and Truman follow their instincts, but we have no clue as to how life will develop. We are, as with Truman, left at the open door. And certainly there is nary a hint of Incarnation. Eliot is correct.

To use more conventional theological language, Weir rejects the objectification of the Spirit, whether through word or concrete action. This is an error both in spirit and Spirit. Head, heart, and hands ultimately need integration and were created together. Similarly, Christian theology links Word and Spirit; it rejects any gnostic mysticism. It is important to discover the Spirit's signature on life. To borrow a phrase from John Updike, if the Spirit's signature is "illegible, even if decisive," we are still left wondering, "What then shall we do?"[25] What will Truman do? What will John Book do in Philadelphia? Guy Hamilton gets his girl, but all else is unclear. The apostle John writes, "And the Word became flesh and lived among us, and we have seen his glory, the glory as of a father's only son, full of grace and truth" (John 1:14). This is T. S. Eliot's point about "Incarnation." Mystery remains, but Christians believe that it has taken shape in the person of Jesus so that there can be "prayer, observance, discipline, thought and action." Weir rejects such concretizing of the Spirit, for the church has so often been Spirit/spirit denying. But the consequence of his purging is severe—in the end, nothing more is left than a vague romantic spirituality.

Having said this, having recognized that in and of themselves Weir's stories portray little beyond the vaguely spiritual (though even this "general revelation" should not be discounted), it is also the case that Christians and non-Christians alike have been moved to concrete action by the stories of Weir. His films invite our encounter with the spirit (Spirit) as few others do. Let me share one such theological encounter.

For my wife, Catherine Barsotti, seeing the movie *The Year of Living Dangerously* was a turning point, a conversion. Being immersed in the pain and poverty of Jakarta, seeing it both literally and figuratively through the eyes of Billy Kwan, she could not escape the question that Billy asked Guy. Quoting Tolstoy (who is quoting Luke 3:10), he asked Guy, "What then must we do?" Billy went on to tell Guy that Tolstoy sold all he had to relieve the suffering around him. In the movie, Guy is not persuaded, believing that government leaders and structures should be involved, not him. Billy himself had tried to respond personally, providing money for a young prostitute and her sick child. But when the boy dies from drinking polluted water, Billy can no longer avoid political involvement. Pounding out on his typewriter the same question, "What then must we do?" Billy decides to challenge Sukarno to feed his people. He hangs a banner over a balcony and is killed for his action. Let me quote Cathy directly:

> "What then must we do?" I left the theater with that phrase and the agonizing eyes of the children of Jakarta burned onto the screen of my mind. In Luke 3, we first hear this question as John the Baptist is preaching repentance and calling the people to bear fruit worthy of their conversion. When the crowd doesn't get it and asks,

Australian journalist Guy Hamilton (Mel Gibson) and photographer Billy Kwan (Linda Hunt) are surrounded by political demonstrators. *The Year of Living Dangerously* (d. Weir, 1982). ©1982 MGM/UA Entertainment Co. All rights reserved.

"What then must we do?" he tells them to live ethically and generously: "Whoever has two coats must share with anyone who has none; and whoever has food must do likewise." Or to tax collectors, "Collect no more than the amount prescribed for you" (vv. 11, 13). In Luke 4, we hear Jesus echoing the same ethic and compassion as he begins his ministry with these words: "The Spirit of the Lord is upon me, because he has anointed me to bring good news to the poor. He has sent me to proclaim release to the captives and recovery of sight to the blind, to let the oppressed go free" (v. 18).

A combination of people, events in my life, and the Holy Spirit had prepared me to see this film. It became a turning point, a recovery of sight. The next week I returned to my project at work, appraising a hospital, but I saw the world differently. Within weeks I applied for a leave of absence and within months left for Mexico to work as a short-term missionary. Six months after my return, I resigned my position to start my own appraisal business in which I would work only thirty hours a week so that I could give myself to the youth of my church and community, to the financial and political struggle to build a shelter for women and children in my city, and to study in the area of cross-cultural theology and ministry. The last twenty-two years have included a variety of tasks, jobs, ministries, and people. And it seems that Billy Kwan's, Tolstoy's, and the Bible's question still rings in my ears, "What then must we do?"[26]

For Cathy, the "hints and guesses" of Weir's movie became incarnate as she heard her Savior speak. What followed was "prayer, observance, discipline, thought and action," for the "hint half guessed" became the "gift half understood." She heard her incarnate Lord compelling her to answer the question in concrete ways.

There are a variety of theological responses that we might offer to the movies of Peter Weir. I have provided but three. One's theological response can be either analytical or experiential, word oriented or spirit oriented. By first looking at how the spiritual vision is portrayed in Weir's movies and then comparing it with the book of Ecclesiastes, I have sought to open the conversation. I have also turned to the theology of Sam Keen (and Rudolf Otto) as an initial, external source of insight into the heart of Weir's vision, believing that Weir's, too, is an "apology for wonder." My theological criticism of the films of Peter Weir is a two-way conversation, moving both from film to faith and from faith to film. Finally, I have illustrated the possibilities of an experiential theological criticism by relating the power of a Weir film to spiritually transform one life. As I have argued throughout this book, we are affected spiritually by what we see.

Other avenues of dialogue are also open. Some might, for example, want to look at Weir's treatment of the explicitly religious, to explore Weir's portrayal of Asian or Aboriginal spirituality, or the pacifistic life of the Amish.[27] Such explicitly religious criticism is probably secondary to the central thrust of Weir's power and meaning, but it can also provide insight. How is the receptivity of Eastern and/or indigenous thought an important counter to the West's penchant to control? Which is more effective, the guns of the Philadelphia police or the political power of pacifism? Is the anachronistic way of life of the Amish or the Aborigines relevant to our modern lives? The dialogue might also proceed in this direction.

In C. S. Lewis's *Silver Chair*, two children are transported to the Green Witch's falsely empirical and bounded universe. Puddleglum, their traveling companion, challenges the Green Witch's realism:

Suppose we have only dreamed, or made up, all those things—trees and grass and sun and moon and stars and Aslan himself. Suppose we have. Then all I can say is that, in that case, the made-up things seem a good deal more important than the real ones. Suppose this black pit of a kingdom of yours is the only world. Well, it strikes me as a pretty poor one. And that's a funny thing. . . . Four babies playing a game can make a play-world which licks your real world hollow.[28]

We have returned in our reflection one final time to consider the relationship between the "real" and the "reel." Peter Weir has done us the service of portraying on "reel" what reality might be at some more central region. His movies challenge that "black pit of a kingdom" which rationality and material-ism assume to be the only possible one. His stories remain hints and guesses, but these should not be disparaged. He has provided the occasion for viewers to experience what in traditional theological language is called "common grace." He has given us a *reel spirituality*.

All who have eyes, let them see.

notes

Preface to the Second Edition

1. Rose Pacatte, FSP, conversation at the Luce consultation on theology and film, Fuller Theological Seminary, Pasadena, Calif., December 8, 2005.

2. Terry Lindvall, one of the other participants in the consultation then told the story of one of his students who responded to his exam question ("Where do religion and film intersect in your life?") by writing that he had never looked forward to the premiere of a sermon, nor had he ever gone to a midnight service dressed as his favorite biblical character. Said Lindvall, "We attend to film as our cult."

3. Jim Friedrich, "Looking for God? Go to the Movies," *Episcopal Life*, April 2001, 17.

4. Cf. Steve Nolan, "Understanding Films: Reading in the Gaps," in *Flickering Images: Theology and Film in Dialogue*, ed. Anthony J. Clarke and Paul S. Fiddes, Regents Study Guide 12 (Macon, Ga.: Smyth & Helwys, 2005), 25–26.

5. Jolyon Mitchell, "Theology and Film," in *The Modern Theologians: An Introduction to Christian Theology since 1918*, ed. David F. Ford with Rachel Muers (Oxford: Blackwell, 2005), 736–59.

Introduction

1. Barry Taylor, address at the luncheon for Wilbert Shenk on the occasion of his installation as a professor at Fuller Theological Seminary, Pasadena, Calif., April 13, 1999, audiocassette.

2. John R. W. Stott, *Basic Christianity* (Downers Grove, Ill.: InterVarsity, 1971), 7.

3. Henry David Thoreau, *The Thoughts of Thoreau*, ed. Edwin Way Teale (New York: Dodd, Mead, 1962), 231, quoted in Ken Gire, *The Reflective Life: Becoming More Spiritually Sensitive to the Everyday Moments of Life* (Colorado Springs: Chariot Victor, 1998), 92.

4. Quoted in *Celluloid and Symbols*, ed. John C. Cooper and Carl Skrade (Philadelphia: Fortress, 1970), 15.

5. During a panel discussion at the Nortel Networks Palm Springs International Film Festival (16 January 2000), director Milos Forman continued to voice just such a distinction: "In American films, entertainment comes first and soul-searching comes second . . . if at all. In foreign films, soul-searching comes first, and entertainment second . . . if at all." Jack Garner and Bruce Fessier, "Land of the Film," *Desert Sun*, 18 January 2000, sec. D, 3.

6. See James Monaco for a distinction between film, movies, and cinema in *How to Read a Film*, rev. ed. (New York: Oxford University Press, 1981), 195. Though a distinction is sometimes made in more technical discussions, for our purposes the words *film*, *movies*, and *cinema* will be used interchangeably.

7. Edward Farley, *Theologia: The Fragmentation and Unity of Theological Education* (Philadelphia: Fortress, 1983), 7.

8. Ibid., 29–48.

Chapter 1: The Power of Film

1. *The Barna Update*, 10 July 2004; *Time*, 19 July 2004.

2. Plunkett Research, Ltd., Entertainment and Media Statistics, 2003, http://www.plunkettresearch .com. Quoted in Sally Morgenthaler, "Film and Worship: Windows in Caves and Other Things We Do with Perfectly Good Prisms," *Theology News & Notes* 52, no. 2 (Spring 2005): 13. Cf. *USA Today*, 6 January 2005, sec. D, 8; *New York Times*, 20 December 2004.

3. *El Pais*, 1 April 2005, 1.

4. While 1.4 billion movie tickets were sold in the United States in 2003, 2.9 billion were sold in India. *Newsweek*, 22 December 2003, E19.

5. *Time*, 22 November 2004, 24.

6. Elizabeth Van Ness, *New York Times*, 6 March 2005.

7. I am indebted to writer Ken Gire for showing me this film clip. He also discussed it in his book *Reflections on the Movies: Hearing God in the Unlikeliest of Places* (Colorado Springs: Chariot Victor, 2000).

8. Quoted by Robert G. Konzelman, *Marquee Ministry: The Movie Theater as Church and Community Forum* (New York: Harper & Row, 1971), 13.

9. Martin Scorsese, "Duel in the Sun," in *Private Screenings: Insiders Share a Century of Great Movie Moments*, American Film Institute with Duane Byrge (Atlanta: Turner, 1995), 141.

10. Quoted in Guy Bedouelle, "Eric Rohmer: The Cinema's Spiritual Destiny," *Communio* 6, no. 2 (1979): 280.

11. Margaret Miles, quoted in Christopher Deacy, *Screen Christologies: Redemption and the Medium of Film* (Cardiff: University of Wales Press, 2001), 1.

12. Read Mercer Schuchardt, "Cinema—The New Cathedral of Hollywood: How Films Are Replacing Religion in Our Cinematic Age," http://metaphilm.com/philm.php?id=6_0_2_0, 9 November 2001. Cf. David Lodge, *The Picturegoers* (1960; Harmondsworth, UK: Penguin Books, 1993), 108–9, quoted in Gerard Loughlin, "Looking: The Ethics of Seeing in Church and Cinema," in *Faithfulness and Fortitude: In Conversation with the Theological Ethics of Stanley Hauerwas*, ed. Mark Thiessen Nation and Samuel Wells (Edinburgh: T&T Clark, 2000), 281: One of the characters muses, "Going to church was like going to the cinema: you sat in rows, the notices were like trailers, the supporting sermon was changed weekly. And people went because they always went. You paid at the plate instead of the box-office, and sometimes they played the organ. There was only one big difference: the main feature was always the same."

13. George Miller, quoted in Michael Frost, *Eyes Wide Open: Seeing God in the Ordinary* (Sutherland, NSW, Australia: Albatross Books, 1998), 100.

14. The passion play featured thirteen tableau scenes, each a minute or so in length.

15. *The Temptation of St. Anthony* (d. Méliès, 1898) began with a monk reading a theological document when, suddenly, a naked woman appears. When the monk moves to greet her, however, she becomes a skeleton. Interestingly, St. Anthony is said to have had such temptations.

16. John Updike, *In the Beauty of the Lilies* (New York: Knopf, 1996).

17. John Updike, *The Centaur* (Greenwich, Conn.: Fawcett, Crest, 1962), 201.

18. Paul Woolf, "Turning toward Home," *Image: A Journal of the Arts & Religion* 20 (Summer 1998): 116.

19. Ibid.

20. Ibid.

21. Stanley Hauerwas and William H. Willimon, *Resident Aliens: Life in the Christian Colony* (Nashville: Abingdon, 1989), 15–16. For a fictional account of a similar circumstance, see David Lodge, *The Picturegoers* (Harmondsworth, UK: Penguin Books, 1992), as described in Gerard Loughlin, "Looking: The Ethics of Seeing in Church and Cinema," in *Faithfulness and Fortitude*, 281: "A rather more suburban staging of the conflict was offered by David Lodge in his first novel, *The Picturegoers* (1960), which considers the impact of the local cinema on the Catholic community of Brickley, and the fruitless attempts of Father Kipling to win back his flock from the temptations of what Alex and his drogs will come to know as the 'sinny.' Father Kipling is convinced that the Saturday night flicks are an occasion for sin,

and in a desperate bid to offer a rival attraction, moves the Thursday Benediction to Saturday evening, which results in empty pews."

22. Joel W. Martin and Conrad E. Ostwalt Jr., *Screening the Sacred: Religion, Myth, and Ideology in Popular American Film* (Boulder, Colo.: Westview, 1995), 1.

23. Rosalind Chao, "My Fair Lady," in *Private Screenings: Insiders Share a Century of Great Movie Moments*, American Film Institute with Duane Byrge (Atlanta: Turner, 1995), 29.

24. Ted Baehr notes the same event but reports alternate figures—a drop from $9.5 million to $4.1 million. Ted Baehr, *What Can We Watch Tonight? A Family Guide to Movies* (Grand Rapids: Zondervan, 2003), 15.

25. K. L. Billingsley, *The Seductive Image: A Christian Critique of the World of Film* (Westchester, Ill.: Crossway, 1989), 53.

26. Amy Wallace, "'Ryan' Ends Vets' Years of Silence," *Los Angeles Times*, 6 August 1998, sec. A, 1.

27. Neal Gabler, *Life the Movie: How Entertainment Conquered Reality* (New York: Knopf, 1998), 9.

28. Elia Kazan, *Elia Kazan: A Life* (New York: Knopf, 1988), 381.

29. Clive Marsh and Gaye Ortiz, eds., *Explorations in Theology and Film: Movies and Meaning* (Oxford: Blackwell, 1997), 1.

30. Beverly Beyette, "A Modern-Day Schindler Faces the Consequences," *Los Angeles Times*, 19 August 1998, sec. E, 1; David Haldane, "Swiss Whistle-Blower to Attend Chapman," *Los Angeles Times*, 19 November 1998, sec. B, 5.

31. Gerry Sittser, *A Grace Disguised* (Grand Rapids: Zondervan, 1996), 173. Not all responses by children to the movie *Bambi* are as positive. Stephen King, for example, recalls: "Yet 50 years later I can still remember the sense of dismay I felt when Bambi's mother was killed, leaving the poor little feller alone. I was a single-parent child myself, and I spent many long nights after lights-out thinking about Bambi and wondering what would happen to me if something happened to my mother. I still remember the simple power of the film's most potent line: 'Man was in the forest.'" Stephen King, "Do Movies Matter? (Part 1)," *Entertainment Weekly*, 14 November 2003, 136.

32. There is a coda to the story that Karen Covell shared with me. Speaking in October 1998 at a seminar in Hollywood that Karen attended, Linda Woolverton, the screenwriter of *Beauty and the Beast*, told of her struggle with executives at Disney to keep Belle as a reader, someone whose main love was books. Disney felt that reading was boring when portrayed on the screen. They wanted a more active hobby, something more physical in nature. Linda argued, however, that by making Belle an intelligent woman with a love for literature, the film could provide a stronger, more positive role model for young female viewers. Linda won the argument, and Catherine Sittser benefited.

Chapter 2: A Brief History of the Church and Hollywood

1. Terry Lindvall, *The Silents of God: Selected Issues and Documents in Silent American Film and Religion, 1908–1925* (Lanham, Md.: Scarecrow Press, 2001), xi.

2. Andre Gaudreault and Tom Gunning, quoted in Lindvall, *Silents of God*, xi.

3. For helpful discussions of early religious cinema, see John Baxter, *The Australian Cinema* (Sydney: Angus & Robertson, Pacific Books, 1970), 7–8; Ronald Holloway, *Beyond the Image: Approaches to the Religious Dimension in the Cinema* (Geneva: World Council of Churches, 1977), 45–59. I am dependent on Holloway for much of my discussion of the rise of cinema.

4. "On August 18, 1900, Booth explained in the Salvation Army pamphlet, *War Cry*, that 'These means are employed by the worldling; they form a source of attraction in the theaters and music halls. Why should they be usurped by the enemy of the souls?'" Lindvall, *Silents of God*, 3.

5. Barton W. Currie, "The Nickel Madness," *Harper's Weekly*, 24 August 1907, quoted in F. Miguel Valenti, *More Than a Movie: Ethics in Entertainment* (Boulder, Colo.: Westview, 2000), 49.

6. Herbert Jump, *The Religious Possibilities of the Motion Picture* (New Britain, Conn.: South Congregational Church Private Distribution, 1911), reprinted in Lindvall, *Silents of God*, 54–78. See p. 58.

7. Holloway, *Beyond the Image*, 52.

8. Ibid., 53.

9. Jump, reprinted in Lindvall, *Silents of God*, 56.

10. Quoted in Les Keyser and Barbara Keyser, *Hollywood and the Catholic Church: The Image of Roman Catholicism in American Movies* (Chicago: Loyola University Press, 1984), 20.

11. Ibid., 24.

12. James Skinner, *The Cross and the Cinema: The Legion of Decency and the National Office for Motion Pictures, 1933–1970* (Westport, Conn.: Greenwood, 1993), 18.

13. Quoted in Holloway, *Beyond the Image*, 118.

14. Quoted in Skinner, *Cross and the Cinema*, 35.

15. Skinner, *Cross and the Cinema*, 37.

16. Quoted in John R. May, "Close Encounters: Hollywood and Religion after a Century," *Image: A Journal of the Arts & Religion* 20 (Summer 1998): 88.

17. For a fuller discussion of this period, see Gregory Black, *Hollywood Censored: Morality Codes, Catholics, and the Movies* (New York: Cambridge University Press, 1994); idem., *The Catholic Crusade against the Movies, 1940–1975* (New York: Cambridge University Press, 1997); and Frank Walsh, *Sin and Censorship: The Catholic Church and the Motion Picture Industry* (New Haven: Yale University Press, 1996).

18. Quoted by Ronald Austin, "Sacrificing Images: Violence and the Movies," *Image: A Journal of the Arts & Religion* 20 (Summer 1998): 27.

19. Michael Medved, *Hollywood vs. America: Popular Culture and the War on Traditional Values* (New York: HarperCollins, 1992).

20. Betsy Carter, "Faith, Hope, and Clarity," *AARP Magazine*, November/December 2004, 52.

21. Evangelicals accounted for 9%, down from 9.2% in 1990; Catholics made up 6.2%, down one percentage point from 7.2% in 1990; and mainline Protestants numbered 3.4%, down from 3.9% in 1990.

22. Rodney Clapp, quoted in "Pop Goes Theology," *Publishers Weekly*, 17 November 2003, S10.

23. Sally Morgenthaler, "Film and Worship: Windows in Caves and Other Things We Do with Perfectly Good Prisms," *Theology News & Notes* 52, no. 2 (Spring 2005): 13–15, 25.

24. Ibid.

25. Quoted in Peter Malone with Rose Pacatte, *Lights Camera . . . Faith!: A Movie Lover's Guide to Scripture, A Movie Lectionary—Cycle A* (Boston: Pauline Books & Media, 2001), xi.

26. Pope John Paul II, "Address of John Paul II to the Participants in the Ninth Public Meeting of the Pontifical Academies," http://www.vatican.va/holy_father/john_paul_ii/speeches/2004/november/documents/hf_j, 9 November 2004. Cf. also Pope John Paul's 1999 address to artists about their gifts and responsibilities titled "Letter to Artists." He begins, "To all who are passionately dedicated to the search for new 'epiphanies' of beauty so that through their creative work as artists they may offer these gifts to the world." Cf. also the pamphlet by Cardinal Roger M. Mahony, archbishop of Los Angeles, *Film Makers, Film Viewers: Their Challenges and Opportunities, A Pastoral Letter* (Boston: St. Paul Books & Media, 1992).

27. Bishop T. D. Jakes, quoted in *Time*, 4 October 2004, 95.

28. Richard Corliss, "The Gospel according to Spider Man," *Time*, 16 August 2004, 70–72.

29. Terry Lindvall, "Religion and Film, Part I: History and Criticism," *Communication Research Trends* 23, no. 4 (2004): 3–44, and Terry Lindvall, "Religion and Film, Part II," *Communication Research Trends* 24, no. 1 (2005): 2–40.

30. Recent books by Bryan Stone (*Faith and Film: Theological Themes at the Cinema* [St. Louis: Chalice, 2000]), David Cunningham (*Reading Is Believing: The Christian Faith through Literature and Film* [Grand Rapids: Brazos, 2002], and John May (*Nourishing Faith through Fiction: Reflections of The Apostles' Creed in Literature and Film* [Franklin, Wis.: Sheed & Ward, 2001]) each use film to unpack the Apostles' Creed, for example.

31. Cf. Robert Jewett, *Saint Paul at the Movies: The Apostle's Dialogue with American Culture* (Louisville: Westminster/John Knox, 1993) and *Saint Paul Returns to the Movies: Triumph over Shame* (Grand Rapids: Eerdmans, 1999); Larry Kreitzer, *The New Testament in Fiction and Film: On Reversing the Hermeneutical Flow* (Sheffield, UK: JSOT Press, 1993); *Gospel Images in Fiction and Film: On Reversing the Hermeneutical*

Flow (London: Sheffield Academic Press, 2002), and three additional books published in 1993, 1994, and 2000; and Robert K. Johnston, *Useless Beauty: Ecclesiastes through the Lens of Contemporary Film* (Grand Rapids: Baker, 2004).

32. Peter Malone and Rose Pacatte have compiled three large volumes providing movie suggestions that correlate with lectionary texts for all three cycles of the church's lectionary (*Lights Camera . . . Faith!: A Movie Lover's Guide to Scripture, A Movie Lectionary—Cycle A, Cycle B, Cycle C* [Boston: Pauline Books & Media, 2001, 2002, 2003]), while Craig Brian Larson has co-written two books titled *Movie-Based Illustrations for Preaching & Teaching: 101 Clips to Show and Tell* (with Andrew Zahn) and *More Movie-Based Illustrations for Preaching & Teaching: 101 Clips to Show & Tell* (with Lori Quicke) (Grand Rapids: Zondervan, 2003, 2004).

33. Doug Fields and Eddie James's two volumes, *Videos That Teach* and *Videos That Teach 2* (Grand Rapids: Zondervan, 1999, 2002), and Bryan Belknap's two books, *Group's Blockbuster Movie Illustrations* and *Group's Blockbuster Movie Illustrations: The Sequel* (Loveland, Colo.: Group Publishing, 2001, 2003).

34. Cf. Edward McNulty, *Films and Faith: Forty Discussion Guides* (Topeka, Kans.: Viaticum Press, 1999); Bob Smithouser, *Movie Nights: 25 Movies to Spark Spiritual Discussions with Your Teen* (Wheaton, Ill.: Tyndale, 2002); Robert K. Johnston and Catherine M. Barsotti, *Finding God in the Movies: 33 Films of Reel Faith* (Grand Rapids: Baker, 2004). Web-based resources include Reel Issues, study guides from The Bible Society of Great Britain, http://www.reelissues.org.uk; Cinema in Focus, http://www.cinema infocus.com; Reel Spirituality, http://www.reelspirituality.org; Damaris CultureWatch, http://www .damaris.org/cw/; and Ministry and Media, http://www.ministryandmedia.com.

35. Cf. Edward McNulty, *Praying the Movies: Daily Meditations from Classic Films* (Louisville: Geneva Press, 2001) and *Praying the Movies II: More Daily Meditations from Classic Films* (Louisville: Westminster John Knox, 2003); Sara Anson Vaux, *Finding Meaning at the Movies* (Nashville: Abingdon Press, 1999); Richard A. Burridge, *Faith Odyssey: A Journey through Life* (Grand Rapids: Eerdmans, 2003).

36. Http://www.cmu.ca/library/faithfilm.html.

37. Http://www.christianitytoday.com/movies/features/filmforum.html.

38. Personal correspondence.

Chapter 3: Theological Approaches to Film Criticism

1. The original categorization was developed by Robert Banks and was expanded by the two of us over the several years that we team-taught a class in theology and film at Fuller Theological Seminary during the mid-nineties.

2. Hyman Appelman, introduction to *Movies and Morals*, by Herbert Miles (Grand Rapids: Zondervan, 1947).

3. Miles, *Movies and Morals*, 20.

4. Ibid., 20, 95; Cf. William Romanowski, "John Calvin Meets the Creature from the Black Lagoon: The Christian Reformed Church and the Movies 1928–1966," *Christian Scholar's Review* 25, no. 1 (1995): 47–62. Romanowski provides a historical analysis of the response of one denomination—the Christian Reformed Church (CRC)—to the advent of movies. As early as 1908, congregations were warned of the moral and spiritual dangers of going to the movies. The film industry was considered a moral "bubonic plague." It was only when *The Sound of Music* (1965) came out that the denomination reconsidered its stance, concluding that film and television could be "legitimate cultural medium(s) to be used by the Christian in the fulfillment of the cultural mandate." The church was encouraged in the report to "engage in a responsible critique of the film arts."

5. Carl McClain, *Morals and the Movies* (Kansas City, Mo.: Beacon Hill, 1970), 25.

6. Bryan P. Stone, *Faith and Film: Theological Themes at the Cinema* (St. Louis: Chalice, 2000), 5.

7. Fax from Ted Baehr to Todd Coleman, 3 October 1997.

8. Theodore Baehr, *What Can We Watch Tonight? A Family Guide to Movies* (Grand Rapids: Zondervan, 2003), 18.

9. Theodore Baehr, "A Cacophony of Prime Time Religions?" in *Religion and Prime Time Television*, ed. Michael Suman (Westport, Conn.: Praeger, 1997), 117.

10. Larry W. Poland, *The Last Temptation of Hollywood* (Highland, Calif.: Mastermedia International, 1988), 6.

11. Nikos Kozantzakis, *The Last Temptation of Christ*, trans. P. A. Bien (New York: Simon & Schuster, 1960).

12. Ibid., 146.

13. John L. Allen, "Top Ten Neglected Catholic Stories of 2002," *National Catholic Reporter* 2, no.19 (3 January 2003): n.p. According to Allen, other bishops in the Mexican church were more conciliatory, calling it an "honest movie" and describing it as "a wake-up call for the church to review its procedure for selecting and training priests and being closer to the people."

14. The Catholic Church's use of indulgences again made the news just a few months after *Dogma* was released. As part of its millennial celebration of the Jubilee, or Roman Catholic Holy Year, the pope ceremonially opened the doors of four basilicas where Catholic pilgrims could earn indulgences during the Holy Year (2000). This caused some Protestant leaders to decline sharing in what the pope had set up as an ecumenical event, the opening of the fourth basilica's doors. The archbishop of Canterbury and a representative of the Orthodox patriarch of Constantinople did participate, however.

15. Kevin Smith, quoted in Mick LaSalle, "Kevin Smith's Religious Experience," *San Francisco Sunday Examiner and Chronicle*, 31 October 1999, Datebook, 50.

16. Patrick Scully, quoted in Teresa Watanabe, "Chasing Catholicism," *Los Angeles Times*, 10 November 1999, sec. F, 1.

17. Cliff Rothman, "*Dogma* Opens in New York to Protesters' Jeers, Audience Cheers," *Los Angeles Times*, 6 October 1999, sec. F, 2, 4.

18. Charles Colson, "And the Winner Is: Death, Depravity and Dullness," *Breakpoint Commentary* #050301, 1 March 2005.

19. Barbara Nicolosi, "The 'Passion' Oscar Snub: Revenge of the Blue States?" beliefnet, http://www.beliefnet.com/story/160/story_16008.html. Nicolosi reduces her description of each of the Oscar-nominated movies to a caricature. Her comments concerning *Sideways*, for example, suggest that Nicolosi failed to understand the deeper moral premise of the film, something many other Christian film critics recognized: "[A] movie that glamorizes four alley cats dressed as beautiful people who fornicate and commit adultery with each other, and indulge in various sexual perversions until the movie ends."

20. Barbara Nicolosi, "How 'The Passion' Rattled Hollywood," ZENIT News Agency, http://www.zenit.org/english, 9 December 2004.

21. Charles Colson with Anne Morse, *How Now Shall We Live? Devotional* (Wheaton, Ill.: Tyndale, 2004), 167; Charles Colson, "Sick, Twisted People," *Breakpoint Commentary*, 26 June 2003.

22. Charles Colson, "Finding Good Movies," *Breakpoint Commentary* #71001, 1997; cf. Focus on the Family's Bob Smithouser, *Movie Nights: 25 Movies to Spark Spiritual Discussions with Your Teen* (Wheaton, Ill.: Tyndale, 2002), 4: "[T]he apostle Paul admonished Christians to *avoid* capture through 'hollow and deceptive philosophy.' To use a military model, there are two ways to avoid capture. One is to stay as far away from the enemy as possible. Another is to study the enemy's strategies from a safe distance, then engage that foe so adroitly that you can defend your homestead and also ensure escape. Families seeking wisdom in the latter should find this book extremely helpful." Or to give yet another example, Donald Drew asks whether a Christian should even go to movies. He answers with a cautious affirmative: "It is my conviction that a Christian, providing that his foundations are firm, should see films and become involved in the arts and other forms of knowledge. The Lordship of God in Christ must be seen to extend into all areas of life." Drew also advises his readers that "a Christian should enter the cinema with a solid grasp of who man is and what truth is." Donald Drew, *Images of Man: A Critique of the Contemporary Cinema* (Downers Grove, Ill.: InterVarsity, 1974), 106. The Christian viewer can watch movies, but carefully, from a clearly defined ethical and religious stance.

23. K. L. Billingsley, *The Seductive Image: A Christian Critique of the World of Film* (Westchester, Ill.: Crossway, 1989), xii.

24. John Butler, *TV, Movies, and Morality: A Guide for Catholics* (Huntington, Ind.: Our Sunday Visitor, 1984), 10.

25. Michael Medved, *Hollywood vs. America: Popular Culture and the War on Traditional Values* (New York: HarperCollins, 1992), 242.

26. Mark Hulsether, "Sorting out the Relationships among Christian Values, U.S. Popular Religion, and Hollywood Films," *Religious Studies Review* 25, no. 1 (1999): 3–11.

27. Les Keyser and Barbara Keyser, *Hollywood and the Catholic Church: The Image of Roman Catholicism in American Movies* (Chicago: Loyola University Press, 1984), 94.

28. Ibid., 104, 106.

29. Michael Medved, "Want an Oscar? An 'R' Revs Up Your Chances," *USA Today*, 19 March 1999, sec. A, 9. In a 1997 essay, Medved does recognize recent positive changes since he wrote *Hollywood vs. America* in 1992. He notes that in the 1990s faithful Christians and Jews assumed prominent positions in Hollywood. After the "relentless religion-bashing of the last fifteen years," there has been a "shift to more supportive on-screen treatment of religious themes and characters." He concludes with this assessment: "Hollywood's current status still leaves vast room for improvement, but an exhilarating spirit of change—if not outright rebirth and revival—is already in the air." Since Medved wrote this article, the on-screen treatment of religious themes has continued to be mixed, but often supportive of faith. Yet Medved's caution continues, as evidenced in a 2003 cover story for *USA Today*, which had invited readers to call a toll-free number and respond either Yes or No to the simple statement: "Hollywood no longer reflects—or even respects—the values of most American families." The phone lines were swamped and the vote decisive: 54,000 Yes; 21,000 No. In the article, Medved concludes as he has since he began writing: "Hollywood does have an anti-religious axe to grind, and they continue grinding it despite the fact that it makes no box-office sense." What escapes Medved's reasoning, however, is the fact that Hollywood's penchant for adult-themed stories might have motives other than religious loathing or box-office success. Perhaps moviemakers, like novelists who do not write mainly for "families" or artists who do not paint simply for intergenerational viewers, might also desire to tell adult-themed stories rooted in the full range of life's realities, portraying its paradoxes and problems, even while seeking something more.

30. Margaret Miles, *Seeing and Believing: Religion and Values in the Movies* (Boston: Beacon, 1996), 4.

31. Ibid., 15.

32. John C. Lyden, *Film as Religion: Myths, Morals, and Rituals* (New York: New York University Press, 2003), 32.

33. T. S. Eliot, "Religion and Literature," in *Religion and Modern Literature: Essays in Theory and Criticism*, ed. G. B. Tennyson and Edward E. Ericson Jr. (Grand Rapids: Eerdmans, 1975), 21.

34. R. W. B. Lewis, "Hold on Hard to the Huckleberry Bushes," in *Religion and Modern Literature: Essays in Theory and Criticism*, ed. G. B. Tennyson and Edward E. Ericson Jr. (Grand Rapids: Eerdmans, 1975), 55.

35. J. C. Friedrich von Schiller, *On the Aesthetic Education of Man*, trans. Reginald Snell (London: n.p., 1954), quoted in Herbert Read, *The Redemption of the Robot: My Encounter with Education through Art* (New York: Trident, 1966), italics original. Cf. Robert K. Johnston, *The Christian at Play* (Grand Rapids: Eerdmans, 1983).

36. Amos Wilder, *Theology and Modern Literature* (Cambridge, Mass.: Harvard University Press, 1958), 29, quoted in Robert K. Johnston, "Christian Theology and Literature: Correlation or Co-Relation?" in *Collection of Papers Celebrating Professor Hiromu Shimizu's Retirement*, ed. Sachiko Yoshida (Kyoto: Apollon, 1991), 15.

37. Roy Anker, *Catching Light: Looking for God in the Movies* (Grand Rapids: Eerdmans, 2004).

38. Peter Malone, with Rose Pacatte, *Lights Camera . . . Faith!: A Movie Lover's Guide to Scripture, A Movie Lectionary—Cycle A, Cycle B, Cycle C* (Boston: Pauline Books & Media, 2001, 2002, 2003).

39. Brian Godawa, *Hollywood Worldviews: Watching Films with Wisdom and Discernment* (Downers Grove, Ill.: InterVarsity, 2002), 177.

40. Tim Cawkwell, *The Filmgoer's Guide to God* (London: Darton, Longman & Todd, 2004), 3.

41. The phrase is Benjamin Brus's, private correspondence, 29 October 2002.

42. The interest in theology and film dialogue can be traced to the 1960s and early 1970s when seminarians and pastors discovered in the films of such European directors as Fellini, Bergman, Buñuel,

and Antonioni, stories of existential depth and significance. One of my own seminary courses during this time was a theology and film class taught for a consortium of theological schools in the Chicago area in which one of our guest lecturers was Roger Ebert. The syllabus had just these directors (along with Kubrick). As might be expected, a spate of books soon followed that promoted dialogue between theology and cinema. Robert Konzelman's *Marquee Ministry: The Movie Theater as Church and Community Forum* (1971), William Jones's *Dialogue with the World* (1964) and *Sunday Night at the Movies* (1967), Roger Kahle and Robert Lee's *Popcorn and Parable* (1971), James Wall's *Church and Cinema: A Way of Viewing Film* (1971), Stanford Summers's *Secular Films and the Church's Ministry* (1969), and W. R. Robinson's edited collection, *Man and the Movies* (1969) are all examples. Most of these books were written with a practical emphasis and provided help for the person setting up film programs or festivals in local churches, viewing movies as a resource for Christian education programs. But even given their goals, the consistent critical stance of these books is that of two-way conversation; it is dialogue.

Perhaps the best of such books is an edited volume by John Cooper and Carl Skrade titled *Celluloid and Symbols* (1970), which includes a number of articles about film written from a theological perspective. The chapter titles are self-explanatory: James Wall wrote on "Biblical Spectaculars and Secular Man"; William Hamilton's title was "Bergman and Polanski on the Death of God"; for Anthony Schillaci, it was "Bergman's Vision of Good and Evil"; and for Harvey Cox, "The Purpose of the Grotesque in Fellini's Films." Cox, for example, specifically addresses the essential role of Christianity in Italian films, especially those of Fellini. Setting the stage for his comments, he writes: "[T]he Italians I met, and this includes Fellini, are not, to put it mildly, indifferent to religion. Some of them, especially the most strident atheists, seem almost obsessed with it. Fellini's pictures include an enormous range of religious themes and personages, from the swindlers dressed like priests in *Il Bidone* and the processions in *La Strada* and *Nights of Cabiria*, to the dangling statue of Christ that opens *La Dolce Vita*. Italy is a country where Catholicism resides not in the head but in the entrails. Everybody has not just a strong opinion about Christianity but fevered feelings as well." Harvey G. Cox, "The Purpose of the Grotesque in Fellini's Films," in *Celluloid and Symbols*, ed. John C. Cooper and Carl Skrade (Philadelphia: Fortress, 1970, 1991), 91.

Schillaci finds much the same to be the case in Bergman's movies, where religious problems are continuously alive. Bergman might see good and evil as residing together, yet there is still a longing for wholeness that is profoundly theological and based on his reaction to Christian theology.

Skrade sums up his intention for the essays in this volume in these words: "[I]f the study of theology and films is to be of any value in our attempts to reunite the God-question and the man-question, the church and the world, both the discipline of theology and the art of the cinema must be allowed their freedom. Instead of returning to some form of monologue in which theology would preach to cinema—or vice versa—both the discipline and the art must be allowed to speak their piece: that is, the goal must be dialogue." Carl Skrade, "Theology and Films," in *Celluloid and Symbols*, ed. Cooper and Skrade, 22.

Both Cooper and Skrade recognize that it is insufficient and perhaps dishonest simply to use a movie to make a point or to illustrate a theological truth. Viewers must let the movie work its charm, enlightening and/or disturbing them. Only then can it have a chance to deepen their understanding of reality (and perhaps even Reality).

43. Bernard Brandon Scott, *Hollywood Dreams and Biblical Stories* (Minneapolis: Fortress, 1994).

44. Robert Jewett, *Saint Paul Returns to the Movies: Triumph over Shame* (Grand Rapids: Eerdmans, 1999), 20.

45. Robert Jewett, *Saint Paul at the Movies: The Apostle's Dialogue with American Culture* (Louisville: Westminster/John Knox, 1993), 7.

46. Ibid., 11.

47. Robert K. Johnston, *Useless Beauty: Ecclesiastes through the Lens of Contemporary Film* (Grand Rapids: Baker, 2004); Richard A. Burridge, *Faith Odyssey: A Journey through Life* (Grand Rapids: Eerdmans, 2003).

48. Bryan Stone, *Faith and Film*, 7.

49. John R. May, *Nourishing Faith through Fiction: Reflections of the Apostles' Creed in Literature and Film* (Franklin, Wis.: Sheed & Ward, 2001), ix.

50. David S. Cunningham, *Reading Is Believing: The Christian Faith through Literature and Film* (Grand Rapids: Brazos, 2002), 22.

51. James M. Wall, "Biblical Spectaculars and Secular Man," in *Celluloid and Symbols*, ed. Cooper and Skrade, 52.

52. Lloyd Baugh, *Imaging the Divine: Jesus and Christ-Figures in Film* (Kansas City, Mo.: Sheed & Ward, 1997), 112.

53. Nathaniel Dorsky, "Devotional Cinema," in *The Hidden God: Film and Faith*, ed. Mary Lea Bandy and Antonio Monda (New York: Museum of Modern Art, 2003), 261, 264.

54. Neil P. Hurley, *Theology through Film* (New York: Harper & Row, 1970), 3.

55. See Robert K. Johnston and Catherine M. Barsotti, *Finding God in the Movies: 33 Films of Reel Faith* (Grand Rapids: Baker, 2004), 19–20.

56. Gareth Higgins, *How Movies Helped Save My Soul: Finding Spiritual Fingerprints in Culturally Significant Films* (Lake Mary, Fla.: Relevant Books, 2003), xix.

57. Ibid., 79.

58. Ibid., 87, 89, 90.

59. Ibid., 30.

60. Tony Campolo, foreword to Higgins, *How Movies Helped Save My Soul*, x–xi.

61. Marcel Proust (1910), quoted in Higgins, *How Movies Helped Save My Soul*, xv.

62. Clive Marsh, *Cinema & Sentiment: Film's Challenge to Theology* (Bletchley, Milton Keynes, UK: Paternoster, 2004), ix.

63. Ibid., 35.

64. Ibid., 134.

65. Ibid., 39, 94.

66. James Wall provides another example of appropriation, going further than Marsh in broadening up his definition of religion. He concludes his reflections on "Biblical Spectaculars and Secular Man" by commenting optimistically on the secular person who is no longer interested in pietistic presentations of Jesus: "He will, however, be open to the evocative power of a film which celebrated humanity, and thereby calls us all to receive the gift of life. His openness, I submit, is further indication that secular man is deeply religious, so long as he is permitted to define his religion in terms of meaningful living" (Wall, "Biblical Spectaculars," 60).

Wall, the editor of *The Christian Century* for more than a quarter of a century, believes that a film's vision "can be said to be 'religious' in the Christian sense if it celebrates humanity or if it exercises with conviction a strong agony over moments where humanity is actually distorted" (ibid., 56). It is the affective power of film (note his language—"celebrates," "strong agony") to portray humanity convincingly that interests Wall, though his strong dialogical tone in most of his film reviews and discussion suggests that he also fits as an example of those who seek "dialogue." For Wall, there is no need for explicitly religious symbols or forms. If a movie speaks to the human condition with an authenticity shared by those who are religious, it is enough. Thus, *Who's Afraid of Virginia Woolf?* (1966) is a "religious" movie because it celebrates humanity in a manner compatible with the way Wall himself views humanity, given his location within the historic Christian community.

Though I understand Wall's intention as he seeks to let a movie's vision of life deepen and extend his theology, I would refrain from calling such a film "religious." Such labeling seems dishonest regarding the intent of the movie. It is better to describe the film as "religion-like," as Marsh does, or to say it functions similar to religion in calling forth a response from the viewer.

67. Thomas Martin, *Images and the Imageless: A Study in Religious Consciousness and Film* (Lewisburg, Pa.: Bucknell University Press, 1981), 63.

68. G. William Jones, *Sunday Night at the Movies* (Richmond: John Knox, 1967), 40.

69. Gerardus van der Leeuw, *Sacred and Profane Beauty: The Holy in Art*, trans. David E. Green (Nashville: Abingdon, 1963), 266.

70. Ibid., 337.

71. Ibid., 266.

72. John R. May, "Religion and Film: Recent Contributions to the Continuing Dialogue," *Critical Review of Books in Religion* 9 (1996): 105–21.

73. Ibid., 117.

74. Marshall Allen, "Schools Work to Return Faith to Film," *Pasadena Star News,* August 29, 2004, sec. 1, 1; private correspondence.

75. Andrew Greeley, *God in Popular Culture* (Chicago: Thomas More, 1988), 250; Andrew Greeley, *The Catholic Imagination* (Berkeley: University of California Press, 2000), 1.

76. Richard McBrien, quoted in Vincent Miller, *Consuming Religion: Christian Faith and Practice in a Consumer Culture* (New York: Continuum, 2004), 189.

77. Greeley, *God in Popular Culture,* 250.

78. David Tracy, *The Analogical Imagination* (New York: Crossroad, 1982).

79. Greeley, *The Catholic Imagination,* 5.

80. Andrew Greeley, *Religion as Poetry* (New Brunswick, N.J.: Transaction, 1996), 50–51.

81. Greeley, *God in Popular Culture,* 250; Cf. Albert J. Bergesen and Andrew M. Greeley, *God in the Movies* (New Brunswick, N.J.: Transaction, 2000). Other Catholic theologians and film critics argue in similar ways. Richard Blake, for example, recognizes the need for the church "to broaden the question of religion and film from morality" (Richard Blake, "From Peepshow to Prayer: Toward a Spirituality of the Movies," *Journal of Religion and Film* 6, no. 2 [October 2002]: n.p.). The religious dimension of film is not to be found either in the moviemaker's intention or in overtly religious content but in the observer-critic's experience (Richard Blake, "Secular Prophecy in an Age of Film," *Journal of Religious Thought* 27, no. 1 [Spring–Summer 1970]: 72). Or again, Thomas Martin argues that Christian witness must engage the larger society at a deeper level than that of ideas alone. Film, as "an art of moving pictures," has "a greater ability to produce a total environment than either painting or photography because it can include in its form more of the ingredients of a normal setting" (Martin, *Images and the Imageless,* 46). As a visual medium that occupies a large part of the average person's life, film has a tremendous impact on the images that govern one's awareness. Moreover, because it has the ability to dramatize, celebrate, and present the full range of human experience, it extends human vision to include that which might otherwise pass unnoticed. In these ways, movies have the "ability to awaken a sense of awe and wonder in the beholder" (ibid., 52). If he had been writing his book today, Martin might have been thinking of the little boy in *Cinema Paradiso* (1988) or of Essie in John Updike's novel *In the Beauty of the Lilies.* Such wonder, writes Martin, "is necessary in laying the foundation for religious consciousness in a culture which tends to reduce experience to 'one damn thing after another'" (ibid.).

82. Roger Ebert, preface to Bergesen and Greeley, *God in the Movies,* viii.

83. David Dark, *Everyday Apocalypse: The Sacred Revealed in Radiohead, The Simpsons and Other Pop Culture Icons* (Grand Rapids: Brazos, 2002). Cf. David Dark, *The Gospel According to America: A Meditation on a God-blessed, Christ-haunted Idea* (Louisville: Westminster John Knox, 2005). See especially chapter 6 with its perceptive discussion of *The Straight Story* (1999) and *Sunset Boulevard* (1950).

84. Edward N. McNulty, *Praying the Movies II: More Daily Meditations from Classical Films* (Louisville: Westminster John Knox, 2003), 13.

85. Paul Schrader, *Transcendental Style in Film: Ozu, Bresson, Dreyer* (New York: Da Capo, 1972), 3.

86. Ibid., 7.

87. Paul Schrader, quoted in Craig Detweiler and Barry Taylor, *A Matrix of Meanings: Finding God in Pop Culture* (Grand Rapids: Baker, 2003), 159.

88. Ibid., 10.

89. Ibid., 160.

90. Ibid., 180–81.

91. Ibid., 181.

92. It is not only the younger generation that is demanding a more culturally relevant style, one rooted in abundance, however. Many of our films that have an international context, either with regard to theme or filmmaker, similarly seek abundant means for invoking wonder in the filmgoing experience. Julie Taymor's wonderfully visual *Frida* (2002), her film biography of the Mexican artist Frida Kahlo, for example, is awash with color and objects and music as she uses Kahlo's paintings, both thematically and

cinematically, to tell her story. As an artist, Kahlo was much admired by the surrealists, for her life and art were both larger than life—her physical suffering, passionate affairs, love of folk culture, and radical politics blended both on canvas and in life. As Margo Jefferson has rightly noted, in *Frida*, Taymor's "glorious visual imagination is rooted in nonnaturalistic, largely non-Western theater traditions. People levitate, disappear and turn into puppets onscreen," just as they did in Kahlo's paintings (Margo Jefferson, "Suddenly Onscreen, It's All about Wonder," *New York Times*, 8 February 2003, n.p.).

To give a second example, from a Spanish-speaking culture, Pedro Almodóvar's award-winning *Talk to Her* (2002), while seemingly suited thematically to the use of sparse means (the movie portrays two comatose women and their caregivers), is anything but sparse. The movie is choreographed like a dance, the color intense, even the stillness is like an intense landscape painting. Like the surrealists, Almodóvar often uses visually extravagant forms to portray his obsession with desire. Once again, Jefferson is helpful in her analysis. She recognizes that Almodóvar has, in this movie, traveled beyond the outrage and extravagance of his previous movies in an effort to elicit wonder. "Wonder is a word we do not use much anymore. . . . But to feel wonder is to be overwhelmed by things beyond our experience and almost beyond our understanding" (ibid.).

93. Terry Lindvall, W. O. Williams, and Artie Terry, "Spectacular Transcendence: Abundant Means in the Cinematic Representation of African American Christianity," *Howard Journal of Communication* 7 (1996): 216.

94. H. Richard Niebuhr, *Christ and Culture* (New York: Harper & Row, 1951).

95. Cf. Glen Stassen, Diane Yeager, and John Howard Yoder, *Authentic Transformation* (Nashville: Abingdon, 1996).

96. Martin E. Marty, foreword to *Hidden Treasures: Searching for God in Modern Culture*, by James M. Wall (Chicago: Christian Century Press, 1997), 7.

97. Andrew Coffin, *World Magazine*, review of *Sideways*, http://www.worldmag.com/displayArticle .cfm?ID=10071, 18 December 2004.

98. Charles Colson, "And the Winner Is: Death, Depravity and Dullness," *Breakpoint Commentary* #050301, 1 March 2005.

99. Dick Staub, CultureWatch, website link for *Sideways*, http://www.dickstaub.com/culturewatch .php?record_id=804, 18 January 2005.

100. Mireya Navarro, "Is a Wine-Soaked Film Too, Er, Rose?" *New York Times*, 20 February 2005, n.p.

101. David DiCerto, Catholic News Service, review of *Sideways*, http://catholicnews.com/data/ movies/04mv429.html.

102. Russ Breimeier, review of *Sideways*, Christianity Today.com, http://www.christianitytoday .com/movies/reviews/sideways.html, 19 November 2004.

103. J. Robert Parks, review of *Sideways*, "Looking Closer," http://promontoryartists.org/looking closer/movie%20reviews/q-z/sideways-jrobert.htm.

104. Darrel Manson, review of *Sideways*, HollywoodJesus.com, http://hollywoodjesus.com/com ments/Darrel/2004/11sideways.html.

105. Craig Detweiler, review of *Sideways*, Metaphilm.com, http://metaphilm.com/philm.php?id=391_ 0_2_0, 19 January 2005.

Chapter 4: Why Look at Film? A Theological Perspective

1. Herbert Jump, *The Religious Possibilities of the Motion Picture* (New Britain, Conn.: South Congregational Church Private Distribution, 1911), reprinted in Terry Lindvall, *The Silents of God: Selected Issues and Documents in Silent American Film and Religion, 1908–1925* (Lanham, Md.: Scarecrow, 2001), 55–56. Cf. the Reverend Dr. Percy Stickney Grant, writing in 1920: "Christ taught his followers by 'Pictures' Parables, we call them. . . . What is the parable of the Prodigal Son but a series of pictures divinely presented? . . . Christ lived and walked among the men of his day. He shared in the life of the common people. . . . If Christ went to the movies would he not say, 'Let my people enjoy this thing. Let my Church employ it. Blessed be that which uplifts, restores, and refreshes the weary souls of men.'"

Percy Stickney Grant, "If Christ Went to the Movies," *Photoplay Magazine* 17, no. 4 (March 1920): 29–30, 121, in Lindvall, *Silents of God*, 233–34.

2. David DiCerto, quoted in Kristen Campbell, "Films Play a Role for Church Groups," *Los Angeles Times,* 16 July 2004, sec. E, 15.

3. Bob Smithouser, *Movie Nights: 25 Movies to Spark Spiritual Discussions with Your Teen* (Wheaton, Ill.: Tyndale, 2002); Doug Fields and Eddie James, *Videos That Teach* (Grand Rapids: Zondervan, 1999); Peter Malone, *On Screen* (Pasay City, Philippines: Paulines Publishing House, 2001), 65.

4. Jolyon Mitchell, "From Morality Tales to Horror Movies: Towards an Understanding of the Popularity of West African Video Film," in *Belief in Media: Cultural Perspectives on Media and Christianity*, ed. Peter Horsfield, Mary Hess, and Adan M. Medrano (Burlington, Vt.: Ashgate, 2004), 116.

5. Cf. Matt Rindge, "Modern Parables: Jesus' Wisdom in Contemporary Film," *Christianity and Theatre* (Fall/Winter 2004): 23–31.

6. Sally McFague, "Parable, Metaphor, and Theology," *Journal of the American Academy of Religion* 42 (1974): 630–31.

7. Mark Noll, Cornelius Plantinga Jr., and David Wells, "Evangelical Theology Today," *Theology Today* 51, no. 4 (1995): 495–507.

8. William G. Kirkwood, "Storytelling and Self-Confrontation: Parables as Communication Strategies," *Quarterly Journal of Speech* 69 (1983): 62.

9. James Carey, "Symbolic Anthropology and the Study of Popular Culture," unpublished essay, quoted by Margaret Miles, "Report on Research Conducted during 1994–95," unpublished paper, 9.

10. Miles, "Report on Research," 10.

11. Michel de Certeau, *The Practice of Everyday Life*, trans. Steven Rendall (Berkeley: University of California Press, 1984).

12. Cf. Peter Berger, ed., *The Desecularization of the World* (Grand Rapids: Eerdmans, 1999).

13. David Hay and Kate Hunt, *Understanding the Spirituality of People Who Don't Go to Church: A Report on the Findings of the Adults' Spirituality Project at the University of Nottingham*, http://www.ctbi.org.uk/downloads/ccom/documents/0008%20David%20Hay%20Final%20Report.doc, August 2000.

14. John Drane, "Contemporary Culture and the Reinvention of Sacramental Spirituality," *The Gestures of God: Explorations in Sacramentality*, ed. Geoffrey Rowell and Christine Hall (New York: Continuum, 2004), 43.

15. David Browne, "Re-conceiving the sacramental." In Rowell and Hall, *Gestures of God*, 31.

16. Cf. Nicholas Lash, *Holiness, Speech and Silence: Reflections on the Question of God* (Burlington, Vt.: Ashgate, 2004).

17. Samuel Taylor Coleridge, quoted in Geoffrey Rowell, "The Significance of Sacramentality," in Rowell and Hall, *Gestures of God*, 10.

18. Walther Zimmerli, "The Place and Limit of the Wisdom in the Framework of the Old Testament Theology," *Scottish Journal of Theology* 17 (1964): 146–58.

19. Cf. Roland E. Murphy, "The Kerygma of the Book of Proverbs," *Interpretation* 20 (January 1966): 3–14.

20. Ibid.

21. Eduard Schweizer, *The Holy Spirit* (Philadelphia: Fortress, 1980), 47.

22. Cf. the definition in *The Oxford English Dictionary*, 10:617: The Spirit is "the active essence or essential power of the Deity, conceived as a creative, animating, or inspiring influence."

23. I have been helped in this summary and that in the next paragraph by Hans Schwartz's article "Reflections on the Work of the Spirit outside the Church," *Neue Zeitschrift für Systematische Theologie und Religionsphilosophie*, ed. Carl Heinz Ratschow, vol. 23 (1985): 197–211.

24. John V. Taylor, *The Go-Between God* (Philadelphia: Fortress, 1972).

25. John Calvin, *Institutes of the Christian Religion*, vol. 1 (Philadelphia: Westminster, 1960), 138 (I.13.14), quoted in Schwartz, "The Work of the Spirit outside the Church," 207–8.

26. Martin Luther, WA 39 II, 198, 21–24 (*Die Promotionsdisputation von Heinrich Schmedenstede: 1542*), quoted in Schwartz, "The Work of the Spirit outside the Church," 206.

27. Martin Luther, WA 40 I, 348, 15–20 (*In epistolam S. Pauli ad Galatas Commentarius 1531*), in his comments on Gal. 3:3, quoted in Schwartz, "The Work of the Spirit outside the Church," 207.

28. The phrase is from Wesley scholar Michael Lodahl, *God of Nature and of Grace: Reading the World in a Wesleyan Way* (Nashville: Abingdon, Kingswood Books, 2003), 136.

29. John Wesley, *NT Notes*, Acts 17:28, quoted in Lodahl, *God of Nature and of Grace*, 117.

30. Karl Barth, *Church Dogmatics*, 4/3.1, *The Doctrine of Reconciliation* (Edinburgh: T&T Clark, 1961), 117.

31. Cf. Paul Tillich, *Systematic Theology,* vol. 3: *Life and the Spirit: History and the Kingdom of God* (Chicago: University of Chicago Press, 1963), 247ff.

32. Jürgen Moltmann, *The Spirit of Life: A Universal Affirmation* (Minneapolis: Fortress, 1992), 3. See also Jürgen Moltmann, *God in Creation: A New Theology of Creation and the Spirit of God* (San Francisco: Harper & Row, 1985).

33. C. S. Lewis, *Surprised by Joy* (New York: Harcourt, Brace & World, Harvest Books, 1955), 238, 180–81.

34. At the end of his life Tillich reflected on his approach to theology. He wrote: "I started with the experiences of the holy and advanced to the idea of God and not the reverse way. Equally important existentially as well as theologically were the mystical, sacramental and aesthetic implications of the idea of the holy, whereby the ethical and logical elements of religion were derived from the experience of the presence of the divine [the Spirit] and not conversely. This made Schleiermacher congenial to me, as he was to Otto." Paul Tillich, *My Search for Absolutes* (San Francisco: Harper & Row, 1967), 28. I thank Craig Detweiler for drawing this Tillich citation to my attention.

35. Paul Tillich, *On the Boundary: An Autobiographical Sketch* (New York: Scribner's Sons, 1966), 27–28.

36. Paul Tillich, *On Art and Architecture*, ed. John Dillenberger and Jane Dillenberger (New York: Crossroad, 1987), 12.

37. Peter Berger, *A Rumor of Angels* (Garden City, N.Y.: Doubleday, Anchor, 1970), 45–75.

38. Robert Jewett, *Saint Paul at the Movies: The Apostle's Dialogue with American Culture* (Louisville: Westminster/John Knox, 1993), 67.

39. Klyne Snodgrass, "Justification by Grace—To the Doers: An Analysis of the Place of Romans 2 in the Theology of Paul," *New Testament Studies* 32, no. 1 (January 1986): 79.

40. Cf. Stan Grenz's conclusion of his article on popular culture's role: "For a large and growing segment of the population, pop culture serves as the chief referent for the cultural task. It provides the central tools by means of which they engage in the age-old task of meaning-making as persons within society. It mediates to them the paradigmatic narrative by means of which and in accordance with which they make sense of their otherwise seemingly senseless lives and thereby construct a sense of personal identity. To the extent that it fulfils this purpose well, pop culture becomes the playground of the Spirit. It serves as an instrument by means of which the divine Spirit nurtures the human spirit." Stanley J. Grenz, "(Pop) Culture: Playground of the Spirit or Diabolical Device," *Cultural Encounters* 1, no. 1 (Winter 2004): 25.

41. The lecture has been published in two different forms: first in Robert McAfee Brown, *The Pseudonyms of God* (Philadelphia: Westminster, 1972), 96–103, and years later in Robert McAfee Brown, *Persuade Us to Rejoice: The Liberating Power of Fiction* (Louisville: Westminster/John Knox, 1992).

42. Justin Martyr, *Second Apology*, 13.

43. Os Guinness, *Dining with the Devil* (Grand Rapids: Baker, 1993), 90.

44. Cf. NRSV rendering: "Do not be conformed to this world, but be transformed by the renewing of your minds, so that you may discern what is the will of God—what is good and acceptable and perfect."

45. Brown, *Persuade Us*, 35.

46. Ibid.

47. For a parallel discussion of Brown's methodology as it applies to literature, see Robert K. Johnston, "Christian Theology and Literature: Correlation or Co-Relation?" in *Collection of Papers Celebrating Professor Hiromu Shimizu's Retirement*, ed. Sachiko Yoshida (Kyoto: Apollon, 1991), 12–22.

48. Dietrich Bonhoeffer, *Letters and Papers from Prison*, ed. Eberhard Bethge, rev. ed. (New York: Macmillan, 1967), 104–5.

49. For a fuller discussion of *American Beauty,* see Robert K. Johnston, "Beyond Futility: *American Beauty* and the Book of Ecclesiastes," in *The Gift of Story: Hope in a Postmodern World*, ed. Emily Griesinger and Mark Eaton (Waco, Baylor University Press, 2006), 85–96.

50. For a fuller discussion of the movie's relation to Ecclesiastes, see Robert K. Johnston, *Useless Beauty: Ecclesiastes through the Lens of Contemporary Film* (Grand Rapids: Baker, 2004), 57–72.

51. John Calvin, *Institutes of the Christian Religion* I.xi.5 and 7, quoted in William Dyrness, "Experiencing God through the Visual: A Methodological Inquiry" (paper presented at the National Consultation on Art and Theology, United Theological Seminary, Minneapolis, Minnesota, September 2002). Dyrness's argument that Calvin's own theology nonetheless allows for the visual, even encourages it, is convincing. Be that as it may, Reformed theologians following on the heels of Calvin used his rhetoric to distance themselves from the image; as Calvin said, pure preaching is "far above the perception of our eyes" (*Institutes* I.xi.12).

52. J. I. Packer, *Knowing God* (Downers Grove, Ill.: InterVarsity, 1973), 38–44.

53. Ibid., 43. Interestingly, few of us are consistent in such pronouncements, and this is as it should be. Bill Dyrness, after quoting these lines from Packer, writes: "But not long ago I heard Packer express the way a recent experience of seeing a dancer in the Ballet Swan Lake moved him to see more deeply than ever the reality of grace." Our experiences, even if we are theologians, often contradict our theory. Dyrness, "Experiencing God through the Visual."

54. Martin Luther, *Luther's Works* (Philadelphia: Fortress, 1958), 40:99, quoted in John W. Cook, "Picturing Theology: Martin Luther and Lucas Cranach," in *Art and Religion: Faith, Form and Reform*, ed. Osmund Overby (Columbia: University of Missouri Press, 1986), 26.

55. Cook, "Picturing Theology," 39.

56. William Dyrness, "Is There a Protestant Aesthetic?" (Wheaton College Aesthetics Lecture, 22 March 2004).

57. See Richard A. Blake, *AfterImage* (Chicago: Loyola University Press, 2000).

58. Mark Noll, "The Evangelical Mind Today," *First Things* 146 (October 2004): 35.

59. Cf. Blake, *AfterImage*.

60. Flannery O'Connor, "Novelist and Believer," in *Manners and Mystery* (New York: Farrar, Straus & Giroux, 1969).

61. H. Richard Niebuhr, *Christ and Culture* (New York: Harper & Row, 1951), 143.

62. Dietrich Bonhoeffer, *Ethics*, ed. Eberhard Bethge (New York: Macmillan, 1955), 101, quoted in David Baily Harned, *Theology and the Arts* (Philadelphia: Westminster, 1966), 148.

63. Harned, *Theology and the Arts*, 149.

64. Paul Tillich, *Systematic Theology* vol. 1 (Chicago: University of Chicago Press, 1951), 40.

65. Paul Tillich, "Art and Ultimate Reality," in *Art, Creativity, and the Sacred: An Anthology in Religion and Art*, ed. Diane Apostolos-Cappadona (New York: Crossroad, 1984), 219–35. This article was originally a lecture at the Museum of Modern Art, New York, 17 February 1959. I found helpful the summary of this lecture given by David Baily Harned in *Theology and the Arts*, 64–68.

66. D. W. Musser and J. L. Price, eds., *The New Handbook of Theology* (Nashville: Abingdon, 1992), 469.

67. John Goldingay, "Biblical Narrative and Systematic Theology," in *Between Two Horizons: Spanning New Testament Studies and Systematic Theology*, ed. Joel B. Green and Max Turner (Grand Rapids: Eerdmans, 2000), 132.

68. Ibid.

69. Martin Buber, *Werke*, vol. 3 (Munich: Kösel, 1963), 71, quoted in Johann Baptist Metz, "A Short Apology of Narrative," trans. David Smith, in *Why Narrative? Readings in Narrative Theology*, ed. Stanley Hauerwas and L. Gregory Jones (Grand Rapids: Eerdmans, 1989), 253.

70. Robert Jewett, *Saint Paul Returns to the Movies: Triumph over Shame* (Grand Rapids: Eerdmans, 1999), 20.

71. Larry J. Kreitzer, *The New Testament in Fiction and Film: On Reversing the Hermeneutical Flow* (Sheffield, UK: JSOT Press, 1993); Larry J. Kreitzer, *The Old Testament in Fiction and Film: On Reversing the Hermeneutical Flow* (Sheffield: Sheffield Academic Press, 1994); Larry J. Kreitzer, *Pauline Images in Fiction and Film: On Reversing the Hermeneutical Flow* (Sheffield, UK: Sheffield Academic Press, 1999); Larry J. Kreitzer, *Gospel Images in Fiction and Film: On Reversing the Hermeneutical Flow* (New York: Continuum, 2002).

72. Philip Yancey, *The Jesus I Never Knew* (Grand Rapids: Zondervan, 1995).

73. Interestingly, the adaptation of Lewis's story to the screen (*The Chronicles of Narnia: The Lion, the Witch and the Wardrobe* [2005]), while a successful movie, subtly changed the focus of the story from Narnia's "deeper magic" to the family bonds of four children. Rather than providing a net to snare something else, the movie was content to point to the content of the Christian gospel while focusing its attention on the children.

74. Paul Tillich, *Systematic Theology*, vol. 1 (Chicago: University of Chicago Press, 1951).

75. Don Browning, *A Fundamental Practical Theology* (Minneapolis: Fortress, 1991), 46; I am indebted to Gordon Lynch's helpful summary of theological approaches to popular culture, *Understanding Theology and Popular Culture* (Oxford: Blackwell, 2005), 99–105, for much of the shape of this paragraph.

76. William Dyrness, "How Does the Bible Function in the Christian Life?" in *The Use of the Bible in Theology: Evangelical Options*, ed. Robert K. Johnston (Atlanta: John Knox, 1985), 159–74.

Chapter 5: Are Movies Art?

1. Quoted in Quentin Schultze et al., *Dancing in the Dark: Youth, Popular Culture, and the Electronic Media* (Grand Rapids: Eerdmans, 1991), 111.

2. For an early, incisive critique of the movie industry, see William F. Lynch, *The Image Industries* (New York: Sheed & Ward, 1959).

3. See David Bayles and Ted Orland, *Art and Fear: Observations on the Perils (and Rewards) of Artmaking* (Santa Barbara, Calif.: Capra, 1993), 74–77.

4. Tim Wright, "A Conversation with Horton Foote," *Image: A Journal of the Arts & Religion* 20 (Summer 1998): 55.

5. Calvin and Hobbes, © 1987 Watterson, printed in *Movie Nights: 25 Movies to Spark Spiritual Discussion with Your Teen* (Wheaton, Ill.: Tyndale, 2002), 3.

6. Cf. Siegfried Kracauer, *Theory of Film* (New York: Oxford University Press, 1960).

7. Dave Kehr, "Dogme: Still Strong, but Less Dogmatic," *New York Times*, 21 March 2004, n.p.

8. Quoted in Craig Detweiler and Barry Taylor, *A Matrix of Meanings: Finding God in Pop Culture* (Grand Rapids: Baker, 2003), 163.

9. Cf. Sergei Eisenstein, *Film Form* (New York: Harcourt, Brace, 1949); Ambros Eichenberger, "Approaches to Film Criticism," in *New Image of Religious Film*, ed. John R. May (Kansas City, Mo.: Sheed & Ward, 1997), 4–5.

10. Iris Murdoch, *The Fire and the Sun* (Oxford: Clarendon, 1977), 86. I am appreciative of my student Craig Detweiler for pointing out Murdoch's comment.

11. I am indebted to Brian Godawa for this observation. Cf. Brian Godawa, *Hollywood Worldviews: Watching Films with Wisdom and Discernment* (Downers Grove, Ill.: InterVarsity, 2002), 17–18.

12. Roy M. Anker, *Catching Light: Looking for God in the Movies* (Grand Rapids: Eerdmans, 2004), 217.

13. Aleksandr I. Solzhenitsyn, *East and West*, trans. Alexis Klimoff et al. (New York: Harper & Row, 1980), 3.

14. Richard A. Blake, *Screening America: Reflections on Five Classic Films* (New York: Paulist, 1991),

15. Cf. Ronald Holloway, *Beyond the Image: Approaches to the Religious Dimension in the Cinema* (Geneva: World Council of Churches, 1977), 25; Les Keyser and Barbara Keyser, *Hollywood and the Catholic Church: The Image of Roman Catholicism in American Movies* (Chicago: Loyola University Press, 1984), xiii; John R. May, "Close Encounters: Hollywood and Religion after a Century," *Image: A Journal of the Arts & Religion* 20 (Summer 1998): 88.

15. As quoted in Keyser and Keyser, *Hollywood and the Catholic Church* (New York: Vintage Books, 1975), xii.

16. "End of an Era as 'Star Wars' Closes," *El Pais*, 20 May 2005 (English supplement to the *International Herald Tribune*), 4.

17. Cf. Lynn Ross-Bryant, *Imagination and the Life of the Spirit: An Introduction to the Study of Religion and Literature* (Chico, Calif.: Scholars Press, 1981), 172.

18. Cf. Giles B. Gunn, "Introduction: Literature and Its Relation to Religion," in *Literature and Religion*, ed. Giles B. Gunn (New York: Harper & Row, 1971), 23.

19. Ibid., 24.

20. Solzhenitsyn, *East and West*, 8.

21. Produced near the end of silent film's golden era, these movies are in many ways the climax of this film genre.

22. Paul Schrader, *Transcendental Style in Film: Ozu, Bresson, Dreyer* (New York: Da Capo, 1972). The quote is found in Gerardus van der Leeuw, *Sacred and Profane Beauty: The Holy in Art*, trans. David E. Green (Nashville: Abingdon, 1963), 333.

23. Martin Scorsese, quoted in Martin Scorsese and Michael Henry Wilson, *A Personal Journey with Martin Scorsese through American Movies* (New York: MiramaxBooks/Hyperion, 1997), 166. The quote was used by Clive Marsh and Gaye Ortiz as the epigraph for their *Explorations in Theology and Film: Movies and Meaning* (Oxford: Blackwell, 1997).

24. Solzhenitsyn, *East and West*, 6.

25. Paul Thomas Anderson, quoted in Julian Wass, "How Goddamn Cool Is Paul Thomas Anderson," *Stanford Daily*, 11 October 2002, n.p.

26. Ibid.

27. Robert Gessner, *The Moving Image* (New York: Dutton, 1970), 19, quoted in Thomas Martin, *Images and the Imageless: A Study in Religious Consciousness and Film* (Lewisburg, Pa.: Bucknell University Press, 1981), 159.

28. James M. Wall, *Church and Cinema: A Way of Viewing Film* (Grand Rapids: Eerdmans, 1971), 33.

29. Dorothy Sayers, "Towards a Christian Aesthetic," in *Unpopular Opinions* (New York: Harcourt, Brace, 1947), 39, quoted in Laura Simmons, "Theology Made Interesting: Dorothy L. Sayers as a Lay Theologian" (Ph.D. diss., Fuller Theological Seminary, 1999), 132–33.

30. Joseph O'Neill, "The Best Novelists, the Worst Movie Adaptations," *New York Times*, 9 November 2003, n.p.

31. Mitchell Stephens, *The Rise of the Image, The Fall of the Word* (New York: Oxford University Press, 1998), xi–xii.

32. I have benefited in my knowledge of this film from the insights of one of my students, Chad Clifford Pecknold.

33. Schrader, *Transcendental Style*, 123.

34. Mark Swed, "The Transcendent Sounds of 'Kundun,'" *Los Angeles Times*, 9 January 1998, sec. F, 12.

35. Cf. Frank Kermode, *The Sense of the Ending: Studies in the Theory of Fiction* (New York: Oxford University Press, 1966).

36. Paul Thomas Anderson, Charlie Rose Transcript, http://www.ptanderson.com/articlesandinterviews/pdl/rose.html.

37. Cubie King, "Punch-Drunk Love: The Budding of an Auteur," Senses of Cinema, file://E:\Punch%20Drunk%20Love%20The%20Budding%20of%20an%20Auteur.html.

38. Jeremy Blake, http://www.ptanderson.com/featurefilms/love/blake/main.html.

39. King, "Punch-Drunk Love."

40. Andrew Greeley, *God in Popular Culture* (Chicago: Thomas More, 1988), 17.

41. Ibid., 252.

42. Craig Detweiler and Barry Taylor, *A Matrix of Meanings: Finding God in Pop Culture* (Grand Rapids: Baker, 2003), 166–67.

Chapter 6: In Film, Story Reigns Supreme

1. Louis Giannetti, *Understanding Movies*, 5th ed. (Englewood Cliffs, N.J.: Prentice Hall, 1990), 300.

2. Jeffrey Katzenberg, quoted in Charles Solomon, "Keeping a Hand In," *Los Angeles Times*, 5 May 2002, Calendar section, 6.

3. Patrick Goldstein, "Sequels Are Fish Food," *Los Angeles Times*, 8 July 2003, sec. E, 4.

4. Robert Newman, quoted in Goldstein, "Sequels Are Fish Food," E4.

5. Frederick Buechner, *Listening to Your Life* (San Francisco: HarperSanFrancisco, 1992), 10.

6. Cf. Conrad Ostwalt, *Secular Steeples: Popular Culture and the Religious Imagination* (Harrisburg, Pa.: Trinity Press, 2003), 148–53.

7. Garrison Keillor, quoted by Ken Gire, *Windows of the Soul: Experiencing God in New Ways* (Grand Rapids: Zondervan, 1996), 120.

8. Ibid.

9. Benjamin Svetkey, "Who Killed the Hollywood Screenplay?" *Entertainment Weekly*, 4 October 1996, 32.

10. Ibid., 34.

11. Okay, *Ocean's Twelve* (2005) was an exception! I suspect everyone's discussion centered on the "stars."

12. The review of *Fly Away Home* appeared originally in *The Covenant Companion*, May 1997, 27. The review of *Amistad* appeared originally in *The Covenant Companion*, March 1998, 33. The review of *Chocolat* appeared originally in *The Covenant Companion*, March 2001, 29.

13. David Augsburger, "Chocolate," in *The Complete Book of Everyday Christianity*, ed. Robert Banks and Paul Stevens (Downers Grove, Ill.: InterVarsity, 1997), 106–7.

14. Cf. Stanley Williams, *The Moral Premise: Harnessing Virtue and Vice for Box Office Success* (Studio City, Calif.: Michael Wiese Productions, 2006), 144–73.

15. Manohla Dargis, "An Irrepressible, Irresistible Rebel on a Roll," *New York Times*, 4 February 2005, n.p.

16. Paul Woolf, "Turning toward Home," *Image: A Journal of the Arts & Religion* 20 (Summer 1998): 123.

17. Wesley Kort, *Narrative Elements and Religious Meaning* (Philadelphia: Fortress, 1975).

18. C. S. Lewis's book for children, from which the movie was adapted, has as its central "character" Narnia itself. That is, it is the atmosphere—an alternate world filled with plashing oceans and loyal fauns, where a "deep magic" awaits overturning by a "deeper magic"—that carries the power and meaning of the story. In the successful film adaptation, the children, whom Lewis had made ordinary so as not to compete with Narnia, are much more developed, their emotions emphasized by repeated close-ups and their desire to keep their family intact transformed into the emotional heart of the movie. Aslan thus becomes more the means of Edmund being rescued from the White Witch than someone who fills viewers with awe and "joy."

19. Jon Boorstin, *Making Movies Work: Thinking like a Filmmaker* (Los Angeles: Silman-James, 1995), 154.

20. Northrop Frye, *Anatomy of Criticism* (Princeton, N.J.: Princeton University Press, 1957), 53.

21. Cf. Nathan Scott Jr., *The Broken Center* (New Haven: Yale University Press, 1966), 4.

22. T. S. Eliot, "Religion and Literature," in *Religion and Modern Literature: Essays in Theory and Criticism*, ed. G. B. Tennyson and Edward E. Ericson Jr. (Grand Rapids: Eerdmans, 1975), 25.

23. Walter J. Ong, "Voice as Summons for Belief: Literature, Faith, and the Divided Self," in *Literature and Religion*, ed. Giles B. Gunn (New York: Harper & Row, 1971), 72.

24. Bill Blizek and Ronald Burke, "'The Apostle': An Interview with Robert Duvall," *Journal of Religion and Film* 2, no. 1 (1997): 8.

25. Quoted in Thomas Martin, *Images and the Imageless: A Study in Religious Consciousness and Film* (Lewisburg, Pa.: Bucknell University Press, 1981), 18. See Norwood Russell Hanson, *Patterns of Discovery: An Inquiry into the Conceptual Foundations of Science* (Cambridge: Cambridge University Press, 1961).

26. Giles Gunn, "Introduction: Literature and Its Relation to Religion," in *Literature and Religion*, ed. Gunn, 24.

27. Boorstin, *Making Movies Work*.

28. Cf. Stephen Farber, "True Knockouts Need an Emotional Punch," *Los Angeles Times*, 9 February 2003, sec. E, 8.

29. Charles Baxter, "Breaking the Body Open: *The Night of the Hunter,*" in *Writers at the Movies: Twenty-six Contemporary Authors Celebrate Twenty-six Memorable Movies*, ed. Jim Shepard (New York: HarperCollins, Perennial, 2000), 47.

30. Ibid., 48.

31. Robert Jewett, *Saint Paul at the Movies: The Apostle's Dialogue with American Culture* (Louisville: Westminster/John Knox, 1993), 32.

32. Boorstin, *Making Movies Work*, 162.

33. Woody Allen, *Woody Allen on Woody Allen: In Conversation with Stig Bjorkman* (New York: Grove, 1995), 208, italics mine.

34. Ibid., 225.

35. Ibid., 223.

36. Woody Allen, quoted in Eric Lax, *Woody Allen: A Biography* (New York: Random House, Vantage, 1991), 362.

37. For a fuller dialogue, see Robert K. Johnston, *Useless Beauty: Ecclesiastes through the Lens of Contemporary Film* (Grand Rapids: Baker, 2004), 35–56.

Chapter 7: Image and Music

1. Lynn Ross-Bryant, *Imagination and the Life of the Spirit: An Introduction to the Study of Religion and Literature* (Chico, Calif.: Scholars Press, 1981), 90.

2. I have found useful Graham Roberts and Heather Wallis, *Introducing Film* (London: Arnold, 2001), and Warren Buckland, *Teach Yourself: Film Studies* (Chicago: Contemporary Books, McGraw-Hill, 2003), as well as the standard introductions to the field: Nathan Abrams, Ian Bell, and Jan Udris, *Studying Film* (London: Arnold, 2001); David Bordwell and Kristin Thompson, *Film Art: An Introduction*, 4th ed. (New York: McGraw-Hill, 1993); James Monaco, *How to Read a Film*, rev. ed. (New York: Oxford University Press, 1981).

3. Cf. Jon Boorstin, *Making Movies Work: Thinking like a Filmmaker* (Los Angeles: Silman-James, 1995), 65–66.

4. Sergei Eisenstein, *The Film Sense*, trans. and ed. Jay Leyday (New York: Harcourt, Brace & World, 1947), 4, quoted in Roger Kahle and Robert E. Lee, *Popcorn and Parable* (Minneapolis: Augsburg, 1971), 23.

5. Andrey Tarkovsky, *Sculpting in Time* (Austin: University of Texas Press, 1986), 63–64.

6. *Hitchcock on Hitchcock*, 255–56, quoted in Buckland, *Teach Yourself*, 19.

7. Cf. Andre Bazin, *What Is Cinema?* (Berkeley: University of California Press, 1967).

8. Richard Schickel, "Conditional Knockout," *Time*, 11 October 1999, 83.

9. Wally Pfister, quoted in Bob Fisher, "The New Generation: Wally Pfister," *ICG Magazine* 73, no. 11 (November 2002): 43.

10. Cf. Ed Eberle, "The Man from Planet X," *ICG Magazine* 72, no. 11 (November 2001): 30–33.

11. Christopher Doyle, quoted in Robert Mackey, "Cracking the Color Code of 'Hero,'" *New York Times*, 15 August 2004, n.p.

12. Rodrigo Prieto, quoted in Bob Fisher, "Uneasy Street," *ICG Magazine* 73, no.12 (December 2002): 49.

13. For an interesting article on the subject, see Elvis Mitchell, "A Year for Images That Will Linger," *New York Times*, 4 January 2004, n.p.

14. George Lucas, quoted in Martin Scorsese and Michael Henry Wilson, *A Personal Journey with Martin Scorsese through American Movies* (New York: MiramaxBooks/Hyperion, 1997), 91.

15. Ibid., 94.

16. George Lucas, quoted in Aljean Harmetz, "Star Wars is 10, and Lucas Reflects," *New York Times*, 21 May 1987, 22, quoted in Quentin Schultze et al., *Dancing in the Dark: Youth, Popular Culture, and the Electronic Media* (Grand Rapids: Eerdmans, 1991), 128–29.

17. Nathaniel Dorsky, "Devotional Cinema," in *The Hidden God: Film and Faith*, eds. Mary Lea Bandy and Antonio Monda (New York: Museum of Modern Art, 2003), 276–77.

18. Paul Ricoeur, quoted in Peter Mann, "Religious Symbolism and Mass Communication," in *Media, Culture and Catholicism*, ed. Paul A. Soukup (Kansas City, Mo.: Sheed & Ward, 1996), 116.

19. Cf. David Dark, *Everyday Apocalypse* (Grand Rapids: Brazos, 2002), 78–95.

20. Robert Towne, quoted in Stephen Farber, "Savviest Filmmakers Put Last Things First," *Los Angeles Times*, 27 August 2001, sec. F, 1.

21. Jack Epps, quoted in Bob Baker, "The Last Word in Films," *Los Angeles Times*, 11 August 2003, sec. E, 8.

22. An alternate ending was filmed (it is available on the movie's DVD version) that follows the car into the canyon, where it crashes. The realism of the scene was rejected in the editing of the movie, for it destroyed the story's intended message of liberation.

23. The importance of film music is also being recognized by the music profession. In France, for example, in 2001, the Orchestre National de Lyon created a series of cinema concerts, while at the Theatre des Champs-Elysées, the Orchestre Lamoureux presented a concert of Gustav Mahler and Bernard Herrmann (the film composer of countless film scores beginning with *Citizen Kane* [1940] and ending with *Taxi Driver* [1976], with a number of Hitchcock movies in between). More recently, John Debney's original score for *The Passion of the Christ* (2004) was a surprising bestseller in the months surrounding the release of the film.

24. Aaron Copeland, "The Aims of Music for Films," *New York Times*, 10 March 1940, summarized in Pauline Reay, *Music in Film: Soundtracks and Synergy* (London: Wallflower, 2004), 32.

25. Barry Taylor, "The Color of Sound: Music and Meaning-Making in Film," *Theology News & Notes* 52, no. 2 (Spring 2005): 9–12.

26. John Ottman, quoted in Jon Burlingame, "They Shoot, He Scores (and Snips)," *Los Angeles Times*, 4 May 2003, sec. E, 29.

27. For a discussion of Kubrick's use of music, see Vincent Lo Brutto, *Stanley Kubrick: A Biography* (New York: Da Capo, 1997); and Thomas Allen Nelson, *Kubrick: Inside a Film Artist's Maze* (Bloomington: Indiana University Press, 1982).

28. For a fuller discussion of *Magnolia* and its music, see Robert K. Johnston, *Useless Beauty: Ecclesiastes through the Lens of Contemporary Film* (Grand Rapids: Baker, 2004), 73–91. See also Reay, *Music in Film*, 59–73.

29. Paul Thomas Anderson, *Magnolia: The Shooting Script* (New York: Newmarket, 2000), 198.

30. Paul Thomas Anderson, quoted in Mark Olsen, "Singing in the Rain," *Sight and Sound* 8, no. 1 (March 2000): 28.

Chapter 8: Becoming a Film Critic

1. Richard A. Blake, *Screening America: Reflections on Five Classic Films* (New York: Paulist, 1991), 4.

2. Devin Gordon, "Monsters' Ball," *Newsweek*, 28 March 2005, 52.

3. Bob Weinstein, quoted in David M. Halbfinger, "'Sin City,' a Film in Bloody Noir," *New York Times*, 31 March 2005, n.p.

4. Orson Welles, quoted in Louis Giannetti, *Understanding Movies*, 5th ed. (Englewood Cliffs, N.J.: Prentice Hall, 1990), 330.

5. Martin Scorsese, in Martin Scorsese and Michael Henry Wilson, *A Personal Journey with Martin Scorsese through American Movies* (New York: MiramaxBooks/Hyperion, 1997), 33. In my discussion of how the Western changed to reflect the changing shape of American culture, I am dependent on Scorsese's insightful comments.

6. Ibid., 40.

7. Cf. Will Wright, *Six Guns and Society: A Structural Study of the Western* (Berkeley: University of California Press, 1975), 97.

8. Tom Ryall, "Teaching through Genre," *Screen Education* 17 (1975): 27–28, quoted in Peter Hutchings, "Genre Theory and Criticism," in *Approaches to Popular Film*, ed. Joanne Hollows and Mark Jancovich (Manchester: Manchester University Press, 1995), 65–66.

9. Wright, *Six Guns*, 34.

10. Ibid., 48–49.

11. Jean Renoir, quoted in Blake, *Screening America*, 181.

12. Robert Banks, "The Drama of Salvation in George Stevens's *Shane*," in *Explorations in Theology and Film: Movies and Meaning*, ed. Clive Marsh and Gaye Ortiz (Oxford: Blackwell, 1997), 59–72.

13. See Geoffrey Hill, *Illuminating Shadow: The Mythic Power of Film* (Boston: Shambhala, 1992), 118–36.

14. Banks, "The Drama of Salvation," 65.

15. For example, Sony Pictures Classics, Paramount Classics, Warner Independent, Focus Features, Fox Searchlight, Miramax. In 2004, their movies included *Hotel Rwanda, The Motorcycle Diaries, Sideways, A Very Long Engagement, House of Flying Daggers, Being Julia, Garden State, Napoleon Dynamite, Eternal Sunshine of the Spotless Mind.*

16. David Bayles and Ted Orland, *Art and Fear: Observations on the Perils (and Rewards) of Artmaking* (Santa Barbara, Calif.: Capra, 1993), 116.

17. Wassily Kandinsky, "Concerning the Spiritual in Art," in *Art, Creativity, and the Sacred: An Anthology in Religion and Art*, ed. Diane Apostolos-Cappadona (New York: Crossroad, 1984), 7 n. 1.

18. It is important not to confuse the director's point of view with the implied narrator. An author's statement on a movie can help us understand what went into the creation of the film, but it can never take the place of the movie itself.

19. Sherman Alexie, quoted by Jeffrey Ressner, "They've Gotta Have It," *Time*, 29 June 1998.

20. Chris Eyre, quoted in Julien R. Fielding, "Native American Religion and Film: Interviews with Chris Eyre and Sherman Alexie," *Journal of Religion and Film* 7, no. 1 (April 2003): n.p.

21. Sherman Alexie, quoted in Fielding, "Native American Religion," n.p.

22. For the discussion of Christian symbolism in the movie, I have been helped by Fielding's discussion and his interviews with Chris Eyre and Sherman Alexie (ibid.).

23. Lester D. Friedman, *The Jewish Image in American Film* (Secaucus, N.J.: Citadel, 1987), 229.

24. Woody Allen, *Woody Allen on Woody Allen: In Conversation with Stig Bjorkman* (New York: Grove, 1995), 263.

25. In *Woody Allen, Side Effects* (New York: Random House, 1980).

26. Michael Hauge, *Writing Screenplays That Sell* (New York: HarperCollins, 1991), 74, quoted in Stanley D. Williams, *The Moral Premise: Harnessing Virtue and Vice for Box Office Success* (Studio City, Calif.: Michael Wiese Productions, 2006), 53. For much of the description of a movie's theme that follows, I am indebted to Stan Williams.

27. Jon Boorstin, *Making Movies Work: Thinking like a Filmmaker* (Los Angeles: Silman-James, 1995), 162.

28. James Stewart, foreword to *Private Screenings: Insiders Share a Century of Great Movie Moments*, by the American Film Institute with Duane Byrge (Atlanta: Turner, 1995), 7–8.

29. Williams, *The Moral Premise*, 50.

30. Three recent books that turn to films in order to illustrate and discuss philosophical ideas and themes are Mary Litch's *Philosophy through Film* (London: Routledge, 2002); Christopher Falzon's *Philosophy Goes to the Movies: An Introduction to Philosophy* (London: Routledge, 2002); and Dean Kowalski's *Classic Questions and Contemporary Film: An Introduction to Philosophy* (New York: McGraw-Hill, 2005). Here, too, a thematic approach is taken toward the movies reviewed. Kowalski uses nineteen movies (e.g., *The Matrix, Bruce Almighty, Being John Malkovich, The Matrix Reloaded, Crimes and Misdemeanors, Life Is Beautiful, Lord of the Flies*) as case studies for considering such topics as skepticism; God; mind, body, and consciousness; freedom, determinism, and foreknowledge; ethics; and human nature. Falzon similarly uses movies to help investigate philosophical themes. Descartes' argument that we are deceived

by an evil genius is enfleshed in movies like *The Truman Show* (1998) and *The Matrix* (1999), and Plato's cave imagery provides thematic direction for *Cinema Paradiso* (1988). Hitchcock's *Rear Window* (1954) explores what we actually see, and *Rashomon* (1950) and *Twelve Angry Men* (1957) explore questions of truth. Descartes' dualism finds expression in *Being John Malkovich* (1999), among others, and questions of personal identity are central in *The Return of Martin Guerre* (1983). Here is a variation of thematic criticism, though it risks reducing film to illustration of ideas otherwise generated.

31. Cf. Nora Zamichow, "Psychologists Are Giving Film Therapy Thumbs Up," *Los Angeles Times*, 4 July 1999, sec. A, 1, 12; and Gary Solomon, *The Motion Picture Prescription* (Santa Rosa, Calif.: Aslan, 1995). Solomon reviews two hundred movies "to help you heal life's problems."

32. Arnold Penenberg, foreword to *Reel Life/Real Life: A Video Guide for Personal Discovery*, by Mary Ann Horenstein et al. (Kendall Park, N.J.: Fourth Write, 1994).

33. Sara Anson Vaux, *Finding Meaning at the Movies* (Nashville: Abingdon, 1999), xi, xii.

34. Larry Sturhahn, "*One Flew over the Cuckoo's Nest*: An Interview with Director Milos Forman," *Filmmakers Newsletter* 9, no. 2 (December 1975): 31.

35. Milos Forman and Jan Novak, *Turnaround: A Memoir* (New York: Villard, 1994), 204.

36. John Broder and Katharine Seelye, *International Herald Tribune*, 11 May 1999, 2.

37. Roger Ebert of the *Chicago Sun-Times* writes, "[S]ome of the most brutal, unremitting, nonstop violence ever filmed." Kenneth Turan of the *Los Angeles Times* says, "Fight Club's level of visceral violence, its stomach-turning string of bloody and protracted bare-knuckles brawls, make it more than worthy of an NC-17." And Joe Morgenstern of the *Wall Street Journal* summarizes the movie in these words: "[A]n arresting, eventually appalling excursion into social satire by way of punishing violence. . . . A theater of cruelty that Artaud couldn't have foreseen: not just frenzied fist-fighting but mutilation, torture and exultant demolition." See Neil Jurgensen, "The 'Fight Club' Debate: Just What Is the Message Here?" *Los Angeles Times*, 1 November 1999, sec. F, 3.

38. Quoted in Amy Wallace, "Is Hollywood Pulling Punches?" *Los Angeles Times*, 26 December 1999, Calendar section, 5, 92.

39. Edward R. Murrow, quoted in William F. Lynch, *The Image Industries* (New York: Sheed & Ward, 1959), 37 n. 1.

40. Laura Mulvey, "Visual Pleasure and Narrative Cinema," *Screen* 16, no. 3 (1975): 6–18.

41. Cf. bell hooks, *Black Looks: Race and Representation* (London: Turnaround, 1992), 122–23.

Chapter 9: Responding to Film Ethically: Moving beyond the Rating System

1. Harvey Cox, *When Jesus Came to Harvard: Making Moral Choices Today* (Boston: Houghton, Mifflin, 2004), 7, 8, 25.

2. Ibid.

3. Kenneth Turan, "Time for an Adult Conversation about R's Failure," *Los Angeles Times*, 2 October 2000, sec. F, 1, 6.

4. Jack Valenti, "The Voluntary Movie Rating System," Motion Picture Association of America (on-line), http://www.mpaa.org/ratings.html, 22 February 1997, quoted in Stan Williams, "Cinema's Divine Destiny" (unpublished manuscript), 56.

5. For a discussion of the Bible's treatment of sex and violence, see Anton Karl Kozlovic, "Religious Film Fears 2: Cinematic Sinfulness," *Quodlibet Journal* 5, no. 4 (October 2003): n.p.; Brian Godawa, *Hollywood Worldviews: Watching Films with Wisdom and Discernment* (Downers Grove, Ill.: InterVarsity, 2002), 187–208.

6. One must hasten to add, however, that when a movie's "larger intention" rather than its "raw data" was used by review boards in an earlier era, Cecil B. DeMille became notorious for combining enough piety with his depictions of debauchery to put a thin religious gloss over otherwise salacious scenes. And the ratings were hardly better.

7. To give a famous (infamous?) example, *Midnight Cowboy* (1969) won the Oscar for Best Picture, despite being given an X rating (the earlier NC-17) by Valenti's Rating Board. After being judged to have artistic merit by winning an Oscar, the movie was re-rated by the MPAA and reassigned an R, even

though not one frame was altered. Even the Ratings Board could not stay only with the "raw data" in this case. Such inconsistency is simply confusing for all involved.

8. Cf. the comments of Janet Robinson, the chairwoman of the Ontario Film Review Board in Canada: "This is my opinion only, but here in Canada we are a little bit more lax on the sexual aspect of [entertainment products] and we're harder on violence. In the States, I think it's the direct opposite. If you show the least little bit of nudity in the States, the Bible Belt down in mid-America just has an absolute fit. Well, for heaven's sakes, we all have breasts, we all have sex, but we're not all violent up here." Quoted in Scott Colbourne, "Battle Heating Up over Gaming Content," *Globe and Mail*, 27 July 2005, R2. In Europe, similarly, there are an increasing number of movies that have transgressed traditional sexual taboo barriers with little public outrage or even interest.

9. The examples that follow are taken from Adena Halpern, "A Moving Target," *New York Times*, 24 October 2004.

10. Jim Salter, "Hollywood Isn't Buckling Up, New Study Says," *Aspen Daily News*, 31 August 2001, 16.

11. Pope John Paul II, quoted in Michael Paulson, "U.S. Catholic Bishops Taking On Death Penalty," *International Herald Tribune*, 22 March 2005, 7.

12. Charles Colson, "Walk a Green Mile in Their Shoes," *BreakPoint Commentary* #000221, 2000.

13. Daniel Defoe, *Moll Flanders* (London, 1772), quoted in Steve Turner, *Imagine: A Vision for Christians in the Arts* (Downers Grove, Ill.: InterVarsity, 2001), 40.

14. Diane Lane, quoted in Julie K. L. Dam, "The Naked Truth about Flesh in Films: Who Strips? Who Won't? Who Wishes They Hadn't?" *People*, 9 December 2002, http://www.cnn.com/2002/SHOW BIZ/Movies/12/09/people.cel.nudity/index.html.

15. Quoted in Dam, "The Naked Truth."

16. The phrase is Gordon Lynch's, who borrowed it from Michael Dyson. Gordon Lynch, *Understanding Theology and Popular Culture* (Oxford: Blackwell, 2005), ix.

17. Mitch Avila, "Responding Emotionally to Film," *Theology News & Notes* 52, no. 2 (Spring 2005): 22–25.

18. Cf. Frank Burch Brown, *Good Taste, Bad Taste, and Christian Taste: Aesthetics in Religious Life* (New York: Oxford University Press, 2000), xi.

19. Dietrich Bonhoeffer, *Letters and Papers from Prison*, ed. Eberhard Bethge, enlarged ed. (New York: Macmillan, 1971), 198.

20. Pat Robertson and Tom DeLay, quoted in Daniel Eisenberg, "Lessons of the Schiavo Battle," *Time*, 4 April 2005, 23.

21. The theme of *The Interpreter* (2005) is not synonymous with its plot, which centers on the assassination of an African president. Rather, it is the embodiment of the proverb, "vengeance is a lazy form of grief." *Jaws* (1975) is not really about sharks, though they fill the story line. Rather, characters and audience alike are forced to confront their primal fears.

22. James Berardinelli, review of *The Sea Inside*, http://movie-reviews.colossus.net/movies/s/sea_inside.html.

23. Kimberley Jones, *The Sea Inside*, http://www.austinchronicle.com/gyrobase/Calendar/Film?Film=oid%3A259839], 5 February 2005.

24. Roger Ebert, "*The Sea Inside*: One Quadriplegic's Dilemma: Life or Death," http://rogerebert.suntimes.com/apps/pbcs.dll/article?AID=/20041216/REVIEWS/4113000, 16 December 2004.

25. It is interesting to note that the production designer for the movie, Henry Bumstead, is ninety, while the author of the book on which the movie is based, Jerry Boyd, was sixty-nine when the book came out. The movie has the tone of the wisdom of age throughout.

26. Andrew Coffin, quoted in Jeffrey Overstreet, *Million Dollar Baby: What Other Critics Are Saying*, http://www.christianitytoday.com/movies/reviews/milliondollarbaby.html, 13 January 2005. Cf. Andrew Coffin, review of *Million Dollar Baby*, *World Magazine*, http://www.worldmag.com/subscriber/display article.cfm?id=10240, 14 January 2005.

27. Christopher Lyon, review of *Million Dollar Baby*, pluggedin.online, http://www.pluggedinonline.com/movies/movies/a0002027.cfm.

28. Annabelle Robertson, "'Million Dollar Baby' Destined to Elicit Praise," crosswalk.com, http://www.crosswalk.com/fun/1308295.html.

29. Charles Colson, "Fighting for What's Important," *BreakPoint Commentary*, 11 February 2005.

30. Michael Medved, "The 'Suicide Solution' Suddenly Seems Trendy," *USA Today*, 9 March 2005, Sec. A, 11.

31. Diane Shreve Singer, "Surrendering to Grief," *BreakPoint Commentary*, 28 February 2005.

32. Marcie Roth, quoted in Sharon Waxman, "Groups Criticize 'Baby' for Message on Suicide," *New York Times*, 31 January 2005, http://query.nytimes.com/mem/tnt.html?tntget=2005/01/31/movies131baby.html&tntemail.

33. Clint Eastwood, quoted in Waxman, "Groups Criticize 'Baby.'"

34. Katie Dallam, quoted in Rick Lyman, "Far from Hollywood, Boxer Whose Dreams Really Died in the Ring," *New York Times*, 9 March 2005, sec. A, 1, 19.

35. Roger Ebert, quoted in Waxman, "Groups Criticize 'Baby.'"

Chapter 10: Responding to Movies Theologically

1. T. S. Eliot, "Religion and Literature," in *Religion and Modern Literature: Essays in Theory and Criticism*, ed. G. B. Tennyson and Edward E. Ericson Jr. (Grand Rapids: Eerdmans, 1975), 21–30.

2. Cf. Roger Wedell, "Berdyaev and Rothko: Transformative Visions," in *Art, Creativity, and the Sacred: An Anthology in Religion and Art*, ed. Diane Apostolos-Cappadona (New York: Crossroad, 1984), 304.

3. David John Graham, "The Uses of Film in Theology," in *Explorations in Theology and Film: Movies and Meaning*, ed. Clive Marsh and Gaye Ortiz (Oxford: Blackwell, 1997), 41–42.

4. James Wall, *Church and Cinema: A Way of Viewing Film* (Grand Rapids: Eerdmans, 1971), 34.

5. Martin Buber, *I and Thou*, 2nd ed. (New York: Scribner's Sons, 1958), 4.

6. Rudolf Otto, *The Idea of the Holy* (New York: Oxford University Press, 1958), 12–40.

7. Martha Nussbaum, *Love's Knowledge* (Oxford: Oxford University Press, 1990), 379.

8. T. S. Eliot, *The Complete Poems and Plays, 1909–1950* (New York: Harcourt, Brace & World, 1971), 119. Eliot also uses the image in "Triumphal March," stanza one of *Coriolan* (ibid., 86).

9. Wallace Stevens, *Collected Poems* (New York: Knopf, 1955), 209, quoted in Robert N. Bellah, "Transcendence in Contemporary Piety," in *Transcendence*, ed. Herbert W. Richardson and Donald R. Cutler (Boston: Beacon, 1969), 89.

10. Quoted in Roy M. Anker, "Movies and the Mystery of God's Love," *The Banner*, 11 October 1999, 14–17.

11. Peter Berger, *A Rumor of Angels* (Garden City, N.Y.: Doubleday, Anchor, 1970), 57–60.

12. John Updike, "Packed Dirt, Churchgoing, a Dying Cat, a Traded Car," in *Pigeon Feathers and Other Stories* (Greenwich, Conn.: Fawcett, Crest, 1962), 172.

13. Houston Smith, "The Reach and the Grasp: Transcendence Today," in *Transcendence*, ed. Richardson and Cutler, 2.

14. Don Browning, quoted by Winston Gooden, "Spiritual Themes in Psychotherapy," Installation address for the Evelyn and Frank Freed Chair of Psychotherapy, Fuller Theological Seminary, 30 November 2004.

15. David Hay, *Exploring Inner Space: Scientists and Religious Experience* (London: Mowbray, 1987), 16.

16. David Hay and Kate Hunt, *Understanding the Spirituality of People Who Don't Go to Church: A Report of the Adults' Spirituality Project at the University of Nottingham* (Nottingham: University of Nottingham, 2000), foreword.

17. Ibid., 207.

18. Wallace Stevens, *Opus Posthumous* (New York: Knopf, 1957), 237, quoted in Robert N. Bellah, "Transcendence in Contemporary Piety," in *Transcendence*, ed. Richardson and Cutler, 86.

19. Nathan Scott Jr., *The Broken Center* (New Haven: Yale University Press, 1966), 204–5.

20. Julius Lester, quoted in Martin Marty, *Context: Martin Marty on Religion and Culture* 28, no. 11 (1 June 1996): 2.

21. Kathleen Norris et al., "Screening Mystery: A Symposium," *Image: A Journal of the Arts & Religion* 20 (Summer 1998): 36.

22. Ibid., 41.

23. Paul Schrader, *Transcendental Style in Film: Ozu, Bresson, Dreyer* (New York: Da Capo, 1972), 6.

24. Harvey Cox, "The Purpose of the Grotesque in Fellini's Films," in *Celluloid and Symbols*, ed. John Cooper and Carl Skrade (Philadelphia: Fortress, 1970), 99.

25. Ken Gire, *Windows of the Soul: Experiencing God in New Ways* (Grand Rapids: Zondervan, 1996), 118–19. One of my students related to me that it was the same scene that as a depressed adolescent made him weep as well. The movie was the first R-rated movie he had seen. He went because his uncle was in the film. And as he followed the struggles of the Richard Gere character, he was both inspired and encouraged.

26. Cf. Michael Bird, "Film as Hierophany," in *Religion in Film*, ed. John R. May and Michael Bird (Knoxville: University of Tennessee Press, 1982), 3–22.

27. Andrew Greeley, *God in Popular Culture* (Chicago: Thomas More, 1988), 245–49.

28. Ibid., 246ff.

29. C. S. Lewis, *The Pilgrim's Regress* (Grand Rapids: Eerdmans, 1958), 171.

30. Greeley, *God in Popular Culture*, 250.

31. William Dyrness, "Response to Margaret Miles' Report on Research" (unpublished manuscript), 3.

32. Quoted in James Wall, *Hidden Treasures: Searching for God in Modern Culture* (Chicago: Christian Century Press, 1997), 28.

33. Ibid.

34. Cf. Clive Marsh and Gaye Ortiz, "Theology beyond the Modern and the Postmodern: A Future Agenda for Theology and Film," in *Explorations in Theology and Film*, ed. Marsh and Ortiz, 249.

35. Ernest Ferlita and John R. May, *Film Odyssey: The Art of Film as Search for Meaning* (New York: Paulist, 1976), 14.

36. "Meet Me in Zihuatanejo: A Meditation on Friendship," *Covenant Companion* 84, no. 9 (September 1995): 12–13, 39.

37. "Has God Gone Hollywood with the Apocalypse?" *Covenant Companion* 88, no. 1 (January 1999): 22–24.

38. Dietrich Bonhoeffer, *Letters and Papers from Prison*, ed. Eberhard Bethge, enlarged ed. (New York: Macmillan, 1972), 193. For a book-length study that puts contemporary film into conversation with the Old Testament book of Ecclesiastes, see Robert K. Johnston, *Useless Beauty: Ecclesiastes through the Lens of Contemporary Film* (Grand Rapids: Baker, 2004).

39. John Drane, "Making Theology Practical: Three Recent Movies and the Contemporary Spiritual Search" (inaugural lecture as professor of practical theology, University of Aberdeen, Aberdeen, Scotland, 1998).

40. Conrad E. Ostwalt Jr., "Visions of the End: Secular Apocalypse in Recent Hollywood Film," *Journal of Religion and Film* 2, no. 1 (1998): n.p.

41. For a more complete discussion see Robert K. Johnston, "Transformative Viewing: Penetrating the Story's Surface," in *Re-Viewing Theology and Film*, ed. Robert K. Johnston (Grand Rapids: Baker, forthcoming).

42. It is the case that this fourfold method was fluid, with countless variations in practice, and was more often implicit than explicit. The publication of De Lubac's magisterial study, *Medieval Exegesis* (1998), points out the wide variations. Yet as Kevin Hughes argues, "De Lubac . . . argues that ancient and medieval Christians carried out an interpretive practice, or, even more, a reality of the relationship between Scripture and the life of faith, that they may not fully have comprehended." "The 'Fourfold Sense': De Lubac, Blondel and Contemporary Theology," *Heythrop Journal* 42 (2001): 451–62.

43. Cf. Flannery O' Connor, "The Nature and Aim of Fiction," in Flannery O'Connor, *Mystery and Manners*, eds. Sally and Robert Fitzgerald (New York: Farrar, Straus & Giroux, 1969), 72–73: "The kind of vision the fiction writer needs to have, or to develop, in order to increase the meaning of his story is called anagogical vision, and that is the kind of vision that is able to see different levels of reality in one image or one situation. The medieval commentators on Scripture found three kinds of meaning

in the literal level of the sacred text: one they called allegorical, in which one fact pointed to another; one they called tropological, or moral, which had to do with what should be done; and one they called anagogical, which had to do with the Divine life and our participation in it. Although this was a method applied to biblical exegesis, it was also an attitude toward all of creation, and a way of reading nature which included most possibilities, and I think it is this enlarged view of the human scene that the fiction writer has to cultivate if he is ever going to write stories that have any chance of becoming a permanent part of our literature."

44. Cf. Northrop Frye, "Reconsidering Levels of Meaning," *Christianity and Literature* 54, no. 3 (Spring 2005): 397–421.

45. Cf. my book *Useless Beauty*, where the encounter with such movies as *American Beauty* and *Magnolia* provides an evocation of beauty/Beauty, which resonates personally, compels communal sympathy and action, and evokes a participation in the transcendent.

46. Cf. Tony Wheeler, "Where Penguins Rule the Roost," *Los Angeles Times,* 4 December 2005, sec. L, 9. In this full-page feature on penguins in the travel section, the article's writer begins, "So if you've seen 'March of the Penguins' and now want to see those fabulous fowl, it's easier (and cheaper) than it has ever been."

47. Lennard J. Davis, "Penguins: A Poor Case for Intelligent Design, Family Values," *Chicago Tribune*, 6 November 2005, section 2, 3.

48. Ibid.

49. Ibid.

50. Karl Rahner, "Poetry and the Christian," *Theological Investigations*, vol. 4 (London: Darton, Longman & Todd, 1967), 357–61.

Chapter 11: An Exercise in Dialogue: The Movies of Peter Weir

1. C. S. Lewis, "On Stories," in *Essays Presented to Charles Williams*, ed. C. S. Lewis (Grand Rapids: Eerdmans, 1966), 101.

2. John Ruskin, quoted in *Celluloid and Symbols*, ed. John C. Cooper and Carl Skrade (Philadelphia: Fortress, 1970), 15.

3. Peter Weir, quoted in Sue Mathews, *35mm Dreams* (Ringwood, Victoria, Australia: Penguin, 1984), 102.

4. Ibid., 105.

5. Peter Weir, quoted in Marek Haltof, *Peter Weir: When Cultures Collide* (New York: Twayne, 1996), 28.

6. Ibid., 34.

7. Cf. Sven Birkerts, "Escape from Pleasantville!" *American Graffiti*, 4 November 1998, in Atlantic Unbound (http://www.theatlantic.com), the Internet site for the *Atlantic Monthly*.

8. Weir, quoted in Mathews, *35mm Dreams*, 98.

9. Ibid., 107.

10. Ibid., 87.

11. Cf. Haltof, *Peter Weir*, 130.

12. Weir, quoted in Pat McGilligan, "Under Weir and Theroux," *Film Comment* 22 (1986): 30.

13. I am indebted to one of my former students, Chad Pecknold, for pointing out to me the original context for the composition of Gorecki's symphony. He also has provided the English translations of the songs Gorecki uses, as well as a summary of music criticism.

14. Walter Ong, "Voice as Summons for Belief: Literature, Faith, and the Divided Self," in *Literature and Religion*, ed. Giles B. Gunn (New York: Harper & Row, 1971), 72.

15. Nathan A. Scott Jr., "The Rediscovery of Story in Recent Theology and the Refusal of Story in Recent Literature," in *Art/Literature/Religion: Life on the Borders*, ed. Robert Detweiler (Chico, Calif.: Scholars Press, 1983), 153.

16. Elizabeth Barrett Browning, *Aurora Leigh, and Other Poems* (New York: James Miller, 1866), 263, 265, 266.

17. Sam Keen, *Apology for Wonder* (New York: Harper & Row, 1969), 130.

18. Sam Keen, "My New Carnality," *Psychology Today* 4 (October 1970): 59.

19. Sam Keen, *To a Dancing God* (New York: Harper & Row, 1970), 82–86.

20. Sam Keen, "Hope in a Posthuman Era," *Christian Century*, 25 January 1967, 106–9.

21. Keen, *Apology for Wonder*, 188.

22. Rudolf Otto, *The Idea of the Holy* (Oxford: Oxford University Press, 1971), 12–40.

23. T. S. Eliot, *The Complete Poems and Plays, 1909–1950* (New York: Harcourt, Brace & World, 1971), 136.

24. Ibid.

25. Cf. John Updike, "Packed Dirt, Churchgoing, a Dying Cat, a Traded Car," in *Pigeon Feathers and Other Stories* (Greenwich, Conn.: Fawcett, Crest, 1962), 172.

26. Robert K. Johnston and Catherine M. Barsotti, "The Year of Living Dangerously," in *Finding God in the Movies: 33 Films of Reel Faith* (Grand Rapids: Baker, 2004), 262–63.

27. Cf. Robert Hostetter, "A Controversial 'Witness,'" *Christian Century*, 10 April 1985, 341–42.

28. C. S. Lewis, *The Silver Chair* (New York: Macmillan, Collier, 1970), 159.

selected
bibliography of
theology and film

Abrams, Nathan, Ian Bell, and Jan Udris. *Studying Film*. London: Arnold, 2001.

Aichele, George, ed. *Culture, Entertainment, and the Bible*. Sheffield, UK: Sheffield Academic Press, 2000.

Aichele, George, and Richard Walsh, eds. *Screening Scripture: Intertextual Connections between Scripture and Film*. Harrisburg, Pa.: Trinity Press International, 2002.

Aldridge, William. "Franco Zeffirelli on Telling the Story of Christ from Its Real Roots." *Screen International* 48 (7 August 1976): 9.

Allen, Woody. *Woody Allen on Woody Allen: In Conversation with Stig Bjorkman*. New York: Grove, 1995.

American Film Institute (with Duane Byrge). *Private Screenings: Insiders Share a Century of Great Movie Moments*. Atlanta: Turner, 1995.

Anker, Roy M. *Catching Light: Looking for God in the Movies*. Grand Rapids: Eerdmans, 2004.

———. "Movies and the Mystery of God's Love." *The Banner*, 11 October 1999, 14–17.

Apostolos-Cappadona, Diane, ed. *Art, Creativity, and the Sacred: An Anthology in Religion and Art*. New York: Crossroad, 1984.

———. "From Eve to the Virgin and Back Again: The Image of Woman in Contemporary (Religious) Film." In May, *New Image of Religious Film*, 111–27.

Austin, Ronald. "Editorial Statement: Screening Mystery." *Image: A Journal of the Arts & Religion* 20 (Summer 1998): 3–5.

———. "Sacrificing Images: Violence and the Movies." *Image: A Journal of the Arts & Religion* 20 (Summer 1998): 23–28.

———, ed. "Screening Mystery: The Religious Imagination in Contemporary Film." *Image: A Journal of the Arts & Religion* 20 (Summer 1998).

317

Avila, Mitch. "Responding Emotionally to Film." *Theology News & Notes* 52, no. 2 (Spring 2005): 22–25.

Baehr, Theodore. "A Cacophony of Prime Time Religions?" In Suman, *Religion and Prime Time Television*, 117–29.

———. *The Media-Wise Family*. Colorado Springs: Chariot Victor, 1998.

———. *What Can We Watch Tonight? A Family Guide to Movies*. Grand Rapids: Zondervan, 2003.

Bandy, Mary Lea, and Antonio Monda, eds. *The Hidden God: Film and Faith*. New York: Museum of Modern Art, 2003.

Banks, Robert. "The Drama of Salvation in George Stevens's *Shane*." In Marsh and Ortiz, *Explorations in Theology and Film*, 59–72.

Barthes, Roland. "The Death of the Author." In *Image/Music/Text*, trans. Stephen Heath, 142–48. London: Fontana/Collins, 1977.

Baugh, Lloyd. *Imaging the Divine: Jesus and Christ-Figures in Film*. Kansas City, Mo.: Sheed & Ward, 1997.

Bausch, Michael G. *Silver Screen, Sacred Story: Using Multimedia in Worship*. Bethesda, Md.: Alban Institute, 2002.

Baxter, John. *The Australian Cinema*. Sydney: Angus & Robertson, Pacific Books, 1970.

Bazin, Andre. *What Is Cinema?* Berkeley: University of California Press, 1967.

Beal, Timothy K., and Tod Linafelt, eds. *Mel Gibson's Bible: Religion, Popular Culture, and the Passion of the Christ*. Chicago: University of Chicago Press, 2006.

Belknap, Bryan. *Group's Blockbuster Movie Illustrations*. Loveland, Colo.: Group Publishing, 2001.

———. *Group's Blockbuster Movie Illustrations: The Sequel*. Loveland, Colo.: Group Publishing, 2003.

Bergesen, Albert J., and Andrew M. Greeley. *God in the Movies*. New Brunswick, N.J.: Transaction, 2000.

Beyette, Beverly. "A Modern-Day Schindler Faces the Consequences." *Los Angeles Times*, 19 August 1998, sec. E, 1.

Billingsley, K. L. *The Seductive Image: A Christian Critique of the World of Film*. Westchester, Ill.: Crossway, 1989.

Bird, Michael. "Film as Hierophany." In May and Bird, *Religion in Film*, 3–22.

Black, Gregory. *The Catholic Crusade against the Movies, 1940–1975*. New York: Cambridge University Press, 1997.

———. *Hollywood Censored: Morality Codes, Catholics, and the Movies*. New York: Cambridge University Press, 1994.

Blake, Richard A. *AfterImage*. Chicago: Loyola University Press, 2000.

———. "From Peepshow to Prayer: Toward a Spirituality of the Movies." *Journal of Religion and Film* 6, no. 2 (October 2002).

———. *Screening America: Reflections on Five Classic Films*. New York: Paulist, 1991.

———. "Secular Prophecy in an Age of Film." *Journal of Religious Thought* 27, no. 1 (Spring–Summer 1970).

Blizek, Bill, and Ronald Burke. "'The Apostle': An Interview with Robert Duvall." *Journal of Religion and Film* 2, no. 1 (1997): 8.

Boatwright, Phil. *The Movie Reporter: Know before You Go (Film/Video Reviews from a Christian Perspective)*. Thousand Oaks, Calif.: Central Christian, 1997.

Bobker, Lee R. *Elements of Film*. New York: Harcourt, Brace & World, 1969.

Boorstin, Jon. *Making Movies Work: Thinking like a Filmmaker*. Los Angeles: Silman-James, 1995.

Bordwell, David, and Kristin Thompson. *Film Art: An Introduction*. 4th ed. New York: McGraw-Hill, 1993.

Boyd, Malcolm. "Theology and the Movies." *Theology Today* 14 (October 1957): 359–75.

Boyum, Joy Gould, and Adrienne Scott. *Film as Film: Critical Responses to Film Art*. Boston: Allyn & Bacon, 1971.

Brewer, H. Michael. *Who Needs a Superhero? Finding Virtue, Vice, and What's Holy in the Comics*. Grand Rapids: Baker, 2004.

Brown, Frank Burch. *Good Taste, Bad Taste, and Christian Taste: Aesthetics in Religious Life*. New York: Oxford University Press, 2000.

Browne, David. "Film, Movies, Meaning." In Marsh and Ortiz, *Explorations in Theology and Film*, 9–20.

———. "Re-conceiving the sacramental." In Rowell and Hall, *Gestures of God*, 21–36. London: Continuum, 2004.

Bryant, M. Darrol. "Cinema, Religion, and Popular Culture." In May and Bird, *Religion in Film*, 101–14.

Buckland, Warren. *Film Studies*. 2nd ed. New York: McGraw-Hill, Teach Yourself, 2003.

Burridge, Richard A. *Faith Odyssey: A Journey through Life*. Grand Rapids: Eerdmans, 2003.

Butler, Ivan. *Religion in the Cinema*. New York: Barnes, 1969.

Butler, John. *TV, Movies, and Morality: A Guide for Catholics*. Huntington, Ind.: Our Sunday Visitor, 1984.

Bywater, Tim, and Thomas Sobchack. *Introduction to Film Criticism: Major Critical Approaches to Narrative Film*. New York: Longman, 1989.

Cawkwell, Tim. *The Filmgoer's Guide to God*. London: Darton, Longman & Todd, 2004.

Chetwynd, Josh. "Escaping 'R' Bondage." *USA Today*, 22 November 1999, sec. D, 1, 2.

Christianson, Eric S., Peter Francis, and William R. Telford, eds. *Cinéma Divinité: Religion, Theology and the Bible in Film*. London: SCM Press, 2005.

Clarke, Anthony J., and Paul S. Fiddes, eds. *Flickering Images: Theology and Film in Dialogue*. Macon, Ga.: Smyth & Helwys, 2005.

Claussen, Dane S., ed. *Sex, Religion, Media*. Lanham, Md.: Rowman & Littlefield, 2002.

Cooper, John C. "The Image of Man in the Recent Cinema." In Cooper and Skrade, *Celluloid and Symbols*, 25–40.

Cooper, John C., and Carl Skrade, eds. *Celluloid and Symbols*. Philadelphia: Fortress, 1970.

Cootsona, Greg. "Jesus the God of Justice and Compassion in Pasolini's *The Gospel according to Matthew*." *Radix* 23, no. 1 (1994): 8–9, 26.

Coppenger, Mark. "A Christian Perspective on Film." In *The Christian Imagination*, ed. Leland Ryken, 285–302. Grand Rapids: Baker, 1981.

Corley, Kathleen E., and Robert L. Webb, eds. *Jesus and Mel Gibson's "The Passion of the Christ": The Film, the Gospels, and the Claims of History*. New York: Continuum, 2004.

Cox, Harvey. "The Purpose of the Grotesque in Fellini's Films." In Cooper and Skrade, *Celluloid and Symbols*, 89–106.

Crofts, Stephen. "Authorship and Hollywood." *Wide Angle* 5, no. 3 (1982): 16–23.

Culkin, John M. "Film and the Church." In *Communication for Churchmen*, vol. 2, *Television-Radio-Film for Churchmen*, ed. B. F. Jackson Jr., 201–56. Nashville: Abingdon, 1968.

Cunneen, Joseph. *Robert Bresson: A Spiritual Style in Film*. New York: Continuum, 2003.

Cunningham, David S. *Reading Is Believing: The Christian Faith through Literature and Film*. Grand Rapids: Brazos, 2002.

Cunningham, Philip A., ed. *Pondering the Passion: What's at Stake for Christians and Jews?* Lanham, Md.: Rowman & Littlefield, 2004.

Dark, David. *Everyday Apocalypse: The Sacred Revealed in Radiohead, The Simpsons, and Other Pop Culture Icons*. Grand Rapids: Brazos, 2002.

Deacy, Christopher. *Screen Christologies: Redemption and the Medium of Film*. Cardiff: University of Wales Press, 2001.

Detweiler, Craig, and Barry Taylor. *A Matrix of Meanings: Finding God in Pop Culture*. Grand Rapids: Baker, 2003.

Detweiler, Robert, ed. *Art/Literature/Religion: Life on the Borders*. Chico, Calif.: Scholars Press, 1983.

Dickinson, Kay, ed. *Movie Music, The Film Reader*. London: Routledge, 2003.

Dorsky, Nathaniel. "Devotional Cinema." In Bandy and Monda, *Hidden God*, 260–80.

Drane, John. "Making Theology Practical: Three Recent Movies and the Contemporary Spiritual Search." Inaugural lecture as professor of practical theology, University of Aberdeen, Aberdeen, Scotland, 1998.

Drew, Donald J. *Images of Man: A Critique of the Contemporary Cinema*. Downers Grove, Ill.: InterVarsity, 1974.

Dyrness, William. "Experiencing God through the Visual: A Methodological Inquiry." Paper presented at the National Consultation on Art and Theology conference, United Theological Seminary, Minneapolis, Minnesota, September 2002.

———. "Is There a Protestant Aesthetic?" Wheaton College Aesthetics Lecture, March 22, 2004.

———. "Response to Margaret Miles' Report on Research." Unpublished manuscript.

Eichenberger, Ambros. "Approaches to Film Criticism." In May, *New Image of Religious Film*, 3–16.

Eisenstein, Sergei. *Film Form*. New York: Harcourt, Brace, 1949.

———. *The Film Sense*. Trans. and ed. Jay Leyday. New York: Harcourt, Brace & World, 1942.

Falzon, Christopher. *Philosophy Goes to the Movies: An Introduction to Philosophy*. London: Routledge, 2002.

Ferlita, Ernest. "The Analogy of Action in Film." In May and Bird, *Religion in Film*, 44–58.

———. "Film and the Quest for Meaning." In May and Bird, *Religion in Film*, 115–31.

Ferlita, Ernest, and John R. May. *Film Odyssey: The Art of Film as Search for Meaning*. New York: Paulist, 1976.

Field, Alex. *HP: The Hollywood Project*. Lake Mary, Fla.: Relevant Books, 2004.

Fields, Doug, and Eddie James. *Videos That Teach*. Grand Rapids: Zondervan, 1999.

———. *Videos That Teach* 2. Grand Rapids: Zondervan, 2002.

Foote, Horton. "A Conversation with Horton Foote." *Image: A Journal of the Arts & Religion* 20 (Summer 1998): 45–57.

Forest, Ben, with Mary Kay Mueller. *God Goes to Hollywood: A Movie Guide for the Modern Mystic*. Lincoln: Writers Club Press, 2000.

Forman, Milos, and Jan Novak. *Turnaround: A Memoir*. New York: Villard, 1994.

Foss, Bob. *Filmmaking: Narrative & Structural Techniques*. Los Angeles: Silman-James Press, 1992.

Fraser, Peter. *Images of the Passion: The Sacramental Mode in Film*. Westport, Conn.: Praeger, 1998.

Fredriksen, Paula, ed. *On The Passion of the Christ: Exploring the Issues Raised by the Controversial Movie*. Berkeley: University of California Press, 2006.

Friedman, Lester D. *The Jewish Image in American Film*. Secaucus, N.J.: Citadel, 1987.

Frost, Michael. *Eyes Wide Open: Seeing God in the Ordinary*. Southerland, NSW, Australia: Albatross Books, 1998.

Frost, Michael, and Robert Banks. *Lesson from Reel Life: Movies, Meaning and Myth-Making*. Adelaide, SA, Australia: Openbook, 2001.

Gabler, Neal. *Life the Movie: How Entertainment Conquered Reality*. New York: Knopf, 1998.

Gallagher, Sharon. "Faith in Film." *Radix* 23, no. 1 (1994): 10–11, 27.

Garner, Jack, and Bruce Fessier. "Land of the Film." *Desert Sun*, 18 January 2000, sec. D, 3.

Giannetti, Louis. *Understanding Movies*. 5th ed. Englewood Cliffs, N.J.: Prentice Hall, 1990.

Gire, Ken. *Reflections on the Movies: Hearing God in the Unlikeliest of Places*. Colorado Springs: Chariot Victor, 2000.

———. *The Reflective Life: Becoming More Spiritually Sensitive to the Everyday Moments of Life*. Colorado Springs: Chariot Victor, 1998.

———. *Windows of the Soul: Experiencing God in New Ways*. Grand Rapids: Zondervan, 1996.

Girgus, Sam B. *The Films of Woody Allen*. Cambridge: Cambridge University Press, 1993.

Godawa, Brian. *Hollywood Worldviews: Watching Films with Wisdom and Discernment*. Downers Grove, Ill.: InterVarsity, 2002.

Graham, David John. "The Uses of Film in Theology." In Marsh and Ortiz, *Explorations in Theology and Film*, 35–44.

Greeley, Andrew. *The Catholic Imagination*. Berkeley: University of California Press, 2000.

———. *God in Popular Culture*. Chicago: Thomas More, 1988.

———. *Religion as Poetry*. New Brunswick, N.J.: Transaction, 1995.

Green, Joel. "The Death of Jesus: Franco Zeffirelli's Perspective." *Radix* 23, no. 1 (1994): 4–7, 22–24.

Grenz, Stanley J. "(Pop) Culture: Playground of the Spirit or Diabolical Device." *Cultural Encounters* 1, no. 1 (Winter 2004): 7–35.

Haltof, Marek. *Peter Weir: When Cultures Collide*. New York: Twayne, 1996.

Hames, Peter. "Forman." In *Five Filmmakers*, ed. Daniel J. Goulding. Bloomington: Indiana University Press, 1994.

Hamilton, William. "Bergman and Polanski on the Death of God." In Cooper and Skrade, *Celluloid and Symbols*, 61–74.

Harned, David Baily. *Theology and the Arts*. Philadelphia: Westminster, 1966.

Hasenberg, Peter. "The 'Religious' in Film: From King of Kings to The Fisher King." In May, *New Image of Religious Film*, 41–56. Kansas City, Mo.: Sheed & Ward, 1997.

Hauerwas, Stanley, and L. Gregory Jones, eds., *Why Narrative? Readings in Narrative Theology*. Grand Rapids, Eerdmans, 1989.

Hauge, Michael. *Writing Screenplays That Sell*. New York: HarperCollins, 1991.

Higgins, Gareth. *How Movies Helped Save My Soul: Finding Spiritual Fingerprints in Culturally Significant Films*. Lake Mary, Fla.: Relevant Books, 2003.

Hill, Geoffrey. *Illuminating Shadow: The Mythic Power of Film*. Boston: Shambhala, 1992.

Hill, John, and Pamela Church Gibson, eds. *Film Studies: Critical Approaches*. New York: Oxford University Press, 2000.

Holloway, Ronald. *Beyond the Image: Approaches to the Religious Dimension in the Cinema*. Geneva: World Council of Churches, 1977.

Hollows, Joanne, and Mark Jancovich, eds. *Approaches to Popular Film*. Manchester: Manchester University Press, 1995.

hooks, bell. *Reel to Real: Race, Sex, and Class at the Movies*. London: Routledge, 1996.

Horenstein, Mary Ann, Brenda Rigby, Marjorie Flory, and Vicki Gershwin. *Reel Life/Real Life: A Video Guide for Personal Discovery*. Kendall Park, N.J.: Fourth Write, 1994.

Hostetter, Robert. "A Controversial 'Witness.'" *Christian Century*, 10 April 1985, 341–42.

Howard, David, and Edward Mabley. *The Tools of Screenwriting: A Writer's Guide to the Craft and Elements of a Screenplay*. New York: St. Martin's Press, 1993.

Hulsether, Mark. "Sorting out the Relationships among Christian Values, U.S. Popular Religion, and Hollywood Films." *Religious Studies Review* 25, no. 1 (January 1999): 3–11.

Hurley, Neil P. "Cinematic Transformations of Jesus." In May and Bird, *Religion in Film*, 61–78.

———. *Theology through Film*. New York: Harper & Row, 1970.

Jasper, David. "On Systematizing the Unsystematic: A Response." In Marsh and Ortiz, *Explorations in Theology and Film*, 235–44.

Jewett, Robert. *Saint Paul at the Movies: The Apostle's Dialogue with American Culture*. Louisville: Westminster/John Knox, 1993.

———. *Saint Paul Returns to the Movies: Triumph over Shame*. Grand Rapids: Eerdmans, 1999.

Johnston, Robert K. "Beyond Futility: *American Beauty* and the Book of Ecclesiastes." In *The Gift of Story: Hope in a Postmodern World*, eds. Emily Griesinger and Mark Eaton, 85–96. Waco: Baylor University Press, 2006.

Johnston, Robert K. *The Christian at Play*. Grand Rapids: Eerdmans, 1983.

———. *Useless Beauty: Ecclesiastes through the Lens of Contemporary Film*. Grand Rapids: Baker, 2004.

Johnston, Robert K., and Catherine M. Barsotti. *Finding God in the Movies: 33 Films of Reel Faith*. Grand Rapids: Baker, 2004.

Johnston, Robert K. ed. "Re-Viewing Theology and Film," *Theology News & Notes* 52, no. 2 (Spring 2005).

Jones, G. William. *Dialogue with the World*. Wilmette, Ill.: Films Incorporated, 1964.

———. *Sunday Night at the Movies*. Richmond: John Knox, 1967.

Kahle, Roger, and Robert E. Lee. *Popcorn and Parable*. Minneapolis: Augsburg, 1971.

Kassabian, Anahid. *Hearing Film: Tracking Identifications in Contemporary Hollywood Film Music*. New York: Routledge, 2001.

Kazan, Elia. *Elia Kazan: A Life*. New York: Knopf, 1988.

Kenny, Glenn. "Are We There Yet?" *Premiere*, February 1999, 91–95.

Keyser, Les, and Barbara Keyser. *Hollywood and the Catholic Church: The Image of Roman Catholicism in American Movies*. Chicago: Loyola University Press, 1984.

Kitses, Jim. *Horizons West*. Bloomington: Indiana University Press, 1969.

Konzelman, Robert G. *Marquee Ministry: The Movie Theater as Church and Community Forum*. New York: Harper & Row, 1971.

Kopplin, David. "Program Notes (for The Wind)." *Los Angeles Philharmonic*, October 1998, 14–17.

Kowalski, Dean. *Classic Questions and Contemporary Film: An Introduction to Philosophy*. New York: McGraw-Hill, 2005.

Kracauer, Siegfried. *Theory of Film*. New York: Oxford University Press, 1960.

Kraemer, Christine Hoff. "From Theological to Cinematic Criticism: Extricating the Study of Religion and Film from Theology." *Religious Studies Review* 30, no. 4 (2004): 243–50.

Kreitzer, Larry J. *Gospel Images in Fiction and Film: On Reversing the Hermeneutical Flow*. London: Sheffield Academic Press, 2002.

———. *The New Testament in Fiction and Film: On Reversing the Hermeneutical Flow*. Sheffield, UK: JSOT Press, 1993.

———. *The Old Testament in Fiction and Film: On Reversing the Hermeneutical Flow*. Sheffield, UK: Sheffield Academic Press, 1994.

———. *Pauline Images in Fiction and Film: On Reversing the Hermeneutical Flow*. Sheffield, UK: Sheffield Academic Press, 1999.

Landres, J. Shawn, and Michael Berenbaum, eds. *After the Passion Is Gone: American Religious Consequences*. Walnut Creek, Calif.: AltaMira Press, 2004.

Larson, Craig Brian, with Andrew Zahn. *Movie-Based Illustrations for Preaching & Teaching: 101 Clips to Show and Tell*. Grand Rapids: Zondervan, 2003.

Larson, Craig Brian, with Lori Quicke. *More Movie-Based Illustrations for Preaching & Teaching: 101 Clips to Show and Tell*. Grand Rapids: Zondervan, 2004.

Lax, Eric. *Woody Allen: A Biography*. New York: Random House, Vantage, 1991.

Lewerenz, Spencer, and Barbara Nicolosi, eds. *Behind the Screen: Hollywood Insiders on Faith, Film, and Culture*. Grand Rapids: Baker, 2005.

Lindvall, Terry. "The Organ in the Sanctuary: Silent Film and Paradigmatic Images of the Suspect Clergy." In Claussen, *Sex, Religion, Media*, 139–52.

————. "Religion and Film, Part I: History and Criticism." *Communication Research Trends* 23, no. 4 (2004): 3–44.

————. "Religion and Film, Part II," *Communication Research Trends* 24, no. 1 (2005): 3–43.

————. *The Silents of God: Selected Issues and Documents in Silent American Film and Religion, 1908–1925*. Lanham, Md.: Scarecrow Press, 2001.

Lindvall, Terry, W. O. Williams, and Artie Terry. "Spectacular Transcendence: Abundant Means in the Cinematic Representation of African American Christianity." *Howard Journal of Communication* 7 (1996): 205–220.

Litch, Mary. *Philosophy through Film*. London: Routledge, 2002.

Lo Brutto, Vincent. *Stanley Kubrick: A Biography*. New York: Da Capo, 1997.

Lodge, David. *The Picturegoers*. Harmondsworth, UK: Penguin Books, 1992.

Loughlin, Gerard. *Alien Sex: The Body and Desire in Cinema and Theology*. Oxford: Blackwell, 2004.

Lyden, John C. *Film as Religion: Myths, Morals, and Rituals*. New York: New York University Press, 2003.

Lynch, Gordon. *Understanding Theology and Popular Culture*. Oxford: Blackwell, 2005.

Lynch, William F. *The Image Industries*. New York: Sheed & Ward, 1959.

MacDonald, Alan. *Films in Close-Up: Getting the Most from Film and Video*. Leicester, UK: Inter-Varsity, Frameworks, 1991.

Mahony, Cardinal Roger M. *Film Makers, Film Viewers: Their Challenges and Opportunities, A Pastoral Letter*. Boston: St. Paul Books & Media, 1992.

Malone, Peter, ed. "From Back Pews to Front Stalls: The Churches in 100 Years of Australian Cinema." *Compass Review of Topical Theology* (Spring 1996): 1–67.

————. "Jesus on Our Screens." In May, *New Image of Religious Film*, 57–71.

————. *Movie Christs and Antichrists*. New York: Crossroad, 1990.

————. *On Screen*. Pasay City, Philippines: Pauline Publishing House, 2001.

Malone, Peter, with Rose Pacatte. *Lights Camera . . . Faith!: A Movie Lover's Guide to Scripture, A Movie Lectionary—Cycle A*. Boston: Pauline Books & Media, 2001.

————. *Lights Camera . . . Faith!: A Movie Lover's Guide to Scripture, A Movie Lectionary—Cycle B*. Boston: Pauline Books & Media, 2002.

————. *Lights Camera . . . Faith!: A Movie Lover's Guide to Scripture, A Movie Lectionary—Cycle C*. Boston: Pauline Books & Media, 2003.

Marsh, Clive. *Cinema & Sentiment: Film's Challenge to Theology*. Bletchley, Milton Keynes, UK: Paternoster, 2004.

————. "Did You Say 'Grace'? Eating in Community in *Babette's Feast*." In Marsh and Ortiz, *Explorations in Theology and Film: Movies and Meaning*, 207–18.

————. "Film and Theologies of Culture." In Marsh and Ortiz, *Explorations in Theology and Film*, 21–34.

————. "The Spirituality of *Shirley Valentine*." In Marsh and Ortiz, *Explorations in Theology and Film*, 193–206.

Marsh, Clive, and Gaye Ortiz, eds. *Explorations in Theology and Film: Movies and Meaning*. Oxford: Blackwell, 1997.

————. "Theology beyond the Modern and the Postmodern: A Future Agenda for Theology and Film." In Marsh and Ortiz, *Explorations in Theology and Film*, 245–56.

Martin, Joel W., and Conrad E. Ostwalt Jr. *Screening the Sacred: Religion, Myth, and Ideology in Popular American Film*. Boulder, Colo.: Westview, 1995.

Martin, Thomas M. *Images and the Imageless: A Study in Religious Consciousness and Film*. Lewisburg, PA: Bucknell University Press, 1981.

Marty, Martin. *Context: Martin Marty on Religion and Culture* 28, no. 11 (1 June 1996).

Mathews, Sue. *35mm Dreams*. New York: Penguin, 1984.

May, John R. "Close Encounters: Hollywood and Religion after a Century." *Image: A Journal of the Arts & Religion* 20 (Summer 1998): 87–100.

————. "Contemporary Theories regarding the Interpretation of Religious Film." In May, *New Image of Religious Film*, 17–40.

————. "The Demonic in American Cinema." In May and Bird, *Religion in Film*, 79–100.

————, ed. *New Image of Religious Film*. Kansas City, Mo.: Sheed & Ward, 1997.

————. *Nourishing Faith through Fiction: Reflections of the Apostles' Creed in Literature and Film*. Franklin, Wis.: Sheed & Ward, 2001.

————. "Religion and Film: Recent Contributions to the Continuing Dialogue." *Critical Review of Books in Religion* 9 (1996): 105–21.

————. "Visual Story and the Religious Interpretation of Film." In May and Bird, *Religion in Film*, 23–43.

May, John R., and Michael Bird, eds. *Religion in Film*. Knoxville: University of Tennessee Press, 1982.

Mazur, Eric Michael, ed. *Art and the Religious Impulse*. Lewisburg, Pa.: Bucknell University Press, 2002.

McClain, Carl. *Morals and the Movies*. Kansas City, Mo.: Beacon Hill, 1970.

McFarlane, Brian, and Geoff Mayer. *New Australian Cinema: Sources and Parallels in American and British Film*. Cambridge: Cambridge University Press, 1992.

McGilligan, Pat. "Under Weir and Theroux." *Film Comment* 22 (1986): 23–32.

McNulty, Edward. *Films and Faith: Forty Discussion Guides*. Topeka, Kans.: Viaticum Press, 1999.

————. *Praying the Movies: Daily Meditations from Classic Films*. Louisville: Geneva Press, 2001.

————. *Praying the Movies II: More Daily Meditations from Classic Films*. Louisville: Westminster John Knox, 2003.

———. *Visual Parables*. (A monthly magazine; view samples from the current issue at www .visualparables.com.)

Medved, Michael. "Hollywood Makes Room for Religion." In Suman, *Religion and Prime Time Television*, 111–16.

———. *Hollywood vs. America: Popular Culture and the War on Traditional Values*. New York: HarperCollins, 1992.

———. "Want an Oscar? An 'R' Revs Up Your Chances." *USA Today*, 19 March 1999, sec. A, 9.

Middleton, Darren J. N., ed. *Scandalizing Jesus? Kazantzakis's "The Last Temptation of Christ" Fifty Years On*. New York: Continuum, 2005.

Miles, Herbert. *Movies and Morals*. Grand Rapids: Zondervan, 1947.

Miles, Margaret. "Report on Research Conducted during 1994–95." Unpublished manuscript.

———. *Seeing and Believing: Religion and Values in the Movies*. Boston: Beacon, 1996.

———. "'What You See Is What You Get': Religion on Prime Time Fiction Television." In Suman, *Religion and Prime Time Television*, 37–46.

Mitchell, Jolyon. "Theology and Film." In *The Modern Theologians: An Introduction to Christian Theology since 1918*, eds. David F. Ford and Rachel Muers, 736–59. 3rd. ed. Oxford: Blackwell, 2005.

Monaco, James. *How to Read a Film*. Rev. ed. New York: Oxford University Press, 1981.

Morgenthaler, Sally. "Film and Worship: Windows in Caves and Other Things We Do with Perfectly Good Prisms." *Theology News & Notes* 52, no. 2 (Spring 2005): 13–15, 25.

Morris, Michael. "Looking for Reel Religion." *Image: A Journal of the Arts & Religion* 20 (Summer 1998): 72–78.

Mulvey, Laura. "Visual Pleasure and Narrative Cinema." *Screen* 16, no. 3 (1975): 6–18.

Neale, Steve. *Genre and Hollywood*. London: Routledge, 2000.

Nelson, John Wiley. *Your God Is Alive and Well and Appearing in Popular Culture*. Philadelphia: Westminster, 1976.

Nelson, Thomas Allen. *Kubrick: Inside a Film Artist's Maze*. Bloomington: Indiana University Press, 1982.

Niccol, Andrew. *The Truman Show: The Shooting Script*. New York: Newmarket, 1998.

Nolan, Steve. "The Books of the Films: Trends in Religious Film-Analysis." *Literature and Theology* 12, no. 1 (1998): 1–15.

Noll, Mark, Cornelius Plantinga Jr., and David Wells. "Evangelical Theology Today." *Theology Today* 51, no. 4 (1995): 495–507.

Oropeza, B. J., ed. *The Gospel according to Superheroes: Religion and Popular Culture*. New York: Peter Lang, 2005.

Ostwalt, Conrad. *Secular Steeples: Popular Culture and the Religious Imagination*. Harrisburg, Pa.: Trinity Press, 2003.

———. "Visions of the End: Secular Apocalypse in Recent Hollywood Film." *Journal of Religion and Film* 2, no. 1 (1998): n.p.

Plate, S. Brent, ed. *Religion, Art, and Visual Culture: Cross-Cultural Reader*. New York: Palgrave, 2002.

————, ed. *Representing Religion in World Cinema*. New York: Palgrave Macmillan, 2003.

Poland, Larry W. *The Last Temptation of Hollywood*. Highland, Calif.: Mastermedia International, 1988.

Postman, Neil. *Amusing Ourselves to Death: Public Discourse in the Age of Show Business*. New York: Penguin, 1985.

Pungente, John, and Monty Williams. *Finding God in the Dark: Taking the Spiritual Exercises of St. Ignatius to the Movies*. Boston: Pauline Books & Media, 2004.

Rayner, Jonathan. *The Films of Peter Weir*. New York: Cassell, 1998.

Reay, Pauline. *Music in Film: Soundtracks and Synergy*. London: Wallflower, Short Cuts Series, 2004.

Reinhartz, Adele. *Scripture on the Silver Screen*. Louisville: Westminster John Knox, 2003.

Rendleman, Todd. "'I didn't need to see the tattooed lady takin' it off': Evangelicals and Representations of Sexuality in Contemporary Film." In Claussen, *Sex, Religion, Media*, 91–100.

Rindge, Matt. "Modern Parables: Jesus' Wisdom in Contemporary Film." *Christianity and Theatre* (Fall/Winter 2004): 23–31.

Roberts, Graham, and Heather Wallis. *Introducing Film*. London: Arnold, 2001.

Robinson, W. R., ed. *Man and the Movies*. Baltimore: Penguin, 1969.

Romanowski, William. "John Calvin Meets the Creature from the Black Lagoon: The Christian Reformed Church and the Movies 1928–1966." *Christian Scholar's Review* 25, no. 1 (1995): 47–62.

Ross, T. J. *Film and the Liberal Arts*. New York: Holt, Rinehart & Winston, 1970.

Runions, Erin. *How Hysterical: Identification and Resistance in the Bible and Film*. New York: Palgrave Macmillan, 2003.

Schaeffer, Franky. *Addicted to Mediocrity: 20th Century Christians and the Arts*. Wheaton, Ill.: Crossway, 1985.

Schillaci, Anthony. "Bergman's Vision of Good and Evil." In Cooper and Skrade, *Celluloid and Symbols*, 75–88.

Schrader, Paul. *Transcendental Style in Film: Ozu, Bresson, Dreyer*. New York: Da Capo, 1972. First published 1972 by University of California Press.

Schultze, Quentin, et al. *Dancing in the Dark: Youth, Popular Culture, and the Electronic Media*. Grand Rapids: Eerdmans, 1991.

Scorsese, Martin, and Michael Henry Wilson. *A Personal Journey with Martin Scorsese through American Movies*. New York: Miramax Books/Hyperion, 1997.

Scott, Bernard Brandon. *Hollywood Dreams and Biblical Stories*. Minneapolis: Fortress, 1994.

Seay, Chris, and Greg Garrett. *The Gospel Reloaded: Exploring Spirituality and Faith in the Matrix*. Colorado Springs: Piñon Press, 2003.

Shaw, David. "Thumbs Up or Down on Movie Critics?" *Los Angeles Times*, sec. A, 1, 16, 17.

Shepard, Jim, ed. *Writers at the Movies: Twenty-six Contemporary Authors Celebrate Twenty-six Memorable Movies*. New York: HarperCollins, Perennial, 2000.

Shiach, Don. *The Films of Peter Weir: Visions of Alternative Realities*. London: Letts, 1993.

Skinner, James. *The Cross and the Cinema: The Legion of Decency and the National Office for Motion Pictures, 1933–1970*. Westport, Conn.: Greenwood, 1993.

Skrade, Carl. "Theology and Films." In Cooper and Skrade, *Celluloid and Symbols*, 1–24.

Smith, Jeffrey A. "Hollywood Theology: The Commodification of Religion in Twentieth-Century Films." *Religion and American Culture* 11, no. 2 (Summer 2001): 191–231.

Smithouser, Bob. *Movie Nights: 25 Movies to Spark Spiritual Discussions with Your Teen*. Wheaton, Ill.: Tyndale, 2002.

Solomon, Gary. *The Motion Picture Prescription*. Santa Rosa, Calif.: Aslan, 1995.

Solomon, Stanley. *Beyond Formula: American Film Genres*. New York: Harcourt, Brace, Jovanovich, 1976.

Soukup, Paul A., ed. *Media, Culture and Catholicism*. Kansas City, Mo.: Sheed & Ward, 1996.

Stephens, Mitchell. *The Rise of the Image, the Fall of the Word*. New York: Oxford University Press, 1998.

Stern, Richard C., Clayton N. Jefford, and Guerric Debona. *Savior on the Silver Screen*. New York: Paulist, 1999.

Stone, Bryan P. *Faith and Film: Theological Themes at the Cinema*. St. Louis: Chalice, 2000.

Storey, John. *Cultural Studies and the Study of Popular Culture*. 2nd ed. Athens: University of Georgia Press, 2003.

Sturhahn, Larry. "*One Flew over the Cuckoo's Nest*: An Interview with Director Milos Forman." *Filmmakers Newsletter* 9, no. 2 (December 1975): 26–31.

Suman, Michael, ed. *Religion and Prime Time Television*. Westport, Conn.: Praeger, 1997.

Summers, Stanford. *Secular Films and the Church's Ministry*. New York: Seabury, 1969.

Svetkey, Benjamin. "Who Killed the Hollywood Screenplay?" *Entertainment Weekly*, 4 October 1996, 32–39.

Swed, Mark. "The Transcendent Sounds of 'Kundun.'" *Los Angeles Times*, 9 January 1998, sec. F, 12, 14.

Tarkovsky, Andrey. *Sculpting in Time: Reflections on the Cinema*. Trans. Kitty Hunter-Blair. Austin: University of Texas Press, 1986.

Taylor, Barry. "The Color of Sound: Music and Meaning-Making in Film." *Theology News & Notes* 52, no. 2 (Spring 2005): 9–12.

Teague, Raymond. *Reel Spirit: A Guide to Movies That Inspire, Explore and Empower*. Unity Village, Mo.: Unity House, 2000.

Telford, William. "Jesus Christ Movie Star: The Depiction of Jesus in the Cinema." In Marsh and Ortiz, *Explorations in Theology and Film*, 115–40.

Tompkins, Jane. *West of Everything*. New York: Oxford University Press, 1992.

Turner, Steve. *Imagine: A Vision for Christians in the Arts*. Downers Grove, Ill.: InterVarsity, 2001.

Updike, John. *In the Beauty of the Lilies*. New York: Knopf, 1996.

Valenti, F. Miguel. *More than a Movie: Ethics in Entertainment*. Boulder, Colo.: Westview, 2000.

Vaux, Sarah Anson. *Finding Meaning at the Movies*. Nashville: Abingdon, 1999.

Wall, James M. "Biblical Spectaculars and Secular Man." In Cooper and Skrade, *Celluloid and Symbols*, 51–60.

———. *Church and Cinema: A Way of Viewing Film*. Grand Rapids: Eerdmans, 1971.

———. *Hidden Treasures: Searching for God in Modern Culture*. Chicago: Christian Century Press, 1997.

Wallace, Amy. "Do Movie Ratings Need New Categories?" *Los Angeles Times*, 10 August 1999, sec. F, 1, 4, 5.

———. "Is Hollywood Pulling Punches?" *Los Angeles Times*, 26 December 1999, Calendar section, 5, 92.

———. "'Ryan' Ends Vets' Years of Silence." *Los Angeles Times*, 6 August 1998, sec. A, 1.

Walsh, Frank. *Reading the Gospels in the Dark: Portrayals of Jesus in Film*. Harrisburg, Pa.: Trinity Press International, 2003.

———. *Sin and Censorship: The Catholic Church and the Motion Picture Industry*. New Haven: Yale University Press, 1996.

Walsh, Richard. *Finding St. Paul in Film*. New York: T&T Clark, 2005.

Williams, Peter. "Review Essay: Religion Goes to the Movies." *Religion and American Culture: A Journal of Interpretation* 10, no. 2 (2000): 225–39.

Williams, Stanley. *The Moral Premise: Harnessing Virtue and Vice for Box Office Success*. Studio City, Calif.: Michael Wiese Productions, 2006.

Woolf, Paul. "Turning toward Home." *Image: A Journal of the Arts & Religion* 20 (Summer 1998): 115–23.

Wright, Will. *Six Guns and Society: A Structural Study of the Western*. Berkeley: University of California Press, 1975.

Yancey, Phillip. *The Jesus I Never Knew*. Grand Rapids: Zondervan, 1995.

Zamichow, Nora. "Psychologists Are Giving Film Therapy Thumbs Up." *Los Angeles Times*, 4 July 1999, sec. A, 1, 12.

Zwick, Reinhold. "The Problem of Evil in Contemporary Film." In May, *New Image of Religious Film*, 72–94.

movies cited

Ben Hur (d. Olcott, 1907) 42
Bend It Like Beckham (d. Chadha, 2002) 222
Bidone, Il (d. Fellini, 1955) 298
Big Kahuna, The (d. Swanbeck, 1999) 134
Big Momma's House (d. Gosnell, 2000) 211
Billy Elliot (d. Daldry, 2000) 154, 220
Birth of a Nation, The (d. Griffith, 1915) 164
Black Hawk Down (d. Scott, 2001) 153
Black Stallion, The (d. Ballard, 1979) 139
Blade Runner (d. Scott, 1982) 175
Blair Witch Project, The (d. Myrick and Sánchez, 1999) 134, 273
Blonde Venus (d. Sternberg, 1932) 46
Blowup (d. Antonioni, 1966) 49
Blue Streak (d. Mayfield, 1999) 221
Bonnie and Clyde (d. Penn, 1967) 49
Boot, Das (d. Petersen, 1981) 155
Born on the Fourth of July (d. Stone, 1989) 72
Bourne Identity, The (d. Liman, 2002) 187, 212
Bourne Supremacy, The (d. Greengrass, 2004) 187, 212
Boxer, The (d. Sheridan, 1997) 232
Boys Town (d. Taurog, 1938) 62
Breakfast at Tiffany's (d. Edwards, 1961) 128
Breakfast Club, The (d. Hughes, 1985) 134
Breaking the Waves (d. von Trier, 1996) 120, 242
Bridge on the River Kwai, The (d. Lean, 1957) 81
Bringing Out the Dead (d. Scorsese, 1999) 77, 134
Broadway Danny Rose (d. Allen, 1984) 148–49, 164, 200
Brokeback Mountain (d. Lee, 2005) 15
Bruce Almighty (d. Shadyac, 2003) 25, 120, 136, 202, 224, 310n30
Bull Durham (d. Shelton, 1988) 22, 61, 65, 104, 174, 249
Butch Cassidy and the Sundance Kid (d. Hill, 1969) 50, 189

Caged Heat (d. Demme, 1974) 23
Calendar Girls (d. Cole, 2003) 219

Call to Arms, The (d. Griffith, 1910) 29
Cape Fear (d. Scorsese, 1991) 71
Casablanca (d. Curtiz, 1942) 201
Catch-22 (d. Nichols, 1970) 215
Celebration, The (d. Vinterberg, 1998) 119
Chariots of Fire (d. Hudson, 1981) 65, 98, 179
Charlie's Angels: Full Throttle (d. McG, 2003) 136
Chicago (d. Marshall, 2002) 148
Chinatown (d. Polanski, 1974) 175, 183, 220
Chocolat (d. Hallström, 2000) 65, 142–44, 307n12
Chorus, The [Les Choristes] (d. Barratier, 2004) 109
Chronicles of Narnia, The: The Lion, the Witch and the Wardrobe (d. Adamson, 2005) 15, 32, 67, 110, 146, 251, 305n75
Cinderella Man (d. Howard, 2005) 234
Cinema Paradiso (d. Tornatore, 1988) 30, 300n81, 311n30
Citizen Ruth (d. Payne, 1996) 31, 228
City Lights (d. Chaplin, 1931) 239
Clockwork Orange, A (d. Kubrick, 1971) 180
Cold Mountain (d. Minghella, 2003) 169, 212
Color Purple, The (d. Spielberg, 1985) 77, 90
Cool Hand Luke (d. Rosenberg, 1967) 69, 251
Cooler, The (d. Kramer, 2003) 219
Cotton Patch Gospel (d. Treyz and Meece, 1988) 69
Country (d. Pearce, 1984) 32, 134
Crash (d. Haggis, 2005) 145
Crimen del Padre Amaro, El (d. Carrera, 2002) 58
Crimes and Misdemeanors (d. Allen, 1989) 157–62, 172, 199, 200, 201, 310n30

Dances with Wolves (d. Costner, 1990) 32, 198, 222
Da Vinci Code, The (d. Howard, 2006) 23
Dead Man Walking (d. Robbins, 1995) 69, 148, 183, 223, 226, 228, 242

Last Tycoon, The (d. Kazan, 1976) 33
Last Wave, The (d. Weir, 1977) 269, 270, 272, 273, 274, 277, 278, 279
Lawrence of Arabia (d. Lean, 1962) 71
Left Behind (d. Sarin, 2000) 121, 124
Left-Handed Gun, The (d. Penn, 1958) 189
Legally Blonde 2: Red, White & Blonde (d. Herman-Wurmfield, 2003) 136
Legend of Bagger Vance, The (d. Redford, 2000) 90
Liar, Liar (d. Shadyac, 1997) 120
Life as a House (d. Winkler, 2001) 70–71
Life Is Beautiful (d. Benigni, 1998) 24, 121, 131, 154, 243, 247–49, 310n30
Limey, The (d. Soderbergh, 1999) 134
Lion King, The (d. Allers and Minkoff, 1994) 136
Little Big Man (d. Penn, 1970) 222
Little Caesar (d. LeRoy, 1930) 46
Little Mermaid, The (d. Clements and Musker, 1989) 136
Lone Star (d. Sayles, 1996) 222
Lord of the Flies (d. Hook, 1990) 310n30
The Lord of the Rings: The Fellowship of the Ring (d. Jackson, 2001) 32, 67, 118
The Lord of the Rings: The Two Towers (d. Jackson, 2001) 32, 67, 118
The Lord of the Rings: The Return of the King (d. Jackson, 2003) 32, 67, 118, 212
Love and Death (d. Allen, 1975) 201

M*A*S*H (d. Altman, 1970) 32
Magdalene Sisters, The (d. Mullan, 2002) 58
Magnificent Seven, The (d. Sturges, 1960) 202
Magnolia (d. Anderson, 1999) 67, 74, 90, 109, 126, 134, 145, 174, 175, 176, 181–83, 212, 309nn28–29, 315n45
Maid in Manhattan (d. Wang, 2002) 222
Man Called Horse, A (d. Silverstein, 1970) 222
Man Who Wasn't There, The (d. Coen, 2001) 169
Man without a Past, The [Mies vailla menneisyyttä] (d. Kaurismäki, 2002) 212

Manchurian Candidate, The (d. Demme, 2004) 137, 212
Manhattan (d. Allen, 1979) 199
March of the Penguins (d. Jacquet, 2005) 262–66, 315n46
Mariachi, El (d. Rodriguez, 1992) 196
Master and Commander: The Far Side of the World (d. Weir, 2003) 212, 269, 270, 271, 272, 273, 274, 275, 277
Match Point (d. Allen, 2005) 160
Matrix, The (d. Wachowski and Wachowski, 1999) 50, 67, 76, 109, 134, 172, 210, 211, 310n30, 311n30
Matrix Reloaded, The (d. Wachowski and Wachowski, 2003) 310n30
Memento (d. Nolan, 2000) 145, 212
Midnight Cowboy (d. Schlesinger, 1969) 311n7
Midsummer Night's Sex Comedy, A (d. Allen, 1982) 201
Million Dollar Baby (d. Eastwood, 2004) 99, 109, 121, 227, 232–37, 312nn26–27, 313n28
Miracle Maker, The (d. Hayes and Sokolov, 2000) 69
Missing, The (d. Howard, 2003) 13
Mission, The (d. Joffé, 1986) 65
Mission: Impossible (d. De Palma, 1996) 138, 144, 187
Mission: Impossible 2 (d. Woo, 2000) 31
Mississippi Burning (d. Parker, 1988) 32
Monster (d. Jenkins, 2003) 212
Monster's Ball (d. Forster, 2001) 67, 118, 146, 309n2
Monsters, Inc. (d. Docter and Silverman, 2001) 135
Moon Is Blue, The (d. Preminger, 1953) 48
Mosquito Coast, The (d. Weir, 1986) 269, 272, 275, 277
Motorcycle Diaries, The (d. Salles, 2004) 310n15
Moulin Rouge! (d. Luhrmann, 2001) 148
Mr. Holland's Opus (d. Herek, 1995) 108
Mr. Smith Goes to Washington (d. Capra, 1939) 203
Mulan (d. Bancroft and Cook, 1998) 135
Mulholland Drive (d. Lynch, 2001) 212

My Best Friend's Wedding (d. Hogan, 1997) 175

My Fair Lady (d. Cukor, 1964) 31

My Family [Mi Familia] (d. Nava, 1995) 222

My Night with Maud (d. Rohmer, 1969) 249

Mystic River (d. Eastwood, 2003) 212

Napoleon Dynamite (d. Hess, 2004) 310n15

Nashville (d. Altman, 1975) 145

Network (d. Lumet, 1976) 71

New York Stories (d. Allen, Coppola, and Scorsese, 1989) 201

Night of the Hunter, The (d. Laughton, 1955) 154, 172–73, 176, 308n29

Nights of Cabiria [Le Notti di Cabiria] (d. Fellini, 1957) 298n42

Nixon (d. Stone, 1995) 71

No Man's Land (d. Tanovic, 2001) 148, 222

Norte, El (d. Nava, 1983) 222

Notebook, The (d. Cassavetes, 2004) 212

Officer and a Gentleman, An (d. Hackford, 1982) 247

Once Upon a Time in Mexico (d. Rodriguez, 2003) 196

Once Upon a Time in the West (d. Leone, 1968) 71

One Flew over the Cuckoo's Nest (d. Forman, 1975) 69, 71, 93, 153, 157, 195, 205–8, 235, 251, 311n34

On the Waterfront (d. Kazan, 1954) 33

Open City (d. Rossellini, 1946) 245

Open Range (d. Costner, 2003) 189

Outlaw, The (d. Hughes, 1943) 47–48

Passion of Joan of Arc, The [La Passion de Jeanne d'Arc] (d. Dreyer, 1928) 69, 124, 130, 242

Passion of the Christ, The (d. Gibson, 2004) 15, 60, 65, 68, 69, 109, 154, 155, 263, 309n23

Passion Play of Oberammergau, The (1898) 28, 42

Patch Adams (d. Shadyac, 1998) 222, 259

Pawnbroker, The (d. Lumet, 1965) 48

Paycheck (d. Woo, 2003) 212

People vs. Larry Flynt, The (d. Forman, 1996) 207

Perfect Storm, The (d. Petersen, 2000) 222

Pianist, The (d. Polanski, 2002) 72

Picnic at Hanging Rock (d. Weir, 1975) 269, 270, 272, 273, 279, 280

Pink Panther, The (d. Edwards, 1963) 131

Pink Panther, The (d. Levy, 2006) 131

Pirates of the Caribbean: The Curse of the Black Pearl (d. Verbinski, 2003) 25

Places in the Heart (d. Benton, 1984) 32, 98, 134, 167, 243, 249, 250

Platoon (d. Stone, 1986) 32, 72, 153

Play It Again, Sam (d. Ross, 1972) 201

Pleasantville (d. Ross, 1998) 194, 273, 315n7

Pocahontas (d. Gabriel and Goldberg, 1995) 189

Psycho (d. Hitchcock, 1960) 104, 165, 179

Public Enemy (d. Wellman, 1931) 46

Pulp Fiction (d. Tarantino, 1994) 23, 145, 222

Punch-Drunk Love (d. Anderson, 2002) 126, 131–33, 306n37, 306n39

Purple Rose of Cairo, The (d. Allen, 1985) 14, 134, 200, 201

Quills (d. Kaufman, 2000) 71

Quo Vadis (d. Guazzoni, 1912) 42

Raging Bull (d. Scorsese, 1980) 77, 104, 125, 232

Ragtime (d. Forman, 1981) 207

Raiders of the Lost Ark (d. Spielberg, 1981) 174

Rain Man (d. Levinson, 1988) 222

Rapture, The (d. Tolkin, 1991) 63

Rashomon (d. Kurosawa, 1950) 311n30

Ray (d. Hackford, 2004) 109

Rear Window (d. Hitchcock, 1954) 311n30

Rebel without a Cause (d. Ray, 1955) 222

Requiem for a Dream (d. Aronofsky, 2000) 137, 220

Reservoir Dogs (d. Tarantino, 1992) 71

Return of Martin Guerre, The (d. Vigne, 1982) 311n30

Risky Business (d. Brickman, 1983) 31

River, The (d. Rydell, 1984) 32

Talk to Her [Hable con ella]
(d. Almodóvar, 2002) 301n92
Tarzan (d. Lima and Buck, 1999) 137, 189
Taxi Driver (d. Scorsese, 1976) 57, 71, 77,
125, 222, 309n23
Team America: World Police (d. Parker,
2004) 220, 221
Temptation of St. Anthony, The (d. Méliès,
1898) 28, 292n15
Ten Commandments, The (d. DeMille,
1923) 44
Tender Mercies (d. Beresford, 1983) 98, 99,
118, 243
Terminator 3: Rise of the Machines
(d. Mostow, 2003) 136
Thelma & Louise (d. Scott, 1991) 63, 99,
120, 175, 176–77, 187
There's Something about Mary (d. Farrelly
and Farrelly, 1998) 220
Thin Red Line, The (d. Malick, 1998) 222
Third Miracle, The (d. Holland, 1999) 21,
109, 134
Thomas Crown Affair, The (d. McTiernan,
1999) 23
Three Kings (d. Russell, 1999) 210
Titanic (d. Cameron, 1997) 33, 136, 153,
156, 190, 251, 261–62
To End All Wars (d. Cunningham, 2001) 66
To Kill a Mockingbird (d. Mulligan, 1962)
118
Tokyo Story (d. Ozu, 1953) 98
Touch (d. Schrader, 1997) 75
Toy Story (d. Lasseter, 1995) 135
Toy Story 2 (d. Lasseter and Brannon, 1999)
135
Traffic (d. Soderbergh, 2000) 168
Treasure Planet (d. Clement and Musker,
2002) 135
Trip to Bountiful, The (d. Masterson, 1985)
118
True Grit (d. Hathaway, 1969) 189
Truman Show, The (d. Weir, 1998) 33, 76,
269, 270, 271, 272, 273, 275, 276, 277,
278, 281, 311n30
Twelve Angry Men (d. Lumet, 1957) 311n30

Ulee's Gold (d. Nuñez, 1997) 137
Unfaithful (d. Lyne, 2002) 225

Unforgiven (d. Eastwood, 1992) 23, 190,
234
Unmarried Woman, An (d. Mazursky,
1978) 204
Usual Suspects, The (d. Singer, 1995) 71,
176

Vanilla Sky (d. Crowe, 2001) 212
Very Long Engagement, A [Un long di-
manche de franceilles] (d. Jeunet, 2004)
310n15

Wag the Dog (d. Levinson, 1997) 273
War of the Worlds (d. Spielberg, 2005) 154
Waterworld (d. Reynolds, 1995) 257
We Were Soldiers (d. Wallace, 2002) 146,
153, 222
When Harry Met Sally (d. Reiner, 1989)
136, 220
Who's Afraid of Virginia Woolf?
(d. Nichols, 1966) 48, 229n66
Wild Bunch, The (d. Peckinpah, 1969) 71,
189
Wind, The (d. Sjöström, 1928) 124
Winged Migration [Le peuple migrateur] (d.
Perrin, 2003) 265
Witches of Eastwick, The (d. Miller, 1987)
28
Witness (d. Weir, 1985) 189, 269, 270,
272, 274, 275, 277, 279, 280, 282
Wizard of Oz, The (d. Fleming, 1939) 147,
168
Woman, Thou Art Loosed (d. Schultz,
2004) 51, 109
Working Girl (d. Nichols, 1988) 214–16

X-Men (d. Singer, 2000) 19, 147
X2: X-Men United (d. Singer, 2003) 136,
147, 179
X-Men: The Last Stand (d. Ratner, 2006) 147

Year of Living Dangerously, The (d. Weir,
1982) 57, 269, 270, 271, 273, 274,
278, 282, 285, 287–89, 316n26

Zelig (d. Allen, 1983) 200

subject index

Acts, 106
Adorno, Theodor W., 117
Aeschylus, 127
aesthetics, 227, 239
African Americans, 77, 140–42
Agassi, Andre, 33
Alexie, Sherman, 197–98
Alighieri, Dante, 104, 261
Allen, John L., 296n13
Allen, Woody
  analysis of, 157–62, 199–201
  covert Christian perspective via, 98
  filmmaking, 151, 172
  point of view, 95, 148–49
  themes, 196, 199
Almodóvar, Pedro, 152, 196, 301n92
Altman, Robert, 145, 196
ambiguity, 277
Amenábar, Alejandro, 229–30
Anderson, Paul Thomas,
  artistic expression, 131–32
  on audience, 126
  intertextuality, 196
  music in *Magnolia*, 181–82
  opening of *Magnolia*, 174
  structure of *Magnolia*, 145
Anderson, Wes, 77, 195
Anker, Roy, 66, 121, 252
Antonioni, Michelangelo, 49
Apostles' Creed, 68
Appelman, Hyman, 57
appropriation of films, 70–74, 81, 299n66

Aquinas, 104
Aratus of Soli, 91
Arbuckle, "Fatty," 45
archetype, 193–94
Aristotle, 179, 188, 203
Armstrong, Gillian, 196
art
  aesthetics and, 239
  artist and, 195
  communion via, 149
  education and entertainment, 121
  faith and, 29
  film and, 132–34
  Heidelberg School, 279
  Holy Spirit and, 96
  and life, 123, 199–201
  morality and, 207
  religion and, 73, 244
  and transcendence, 76, 122, 126
Assyrians, 99–100
Atkinson, George, 49–50
atmosphere, 147, 158, 164, 278
audience
  in critical analysis of film, 149–50, 152–56
  genre and, 187, 190
  in theater, 210
Augsburger, David, 144
Augustine, 98, 103
Austin, Ronald, 245
auteur criticism
  benefit, 150, 196
  biography, 196–98

339

Dougherty, Dennis Joseph (archbishop of Philadelphia), 46
Douglas, Kirk, 30
Douglas, Michael, 175, 273
Doyle, Christopher, 168
Drane, John, 90, 258
Drew, Donald, 296n22
Dreyer, Carl Theodor, 67, 77, 124–25, 130
Dunaway, Faye, 220
Duvall, Robert, 119, 151, 258
Duvall, Shelly, 132
DVD, 50
Dyrness, William, 104, 111, 250, 304n51

Eames, Charles, 117
Eastman, George, 41
Eastwood, Clint, 188, 190, 196, 232, 234
Ebert, Roger
  on *Beauty and the Beast*, 36
  on *Chocolat*, 143
  evaluation of films, 155, 185
  on moral choices in film, 236–37
  perspective of, 252
  on ratings, 218,
  on *The Sea Inside*, 230–31
  on *Touch*, 75–76
Ecclesiastes
  films in dialogue with, 67–68
  friendship and, 253–56
  God in complexity, 161–62
  goodness of life, 92, 102, 283
  Peter Weir's films and, 289
  vanity, 225
Edison, Thomas, 41
Eisenstein, Sergei, 165
Eliot, T. S.
  on aesthetics, 239
  on audience, 149–50
  on criticism, 252
  on image, 286
  on incarnation, 287
  on reading literature, 64–65
  spiritual influence of, 245
  on transcendence, 243
Elmer, Gregory, 38–39, 74, 245, 250
Emerging Church movement, 50
Episcopal Committee on Motion Pictures, 46

"ethical patience," 226, 231
euthanasia, 228, 234
Evagrius, 102
Evangelical Covenant Church, 138
evangelicals and Catholics, 104
evangelism via film, 51
evil, 259–60
experience, theology and, 111, 113
Eyre, Chris, 197–98

Fairbanks, Douglas, 45
Fairbanks, Douglas, Jr., 46
faith
  aesthetic experience of, 64
  art and, 29
  and culture, 87, 111, 217
  film and, 67
  moviegoing and, 14, 28, 64–65
  story and, 219
  truth and, 162
Falconetti, Maria, 124
family, 263
Farley, Edward, 24
Farrow, Mia, 199
Fellini, Federico, 23, 48–49, 151, 174, 246
feminist criticism, 214, 240
Ferlita, Ernest, 251–52
Field, Sally, 32, 249
Fields, Doug, 88
film
  action in response, 287
  advances in technology, 25–26
  analysis, 149–57, 186f8.1, 240
  apostle Paul and, 67, 96–97, 108
  art and, 117, 127–33, 135
  audience and, 135, 149–50, 152–56
  Bible and, 67–68
  biblical interpretation and, 261
  books on, 51–52
  Christ-figures in, 68–69, 110, 157, 193, 206–8, 251
  Christians and, 22–23, 52, 223–26, 296n22
  coherence, 195
  color in, 133, 168–69
  commercialism, 117–18
  communication and, 126–27

Newman, John Henry Cardinal, 225
Newman, Robert, 136, 189
Nichols, Mike, 196, 215
Nicholson, Jack, 93, 153, 183, 220
Nicolosi, Barbara, 60, 64
Niebuhr, H. Richard, 78, 105
Nolan, Christopher, 145, 212
Nolan, Sydney, 279
Noll, Mark, 88, 103–4
numinous, 242. *See also* transcendence
Nussbaum, Martha, 243

Oberammergau, 28
O'Connor, Flannery, 104
O'Connor, John Joseph (archbishop of New York), 59
Oh, Sandra, 82
O'Neill, Joseph, 128
Ong, Walter, 150, 281
Organization Catholique Internationale du Cinéma, 88
Origen, 99
Orland, Ted, 195
Ortiz, Gaye, 66, 205, 253
Osbournes, 33
Ostwalt, Conrad, Jr., 73, 253, 259
O'Toole, Peter, 37
Ottman, John, 179
Otto, Rudolf, 242, 285, 289
Overstreet, Jeffrey, 52
Ozu, Yasujiro, 77, 98

Pacatte, Rose, 13, 66
Pacino, Al, 167
Packer, James, 102–3
Paquin, Anna, 139
parable, 87–88, 106
Parker, Trey, 221
Pasolini, Pier Paolo, 68
"path of beauty," 51
Paul (the apostle)
  and the Athenians, 91
  on purity, 225
  and theological dialogue with films, 67, 96–97
  theology and narrative, 106–8
  viewpoint, 224

Payne, Alexander
  auteur criticism and, 195–96
  Citizen Ruth, 228
  humanity in films of, 98
  Omaha in films of, 31–32
  Sideways, 81–82
Pearce, Roy Harvey, 123
Penn, Arthur, 189
Penn, Sean, 148, 183, 202
Perlman, Itzhak, 131
Perry, Joseph, 42
Peterson, Eugene, 99
Pfister, Wally, 167–68
Picasso, 106, 226
Pickford, Mary, 43, 45
Pitt, Brad, 211
Pius XII, Pope, 58
Pixar, 135
Plantinga, Cornelius, Jr., 88, 103
plot
  movement of, 163
  in Peter Weir's films, 277
  in story and film, 146, 156, 201–2
  Woody Allen on, 161
point of view
  in Peter Weir's films, 279–81
  vehicles of, 147–48, 174, 180, 182–83
  in Woody Allen films, 148–49, 159–60
Poland, Larry, 58
Polhemus, Robert, 196
pornography, 156
Porter, E. S., 164
Portman, Natalie, 130
postmodernism, 69, 90
preaching, 111
Preminger, Otto, 48
Prieto, Rodrigo, 169
Production Code, 47–49, 62
Protestant theology
  characteristics, 75
  image and, 102–5,
  spirit, 282–83
Proust, Marcel, 72
Proverbs, 92, 260
Psalms, 92, 114–15, 232
Puccini, 230
Purcell, 180
purity, 225

sexuality in film, 47, 219–20, 312n8
Shadyac, Tom, 120
Shelton, Ron, 103–4
Shyamalan, M. Night, 195
Simmons, Jean, 30
Simon and Garfunkel, 180
Singer, Bryan, 179
Singer, Diane, 236
Siskel, Gene, 185
Sittler, Joseph, 250
Sittser, Catherine, 152, 245, 293n32
Sittser, Gerry, 36–37
Sjöström, Victor, 124
Skinner, James, 46
Sklar, Robert, 122
Smith, Anna Nicole, 33
Smith, Kevin, 59
Smithouser, Bob, 88, 296n22
Snodgrass, Klyne, 97
Soderbergh, Stephen, 168
Solzhenitsyn, Aleksandr, 122, 124, 126
Spacek, Sissy, 32
Spellman, Francis Joseph (archbishop of
    New York), 48
Spielberg, Steven
    Amistad, 140–41
    as auteur, 152
    filmmaking of, 154
    opening, 174
    perspective of, 196
    Saving Private Ryan, 32, 79, 81
    Schindler's List, 35
spirituality
    chancing the sacred, 208–10
    film and, 52–53, 72, 90–91, 125
    in Peter Weir's films, 283–86
    search for, 22
    universal, 90
    Western, 272
Stallone, Sylvester, 31
Starr, Ken, 259
Stephens, Mitchell, 129
Stevens, George, 68, 192–94
Stevens, Wallace, 243–44
Stewart, Jimmy, 203
Stewart, Martha, 33
Stone, Bryan, 57, 68, 205
Stone, Sharon, 220

story
    analyzing, 137–38, 144–45, 145–50, 160
    appeal, 217
    audience, 250
    centrality of, in film, 14, 135
    communion with and through, 149–50
    elements in service to, 183
    ethics and, 217
    faith and, 218
    indirect, 110
    in Judaism, 107–8
    narrative criticism, 157–62
    pace and action, 138
    and performance, 108
    power of, 245
    self awareness via, 136, 156, 204–5
    technique in film, 14
    theology and, 91, 106–10
    visual style, 77, 300n92
    wonder through, 285
    See also parable
Stott, John R. W., 22
Strauss, Richard, 32, 180
Sundance Film Festival, 109–10, 129, 137,
    197
Svetkey, Benjamin, 138, 144
Swank, Hilary, 232–33
Swed, Mark, 131
Swinton, Tilda, 32
symbol, 172, 175

Tada, Joni Eareckson, 235
Tally, Thomas, 42
Tarantino, Quentin, 145, 152, 196,
    211–12
Tarkovsky, Andrei, 67, 165
Taylor, Barry, 21–22, 134, 179
Taylor, Jim, 81
Taylor, John, 94
Taymor, Julie, 300n92
television, 49
Terry, Artie, 77
theater, 44, 155
thematic criticism
    the critical axis, 251
    film and other texts, 201–5
    focus of, 150, 186
theme, 201–5, 228, 268